D0204022

DANCING WOMEN

In this compelling and lively book Sally Banes recasts canonical dance history since the early nineteenth century in terms of a feminist perspective. Setting the creation of specific dances in socio-political and cultural context, *Dancing Women* shows that choreographers have created representations of women that are shaped by society's continuing debates about sexuality and female identity.

Banes raises questions about issues of representation in dance, showing that the relationship of performance to storyline is a complex one, and reveals that over and over again, in both ballet and modern dance, women characters on the dance stage are enmeshed in various permutations of "the marriage plot."

In *Dancing Women*, Banes uses an interpretive strategy different from that of other feminist dance historians, finding a much more complex range of cultural representations of gender identities. Investigating women's images ranging from seductive sylphs to reluctant brides to tyrannical mothers, Banes suggests how "female microcosms" – girlhood friends, fairy godmothers, or avenging unclean spirits – create both positive and negative pictures of women's communities and how women dancing solo challenge social norms.

Sally Banes is the Marian Hannah Winter Professor of Theatre History and Dance Studies at the University of Wisconsin-Madison and is an internationally known writer and lecturer on dance.

DANCING WOMEN

Female bodies on stage

Sally Banes

London and New York

First published 1998
by Routledge
11 New Fetter Lane, London EC4P 4EE

Simultaneously published in the USA and Canada
by Routledge
29 West 35th Street, New York, NY 10001

Typeset in Baskerville by Keystroke, Jacaranda Lodge, Wolverhampton
Printed and bound in Great Britain by Biddles Ltd, Guildford and King's Lynn

British Library Cataloguing in Publication Data
A catalogue record for this book is available from the British Library

Library of Congress Cataloguing in Publication Data
Banes, Sally.
Dancing women : female bodies on stage / Sally Banes.
p. cm.
Includes bibliographical references and index.
1. Women dancers. 2. Women—Identity. 3. Sex in dance. 4. Body, Human. I. Title.
GV199.4.B35 1998
792.8′082—dc21 97–24496
CIP

ISBN 0–415–09671–5 (hbk)
ISBN 0–415–11162–5 (pbk)

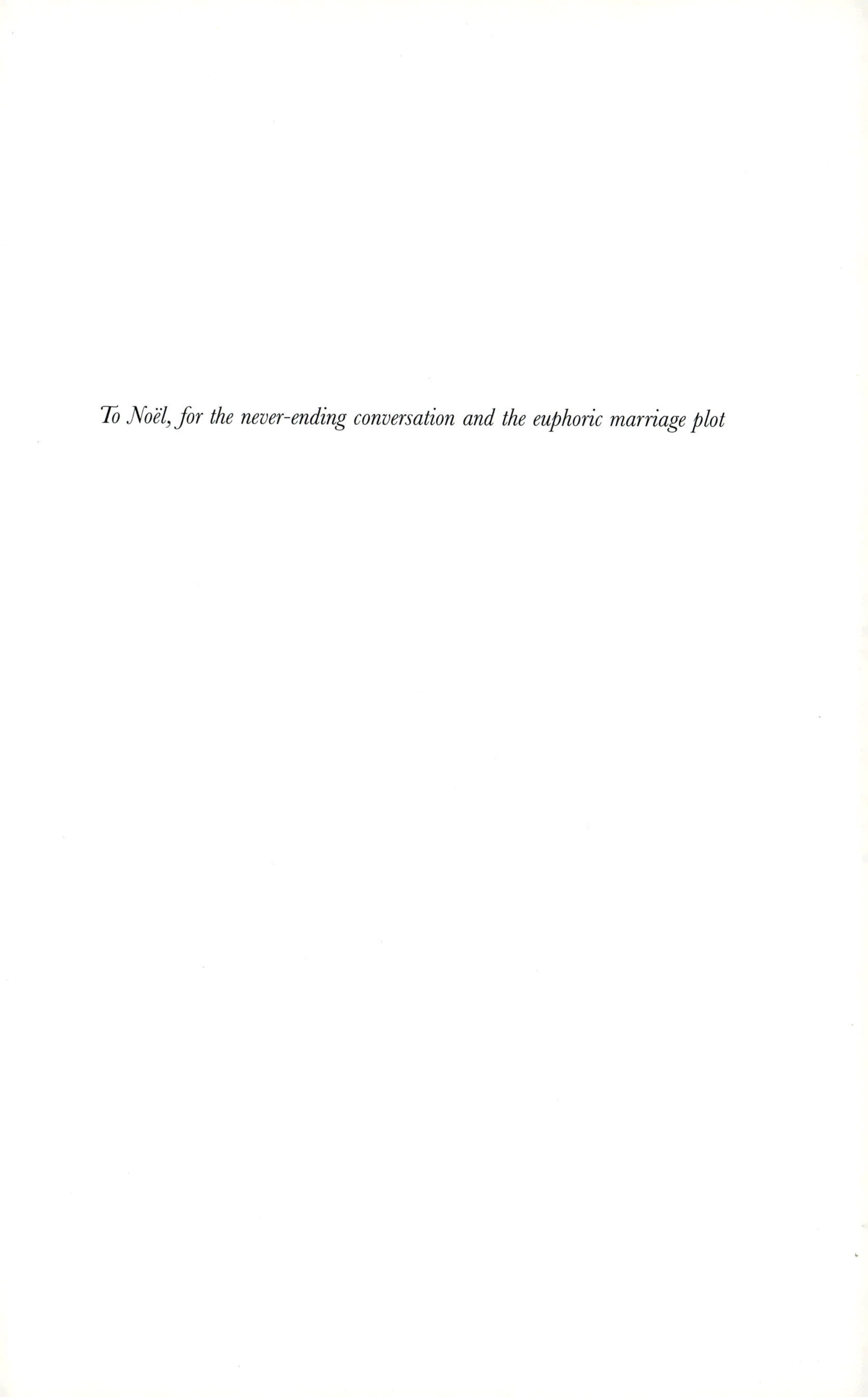

To Noël, for the never-ending conversation and the euphoric marriage plot

CONTENTS

LIST OF PLATES

ACKNOWLEDGMENTS

I would like to thank the following individuals for their help in the research, writing, and preparation of this book: Erik Aschengreen, Helen and Daniel Banes, Barbara Barker, Gigi Bennahum, Susan Bernstein, David Bordwell, Buff Brennan, Ramsay Burt, James Carroll, Laurie Beth Clark, Susan Cook, Arlene Croce, Stephen Davies, Jill Dolan, Alison East, Sorella Englund, Sharon Friedland, Beth Genné, Isabelle Ginot, Linda Gordon, Robert Greskovic, Linda Caruso Haviland, Deborah Jowitt, Janet Lansdale, Li Chiao-Ping, Alastair Macaulay, Susan Manning, Elaine Marks, Carol Martin, Judy Mitoma, Monica Moseley, Madeleine Nichols, Cecilia Olsson, Jane Pritchard, Douglas Rosenberg, Laurence Senelick, Marc Silberman, Elizabeth Souritz, Mike Vanden Heuvel, Karen Vedel, Juliette Willis, and Phillip Zarrilli. I also want to thank all my colleagues in the Theatre and Drama Department and the Dance Program at the University of Wisconsin-Madison for their support and for nominating me for various grants that allowed me to pursue my research. I owe a special debt of gratitude to the students in my dance history courses at the University of Wisconsin who helped me work out some of the ideas in this book.

I have worked on *Dancing Women* at numerous archives over the past six years and am indebted to the helpful staff members there: the Dance Collection at the New York Public Library for the Performing Arts; the Performing Arts Library and Museum, San Francisco; the Royal Theatre Archive and Library, Copenhagen; the Theater Museum, Copenhagen; the Royal Opera House Archives, London; the Ballet Rambert Archives; the Harvard Theatre Collection; the Theater Museum, St. Petersburg; and the Bakhrushin Theater Museum, Moscow. I am grateful both to those institutions and also to the Stiftung Archiv der Akademie der Künste, Berlin, and the House Foundation for the Arts for supplying illustrations.

Parts of this book have been developed through talks given at the University of California-Los Angeles, Swarthmore College, Bryn Mawr College, the New Arts Program of Kutztown at the Painted Bride, the University of Copenhagen, Dans i Dialog at Dansenhus (Copenhagen), the University of Stockholm, Danshögskolan (Stockholm), Montpellier Danse, the Institute for Research on Women and Gender at the University of Michigan, the School of Performing

Arts (Auckland, New Zealand), the University of Surrey, and, at the University of Wisconsin-Madison, the Institute for Research in the Humanities and the Women's Studies Research Center. I appreciate the opportunities for refining my ideas provided by those invitations and audiences.

I am especially grateful for the semester I spent as a fellow at the Institute for Research in the Humanities at the University of Wisconsin, which allowed me to pursue writing full-time and to engage in very fruitful conversations with the other fellows there about my work. I thank, as well, the members of the Performance Studies group at the University of Wisconsin, who provided feedback and support.

This book could not have been written without the financial support I received from a fellowship from the National Endowment for the Humanities; a Howard D. Rothschild Fellowship in Dance from the Harvard Theatre Collection; and grants from the University of Wisconsin Graduate School and Vilas Associates Fund.

I am much obliged to my first editor at Routledge, Julia Hall, for suggesting that I write this book and to my second editor, Talia Rodgers, for her enthusiasm in the final stages of the project. Joan Acocella has been a faithful friend and colleague throughout, and Lynn Garafola has generously supported me in so many ways – archival, editorial, intellectual, and sororal. Mary Evans has helped me keep my focus. Finally, I am more thankful than words can convey to my husband, Noël Carroll, who collaborated with me on one segment of Chapter 1, who helped me think through every part of the book, and whose imagination, curiosity, erudition, perspicacity, decisiveness, patience, impatience, and humor continue to inspire me and bolster me in every way.

Some sections of this book have already been published or will be published separately, and I would like to thank the editors for allowing me to incorporate that material. Parts of Chapter 1 appear as "Marriage and the Inhuman: *La Sylphide*'s Narratives of Domesticity and Community" (with Noël Carroll), in Lynn Garafola, ed., *Re-Thinking the Sylph: New Perspectives on the Romantic Ballet*, Studies in Dance History (Hanover, NH: Wesleyan University Press/University Press of New England, 1997); parts of Chapter 4 appear in "*Firebird*, the Asian Bloodline, and the Body Politic," in Lynn Garafola and Nancy Van Norman Baer, eds., *The Ballets Russes and Its World* (New Haven, CT: Yale University Press, 1998); and parts of the Envoi were published as "Feminism and American Postmodern Dance," in *Ballett International/Tanz Aktuell* (June 1996) and as "Postmodernism, the Emotions, and the Dancing Body," in Gerhard Hoffmann and Alfred Hornung, eds., *Emotion in Postmodernism*, American Studies, Vol. 74 (Heidelberg: Universitätsverlag C. Winter, 1997).

NOTE ON TRANSLITERATION

There are various methods of transliterating from the Cyrillic to the Latin alphabet. Following standard practice in transliterating Russian names and titles, I have used the more familiar (to Western eyes) spellings in the text in order not to confuse the reader, whereas in the notes, I have followed a modified Library of Congress transliteration system. However, where I am citing works already published in English translation, readers will notice some discrepancies in spelling. Thus, for instance, Vera Krasovskaia also appears as Vera Krassovskaya, since her name appears in two different versions on the title pages of two different works in English.

INTRODUCTION

In this book, I attempt to recast canonical dance history since the mid-nineteenth century in terms of a feminist perspective. Although women are featured prominently in most books written about the theatrical dancing of the last two centuries, only in the past few years have dance historians begun to write specifically feminist histories of the artform. With this book I hope to contribute one thread to that discussion, a thread that at times tangles with some earlier feminist writings.

The book is divided into six chapters covering the Western, predominantly Euro-American dance canon. There are chapters on: the mid-nineteenth-century Romantic ballet in France and Denmark; the late nineteenth-century Russian Imperial ballet; the American forerunners of modern dance at the turn of the century; early modern ballet of the first decades of the twentieth century (as represented by Diaghilev's Ballets Russes in Paris); historical modern dance of the 1920s, 1930s, and 1940s in Germany and the United States; and contemporary ballet from the 1930s to the 1950s in Europe and the United States. Thus the book starts when ballet as we know it – with women ascendant – began, and it ends with the establishment of the canonical modern dance and modern ballet that still shape choreography today.

In each chapter I focus on one or several dances, in order to retell the story of Western theatrical dancing from a woman-centered perspective. I analyze how representations of women are constructed in major works of the theatrical dance canon written by both men and women. Setting the creation of these works in socio-political and cultural context, I show that choreographers have created images of women that are shaped by – and that in part shape – society's continuing debates about sexuality and female identity. I argue that the dance stage has often reflected and reinforced, but has also formed and in some cases criticized cultural conceptions of corporeality – in particular, conceptions of women's bodies and identities – and that through dance, men's attitudes toward women and women's attitudes about themselves are literally given body on stage.

The book concludes with a postscript on feminism and postmodern dance from the 1960s to the present that briefly extends my analysis of the canon by exploring strategies that have been used by recent choreographers to problematize both dance discourse and gender discourse, and that suggests ways in which choreographers recently have created representations of gender diversity along ethnic lines, as more persons of color have entered the arena of concert dancing.

My methodology in researching and writing this book may be characterized as close analyses of choreography, situated in artistic, socio-political, and economic contexts. The close analyses are partly based on examinations of dance elements: postures, gestures, steps; the use of space, time, weight, and flow; aspects of solo, duet, and group interactions; and music, costumes, and sets. These are interpreted, loosely along the lines of Erving Goffman's *Gender Advertisements*, in terms of their meaning in the gender codes of Western culture.[1] Although I often use biographical information to illuminate my interpretations of the dances, I am less interested in the sociology of women's lives as dancers or choreographers than in the ways in which choreography and performance create cultural representations of gender identities.

Like so many women involved in dance, I long felt that an explicit feminist analysis was simply unnecessary in a highly feminized field, where many of the leading figures – both artists and scholars – are women. However, over the past several years, both the field of dance practice and the critical discourse surrounding it have changed in ways that foreground feminist consciousness. On the one hand, the current generation of choreographers has been inserting issues of feminist identity in their dances. On the other hand, a younger generation of dance scholars has put the issue of feminist analysis on the table as an issue for urgent debate in our field.

As I noted earlier, the discipline of dance history has only very recently begun to be examined from a feminist perspective, and there are very few models. Much work needs to be done. Indeed, some of the very basic research and interpretation that have been done in other fields – the analysis of women's images in canonical works of literature, for example – has not yet occurred in dance studies. This book is meant to fill in some of these gaps.

Method

My own interpretive strategy is quite different from that of other feminist dance historians, for instance Christy Adair in *Women and Dance: Sylphs and Sirens*, who makes the general claim that ballet is oppressive to women, while modern dance is liberatory, or Ann Daly, who has applied Laura Mulvey's theory of the imposition of the male gaze in cinema to dance.[2] I reject the psychoanalytic model of "the male gaze" as it has been adapted from cinema to dance, since its explanatory power is problematic for cinema, but even more so for dance.[3] And I differ from Adair in that I do not begin with a political agenda that stresses either victimization or celebration, negative or positive representations. The French feminist historian Arlette Farge discusses the sterility of both what she calls the *misérabiliste* interpretation and the celebrationist interpretation of women's roles and representations in history.[4] I agree with her, and find that if one starts neither with an assumption that all women are victims nor with the idea that they are all heroines, and neither with the idea that images of women are all negative nor that they are all positive, but rather, looks closely at the evidence of the works themselves, one actually finds a much more complex range of representations than has previously been suggested.

Of course, close analyses are not the whole picture, for although many of the dances I analyze remain in the repertory today, they still bear traces of the conditions of their making. For instance, in *Giselle*, an 1841 French ballet, a village community of men and women celebrating the harvest in Act I gives way in Act II to a flock of dead, vampire-like, virgin brides-to-be (that is, brides that never were). The heroine of the ballet has died of a broken heart (or perhaps a self-inflicted suicide) upon discovering that her peasant lover has deceived her: he is in reality a nobleman and is engaged to a noblewoman. In analyzing this ballet from a gender perspective, one must understand the themes of cross-class seduction and betrayal in sentimental literature and the *ancien régime*'s harsh economic and sexual realities of *droit du seigneur*, as well as changing ideas in early nineteenth-century France about marriage.

In considering the reluctant bride of Bronislava Nijinska's *Les Noces* (1923), one should know first about the traditional economic barter of women in the Russian peasant class and then about the changing status of women and the new marriage laws – both vehemently resisted by the peasantry – in revolutionary Russia. In looking at Mary Wigman's *Witch Dance* (1926), one thinks about both the history of women's persecution during the witchcrazes in Reformation Germany and the twentieth-century appropriation by Expressionist artists of various "alien" artistic conventions, including medieval and Asian forms, to stage a self-representation of otherness. Martha Graham's *Night Journey* (1947), a retelling of the Oedipus myth from Jocasta's point of view, needs to be analyzed in light of the popularity of Freudian and Jungian analysis in the 1940s, as well as the growth of the feminine mystique in postwar America.

To do close analyses of images is absolutely necessary to understanding the workings of representations – otherwise, one is left with essentializing generalizations about genre conventions. For example, Susan Foster alleges that in the ballet pas de deux the woman is always passively dependent on the man.[5] But there are many classical ballet pas de deux (such as that of Odile – the evil impostor swan – and Siegfried in *Swan Lake* [1895]) in which the woman is depicted as forceful and self-reliant. However, to do only close analyses leaves out not only the artistic conventions and traditions (or their ruptures) that shape the work and make meaning, but also the social and political contexts of women's status, sexual life, work, and education that also construct its sense. In other words, these choreographic representations are not socially or politically free-floating. But on the other hand, they should not be judged as "progressive" or "reactionary" according to current postfeminist values. Moreover, the politics of these dances are complicated, for reactionary monarchical politics or what we might now see as cultural appropriation may coexist with liberatory images of women and of sexuality, as in *The Sleeping Beauty* (1890) and *Radha* (1906). Susan

Manning has pointed out that in early modern dance a "distinct ideological profile . . . marked the paradoxical social function of the form, its ability to contest and to conform at the same time."[6] But I would suggest that this is true not only of early modern dance.

My approach to analyzing choreographic representations is historical and materialist (in the sense of anti-essentialist). While I describe and analyze images and tropes that seem to emerge repeatedly throughout dance history, I do not see them as universal or essential, but rather as produced by historical conditions and a dialogic tradition of artistic practices.[7]

The particular themes and issues of each dance, and the interrelations among the dances, have emerged in my study in the course of close analysis and contextualization. And what I find is that, rather than absolutes, there is a spectrum of ambiguities to explore. Working with the complexities of these ambiguities and paradoxes yields much more exciting questions than previous feminist analyses have indicated. For instance, in the Romantic ballet *La Sylphide*, choreographed in two different versions by Filippo Taglioni (1832) and August Bournonville (1836), the female characters include Effie, the bride-to-be; her girlfriends; her fiancé's mother; Madge, a witch, and her confederates; and the sylph – an aerial nymph – for whom the ballet is named and her "sisters." These characters run the gamut from the aggressive to the assertive, the seductive to the elusive. So, facile generalizations about *the* image of women here are out of the question, and sensitivity to variegated images is apposite.

A close analysis of the choreography of *La Sylphide* reveals that generalizations about images of women in Romantic ballets as passive and ethereal does not come close to capturing the complex range of female characters and their roles in the communities constructed on stage – including two distinctive all-female communities. The sylph, often characterized simply as an angelic "ideal woman," is, as dance historian Erik Aschengreen has pointed out, a complex mixture of fragility, naiveté, and sexual provocation.[8] The cloistered female community of the unattainable, airy sylphs simultaneously suggests the spirituality of nuns and the seductiveness of *demi-mondaines*, while the demonic, ugly witches invert spirituality and repel sexual desire.

The witch in *La Sylphide* is a particularly striking character. Often danced by a man, she is the most powerful figure in the ballet. She often takes up more space than other women, breaks polite codes of movement with her grotesque gestures, and manipulates the actions of young lovers like a puppeteer. Witches perennially recur, not only in Romantic and late nineteenth-century ballets (for instance, Carabosse in *The Sleeping Beauty*), but also in modern dance (Wigman's *Witch Dance* [1926], Graham's *Cave of the Heart* [1946], and the monstrous mother in Doris Humphrey's *With My Red Fires* [1936]). Although each witch is unique, the category of "witch" on the dance stage often embodies an enduring social ambivalence toward old women – their ambiguous status in terms of both sexuality and gender; the respect shown for their wisdom, but at the same time the fear felt regarding the powers and secrets of assertive women who are, according to folklore, knowledgeable about mysterious biological processes and who preside over births and deaths. On stage, these figures are simultaneously outcasts and sources of power. They possess knowledge and skill, yet they often use these for evil ends; their dancing is both grotesque (violating classical lines) and attractive (strong and vitally energized). Positive and negative qualities intermingle in the figure of the witch on the dance stage to form ambiguous images of power and its distortions.

The marriage plot

Over and over again, women characters on the dance stage are enmeshed in what I call "the marriage plot," in both ballet and modern dance. An analysis of the various permutations of the marriage plot, therefore, partly structures my book. I use the word "plot" in the double sense of a narrative and a bourgeois social imperative, what lesbian feminist critics have called "compulsory heterosexuality."[9] I should qualify my use of the term "marriage plot," however. While I do not consider the marriage imperative in Western society to be a consciously authored misogynist or homophobic, top-down conspiracy, I certainly acknowledge the patriarchal basis of the marriage institution as well as the patriarchal expectation that marriage will be most women's fate, and I use the term to allude to that.

Rejecting a reflectionist view of art and culture, I believe that the dances I analyze have participated (and continue to participate) in cultural discourses surrounding marriage. But, somewhat to my surprise, in analyzing a series of dances that I expected uniformly to reinforce the values of patriarchy, I found quite the opposite. In fact, these dances seem to participate in the growing anxiety in Europe and America, at least since the French Revolution, toward marriage as it is peculiarly associated with women's destiny. While individual dances may buck the trend and "push" the marriage plot (in the insidious sense), they are the exception rather than the rule. In fact, even in what is often seen as the conservative arena of the ballet stage, the general trend over the past century and a half has been toward questioning the values of marriage and monogamy. *The Sleeping Beauty*, for instance, proposes a radically different way (for its time) of choosing the marriage partner – as an act of mutual love, rather than as an economic and political transaction between fathers.

There are historical reasons for dance's association with the marriage plot. Ballet's origins lie in danced entertainments at royal weddings in Renaissance Europe.[10] As theatrical dancing became public and professional in the seventeenth century, representations of weddings and marriages – or, tragically, of broken nuptials, by the nineteenth century – became obligatory *in* the ballet, rather than as the social context of its performance. That is, where dances were first embedded in weddings, weddings came to be embedded in dances.

It is also significant that, viewed from this perspective, the forerunners of modern dance at the turn of the century emerge *choreographically* as sexual revolutionaries, for by dancing solos without male partners, they categorically rejected the marriage plot entirely in their dances – even if, like Isadora Duncan, they celebrated maternity. But the next generation of modern dancers – that of Martha Graham – returned to the marriage plot, troubled though it was.

Both ballets and later modern dance repeatedly display communities of young women and the marital passage out of those cloistered "feminine microcosms" into a patriarchal world.[11] And although there are also some representations of women working in dance, they are scarce. Oddly enough, certain images of women absolutely standard to other artforms rarely show up in the dance canon. Notably, domesticity in general – life after marriage – which constitutes an entire genre in painting, rarely appears on the dance stage, for reasons that deserve closer attention.

Analyzing Jane Austen's novels, Louis Menand has written:

> She didn't care a bit about what it was like to be a married woman or a landlord or a professional man or even the suitor of one of her young women. She thought an unattached young woman with intelligence and some degree of physical vibrancy was the most marvelous creature in the world, and that the relations between women like these was a hundred times more poignant than the relations any of them would ever have with a man. What must have made this type so appealing to her, of course, was that this was the only time in their lives in which women like that had an absolute power – if only the power to withhold themselves – over the desires of a man.[12]

In dance, this conspicuous framing of the moment of marital choice is a favored theme. Moreover, the choice of a marriage partner can be seen as standing metaphorically for women's agency in general. In fact, if the marriage plot did not already exist, dance would have had to invent it, for the physical conditions of the vital people portraying the action in dance overdetermine the preeminence of the marriage plot. Although older dancers may still perform in ancillary roles, the central performers in both ballet and modern dance are young women at the peak of their powers as dancers. And on stage their job is to move – to be active. The medium of dance – lively young bodies, with a preponderance of female bodies, in motion – itself militates against depicting sedentary states (like domesticity) and leans instead toward issues of sexuality and the social governance of mating through the marriage institution.

So, in dance, we constantly see brides, their girlfriends, and their mothers, as well as female threats to successful marriages – figured as supernatural or inhuman creatures (like witches, automatons, and bad fairies) in the nineteenth century, but more often as all-too-human (mistresses and rivals) in the twentieth.

There is also a class issue regarding the representations of women in the dances I analyze. The theatrical dance canon comprises dancing on the lyric and concert stage – largely aristocratic or bourgeois venues. Thus the tendency is to represent on stage bourgeois, rather than working-class, values toward sexuality and marriage. This is not to say that bourgeois values are always upheld; they may well be contested. But they structure the conversation, which tends to be far more polite than that of the popular stage. For instance, as I discuss in Chapter 5, Valeska Gert, a cabaret performer who was a contemporary of Mary Wigman's in Germany in the 1920s, like Wigman appropriated the outsider persona of the witch. But in addition, in Gert's repertoire of dance roles was a streetwalker (*Canaille*). Prostitutes rarely populate the high-art dance stage, even in eras when they proliferate in literature, drama, and visual art (although dancers themselves have at times been treated socially and sexually as only a step above ordinary streetwalkers).[13]

To look at women's roles and the marriage plot is to examine kinship networks and to analyze how women fit in (or not) according to the community's rules. These dances tell us stories about whom one should or should not marry, especially in terms of class, but also in terms of incest taboos, endogamy versus exogamy, physical attributes, and disposition.

In analyzing the marriage plot for each dance, I use an interpretive grid that distinguishes between two sets of binary oppositions: whether the outcome of the marriage plot is failure or success; and whether the affective value of the marriage, as it is portrayed in the choreography, is positive (euphoric) or negative (dysphoric). There are subdivisions in these categories, for the affective value of the marriage in a single dance can vary from one character to another (or from the bride to the community) and from internal (the characters' point of view) to external (the narrator/audience's point of view). Usually, a successful marriage creates a comic plot, in Northrop Frye's sense, while a failed marriage leads to tragedy.[14] But adding the element of euphoric/dysphoric value can complicate the meaning of the marriage (or its failure to take place).

For instance, the marriage of convenience in Antony Tudor's *Jardin aux Lilas* (1936) has a successful outcome – the marriage does take place. But because it is a dysphoric event both for the characters in the ballet and for the audience, the dance is a small tragedy, like so many twentieth-century dances about reluctant brides. Yet, other aspects of choreography – like the use of humor – can alter the meaning of a dance. Frederick Ashton's *A Wedding Bouquet* (1937), set to words by Gertrude Stein, which also depicts a marriage of convenience with dysphoric value, becomes comedic through its use of both verbal and choreographic wit. Although ballet is often criticized as embodying a fantasy world, whereas modern dance is seen as more realistic, there is clearly a shared movement since the nineteenth century in both ballet and modern dance toward showing marriage as problematic (dysphoric) and as ripped away from social context – that is, family as well as community.

Dance "texts" as evidence

Dance is, as Agnes de Mille, has exclaimed, "written on the air."[15] It is elusive, and it has been notoriously badly documented prior to the recent invention of inexpensive videotaping technologies. And, of course, because of camera angles, editing, and so forth, film and videotape rarely capture the whole of a dance. We have no standard notation system in Western dance, and even Labanotation, a widely used but cumbersome system, was only perfected in the middle of this century.

Theatrical dancing has historically been an often orally transmitted, face-to-face tradition, in which choreography is passed from one body to another in the rehearsal studio. Our "texts" are more like Homeric epics than Chekhov plays. They rely on human memory, which can be faulty, and each interpreter willy-nilly adds something of her own to the choreography as she passes it along. Therefore, dance "texts" are more malleable, more subject to mutation than those of other performing arts in the West, such as plays and musical compositions, which usually have fixed texts. Authenticity is difficult, if not impossible, to verify in dance history.

At what object, then, does the dance historian look when making her interpretations? My answer may not satisfy historians used to working with written records, but it would sound familiar to archaeologists. We work with shards, traces, memories, contexts, written descriptions, revivals, reconstructions, and speculation, as well as with film and video recordings of individual performances. We then make the best guess we can about what the dance is (or was). Many of the dances I analyze in my book are still (or once again) part of the repertory. I have seen most of them in live performance (sometimes as reconstructions). But that still presents problems, for having seen a dance once or even many times does not allow one to examine it in detail. For detailed choreographic analysis I have relied on film and video records. But unfortunately, even these documents are spotty. The best versions may not exist or may be unavailable for viewing (often for copyright reasons). Still, I have limited my analyses to dances I could study, through motion picture documentation, in order to be able to base my interpretations on close studies of the choreography.

Performance vs. plot

The reason for my insistence on analyzing performances, both live and recorded, rather than libretti, raises an important metacritical issue. Too much is lost in the gap between performance and plot description. There is an important distinction between critical interpretations of plots and analyses of performances. Very often, exactly because choreographic texts are elusive, dance historians rely on literary plots to make their critical interpretations. Privileging plot descriptions over performance descriptions, however, overlooks the most crucial aspect of dance. It is, after all, a *live*, interpretive art. It is not fixed on the page, nor can all its meanings be accurately conveyed through verbal means. And bodies can impart different meanings – sometimes diametrically opposed meanings – than words suggest.

The issue of looking at plot in relation to performance has enormous consequences for interpreting representations of women in choreography. The plot may verbally describe a female character as weak or passive, while the physical prowess of the dancer performing the role may saturate it with agency. Thus, even dances with misogynist narratives or patriarchal themes tend to depict women as active and vital. The Sugarplum Fairy is the benign but extremely powerful supreme ruler of the Land of Sweets in *The Nutcracker* (1892). And one can't help but admire the potency of the Amazons who destroy their male sexual partners in Jerome Robbins's *The Cage* (1951), no matter how disgusting the choreographer clearly finds them.

Recently, debates in opera studies have centered around a similar interpretive crisis. Taking issue with Catherine Clément's contention (in *Opera, or the Undoing of Women*) that operas are misogynist because their plots so often kill off women, Carolyn Abbate asserts that the presence of singing women on stage creates a performance meaning different from that of the literary plot. Abbate writes, "Clément neglected their triumph: the sound of their singing voices. This sound is . . . unconquerable; it cannot be concealed by orchestras, by male singers, or – in the end – by murderous plots."[16] Moreover, Abbate points out that by focusing on the voice rather than instrumental music in her analysis of opera – that is, by focusing on bodily performance rather than the plot or the musical score – she opens a space in musical analysis for two underrated aspects of music: "the *physical* force of music," and the contribution of the performer over "the monological authority of 'the Composer.'"[17] Abbate refers to the singer as "a female authorial voice," "claiming a place as an active subject who sees and speaks." Contesting Mulvey's theory of the "scopophilic ideology" of the male gaze, Abbate maintains that:

> Listening to the female singing voice is a more complicated phenomenon. Visually, the character singing is the passive object of our gaze. But, aurally, she is resonant; her musical speech drowns out everything in range, and we sit as passive objects, battered by that voice. As a voice she slips into the "male/active/subject" position in other ways as well, since a singer, more than any other musical performer, enters into that Jacobin uprising inherent in the phenomenology of live performance and stands before us having wrested the composing voice away from the librettist and composer who wrote the score.[18]

Abbate's position – taking performance as much into account as the opera's plot – is far more attractive than Clément's, which drains opera of its material performance conditions and simply reduces it to the act of mechanically retelling a literary narrative. And Abbate's points are in many ways useful to apply to dance.

In dance, as in music and drama, a score or text provides the skeleton on which the musculature of the individual performer's interpretation is built. The performance aspect is as important a consideration as (if not a *more* important consideration than) the plot to the interpretation of a dance. Indeed, the plot and the performance can come into direct conflict, as when dancers stress nuances of gesture or posture that seem to undermine or render ironic the narrative flow. For instance, as I discuss in Chapter 3, in *Firebird* (1910), the ballet's pseudo-fairytale plot in the opening scene is well known. Prince Ivan, out hunting in the forest, captures the Firebird. To regain her freedom, she gives him a magical feather. Yet in the Royal Ballet film of the ballet, Margot Fonteyn, who was coached in the role by the original Firebird (Tamara Karsavina), behaves in such a way that we see *her* to be manipulating the Prince, in an erotic game of domination.

It may be that Abbate's second point, the wresting of the composing voice by the female opera singer from the librettist and composer, is more germane to ballet than to modern dance, for the histories of these two often independent genres have been separately gendered, as well. Most often ballet choreographers have been men, while the first two generations of modern dance choreographers were populated predominantly by women. Thus the "Jacobin uprising" Abbate triumphantly describes, in which the downtrodden female performers in opera seize power from male creators, would have little relevance to modern dance. Since the separately gendered job hierarchy there favored women, historically, when there was a gendered power struggle, it took the form of men asserting themselves in a world of women.

However, ballet and opera came, so to speak, out of the same womb. The French Romantic ballet was born in Paris on the Opéra stage, where ballets were performed as entr'actes or as codas to the operas. In both artforms, men worked at the top of the creative hierarchy – as librettists, composers, choreographers, and managers – while women worked, alongside more men, at the bottom, as performer/interpreters of various ranks. So the situation of gender inequity in the making of the work was equivalent in ballet and opera, while the potential for female interpretive artists to display skill and power at the bottom was, if anything, even more prevalent in dance than in opera. Statistically speaking, there were usually more female dancers on stage in a ballet than female opera singers in any given opera production.[19]

However, taking Abbate's point even further, dance – even the realm of ballet, with its patriarchal hierarchies – provides still greater opportunities for women dancers to "wrest the composing body" away from the choreographer. For an opera singer's musical text is strictly bound by the composer and librettist, while a dancer may more easily "re-choreograph" her own part. Indeed, especially in the nineteenth century, prima ballerinas were often known to interpolate their own renowned specialty "routines" wholesale into the choreography of ballets written by men.[20]

While my use of Abbate's notion of the "envoicing" – perhaps here, the word "embodying" would be more germane – of women on the dance stage may seem like just another form of celebrationism, I would argue that it is not. For just as anti-anti-pornography feminists are not necessarily pro-pornography, and anti-right-to-lifers are not anti-life, to criticize the tiresome refrain of *misérabilisme* by looking, through performance, at the potential for representing women's agency on stage is not at all the same as perennially finding positive images of women there. Rather, it is to open up the possibility, as I suggested earlier, of more complex representations that may combine negative and positive aspects and that may function both to criticize and to uphold social values in regard to gender.

Conclusion

For reasons of access due to social and economic class (as well, of course, as for reasons of white ethnic hegemony), until the 1960s very few works in the dance canon, either in Europe or the United States, included representations of African American women or other women of color, nor, for the most part, were the dances made by persons of color. And so my study of canonical dances focuses primarily, although not exclusively, on works by European or Euro-American choreographers. The one exception in the canonical dances I analyze is the choreography of Katherine Dunham, an African American trained as an anthropologist as well as a dancer, whose field work in Haiti and other areas of the African diaspora informed her dances. Dunham brought to the American concert dance stage a very different view from that of her peers not only of matriarchy, but of spirituality and witchcraft, with roots in African culture.

Any examination of a received canon necessarily leaves out many valuable works and authors. I do not believe that only dances made by Euro-American choreographers are important. My study also omits dances by the leftist choreographers of the 1930s and 1940s and other significant works marginal to the mainstream of concert and ballet dancing, as well as the vast range of dances in popular culture. My purpose in analyzing the high-art dance canon is not to reinscribe it.[21] But I want to argue that to examine the canon is nevertheless an important project. The canon we have inherited – the dances that have survived for myriad reasons, including both the test of time and the fallibility of human memory as well as the distribution of cultural capital – cannot be wished away by fiat. It is worth analyzing (Marx, after all, dissected capitalism, not communism, in *Capital*), and in fact, much of it is worth keeping – though certainly not to the exclusion of other dances. But what the dance canon leaves out – including various histories of popular, vernacular, and avant-garde dance performances, by both whites and persons of color – would fill many more volumes of feminist analysis and will surely provide topics not only for my own future studies but for those of other dance historians to come.

1

THE ROMANTIC BALLET

La Sylphide, Giselle, Coppélia

The era of the Romantic ballet marks the beginning of women's ascendancy on the dance stage. Themes of the supernatural, exotic folklore, and the quest for the ideal were skillfully realized in the union of scenic effects, diaphanous costumes, shadowy gas lighting, and above all, the expressive use of dance technique, in particular the pointework and lightness of the female dancer, as well as the more earthy, often erotic styles of folkloric character dances. The first major Romantic ballet, *La Sylphide* (1832), according to dance historian Ivor Guest, "sealed the triumph of Romanticism in the field of ballet;" it was, he wrote, "as momentous a landmark in the chronicles of Romantic art as 'The Raft of the "Medusa"' and *Hernani*."[1] The ballet spawned a range of imitations and variations on the theme of the supernatural. It served as a template, ushering in a period, as the French critic Théophile Gautier remarked, when "the Opéra was given over to gnomes, undines, salamanders, elves, nixes, wilis, péris – to all that strange and mysterious folk who lend themselves so marvelously to the fantasies of the *maîtres de ballet*."[2] And the relations in the ballets between humans and these fantastic creatures supplied stories that cast female sexuality and its regulation through the institution of marriage in a fresh light.

But it was not only the formal qualities or even the content of these ballets that set the tone of the Romantic era in ballet. The economic and social conditions of ballet production and reception in France had shifted after the 1830 revolution, for the Opéra was converted from a state-owned and -operated institution into a state-subsidized but privately run commercial enterprise. At the same time, the class make-up of the Opéra audience diversified, and the new, predominantly bourgeois, audiences – many of them raised on the phantasmic and exotic spectacles of Paris boulevard melodramas – exerted an unprecedented box-office power.[3] In the 1830s and 1840s, the Romantic ballet flourished, especially in Paris, but also in other European capitals, including London, Milan, Vienna, St. Petersburg, and Copenhagen. And it brought to the international dance stage the anxieties and concerns of the bourgeois class – including those regarding women, their role in society, and their sexuality.

La Sylphide

La Sylphide, originally choreographed by Filippo Taglioni to music by Jean-Madeleine Schneitzhoeffer and given its premiere at the Paris Opéra in 1832, was a benchmark in ballet history, and it was also a turning-point in the career of Marie Taglioni, the choreographer's daughter and best student.[4] For Taglioni *fille* created the title role of the airy sprite who seduces a Scottish farmer away on his wedding day, into the mystical forest. The ballet showcased the dancer's mastery of technique, her special ability to mask the effort of physical virtuosity

Plate 1 Marie Taglioni in *La Sylphide*, Paris (1837). Devéria lithograph, Edwin Binney 3rd collection, Harvard Theatre Collection, The Houghton Library. Courtesy of the Harvard Theatre Collection.

in order to appear suitably imponderable and ethereal. Gautier compared her to "an idealised form, a poetic personification, an opalescent mist seen against the green obscurity of an enchanted forest."[5] When she toured Russia in 1837, a critic marveled that "it is impossible to describe the suggestion she conveyed of aerial flight, the fluttering of wings, the soaring in the air, alighting on flowers, and gliding over the mirror-like surface of a river."[6] The role catapulted Taglioni to international stardom, and she became indelibly identified with the character of the Sylphide.

The scenario for *La Sylphide* was written by Adolphe Nourrit. A tenor at the Paris Opéra, Nourrit appeared in the leading male role in Meyerbeer's opera *Robert le diable* in 1831, playing opposite Marie Taglioni in a spectral Ballet of the [Dead] Nuns. For *La Sylphide*, Nourrit had been inspired by Charles Nodier's 1822 novella *Trilby, ou le Lutin d'Argail*, set in an ancient Scottish landscape of lochs, mists, and highlands, in which a fisherman's wife falls in love – lethally – with a male elf.[7] Nodier himself was influenced by Sir Walter Scott's fantastic evocations of a medieval Scotland populated by goblins, witches, and sorcerers.

Although Nourrit's scenario is often referred to as an adaptation of Nodier's story, it is also usually said that the two narratives have very little in common, besides the Scottish setting. For one thing, the gender relationships are reversed in *La Sylphide*. For another, *La Sylphide* makes no reference to religion, while *Trilby* involves an exorcism, a pilgrimage, and a ruined cemetery.[8]

What is not usually acknowledged is that the core theme of Nodier's novella – the fatal subversion of marital relations – becomes even more evident in the ballet. In fact, the transgender representation of the elf as a supernatural female figure in *La Sylphide* also recalls Scott's novels and poems, for both the Sylphide, as a seductive enchantress, and the witch, as a soothsayer with mysterious demonic powers, are reminiscent of Scott's women.[9] The very structure of the choreography in *La Sylphide* emblematically narrates the regulation of marriage by the community. Indeed, if *Trilby* exacts 1,000 years of estrangement for infidelity, *La Sylphide* stands as a cautionary tale, admonishing men on pain of death to marry *inside* their own community and not to be lured *outside* their own folk into a world portrayed as Other and inhuman.[10]

La Sylphide, that is, is based upon a radical opposition of love and matrimony within the group – an event that is portrayed as occurring *inside* a cavernous farmhouse – versus love *outside* the folk – love literally outdoors, in the forest regions of the sylphs.[11] Moreover, this difference is further presented as a choice between humanity (the folk), on the one side, and the inhuman (the Sylphide), on the other. Just as Taglioni herself and ballerinas in general might be seen as seductively drawing gentlemen away from their hearths and the heart of their families, and into the Foyer de la Danse, the Sylphide seduces young James away from his wedding into a realm that he barely understands and that he only inhabits at the cost of self-destruction.[12]

In 1834, the Danish choreographer August Bournonville saw Taglioni's *Sylphide* in Paris. He created his own version in 1836 in Copenhagen, to new music by Hermann Løvenskjold. It is Bournonville's version that I will analyze here, because I believe that, although it has been altered in obvious ways over the years, it is still the closest we can come to the original Taglioni version.

La Sylphide is a ballet in two acts. The first act takes place in a commodious farmhouse where James Reuben lives with his widowed mother. It is his wedding or betrothal day.[13] But just before the entrance of Effie, his fiancée, and the wedding guests, James, dozing by the fireplace, is visited by a gossamer vision – the Sylphide.[14] She hovers over his chair, dances out her love for him, kisses him, and then, when he wakes and approaches her, disappears up the chimney. Gurn – James's friend and rival – arrives, then the bride, with her women friends. When James notices Madge, the witch, warming herself at the fireplace, he angrily tells her to leave. But she offers to read the eager young women's futures in their palms. Notably, considering the major theme of *La Sylphide*, all of Madge's predictions concern marriage and procreation: the first young woman, Madge predicts through pantomime, will bear many children who will all flourish; the second, children who will die. The third fortune-seeker is a child, who is slapped for her effrontery: she is too young for such stories. The fourth young maiden is surprised to discover (she mimes embarrassment as she touches her abdomen) that she is already pregnant. Madge tells Effie, the fifth maiden, that her happiness lies with Gurn, not James – a shocking revelation. Marriage stories, it seems, preoccupy the women in this ballet.

Effie goes upstairs to get ready for the wedding ceremony; the guests leave, and suddenly the Sylphide appears again, this time in the window. She tells James she loves him and dances with him flirtatiously. She wraps his scarf around herself and seems to beg for his protection. Gurn watches as James kisses the sprite. When it is time for the others to return, the Sylphide hides in James's armchair, and he covers her with a plaid. Gurn tells the others what he has witnessed and pulls the plaid aside, but the Sylphide is gone. All that remains is a bundled scarf. The rest of the guests arrive and dance in various formations, as the Sylphide, visible only to James, flits among them. As the bridal couple is about to exchange rings, the Sylphide snatches Effie's ring from James's hand and dashes out of the house. He runs after her, leaving the wedding guests stunned.

The second act takes place in a misty forest. Madge summons the other witches, who dance around a boiling cauldron, out of which Madge pulls a scarf. The mist clears, and the Sylphide and James appear. She shows him how she lives and introduces him to a bevy of other sylphs. But as they dance together, she constantly escapes his grasp. James seeks advice from Madge, who gives him the scarf and advises him to wrap it around the Sylphide. This, she explains, will make the Sylphide's wings fall off. But when he captures her, the loss of the Sylphide's wings also marks her death. The sylphs carry her aloft, while the wedding procession of Effie and Gurn crosses the stage. As James falls to the ground, grief-stricken, the witch rises over him triumphantly.[15]

Commentators have often interpreted *La Sylphide* as an allegory of the search for the ideal, as represented by the Sylphide.[16] And such an interpretation is surely borne out in the searching, yearning movements of James, who is so often late in arrival, the sylph having fluttered elsewhere. Yet, it seems that there is also a darker design that is compatible with the incidents of the ballet. It is the story of marriage, of socially licensed sexuality, and of what is possible and impossible, sanctioned and forbidden, with respect to courtship.[17]

The theme of whom one may marry, of course, is a recurring one in Romantic ballet, although it emerges as early as the Pre-Romantic ballet *La Fille Mal Gardée* (1789). It appears, for example, in the major works like *Ondine*, *Alma*, and *Giselle*, as well as in *La Sylphide*. In *Giselle*, the theme of whom one may *not* marry is portrayed most realistically and straightforwardly. One must stick with one's own social class or risk destruction. In *La Sylphide*, perhaps the sylphs represent an aristocratic station to which James ought not aspire. They are certainly *higher* than he, considering their aerial capabilities (not new to this ballet, but nevertheless symbolically potent here). In any case, they, along with the tribe of witches, stand for the Other, for some literally alien group outside what is given as James's natural and appropriate network of affections – so often portrayed as a ring of joyous, folkish dancers.

Within the farmhouse, James is surrounded by his people. And the ballet literalizes the ethnocentric proclivities of peoples to identify themselves as the People and, in consequence, to regard outsiders as not quite human, or, in the case of *La Sylphide*, as downright inhuman – as bewinged creatures sometimes marked by insectile movement and even more generally by "unnatural" movement (i.e., balletic movement which, parenthetically, also connotes aristocratic movement).[18] The action of the ballet, in turn, mobilizes this association of the inside/human/folk in order to cast marriage to outsiders and nonfolk – to sylphs, foreigners, and other nonhumans – as destined to go badly.

So, in terms of its plot, *La Sylphide* is fundamentally about whom one should marry and whom one shouldn't. But it advances this theme in its very structure, not simply in its plot. Symbolically, the ballet presents two options: marriage *inside* the group, which is depicted as human and as sanguine, and marriage or love *outside*, which is portrayed as union with the inhuman and as inevitably tragic. In short, freely borrowing from Lévi-Strauss, one might say that *La Sylphide* is a myth about the regulation of marriage – i.e., it is about whom it is appropriate to marry. Working out the inappropriateness of marrying one of *them* instead of one of *us* – the inhuman rather than a human; the Other rather than a member of the community – not only supplies the thematic motivation for the plot development in *La Sylphide*. It also serves as the basis for the articulation of an overarching choreographic structure of studied and highly connotative contrasts. This is developed in terms of contrasts between the endogamous marriage – within the population of Scots – and the exogamous marriage – between a Scot and a sylph.

In order to analyze the choreographic structure, it will be useful first to discuss the movement structures for the three salient groups in the ballet (the Scots, the witches, and the sylphs). Then I will analyze the choreography for the key individuals (the Sylphide, Effie, James, and Madge) and for their interactions.

In terms of the myth of marriage regulation, the audience is presented with three "tribes," only one of which it is appropriate for humans to marry into, since of the three groups only one is human. Although they have aspects and even steps in common, each of these tribes is marked off by distinctive movement qualities. Even if a particular gesture or step is replicated from one group to another, it does not always have the same look or significance. The same step may be performed in disparate styles, taking on an entirely discrete identity (for instance, both Effie and the Sylphide do rondes de jambes en l'air, but in one case this signals precision and closure, while in the other it suggests weightlessness and porosity). Or, it may be clear that a member of one group is "quoting" the movement as well as the style of another group (as when Gurn flaps his arms and then poses *à la* Sylphide to show the Scots what he has seen, i.e., the Sylphide; or when, in the forest, the Sylphide gestures in the Highland Fling shape and style similar to that seen among the Scots in Act I – right arm held shoulder height, left arm curved solidly over the head – to signal to James her desire to marry him and her willingness to join his clan).

The initial group, the Scots, have two dances in Act I: first, there is the entry of Effie's women friends, and then a dance of the whole community, including both males and females. Each dance is done in a distinctive folkdance style, with allusions to such Scottish dances as the Highland Fling. The women's dance is a brief, brisk ceremonial entry. Two phalanxes of four young women, led by a ninth female dancer, hold their left arms jauntily akimbo in the style we soon come to recognize as characteristic of the Scots. Their right arms, however, hold either the hems of their kilts (suggesting a curtsey) or a gift. They nod their heads or turn them smartly on the beat of the music, and they kick their feet forward as they step, like frisky colts. After the fortune-telling episode and the pas de deux between James and the Sylphide, the women enter in the same formation as before, followed by two phalanxes of men playing bagpipes. Now the entire community dances, making more complex floor patterns, forming and reforming lines, circles, and squares, and dividing up sometimes into couples and sometimes into single-gender groups. Their ability to form these dance figures cooperatively signals their social cohesion.

The dominant movement qualities of the two Scottish dances – earthbound energy, dexterity, and strength contained within limited, hemmed-in spaces – indicate that this is sturdy farming stock. Both men and women wear utilitarian shoes, and the men and women often dance identical steps close to the ground, side by side or facing one another, with arms intertwined or crossed as in a skating formation. At the same time, many of their dance figures are reminiscent of children's games, suggesting a playful spirit of celebration.

We have already seen the delicate Sylphide, wearing a white tulle dress and satin slippers (pointe shoes resembling the dress shoes for evening wear fashionable in the 1830s), dancing alone in a distinctly ethereal, balletic style. When she has danced with James, the two contrasted sharply, and they never touched. Therefore, the folkdance style here, performed by hearty, earthy people wearing bright jackets and plaid kilts and scarves, strongly connotes, first, that the Sylphide does not belong here; their movement, in Labanalysis terms, is bound, while hers is free. And that contrast, taken literally, perhaps explains why James has become obsessed with her, for she seems to represent a realm outside of, and free from, social constraints. Second, the folkdance style signals that this is a community that dances to the same beat and whose steps and hands intricately interlock – metaphorically, a community with shared values, knowledge, and behavior.

Older adults, marriageable youth, and children all take part in the second folkdance. The designs of the choreography emphasize both the theme of matrimony and reproduction within a closed group and the counter-theme of the runaway bridegroom. Almost all the participants in the dance, even the widowed older adults, are potential brides and grooms. In their dance, they not only celebrate the upcoming nuptials of James and Effie, but also show off their own prowess as prospective mates. That there are several generations in the dance promises continuity; through dancing, the children learn the courtship rituals and are initiated into the community. Moreover, various dance figures seem to symbolize matrimonial union sanctioned by and enclosed within the community, as repeatedly couples are formed and reformed out of small groups as well as the whole. When lines of couples cover the space in criss-cross patterns, or when they break apart to form neat rows, images of domesticated landscapes, plowed fields, and the multiplication both of crops and of progeny arise. When all join hands to form a large circle, the community as a whole contains, but does not subsume, individuals, couples, and families. But within this image of equality and unity, something is amiss. For when the group moves into a quadrille, and Effie changes partners, coming "home" she ends up alone, for James, who has run after the Sylphide, is absent from the "home" position.

The second group to appear are the witches, at the beginning of Act II. More a gang than a community, they dance in a circle but, unlike the humans, make no physical contact with one another. Their gestures are angular, asymmetrical, and mechanical; their hands are perennially twisted and splayed, and Madge's fingers are preternaturally long. Although the witches, too, are strong and earth-bound, they are shown as the opposite of the agile humans. Their movements are jerky and spasmodic as they greet one another, crouch by the cauldron, and pass around cups of infernal brew and bolt it down. Snake-like, they press their bellies to the ground. Although they live in nature, they are anything but natural (in the sense of wholesome). Rather, resembling the grotesque figures in Renaissance antimasques, they are monstrous inversions of humanity.

The third "tribe" are the sylphs. Like the witches, they live in nature in a single-sex community, where there can be no reproduction. In fact, the sylphs seem undifferentiated in many respects besides gender. Their movements are not only identical, but extremely symmetrical. They are dressed identically. They look so much alike – as if they were clones – that James can't find his beloved Sylphide when she disappears within the group. If the farmers and the witches are earthbound, the sylphs are airborne. If they are strong, the sylphs are lighter than air. Moving up onto pointe and back down again, taking small vertical jumps and mincing steps (bourrées) that make them appear to hover in place and skim rapidly along the ground, they are more like hummingbirds or moths than women. Their arms float upward weightlessly. The music they dance to has no beat, and its instrumentation – a solo flute and harp – sounds wispy and feminine. In contrast to the humans, their gestures and steps are airy and open; their bodies seem boundaryless and permeable.

The contrast among these three groups is even more starkly drawn in the individual members of the groups whose fates are intertwined in the drama and the ways those individuals interact choreographically. The first character we see dancing is the Sylphide. Her motions are as mercurial as her moods. When the curtain opens, she kneels at James's armchair, in the dainty, contemplative pose – her chin resting on her right hand, her right elbow resting on her left hand – from the well-known painting by G. Lepaulle of the original French version of the ballet. She is by turns gracious, cautious, confident, loving, and mischievous; she moves forward and back from James's chair as if to embody some ambivalence about revealing herself to him; she begins with low, small-scale footwork and then opens into space-devouring leaps; above all, she is never fixed in one place. Her back is flexible, and her movement sequences are extremely fluid. And when she dances in her own habitat, in the second act, her hovering (with the help of some unobtrusive stage machinery) turns into flight. In both spaces, James has trouble catching her or finding her (unlike a wife, who's always at home). In contrast to Madge, who often gestures powerfully downward, the Sylphide's tendency is to move up – into chimneys or trees.

Moreover, it is important to note that the Sylphide has a special relationship to the apertures of the house (the chimney, the window, the door), and that Madge, too, is first sighted at the hearth. Both are liminal figures, who straddle cultural boundaries – inside/outside, natural/supernatural. The Sylphide is not only ambivalent, she is also ambiguous. For although she is childlike, seemingly innocent, and fragile, she also has a seductive, perhaps even demonic side. Dance historian Erik Aschengreen has remarked that in certain interpretations of the ballet, the Sylphide "was directly related to the witch Madge" and that the French critic Jules Janin had found the character "both dangerous and enchanting."[19] That the Sylphide and Madge are never simultaneously present on stage may suggest that they are mysteriously related as reverse images.[20]

After the Sylphide vanishes up the chimney, Effie and her friends enter. Although her part largely involves mime, Effie has one small solo dance, which she does to welcome her wedding guests. Where the Sylphide was tentative, Effie is perfectly at home. She plants herself firmly in the center of the room and, as she opens first her right arm, then her left arm in a wide, open gesture of welcome, she turns to each side to survey the room. In an echo of the opening scene, she too kisses James, who has once again fallen asleep in his chair. But he is startled, rather than enchanted, when he wakes this time. After Effie's friends offer her gifts, she dances. Slowly and deliberately placing her left hand on her hip and her right hand overhead, she performs a few steps of some fancy footwork. Although her leg gestures are similar to the Sylphide's, they seem more mundane. Her crisp delivery, the way her raised foot crosses at her knee or ankle, her close turns, and her sharp changes of direction all give the dance a folkish air. And when her dance ends, she again performs her wide embrace, one arm opening out at a time to include all the guests.[21]

Dancing for her guests, Effie is outwardly directed, presentational in her gestures. Her dancing has a social purpose, just as her sexuality will be channeled toward social reproduction. In contrast, the Sylphide, in her first dance, seems to play by herself and for herself. She touches herself both protectively and provocatively when James approaches her, and although in her second dance she communicates her need for him, it is not clear what form her desire could take. Effie is potentially a mother; the Sylphide certainly is not. In some ways, Effie is sweet and innocent, but she can also be tenacious. She has definite plans for her future, and they include marriage. Furthermore, she will not be a wife entirely dominated by her husband. When James brutally seizes the witch's arm, Effie calms him down, insists that Madge be given a drink of liquor to warm her bones, and begs James to let the witch tell the maidens' fortunes.

A moment before we suddenly see the witch crouching to warm herself at the hearth, James wraps Effie ceremoniously in a plaid scarf, the tartan of his clan. (This scarf, of course, foreshadows another scarf – the poisoned one that serves as the instrument of the Sylphide's death.) When the witch and the guests leave, and Effie goes upstairs to change, the Sylphide returns to the farmhouse, this time through the window. And now, James kneels at her feet. At first she mimes her sadness at James's marriage. But she brightens as she invites James to come home with her to the forest, and her dancing becomes flirtatious. Or perhaps her powers of enchantment are magical; twice she seems to pull James toward the door, but each time he, remembering his vows, resists. She wraps herself in the same portentous scarf that James had wrapped around Effie and looks at him coyly as if to implore him to put her in his fiancée's place during the wedding ceremony. The wedding guests return, do their folkdancing, and the wedding ritual begins, only to be broken when James rushes out the door to follow the Sylphide.

In a sense, James has two broken nuptials. And although each interrupted ceremony takes place in a completely different realm, his two solo dances in the two acts are very similar. He seems literally to jump for joy. And not only does he jump; he jumps high and wide, moving across the stage and taking up so much space that he presses the Scots (in Act I) and the sylphs (in Act II) to the very perimeters of the stage. James also turns while he jumps, executing the most complex steps in the entire ballet.[22] As well, he does rapid, detailed footwork, beating his ankles together and performing entrechats.

However, even though the steps James performs in each solo are similar, they have different meanings in the two different circumstances. In Act I, his solo takes place just after the entry of the wedding guests. It is almost a ritual display of the

Plate 2 Hans Beck as Madge, Valborg Guldbrandsen as Effie, Gustav Uhlendorff as James in Act I of Bournonville's *La Sylphide* (1903). Photograph by Georg Lindstrom. Courtesy of the Royal Theatre Archive and Library, Copenhagen.

bridegroom's favorable qualities. As he holds his arms in a circle above his head (a high fifth port de bras) and then moves the circle downward (a low fifth port de bras), he seems to frame his head and torso, presenting himself as if in a portrait, as if to say "Look how handsome I am, and see how heroic my uplifted chest is!" When he jumps high and turns in mid-air, the community can observe his strength and coordination. When he dispatches his entrechats, they can take stock of his ability for detailed precision, as well as the speed with which he works. His consumption of space signals a distinctively male-coded drive to control territoriality, which in turn connotes power.[23]

In Act II, James performs certain steps slightly differently; for instance, the beats of his ankle resemble the fluttering steps of the sylphs more than the bold, highly controlled footwork of his earlier dance. And he even adopts some of the sylphs' steps. This solo, unlike the solo in the farmhouse, is segmented, its parts alternating with responses from the Sylphide. Thus it is really part of a pas de deux, which, in turn, is sandwiched between group dances by the sylphs. So in the second solo, James seems less to be demonstrating his strength and skills than to be introducing himself, having a challenge dance with his beloved, and then being incorporated into the group.

If James is powerful, here in the forest his nemesis, Madge, proves to be even more so. Crouching by the fire, bending over her cane, or limping toward a seat, in Act I she looks like a helpless old woman, gnarled and crippled. But in the opening scene of Act II, she is in her element. Her arms weave strange incantations over the cauldron's brew. She beckons commandingly for her sister witches to join her. And when they do, her gestures become elated and expostulatory. She thrusts them strongly upward, outward, and downward. She seems, with her arms, to be ranting like a mad scientist or hysterical dictator. The same powerful thrusting gestures later in this act shove Gurn to his knees to propose to Effie, and James to his knees to beg for Madge's help. When James asks Madge's forgiveness for his rude treatment of her in the farmhouse, she draws herself up, gesturing both the pride of one whose dignity was insulted and the exultation of one who will never forgive, but will ultimately achieve her revenge. After the Sylphide's death, the witch lifts her arms above her head and seems to tower over James, showing that she is literally above him.[24] But merely to kill him would not suffice. She pulls him back into semiconsciousness to make him suffer more deeply as he watches the Sylphide's funeral. In the final tableau, she lifts her arms triumphantly as she crouches by James's prone body.

On the one hand, *La Sylphide* operates, in a broad sense, like a cautionary tale, warning that romance outside one's social circle risks destruction and death. Certainly, Bournonville, as well as the Copenhagen society he inhabited, agreed wholeheartedly with that message.[25] But on the other hand, *La Sylphide* indulges forbidden wishes, allowing James to gambol with the woodland sylphs for the best part of the second act before he is killed. In this way, the ballet is reminiscent of so many crime stories whose final moral lesson – that crime does not pay – is preceded by waves of gratifying violence and mayhem. Similarly, *La Sylphide* admonishes against courtship outside the group, but only after painting it in idyllic colors, thus in the last instance taking back with one hand what it has lavishly entertained with the other.[26]

Marriage, of course, has always been an important social theme in Western dancing. In the Renaissance, amateur ballets were mounted at royal wedding ceremonies, whereas with the professionalization of dance in the eighteenth century, representations of weddings were made part of the ballet itself.[27] With *La Sylphide*, however, an important turn is taken, one which profoundly marks the direction of the Romantic ballet. For in *La Sylphide*, as in many of its progeny, the theme of marriage is introduced, only to be subverted in various ways. If eighteenth-century ballets represented wedding ceremonies, Romantic ballets so often show them undermined. *La Sylphide*'s human marriage plot, like that of so many Romantic ballets, fails. But the human marriage plot is also dysphoric, for it seems James could not have been happy married to Effie. Rather than a celebration of the incorporation of the community, *La Sylphide* explores society's anxiety toward the Other, and perhaps toward the institution of marriage itself.

Giselle

The original version of *La Sylphide* was made two years after the July Revolution of 1830 and the establishment of Louis-Philippe's "bourgeois monarchy." *Giselle*, choreographed nearly ten years later, in 1841, embodies even more explicitly the values of that era, not only in terms of gender politics, but also in terms of class conflict and compromise, expressed through a gendered narrative of doomed love across class lines. Depending on how the role of the hero is played, the first act of the ballet may be read as the story either of a peasant girl's seduction and betrayal by a nobleman or of a tragically futile love affair that violates class boundaries – both well-known themes (the latter at least since Rousseau's *La Nouvelle Heloïse* [1761]), asserting similarly anti-aristocratic, democratic values.

The theme of seduction and abandonment, most commonly of a lower-class woman by a nobleman, is anti-aristocratic because it is more than simply a sad tale of love disappointed. It is a form of rape, and rape is not simply a matter of sex, but of political power. The European literary tale of seduction and abandonment speaks in sexual metaphors of the acutely asymmetrical power relations between classes. For the imagery of sexual predation not only invokes the libertinage of the ancien regime, but also stands for other kinds of non-sexual predation – for the social and economic exploitation and bondage of the peasantry and working class. Similarly, the theme of true love that is obstructed by class boundaries criticizes the rigidity of hierarchies and social barriers that insist on strictly endogamous and homogamous marriages.

But *Giselle* is also heir to gothic literature, horror tales, and boulevard melodramas. It adds to the familiar earthly tragedy of foiled love a note of the supernatural and of spiritual dis-ease. In its crucial second act, a regiment of female vampire-figures – the Wilis, ghosts of maidens who died before their wedding days – wreaks revenge on men. But ultimately, class and gender warfare come to an end. An unholy night of terror ends, and with the dawn's light (at the ballet's conclusion) come peace and reconciliation.

Giselle has often been viewed as a story about the universality and transcendence of love, which endures beyond life itself. For instance, Ivor Guest refers to

> the fragility of the heroine, her mind balanced between reason and madness; the hero's love which outlives his passion and stretches out to seek his beloved beyond the tomb; the hopelessness of their love in this life, but the purification which it brings to his soul.[28]

However, there are other ways of understanding *Giselle*. I will argue here that *Giselle* is historically situated and that its love story is tightly bound into its original socio-political milieu. It does not speak of universals, but rather, serves as an allegory for the assertion of bourgeois individuality and as a metaphor for political compromise during a specific period of French history – the era of the "citizen-king" Louis-Philippe, a political regime consciously built on those centrist middle-class principles and rhetoric.

As Evan Alderson has shown, *Giselle* upholds bourgeois values in various ways:

> a woman triumphs, but her power has been channeled in a way that confines male sexual anxiety, subtly condones male aggression, and alleviates male guilt. . . . These same values appear to manifest a deep respect for women (at least for bourgeois wives and daughters) and a profound interest in private experience, especially the domestic emotions. Moreover, they are infused with the sentiment for beauty.

Alderson asserts convincingly that "whatever the avowed social oppositions of Gautier's aestheticism, he has not escaped 'the intolerable world of the bourgeoisie;' he has become its ideologist."[29]

Moreover, as I will argue, *Giselle* represents its heroine as a female nurturer firmly ensconced in the new, private bourgeois domain, turning her back on female community and terrorist feminist activism. The "noble spiritual love" that the ballet celebrates is not the triumph and transcendence of a universal human emotion, but, rather, a political affirmation of the self and of personal agency that is historically rooted, part and parcel of the French bourgeois ideology. Yet, ultimately that individual defiance is muted in a spirit of concession. In the context of the July Monarchy, harmony and reconciliation were less spiritual values than socio-political ones, and *Giselle*'s night of terror that ends with a peaceful sunrise clearly expresses a metaphoric desire for post-revolutionary tranquility – in particular, among women.[30] That the political metaphor is implicit and comes in romantic wrappings – turning inward and speaking of individualized feelings – fits with the new French middle-class preoccupations regarding private life and a bourgeois view of freedom seen as a personal, rather than political, matter.[31]

The Paris Opéra itself was a site where class and gender had always been dramatized. I have already noted that in 1830 the institution had been converted from a state-owned enterprise to a state-subsidized private business and that the class make-up of the audience shifted accordingly, from predominantly aristocratic to mainly upper-middle class. No longer was the auditorium of the Opéra the haunt of aristocrats (a hierarchical replica of the court) or a hunting ground for social and sexual encounters – a place for the public performance of wealth, power, and erotic allure. However, backstage, a different kind of sexual "market" was established under Louis Véron's directorship in the Foyer de la Danse, where certain privileged men, many of them members of the Jockey Club, could now make assignations with the ballet dancers.[32]

In fact, as historian James H. Johnson has observed, the 1831 remodeling of the Opéra symbolized the management's change of policy and patronage by making the auditorium both visually less ostentatious (and thus less allied to aristocratic tastes) and fiscally more lucrative. Véron disciplined his audiences, forbidding spectators to leave their seats during the performance and dimming the house lights, but there was another, internal discipline – the *haut bourgeois* code of politeness – that transformed audience behavior.[33] And what was seen on the stage changed as well. Johnson points out that

> the underlying political messages of the operas [middle-class audiences] saw there . . . flattered just such [a bourgeois] identity, the identity of the respectable middle, the *juste milieu*, neither royalist nor revolutionary, opposed to religious fanaticism while still vaguely believing, dedicated to honor, allied with order, suspicious of the masses.[34]

It is with this system of morality and behavior in mind that we must analyze *Giselle*'s narratives of seduction, betrayal, madness, nuptial tragedy, revenge, and pardon. It will explain why both Albrecht and Giselle are "saved" – why he is not killed by the Wilis, and why she finally rests in peace in her grave.

Giselle was written by Théophile Gautier and Jules-Henri Vernoy de Saint-Georges, inspired by two poems: "De l'Allemagne," by Heinrich Heine, and "Fantômes," from *Les Orientales*, by Victor Hugo. It was set to music by Adolphe Adam. Choreographed by Jules Perrot and Jean Coralli, the ballet was created to showcase Carlotta Grisi, the newest rising star of the Paris Opéra ballet, who was equally adept at dancing vivacious, earthy character dances and aerial, otherworldly roles.[35] She combined in one dancing body the best features of the famous rivals Fanny Elssler and Marie Taglioni, whom Gautier had characterized, respectively, as pagan and Christian.[36] In fact, this distinction holds for the entire ballet *Giselle*, for the first act is Christian and the second is pagan, although the styles of dancing are inverted: the first act is *terre-à-terre* and Elssleresque, while the second act is aerial and Taglioniesque.

Plate 3 Carlotta Grisi in *Giselle* (ca. 1844). Lithograph by Challamel. Courtesy of the Dance Collection, The New York Public Library for the Performing Arts, Astor, Lenox and Tilden Foundations.

In the rustic setting of the German wine-country in Act I, we see Giselle's and Loys's cottages in the foreground.[37] In the original setting, a castle loomed in the distance. The gamekeeper Hilarion, who loves Giselle unsuccessfully, discovers that his rival, Loys, is in reality Duke Albrecht in disguise. Giselle and Albrecht enter and dance their vows of love. That they do the same steps in the same style, side by side, seems to imply that they are equal, and perhaps even suggests that there is no sexual hierarchy in this imagined peasant life, for there is no gender differentiation in their dancing here.

When the lovers are interrupted by Hilarion, Giselle rejects him. They are joined by a group of peasant girls, who arrive to take Giselle to harvest grapes. But she leads them all in a merry folkdance. Albrecht joins in; the fact that he is the only man in the group speaks well for him, for it signals he has been accepted into the community. The young women – the "good sisters" of Giselle's earthly community – skip, hold hands, and look at one another. Their human contact and the angular knees and elbows of their joyous dancing – their *terre-à-terre*, literally earthy dancing – sets them apart from the Wilis, the inhuman "evil sisters" Giselle joins in the second act. Giselle's mother, Berthe, reprimands her for not working and for tempting fate. Berthe recounts the legend of the Wilis, who spirit away girls who love dancing, and she points out that Giselle is particularly vulnerable, for she already has a weak heart.

A royal hunting party enters the scene. The prince asks Berthe to provide them with water and a place to rest. His daughter, Bathilde, is enchanted with Giselle, who immediately confesses to her that she is in love, and Bathilde confides that she, too, is engaged. Giselle, giddy with joy, shows her gullibility and vulnerability in her interaction with Bathilde. While the royal party rests inside Giselle's cottage, a group of peasant youth arrives. They crown Giselle Queen of the Vintage, but in the midst of the merriment, Hilarion reveals Albrecht's deception. The Prince and Bathilde emerge from the cottage, and they recognize Albrecht, who is Bathilde's fiancé. Giselle goes mad, reprising in a tragic, twisted refrain – as if dredging them bitterly from her memory – the steps she had happily danced earlier with Albrecht, and she either dies of a broken heart or kills herself with Albrecht's sword.[38]

Act II takes place in a dank forest, the site of Giselle's tomb. Midnight strikes, and Myrtha, Queen of the Wilis, appears, making her dancing rounds of her dominion. The regal, courtly quality of her dancing and the fact that she dances alone establishes her monarchy. She holds two branches of rosemary, an herb that symbolizes remembrance and fidelity. But in her rancorous empire, these are vindictive, rather than benevolent qualities. After marking her territory, she calls forth her subjects, the ghostly virgins, who make their obeisances to her, and they dance in formation. In contrast to the peasant girls, the Wilis dance with elegantly stretched, attenuated limbs. That the slow, beautiful, aristocratic movements in this ballet belong to evil spirits makes them entrancing in the same way vampires are, for they evince a combination of attraction, especially sexual magnetism, and repulsion. At the end of their dance, moving across the stage in arabesque penchée, they look like animals crawling or insects skimming the lake's surface. One is reminded that God condemned the serpent in the Garden of Eden to crawl forever on the earth.

Finally, Giselle emerges from her tomb to be initiated into their cult. She, too, strikes an arabesque and, spinning in a circle, looks like she is out of control, held in the thrall of an external force. For the first time, she does not enjoy dancing, for she is dancing against her will. She is an emblem of power and agency split apart, for if in Act I she experienced freedom of choice with little social power, in Act II Giselle wields the power with which Myrtha imbues her, but has no freedom. Her limp hands, her backwards jumps, the way her arms or head follow the rest of her body give the impression that she has no volition of her own.

Albrecht arrives to mourn Giselle, and her ghost appears to him and dances with him. At first she is elusive, like the Sylphide was to James, but soon their dancing becomes synchronized. Still, if on earth they danced close together and side by side, here they are more distant and cover more space, although when they do come together, he often lifts her. In this aristocratic realm, not only have their genders crystallized as distinct, but he partners her in ways that make her lofty and celestial. He literally elevates her, exalting her in a way he did not when she was alive.

Hilarion also arrives, and the Wilis dance him to death. That he dances constantly and agitatedly, either partnered by all of the Wilis or alone (with none of them), oscillates between suggesting anonymous promiscuous sex and celibacy. Either way, Hilarion is unlike Albrecht, who is faithful to one partner. But when Myrtha signals that Albrecht is the next victim, Giselle defies her, placing herself in front of her lover as if to shield him. She and Albrecht try to take sanctuary near the cross on her tomb, but Myrtha forces Giselle to dance. She does so slowly, as if hypnotically possessed, and her dancing entices Albrecht away from the protection of the cross.

At first Giselle and Albrecht dance an extended adagio. (The Wilis, lined up on either side, do not seem to notice that this kind of dancing will never exhaust their chosen victim.) This seems like a suspended moment, out of time, when instead of moving the narrative action forward, the dancers are pausing to express an emotional quality. It is a private instant of tenderness and intimacy. Then the music and the dancing speed up, and once again their dancing seems to control them, rather than the other way around. Now it is as if what gave them joy in life – dancing together – has become their curse. Giselle beseeches Myrtha, even bringing her the flowers Albrecht had placed on her grave, but the Queen is relentless in her command. From time to time Albrecht falls down, exhausted, but Myrtha repeatedly forces Giselle to entice him back into dancing with her.

But at last, just as Albrecht falls into a final exhaustion, dawn breaks. The Wilis disappear. In the original scenario, Albrecht rose to place Giselle on a mound of flowers, and as she began to be pulled into the earth, the Prince and Bathilde arrived. Giselle left Albrecht forever, gesturing farewell and signaling her wish that he should marry Bathilde. In the modern version, Giselle returns to her tomb, leaving Albrecht alone. In one staging, he gathers up the flowers he had put on her grave and as he backs away from her tomb, drops them one by one. When the last one is gone, metonymically suggesting that Giselle and he are parted forever, he collapses.[39]

Although Act I is set in Germany, its references to the sexual cruelty of an aristocracy that unfeelingly sows its wild oats among the peasants has unmistakable parallels to the French pre-Revolutionary *ancien régime*, as well as to the Bourbon restoration. While *jus primae noctis* and *droit du seigneur* may or may not have been myths, they are nevertheless powerful social images that stand for the untrammeled greed and lust of the nobility. Perhaps Act I of *Giselle* even recalls the Marquis de Sade's many tales of innocent women raped and discarded by dissolute noblemen. *Giselle*'s first-act narrative also bears similarities to the love plot of Auber's opera *La Muette de Portici* (1828), but without the latter's revolutionary setting.

La Muette de Portici, also known as *Masaniello*, sets its story of impossible love against a backdrop of the 1647 Neapolitan uprising against the Spanish. The mute heroine, Fenella, is seduced and abandoned by Alphonse, son of the Spanish duke. Like Giselle, Fenella kills herself; like Albrecht, Alphonse repents. Although a performance of the opera in Brussels is said to have sparked the Belgian revolution of 1830, Johnson points out that its ultimate message was not revolutionary, but politically moderate, for Fenella's brother, the fisherman Masaniello who had stirred up revolution to defend her honor, ultimately rejects political violence. "Scribe's political message is clear: tyranny of either stripe, royalist or revolutionary, is shameful; there are good, if fallible, aristocrats just as there are decent commoners; however necessary, sudden political change is dangerous, so a prudent middle path is best."[40]

In much the same way, despite the potentially anti-aristocratic theme in *Giselle*, by the end of Act I Albrecht appears to be devastated by Giselle's death, and by the beginning of Act II he is genuinely repentant. This in itself mitigates a revolutionary message, but there are other factors – chief among them Giselle's protection of him and our complete lack of sympathy for his rival, Hilarion – that do so, as well.

It is Act II, however, where the main interest of the ballet lies. Indeed, all of Act I seems to exist only as a pretext for the action in Act II, and this factor, too, stresses the palliative aspect of the narrative. (This should not be surprising, since Gautier's original scenario consisted only of a version of the second act.) The folkish character of the dancing (alternating with storytelling mime) and the portrayal of a human community with its divisions between class and gender in Act I give way to a cold, stern, glittering choreography that takes place in a nether world ruled by women devoid of human distinction – or human feeling. In a variation with feminist significance on the vampire legend, where usually men prey on women, here it is the women who indiscriminately drain men of life.

In Gautier's original description, the Wilis were somewhat distinguishable as dancing girls with various personalities and costumes, corresponding to different sorts of ballet character dances, but they still somehow seemed identical:

> First, with a purring of castanets and a swarming of white butterflies, with a large comb cut out like the interior of a Gothic cathedral, and silhouetted against the moon, comes a cachucha dancer from Seville, a gitana, twisting her hips and wearing finery with cabalistic signs on her skirt – then a Hungarian dancer in a fur bonnet, making the spurs on her boots chatter, as teeth do with cold – then a *bibiaderi* in a costume like Amani's, a bodice with a sandal-wood satchel, gold lamé trousers, belt and necklace of mirror-bright mail, bizarre jewellery, rings through her nostrils, bells on her ankles – and then, lastly, timidly presenting

> herself, a *petit rat* [ballet girl] of the Opéra in practice dress, with a kerchief round her neck and her hands thrust into a little muff. All these costumes, exotic and commonplace, are discoloured and take on a sort of spectral uniformity.[41]

Although eventually the Wilis were dressed identically, in long white tutus, even this early scenario suggests their uncanny property of sameness simultaneously linked to their femininity. That they are dancing virgins, after all, is what they have in common, and so their danger itself seems to come from their clone-like features: their female sex and their interchangeability.

The lightness and soft footwork of the Wilis' dancing and their mothlike costumes, added to their clone-like character, gives them, like the sylphs in *La Sylphide*, an insectile quality. So, too, does their vampiric, preying nature and their characteristic horizontal arabesque penchée. Indeed, they seem to be embodiments of – or at least closely related to – the Greek Furies, blood-sucking "virgin daughters of Night" in Aeschylus' *Oresteia*, who were perhaps originally figured as pestilent buzzing, swarming flies in ancient myth.[42] The Furies tell Orestes, the matricide:

> No, neither Apollo, nor Athena's strength
> will rescue you, perishing, uncared for,
> knowing in your heart no whereabouts of joy,
> the blood sucked from you, fodder for ghosts,
> a shade.
>
> . . .
>
> Come join the dance; let us join in it!
> for we have made our decision
> to reveal the song of hatred:
> how we, the Furies' regiment,
> administer men's fated lives.[43]

Later, Orestes *is* saved by Athena, just as Albrecht is saved by Giselle's protection, although in the ballet the Wilis simply disappear – instead of being transformed, like the Furies, into beneficent household spirits (the Eumenides).

Surely, however elegant they looked on the ballet stage, the Wilis, that threatening mob of spiteful women, must have called up cultural memories of activist women during the Revolution and the Terror – demonstrating, rioting, and taking up arms.[44] Both revolutionary women and Marie Antoinette were characterized at the time as "furies."[45] As dance historian Joellen Meglin points out, "The Romantic ballet communicated a . . . horror of congregations of women. . . . Women acting in concert were characterized as vindictive, wrathful, and remorseless; they were the fearsome oppressed who would vent their fury in judgment of the oppressors. The *corps de ballet* was a kind of irrational mob taking justice into its own hands. . . . Like the hellish women agitators of the Revolution, they tried to exert control over other women against their wills."[46]

If those in the audience remembered their Aeschylus as well as they remembered the violence of revolutions, they might indeed have prayed, along with the Eumenides at the end of Aeschylus's play,

> that never in this city shall stir the noise
> of faction, that is never sated with evils.
> May the dust never drink the black blood
> of fellow citizens, in their lust for revenge,
> hunting for murder to answer murder,
> to the ruin of the city.
> Rather let them give joy for joy
> in harmony, a community united.[47]

This message of peace and reconciliation, coming from the tamed Furies, was what French post-revolutionary audiences wanted to hear from women.[48]

But there is another community of women of whom the Wilis would have reminded audiences. The Wilis, a cloistered, hierarchical company of virgins, were in a sense anti-nuns, dedicated to an unholy mission. This reversal of Christian values in an uncontrollable gang of women could connote sexual as well as political danger. For a group of women who only find pleasure in each other's company and go around killing men might well suggest lesbian "perversions," and the idea that nuns indulged in homosexual activities was already a familiar theme in literature at least since the eighteenth century. In the first scene of de Sade's *L'Histoire de Juliette* (1797), for instance, the adolescent heroine is initiated into sapphic love at her convent school during a small orgy involving the abbess and another pupil. De Sade's motives for writing this scene, of course, were anticlerical, as were Diderot's in *La Religieuse*. Meglin argues that romantic literature repeated these themes, but in order to show the perversity of the revolutionary value of fraternity, symbolized now by sororal love: "illicit relations or incest with a sister, be she a sibling or a sister of the convent, were an obsession and sin célèbre."[49]

Suggestions of questionable goings-on in convents were not unfamiliar on the stage of the Opéra, either. Marie Taglioni's first great triumph had come in a scene reminiscent of the dance of the Wilis, the Ballet of the Nuns in Meyerbeer's opera *Robert le diable*. In it, she danced the role of the debauched abbess Hélène, one of the group of lapsed nuns who arise from their tombs at the Devil's behest, throw off their habits, and dance hedonistically. Hélène uses her sexual charms to entice Robert, the Devil's son and a nobleman, into taking a magic talisman that will win him his beloved. The vices the nuns had practiced in their earthly lives are reenacted in the ballet. "Stirring the cold dust from the tombs, they suddenly throw themselves into delights from their past life; they dance like bacchantes, they gamble like lords and drink like soldiers," wrote the reviewer for the *Revue des deux mondes*.[50] The American Fanny Appleton describes the overall effect of the Ballet of the Nuns:

> It was magnificent and terrific and diabolical and enchanting and everything else fine. The music and the show and the dancing! The famous witch's dance [*sic*], in the freezing moonlight in the ruined abbey, was as impressive as I expected. . . . They drop in like flakes of snow and are certainly very charming witches with their jaunty Parisian figures and most refined pirouettes! . . . The diabolical music and the dead rising from their tombs and the terrible darkness and the strange dance unite to form a stage effect almost unrivalled.[51]

Gautier's description of *Giselle*'s second act shows just how close the Wilis were to the ghosts of the lapsed nuns in *Robert le diable*:

> With her characteristic melancholy grace [Adèle Dumilâtre, in the role of Myrtha] frolics in the pale star-light, which glides over the water like a white mist, poises herself on flexible branches, leaps on the tips of the grass, like Virgil's Camilla, who walked on wheat without bending it, and, arming herself with a magic wand, she evokes the other *Wilis*, her subjects, who come forth with their moonlight veils from the tufted reeds, clusters of verdure, and calixes of flowers to take part in the dance. She announces to them that they are to admit a new *Wili* that night. Indeed, Giselle's shade, stiff and pale in its transparent shroud, suddenly leaps from the ground at Myrtha's bidding. . . . The shroud falls and vanishes. Giselle, still benumbed from the icy damp of the dark abode she has left, makes a few tottering steps, looking fearfully at the tomb which bears her name. . . . All at once, as though she wished to make up for the time wasted in that narrow bed fashioned of six long planks and two short ones, to quote the poet of *Leonore*, she bounds and rebounds in an intoxication of liberty and joy at no longer being weighed down by that thick coverlet of heavy earth.[52]

The image of Wilis as anti-nuns has an anticlerical inflection, but it is recuperated in the Christian quality of Giselle's sufferance and forgiveness of Albrecht.

The Wilis might have recalled yet another group of women for *Giselle*'s audiences: the large numbers of single women, both working class and middle class, who were beginning to cause a number of social anxieties, including those about prostitution, but also about population decline. Feminist historian Claire Goldberg Moses points out that the spinster brought shame on the bourgeois family, that there were extremely limited professional options available to her (partly because she was usually inadequately educated), and that these few opportunities were so competitive and poorly paid they often brought her to the edge of poverty.[53] According to the historian Adeline Daumard, "The old maid was a burden, useless and disdained. In truth, the older spinster woman, almost always with very limited resources, lived so completely on the edge of society that she hardly even belonged to the bourgeoisie."[54] For the working-class woman, who was even less likely to marry, there were fewer options: back-breaking factory work, domestic service, work convents, and prostitution. Even going to prison was a way for these women to get food and shelter.[55]

The normative expectation, at least for bourgeois women, was that all women would get married in order to channel their sexuality "properly" – but in fact a large proportion did not. For working-class women, prostitution was often the only alternative to starvation, and in the first thirty years of the nineteenth century, prostitution – both legal and illegal – flourished. The number of prostitutes in Paris tripled.[56] Therefore what was perceived as the rampant sexuality of single women was a source of enormous cultural anxiety. The Wilis were like a pack of surplus single women – unprocreative old maids (still a sexual threat, since celibacy was as frowned upon in French society at this time as promiscuity) or potential prostitutes.

Indeed, since dancing is often a metaphor for libidinous sexuality, that the Wilis all died from "dancing too much" hints that, while they may have died with their virginity intact, nevertheless, they perished from excess lust. And this suggestion may be borne out in the choreography of *Giselle*. Hilarion, after all, expires because his dancing is not regulated by one partner. As I noted above, he either dances alone (implying celibacy) or is passed along the entire line of Wilis (implying the anonymous promiscuity of illicit sex). Giselle is able to modulate her partner's dancing, and thus to save him; her control of his timing, a metaphor for her efficient management of his sexuality, argues in favor of bourgeois marriage and the new marital values of sexual fidelity.

The character Giselle, of course, hails neither from the French urban working class nor from the bourgeoisie; she is a German peasant. But in the binary established by the ballet, she is "not-aristocratic," and therefore, for the Opéra's audiences, could stand for French bourgeois womanhood. She is not precisely an old maid, since she was engaged to marry in life and died prematurely. Still, the heart of her tragedy is that she could not marry, and that is certainly analogous to the mundane misfortune of the bourgeois spinster.

But at the same time, she is analogous to the working girl. The marriage Giselle had dreamed of could not have taken place in the society she lived in, for not only differences in class status, but also Albrecht's betrothal to another woman kept her apart from her lover. Certainly this was the case for many nineteenth-century French working women who found themselves, if not in love with, at least sexually involved with married men (often their employers) from the upper classes.[57] Since marriage was strictly homogamous in regard to class, these lower-class women could not possibly hope to legitimize either their relationships or the children born of these liaisons.[58] Nevertheless, in the ballet Giselle ultimately does transcend these barriers to become her lover's partner, and this is what allows her finally to rest in peace.

The lovers inhabit two different communities in *Giselle*, and their nuptials seem to be twice broken. But the marriage grid I discussed in the Introduction is more complicated in this ballet than in many others. In the first act, the marriage plot fails both because of Giselle's death and because of Albrecht's elite class origins (as well as his betrothal), and the affective value of that marriage in the human community changes from euphoric to dysphoric when Albrecht's true identity is revealed. In the second act, a new marriage plot in one sense also fails, for Albrecht survives and lives, while Giselle is dead. Unlike Romeo and Juliet, these lovers are not joined in death. Rather, Albrecht will marry Bathilde (at least in the original scenario; in modern versions he is simply alone at the end), although in some way Giselle will also always be "with" him. The affective value of a potential "marriage" between Giselle and Albrecht in the community of Wilis, however, is dysphoric.

Nevertheless, from the author's and audience's point of view, the outcome, although sad, is also euphoric, for Giselle does elude the society of the Wilis and finds peace, while Albrecht survives on earth. And in this sense, their "marriage" does not fail, but actually succeeds – although it only lasts one night. The consummation of that marriage is spiritual, not physical; it is their act of dancing together tenderly while ultimately resisting Myrtha's thrall. Perhaps this complexity of the marriage plot and the oscillation of affect in *Giselle* partly accounts for the ballet's longevity.

Although the ballet is unlike *Romeo and Juliet* in that only one partner dies, in other aspects it resembles Shakespeare's play in ways that are worth examining briefly. Shakespeare's play, too, is often seen as a paean to eternal, universal, transcendent love. And yet, analyzed from a historical point of view, it can be seen as an assertion of the birth of individualism against the feudal epoch. Romeo and Juliet defy the social divisions that forbid their love (between warring families, rather than between *Giselle*'s incompatible classes). Juliet's refusal to comply with the feudal practice of arranged marriages participates in that defiance. The lovers' deaths constitute a tragedy on a personal level, but on a political level they triumph, for they have succeeded in rejecting the outmoded, feudal political system that stifled individual choice in order to further the community's and the family's rigid socio-political codes and interests. Similarly, *Giselle* upholds the right to individual choice, so key to the bourgeois ethos, in the face of hierarchical, autocratic laws regarding both marriage and revenge.

Still, the ending of *Giselle* does not advocate individual rights at the expense of social order, and in this regard, the ballet endorses the political status quo. For finally, as in the bourgeois monarchy itself, there is a *rapprochement* between the aristocracy and its Other. Albrecht, like the French monarchy itself, is not totally absolved of his sins, but rather, he is pardoned; he is reinstated to his former condition, yet – perhaps like Louis-Philippe, or at least like the official images of the citizen-king – somewhat chastened.

As for Giselle, she too is recuperated by the bourgeois domain. Dancing against her will to exhaust Albrecht, yet tenderly ministering to him all the while, she becomes precisely the figure of the consoling caregiver and partner so prized by the emerging bourgeois domestic ideology, set in direct contrast to the unnatural, vengeful, all-too-public Wilis. She is not just Albrecht's dance partner, but his partner in spirit. She becomes one of the Eumenides, a beneficent domestic presence. And, as flutes and harps accompany Giselle's final descent, not into her grave but into a bed of flowers, she seems to be transformed into an angel, freed from the spell of the vindictive Wilis by the consummation of her union with Albrecht.

Anxieties about marriage and about women's sexuality were widespread in France in the 1830s and 40s. The utopian feminist movement that emerged in the 1830s, in particular the Saint-Simonians, called for sexual equality and love outside of the marriage institution, which – despite the rhetoric of bourgeois domesticity – was often simply an economic arrangement between families and which, although seen as woman's only natural fate, deprived her of all legal rights. Feminists advocated civil rights for women and called for the reform of marriage laws, including divorce.[59] *Giselle* assuages those anxieties. Its heroine deserts the ranks of angry celibates in order to become a protective caregiving figure, and her soul is saved by the consummation that takes place on her other-worldly wedding night. But still, she is dead; female self-sacrifice makes male survival possible. (However, it should be noted here that to many contemporary spectators, death ends existence, but to a large proportion of nineteenth-century viewers, of course, death was a doorway – albeit hedged about with dangers – to a greater spiritual life.) Evan Alderson observes, "the erotic is given and yet simultaneously denied. . . . Ideality . . . both captures and subverts [erotic stimulus] in the interests of sentiment and power."[60] Exogamy raises its ugly head, but is conveniently avoided. The ballet is pro-marriage, asserting that one must have a partner – but at the same time, it reminds us that not just any partner will do. *Giselle* presents an individualistic rebellion against the conventions of marriage, only to soften that message with centrist compromise.

Coppélia and the "decline" of French nineteenth-century ballet

It is interesting to note that *La Sylphide*, the first Romantic ballet, stands to *Coppélia* (1870), arguably the last significant nineteenth-century French ballet, as tragedy does to comedy. Both *La Sylphide* and *Coppélia* set up a conflict between a human community and its potential intrusion by a nonhuman (foreign) Other. In *La Sylphide*, the alien is supernatural, while in *Coppélia* alterity is subhuman, a robot. But whereas *La Sylphide* ends in the destruction of both protagonists, *Coppélia* ends in a successful, euphoric marriage and an incorporation of the human couple into the community. *La Sylphide* involves two sets of broken nuptials, but in *Coppélia* Frantz and Swanilda's wedding vows are happily sealed, and the threat to the joy of the human marriage, in the figure of the mechanical doll, is revealed as lifeless and harmless.

In many ways, the contrast in affect of these ballets is suggested by the state of contemporary French politics, for if the 1830s were a decade in search of stability, the late 1860s were a time of prosperity, confidence, and expansion. But the contrast in affect is also connected to sexual politics and to changing views of the institution of marriage itself. The Second Empire was, after all, the birthplace of the French bedroom farce, as epitomized in the playwright Eugène Labiche's various *ménages à trois*; indeed, his *The Happiest of the Three* was written in the same year as *Coppélia*. This period also saw the triumph of the operetta, which satirized and souffléd the tragic love plots of grand opera.[61] In Jacques Offenbach's well-known operetta *La Belle Hélène* (1864), Helen of Troy is a bored Parisian housewife whose affair with Paris (the man) is justified for political reasons. Siegfried Kracauer notes that despite the operetta's tone of doom, "it allowed the accent to be put on eroticism and the gospel of pleasure. . . . In 1865 the whole of France was singing: *Dis-moi, Vénus, quel plaisir trouves-tu/A faire ainsi cascader, cascader la vertu?*"[62] Divorce was still illegal in France, but the licentious Second-Empire attitude toward extramarital sex was a far cry from the bourgeois view of virtue and marriage in *Giselle*.[63]

The scenario for *Coppélia, ou La Fille aux yeux d'émail*, written by Charles Nuitter (the Opéra's archivist), was derived from E.T.A. Hoffmann's fantasia *Der Sandmann*. But unlike the male protagonist of the Hoffmann story, who descends into hallucinations and madness as a result of his misdirected love, Frantz – the male protagonist of the ballet *Coppélia* – is rescued by his fiancée from his obsessive attraction to a life-size automaton. In fact, the fiancée, Swanilda, displaces Frantz as the main character of this ballet. It is she who cleverly impersonates the mechanical doll Coppélia; it is she who saves Frantz from losing his soul during Dr. Coppélius's alchemical experiments. With its lively music, by Léo Delibes, and its sparkling choreography, by Arthur Saint-Léon, the original ballet completely changed the meaning of Hoffmann's story. If *Der Sandmann* was dark and macabre, later serving Freud as a prime example of "the uncanny," *Coppélia* was sunny and effervescent – all brilliant surface – and it had a happy ending. That the role of Frantz was originally danced by a woman *en travesti* – dressed in man's clothing – feminized all the dancing and imbued the ballet with a light, bon-bon flavor.

In Act I, which takes place in a town square in Galicia, Swanilda sees a girl sitting on a balcony, reading a book, in a house opposite her own.[64] In Swanilda's efforts to get Coppélia's attention – she dances, prances, and stamps her foot in frustration – we see both the heroine's qualities and those of the automaton. Swanilda is friendly, lively, curious, clever, funny, tenacious, and passionate; all these traits are expressed by her dancing, and especially by the adroitness, speed, and variety of her footwork.[65] The agility of her legs and feet seems to stand for a nimble mind. Coppélia, on the other hand, is the polar opposite of animated. She is motionless, stony, unable to be roused.

When Frantz appears, Swanilda hides. He greets Coppélia; unlike Swanilda, he does not dance, but mimes his salutation to the new object of his affections.

Coppélia suddenly starts up awkwardly from her chair, leans forward, and moves her arms in a stiff, fitful sequence. Dr. Coppélius appears on the balcony. Swanilda expresses her anger at Frantz's infidelity and is joined by her girlfriends – a group in which she clearly is the vivacious leader. Then all the villagers enter and the group dances a joyous mazurka, to fast, lively music reminiscent of a cancan. Swanilda and Frantz quarrel, and Swanilda dances with her girlfriends. Their sparkling, springy allegro footwork, studded with beats and *changements*, in which no movement is held for more than a few seconds, not only stresses their vitality, but also shows Swanilda's emotional resilience. Unlike Effie or Giselle, when Swanilda thinks she has lost her fiancé's love, she takes action to change the situation.

In Act II, Dr. Coppélius leaves his house, dropping his key, and his house is infiltrated from two directions: Swanilda and her friends use the key to steal into the strange doctor's workshop, while Frantz climbs a ladder to enter through the balcony, in order to woo Coppélia. As the girls wreak havoc in the workshop, bringing a variety of automatons to life, Swanilda discovers that Coppélia is only a human-scale doll, a clockwork robot. But Dr. Coppélius enters, and the girls run away. Swanilda hides in the cabinet where Coppélia is kept. Next Frantz enters the workshop, and Dr. Coppélius drugs him. He prepares to transfer Frantz's soul to the body of Coppélia.

When Dr. Coppélius brings his robot daughter out of the cabinet to complete the transfer, Swanilda appears, disguised as Coppélia. She makes the automaton seem to come to life, as her movement become less angularly mechanical, more rounded and fluent. Dr. Coppélius, delighted that his magic seems to be working, but disgruntled at her increasingly wild behavior, commands Coppélia/ Swanilda to dance for him. He gives her a mantilla, and she performs a sultry Spanish dance; he gives her a tartan, and she does a lively Scottish dance. Her coordination is extraordinary, signaling her humanity.

Meanwhile, Swanilda keeps trying to rouse Frantz. Impatient, she becomes unruly, stamping on Dr. Coppélius's book, throwing the objects in the workshop into disorder, and refusing to obey the alchemist's orders. She is like a machine gone out of control, but she is also a most willful, recalcitrant daughter. Finally, as Frantz wakes up, Swanilda brings out the lifeless, unclothed doll – the real Coppélia – and pulls her lover out of the house, as Dr. Coppélius grieves over his inert robot and his lost experiment.

In the (now-lost) third act, Frantz and Swanilda celebrate their wedding, along with the other village couples. The allegorical figures of Dawn, Prayer, Work (in the persons of a spinner and harvest-women), Discord, War, and Peace all dance *divertissements*, and Hymen presides over the group wedding. Finally, Evening and Night appear, guiding the procession of Pleasure.

The contrast between the robot Coppélia's jerky, irregular spurts of movement and Swanilda's rhythmic, animated, highly articulate and well-balanced leg movements and footwork, coordinated with her gracious arm gestures – i.e., the *humanity* of her dancing – serves to highlight graphically which "woman" is more desirable as a spouse. And the final absorption of the wedding couple into the folk dance figures of the group suggests that the community has ratified this union of human with human.

It is striking that in Act II, Swanilda carries out what might be seen today as a feminist revolution in Dr. Coppélius's workshop, zestily attacking the patriarchal control of the father-figure and flaunting her indocility. When she is disguised as Coppélia, her dancing metaphorically embodies an emancipatory movement from total restriction, dependent on the alchemist's authority, to autonomy, signified by her full range of motion and her impetuous, untameable actions. Yet this sense of freedom is recuperated in the final act, when Swanilda achieves her goal of marriage and reins in her riotous behavior. Thus, as in *La Sylphide*, the audience can enjoy the pleasures of untrammeled behavior, but still arrive peacefully at social harmony by the ballet's end. Still, unlike *La Sylphide* and *Giselle*, this ballet represents women's power not as threatening, but as attractive.

The Romantic ballet flourished all over Europe, but especially in France, between the revolutions of 1830 and 1848, during the bourgeois monarchy of Louis-Philippe, the citizen-king. As I have shown, despite its flirtations with rebellion and its anxieties about social order, the Romantic ballet largely upheld a bourgeois ethos regarding women's roles, women's sexuality, and the institution of marriage. But by the end of the Second Empire in 1870, when *Coppélia* was created, both the political and cultural climates had changed drastically. And so had the ballet stage.

Coppélia marked the end of an era – the conspicuously frivolous Second Empire of Napoleon III. Members of the corps de ballet lifted their skirts to sneak cancan steps into their appointed roles. And after the performances, dandies gathered backstage in the Foyer de la Danse to toast and seduce the ballet girls, in a manner even more flagrant than during the 1830s and 40s. Contemporary observers depict "the man of fashion" in the audience as interested only in the dancer's body, not in the dance. Charles Yriarte, for instance, described the Opéra milieu of 1867, in which even the tragedy of *Giselle* was reduced to frothy "fairylike effects . . . and ethereal *pirouettes*":

> The man of fashion at the Opéra, with his box or his stall, his favourite dancer, his opera-glasses, and his right of entry backstage, has a horror of anything which remains on the bills for a long time, of anything artistic, which must be listened to, respected, or requires an effort to be understood. . . . I wager that eight out of every ten *abonnés* prefer *Pierre de Médicis* to the fourth act of *Les Huguenots*, and *Néméa* to *Guillaume Tell*. And why? Simply because [the dancer] Louise Fiocre shows her limbs in *Pierre*, and her younger sister Eugénie shows much more than that in *Néméa*. . . . To the soothing strains of sweet and lively music your attention can wander from the calves of Mlle Brach or Mlle Carabin to the shoulders of Mme de N——; and during the interval, you can visit

> every box, or receive visitors in your own. That is the real Opéra, the only Opéra possible for this brilliant, light-hearted society.[66]

Novels and memoirs of the period insouciantly paint a picture of the ballet dancer as a *demi-mondaine*. The Comte de Maugny, locating the Foyer de la Danse as the border between the two sexual realms of Paris society, characterized the Opéra dancers as "the Faubourg Saint-Germain, the cream of the *demi-monde*."[67] Of course, the wanton atmosphere of the ballet as a brothel may partly have been a literary fantasy, for as one writer reflected in *Le Figaro* in 1859,

> There is not one Parisian novel which does not introduce a banker or a man of fashion who keeps a ballet girl of the Opéra. But the *Académie de Musique* barely contains thirty *danseuses*, so that even if the *rats* and supers were included, there would be at least a thousand happy admirers for each of them.[68]

However, as dance historian Lynn Garafola has more soberly observed, the majority of ballet dancers were working-class women, and "poverty invites sexual exploitation, especially in a profession of flexible morals." Garafola ties the peculiar sexual situation of the nineteenth-century French ballet dancer to the bourgeoisification of Opéra during the Romantic era and its specific treatment of the dancer's sexuality as yet one more gratifying commodity to proffer its customers. "In the 1830s . . . the backstage of the Paris Opéra became a privileged venue of sexual assignation, officially countenanced and abetted. . . . For the millionaire libertines of the audience . . . performance [was] foreplay to possession" in the "private seraglio" the Opéra had become.[69] By the time of *Coppélia*, at the twilight of the Second Empire, the ostentatious transformation of the Opéra into a sexual marketplace that included the participation even of the Emperor seems to have become complete.[70]

At the same time, during the 1850s and 1860s, the technical prowess of the ballerina increased enormously, fed partly by the discoveries of Carlo Blasis in Milan and the Italian school of ballerinas who appeared on ballet stages all over Europe. Guest has characterized the Second Empire as one of "decadence" for the French ballet precisely because, as the female dancer grew in status, the male dancer's visibility decreased, until finally "his rôles were even taken from him and allotted to a female dancer."[71] Ballerinas dancing the parts of young heroes in male dress lent the ballets of this period a certain piquancy, as they leavened the style of "male" dancing with their rounded bodies and soft, light movements. For not only did women dance in travesty roles in order to create a homogeneous, feminized bodily style on stage – even during "heterosexual" courtship scenes. The abbreviated male costumes also allowed their legs to be bared nightly to the knee (a degree inconceivable in nineteenth-century daily life) and to become admired artistic – and sexual – objects. As Garafola puts it, "the *danseuse en travesti*

[was] that curious androgyne who invoked both the high poetic and the bordello underside of romantic and post-romantic ballet."[72]

Guest condemns travesty dancing as unnatural in explicitly sexual terms: "The triumph of the ballerina was complete, but the decline of the Romantic Ballet was made certain, for the eclipse of the male – evidenced by Degas' neglect of him in his pictures – could only lead, as in life itself, to sterility."[73] And yet, Guest also mentions in passing that this period saw the emergence of the ballet heroine – that is, of the female dancing protagonist who asserts agency – in works like *La Fonti* (1855), *L'Étoile de Messine* (1861), and *La Maschera* (1864). The intrepid Swanilda, in *Coppélia*, is the epitome of the new ballet heroine.

The innovative technical bravura of the ballerina now made representations of powerful ballet heroines possible. And the corresponding physical softening of the male roles, as danced by women in travesty, simultaneously created representations of less forceful men on stage. As Garafola remarks, male dancers were relegated to roles, like Dr. Coppélius, that required acting and mime, rather than dancing – parts that "could be performed by those long past their prime." She writes, "Men on the ballet stage were fine, it seemed, so long as they left its youthful, beardless heroes to the ladies and so long as they were elderly and, presumably, unattractive."[74]

This "inversion" of gender roles, of course, is foregrounded in *Coppélia*, in which Swanilda rescues her foolish fiancé, originally danced by a woman, through her resourcefulness, ingenuity, and bravado and thus also saves her relationship. Garafola sees the travesty dancer as a symbol of women's sexual exploitation both on stage and off stage at the Opéra. Both the removal of the "obstreperous male" from the ballet of the Second Empire and the suggestion of Sapphic love, she argues, cleared the way of any obstacles to the male spectator's enjoyment of his imagined harem.

Yet it is certainly possible, while agreeing that the ballet dancers were sexually exploited and were often presented on stage to be ogled, to see the dynamic of travesty dancing somewhat differently. For one thing, the presence of other men both in erotic artistic representations of women and in actual brothels has probably never prevented male spectators and clients from being sexually aroused. But more importantly, at least in *Coppélia*, travesty dancing's "liberation of the leg" had a double-edged meaning. It was as important to the history of the emancipation of female bodies as it was to the economy of male pleasure.

Guest recounts an anecdote about a ballet girl, Clara Pilvois, who "dared to introduce the wild gyrations of the cancan into one of Mazilier's rehearsals." The balletmaster "was horrified" and reprimanded the dancer, threatening to replace her if she persisted in this outrageous behavior. There then followed a series of disobedient acts: she ignored his warning, danced the forbidden dance again, and was expelled from the rehearsal. But she pleaded to be reinstated. "'Please, please give me back my *pas*,' she begged. 'If you don't, my mother will die when she hears of it.'" And yet, at the very next evening's performance, "the audience were treated to the curious spectacle of one of the nuns in *Robert le Diable* dancing the cancan."[75] This dancer's impudence simultaneously catered to the lascivious tastes of the "men of fashion" in the Opéra audience and asserted the female dancer's independence and authority – her autonomy from the male choreographer.

In *Coppélia*, the new-found freedom of the female body on the ballet stage, although formally assigned to the travesty role of Frantz, is taken up in the choreography by Swanilda. Her celebration of the articulateness of the human leg may, in some ways, emulate the irrepressible cancan dancer. And undeniably it catered to the male voyeurism of nineteenth-century audiences. In those respects, her dancing reflected and, indeed, participated in the sexual hedonism of the Second Empire.

But in other ways, Swanilda's celebration of the articulate leg, and by extension, her indomitable spirit, projects the rising tide of feminist activity in France in the last, liberal years of the Second Empire. And it foreshadows not only the powerful female figures on the Russian ballet stage of the 1890s, but also the attempt, in the feminist dress reform movement of the late nineteenth century, to liberate women's bodies in Western culture at large. If the female leg is a symbol of male desire on the nineteenth-century French ballet stage, it is also the sign of female mobility, outside of hearth and home, in the modern arena of public life.

2

THE RUSSIAN IMPERIAL BALLET

The Sleeping Beauty, The Nutcracker, Swan Lake

Marius Petipa, the French choreographer transplanted to Russia whose name is synonymous with the Russian Imperial ballet, achieved his greatest success with *The Sleeping Beauty* (1890). A compendium of several earlier styles of ballet, *The Sleeping Beauty* sets forth the canon of the classical ballet vocabulary and choreographic structure.[1] Through its plot and its setting, as well as its bodily codes of decorum, the ballet encapsulates the behavior and values of the courtly hierarchy that produced it. Created in reactionary times in Russia, the ballet expresses deeply conservative royalist politics. Its choreographic form crystallizes a gender-coded division of labor that has come to define classical ballet, and it is the most splendid celebration in the Western dance canon of the wedding theme. Thus, one might presume that it would be relentlessly patriarchal. But ironically, *Beauty*'s world is one in which men nearly disappear and women reign supreme, apparently contradicting the gendered messages of the literary versions of fairytales that inspired the ballet.

The ballet *The Sleeping Beauty* was conceived by Ivan Vsevolozhsky, director of the Imperial Theatres from 1881 to 1899, who wrote the scenario, designed the costumes, commissioned the score from Peter Tchaikovsky, and worked closely with Petipa as he choreographed the ballet. Vsevolozhsky wanted to create court ballets as dazzling as those of the French court under Louis XIV, but rather than choosing a classical theme (as Lully might have done), he set his ballet in the time of the Sun King, basing it on a fairytale written by Charles Perrault for Versailles court society. This was a brilliant choice, for Vsevolozhsky thus in a single stroke cross-referenced an array of events and issues. One was the beginning of theatrical dancing as we know it in all the splendor of the French baroque ballet, with its emblems of *civilité.* A second was the royal Russian emulation of the French absolutist court at its zenith. And the third, in a timely way, were various Franco-Russian alliances – from 1755 right up to the treaty being negotiated as the ballet was being made, culminating in the entente cordiale of 1897. Vsevolozhsky looked back – through a French lens – to the eighteenth century in Russia (and the birth of Russian francomania). This period marked a renascence for Russia, a nation that many felt had long slumbered culturally as well as politically. Thus in *The Sleeping Beauty* Vsevolozhsky not only also invoked the Golden Age of France, but also that of the Russian aristocracy, beginning with the reign, 100 years earlier, of Catherine the Great, Russia's own Louis XIV.[2]

This was not the first time *The Sleeping Beauty* had been adapted to the stage. Nineteenth-century British pantomime and French *féeries* served up melodramatic struggles between good and evil, embellished with magical effects and spectacular transformations, as standard fare, and fairytales provided the perfect plots. *The Sleeping Beauty* had been a favorite subject of these popular genres. It had also been the theme of a ballet by Jean Aumer (with a scenario by Eugène Scribe) in Paris in 1829, several elements from which found their way into Vsevolozhsky's scenario.[3]

Many expected the Russian *Sleeping Beauty* to be no more than a despised *féerie*. But the Petipa–Tchaikovsky ballet proved to be more than a frivolous extravaganza. Although the ballet reaches into the past (evincing a retrospectivism that characterized many strata of Russian culture in the 1890s, from the Imperial Theatres to Diaghilev's World of Art movement) and although it was inspired by an "escapist" dance genre, it is very much a late nineteenth-century entity, and it has entered the canon of serious high art.[4]

The ballet may never, as Slavicist Tim Scholl argues, have been directly intended "to gain court favor."[5] (In fact, Tsar Alexander, a francophobe and a Russian nationalist, simply pronounced it "very nice," to Tchaikovsky's consternation.[6]) But clearly the ballet's narratives of dread – surrounding the safety of royal bodies, the urgency of dynastic succession and survival, and royal alliances capable of banishing all evil from the realm – serve as a striking allegory for the obsessions of the Russian empire circa 1890. This was an autocratic kingdom that had been living under strict martial law since Tsar Alexander II's assassination in 1881. To the courtiers witnessing *The Sleeping Beauty*, subject (like all Russians) to the whims of the bureaucracy and the secret police concerning every matter of daily life, the outlawing of ordinary, necessary items such as needles and spindles would not be at all surprising.[7] In the world of *The Sleeping Beauty*, unreasonably repressive prohibitions are rationalized as benignly motivated and therefore legitimate.

Moreover, the fairytale ballet served, like the literary fairytale in the French court of Louis XIV, a more general ideological function – what fairytale scholar Jack Zipes, in analyzing the literary tales, refers to as "an institutionalized symbolic discourse on the civilizing process" that indoctrinates readers to conform to dominant social codes, including table manners, dress, the regulation of the body, sexual relations, and polite speech. Fairytales, that is, served an important pedagogical and political function, for it was possible in seventeenth-century France to move up from the *haute bourgeoisie* to aristocratic circles. At the same time, childhood began to be distinguished as a separate life-stage and a prime locus for socialization. Thus, the fairytale, alongside other manuals for behavior in the form of books and pamphlets, served as a channel of social and political pedagogy.[8]

The late nineteenth century in Russia was a time of political struggle both internally and externally – a time of simultaneous aspirations to a national, uniquely Russian culture and to hegemony in global politics (especially with regard to Western Europe). In many ways, ballet was isolated from these struggles. But, paradoxically, to emulate the manners and mores – literally, the bodily attitudes – of the foreign French court was, in a complex assertion of autonomous political and cultural identity, to refute the standard epithet of Russian backwardness.[9] It was a way to claim elegance, propriety, courtliness, luxury, and political power as Russian attributes just as much as French ones. (But of course, the eighteenth-century French style was an outmoded view of aristocracy, for no court like that existed in nineteenth-century France.) Indeed, if not for the Tsar, at least for other courtiers, the ballet *The Sleeping Beauty* could serve as an imaginative model as well as a marker of royal behavior and hierarchical values, enacting the triumph of order in the realm, and reproducing and reinforcing in a charmed arena values that in reality were constantly questioned and under threat. As dance historian Deborah Jowitt points out, the timely and practical moral of *The Sleeping Beauty* for the Russian courtier was that "a breach in royal courtesy, even to such nasty adversaries as wicked fairies, can allow chaos to upset the orderly flow of events." The world of the court was reflected in the hierarchy of the ballet company: "the ballerina and premier danseur, like the tsar and tsarina, were framed by a select company of soloists (the grand dukes and duchesses) and demi-soloists (court officials, if you like) and by a further stratified corps de ballet."[10] And of course, there was even an imperial court represented on stage, further enhancing the endlessly reflecting mirror images of royal power.[11] Since the Imperial Ballet and the Imperial Theatres were in fact part of the Ministry of the Imperial Court, the tsarist hierarchy of the company was not just symbol, but reality.

A lady-in-waiting to the nineteenth-century Romanov court wrote, regarding the incessant parade of courtly celebrations, ceremonies, and other splendid, obligatory royal displays in vogue since the days of Peter the Great, "Power in Russia is so very complete and majestic while elsewhere, in other countries, only the word remains. Here it bears a religious, and, one may say, supernatural character that acts on the imagination."[12]

The Sleeping Beauty, a ballet about royal power created in the Imperial Theatre for the Russian court, acts on the imagination on multiple levels. Answering complaints that the fairytale theme was trivial (and, furthermore, too foreign), Tchaikovsky's friend Herman Laroche insisted,

> Say what you wish against fairy-tales. You will do away neither with the fact that they have succeeded in taking root in our fantasy in the continuity of generations, nor with the fact that from childhood we became closely linked with them and love them, nor with the fact that we find in them some of the most profound ideas to stir humankind.[13]

In this Laroche echoes Perrault himself, who saw his tales as combining entertainment with moral instruction. "These trifles were not mere trifles . . . they contained a useful moral, and the playful narrative surrounding them had been chosen only to allow the stories to penetrate the mind more pleasantly and in such a manner to instruct and amuse at the same time," Perrault wrote.[14]

The tale – and the ballet – of *The Sleeping Beauty* have been variously interpreted as: a struggle between good and evil; life conquering death; love as the source of life; the perennial passing of the seasons from winter to spring; a related pattern of social and spiritual renewal; the shifting of generations; the survival of the good and the beautiful despite the ravages of time; and the coming of age of a young woman.[15] Although the last aspect might seem the slightest and most mundane, given all those earlier cosmic themes, in fact it looms large when one realizes that it, like the Persephone myth, contains within it not only the story of an individual's maturation, but also the fertility motifs of the seasonal cycle, as well as the themes of life, love, death, renewal, the succession of generations, the passing of time (days, seasons, years), and historical change. (In the ballet, of course, Beauty's name is Aurora – Dawn – signaling a new day.) That is, the macro-themes are contained within what at first glance looks like a micro-theme, and, in fairytale fashion, abstract themes are here given human (or, if not mortal, at least human-shaped) bodies.

That in the ballet an individual woman's story could be fleshed out beyond the one-dimensionality of the literary fairytale and presented as rich, multi-layered, and significant – indeed, as noble – is in itself significant, for several reasons. One is the simple, but striking fact that the biography of a female protagonist could be the central subject of a narrative.[16] Another is that the ballet's authorial team, however unconsciously, restored to a literary fairytale, encrusted with patriarchal accretions, an earlier woman-centered model, told by female storytellers, of an active princess (rather than an active hero and a passive princess).[17] Another, related point is that in an era when women were struggling for political equality, in this ballet a woman-centered world, in which a woman protagonist finds agency and autonomy within a marriage based on mutual love, was represented – again, however unconsciously – as salutary and authoritative. Admittedly, the conventions of ballet had since the Romantic era put women at center stage, for reasons that can only be seen in retrospect as sexist. But for complex reasons, in *The Sleeping Beauty* various historical factors conspired to undermine this legacy of institutional sexism, and to create instead challenging, positive images of female power and autonomy on stage.

The gender of fairytales

Charles Perrault's tales were specifically written for the seventeenth-century French court as gender-coded moral lessons for boys and girls – they were instructions for how to become the perfect aristocrat – and Perrault ended each tale with a moral. The poem that followed his story of *The Sleeping Beauty* counseled deferred gratification. And indeed, all his tales recommend patience for girls – in regard not only to choosing a suitable marriage partner but also to entering the state of matrimony, as well as in regard to life's never-ending tribulations. In Perrault's original tale, Beauty has a life after marriage, and she encounters more problems. In fact, she has no fancy wedding, but quickly and quietly marries her prince right after dinner on the day he wakes her up, and they go right back to bed. Since the princess is not the least bit tired, she and the prince find other things to do than sleep, which activity results nine months later in a child. The prince keeps their marriage secret from his parents, visiting Beauty from time to time, and they have a second child. Eventually, the prince's father dies, and the prince succeeds to the throne, finally bringing Beauty and her two children home to his ogre (that is, cannibalistic) mother. When the new king goes off to war, the mother-in-law orders first one grandchild, then another, then Beauty to be served up as delectable dishes. Each one is saved and hidden in turn by the cook, but in the final scene of the story, the king arrives home just in the nick of time to rescue Beauty and their children – who, having been discovered still alive by his mother, are about to be thrown into a cauldron full of serpents, toads, and other vile creatures.[18]

Perrault's emphasis on the value of patience conforms with what Zipes sees as Perrault's views of woman in general – that she should be "beautiful, polite, graceful, industrious, properly groomed, and [know] how to control herself at all times. . . . She must be passive until the right man comes along to recognize her virtues and marry her."[19] Lilyane Mourey has commented that for Perrault, intelligence in women could be dangerous, and independence even more so, since this could threaten the marriage institution and the family and thus weaken the entire fabric of society. For Perrault, she concludes, personal virtues are completely gender-coded: "Beauty is an attribute of woman, just as intelligence is the attribute of men."[20]

It is this aspect of social indoctrination in and by fairytales to which feminists have objected, and rightly so. In analyzing both the Perrault and Grimm versions of *The Sleeping Beauty*, contemporary feminists have complained that of all the fairytales, this one most drastically endorses female docility and passivity, for what could be more passive than waiting for 100 years for the right man to come along and rescue one? Andrea Dworkin, for instance, castigates fairytales in her book *Woman Hating* for creating negative role models for girls. She writes,

> At some point the Great Divide took place: they (the boys) dreamed of mounting the Great Steed and buying Snow White from the dwarfs: we (the girls) aspired to become that object of every necrophiliac's lust – the innocent, *victimized* Sleeping Beauty, beauteous lump of ultimate sleeping good. Despite ourselves, sometimes knowing, unwilling, unable to do otherwise, we act out the roles we were taught.[21]

In *Kiss Sleeping Beauty Good-Bye*, a study of various fairytales, psychologist Madonna

Kolbenschlag criticizes *The Sleeping Beauty* for modeling female roles for contemporary women as comatose and catatonic.[22]

Sandra Gilbert and Susan Gubar, referring to a different aspect of woman's representations in fairytales – the fairy godmothers and wicked witches who help or obstruct the heroine – posit an "essential but equivocal relationship between the angel-woman and the monster-woman," both of which they find problematic in terms of the social and political status of women.[23] The angel-woman and the monster-woman could correspond to the Lilac Fairy and Carabosse in the ballet *The Sleeping Beauty*. (In Perrault's original fairytale, neither the old, wicked fairy who curses the princess nor the young fairy who mitigates the curse is named or described.) They could also correspond to Odette and Odile in the ballet *Swan Lake*.

However, these extreme characterizations of fairytale heroines seem as one-dimensional and stereotypical as the authors declare the tales to be.[24] Most feminists who discuss fairytales do not discuss the literary history of the tales or their history on the popular stage. The claims themselves are universalizing and ahistorical, as well as evincing an elitist class bias, for these authors seem completely unaware of the social history of the production of French literary fairytales: their origins in the world of working-class female storytellers. In the seventeenth century, fairytales became a marginalized literary genre pioneered and dominated primarily by women. Although these women were aristocrats, what they published were the tales told to them by their peasant nurses; in a sense, the tales were co-authored by women across class lines. The *précieuses*' reworkings of the traditional folktales (for aristocratic and bourgeois audiences) were read as criticisms of prevailing social institutions, especially the practice of arranged marriages.[25]

Moreover, many feminists' knowledge of fairytales seems limited to the stories' sanitized, Americanized, Disney versions (which frequently do eviscerate the tales' original meanings). But as the feminist writer Marina Warner has recently argued, in their time these tales were not one-dimensional, but offered messages of female acquiescence *and* resistance, expressing the contradictory, complex aspirations of their female authors (who were privileged in terms of their class status but constrained by their gender) both to change the rules and to maintain the status quo. And these aristocratic authors brought into an official, literary space an underground vernacular oral thread that for generations, within a patriarchal medieval and early capitalist culture, had voiced (from the peasant's perspective) real female antagonisms, reconciliations, exploitations, fears, hopes, and fantasies, as well as an ongoing struggle between classes.[26]

Indeed, given the history of female authorship of these tales, as they passed from the oral to the written tradition and became upwardly mobile in class terms, the attempt by the king in *The Sleeping Beauty* to outlaw spindles takes on new light. It was common practice for storytellers to tell their tales where women gathered together to do monotonous work, such as spinning and laundering. This was a way to entertain the group while they worked in a communal fashion, either in or out of the home. Hence the terms "to spin a tale," "to weave a plot."[27] The two activities – spinning and storytelling – went hand in glove. Moreover, both before and after industrialization, the textile industry was primarily a women's domain, especially in France. The spinster – that is, the woman with the distaff (a term that has come to mean women's concerns, or simply that which relates to women) – was also the teller of tales. Often, she was seen as merely an old gossip, a chatterbox. But, as Warner points out, the word "gossip" once meant "godmother," and intimated close friendship and caring. To speak of gossip is to speak of informal networks of women's wisdom about "the control of fertility and mortality, through skills like midwifery, and the direction of attitudes and alliances and interests." So it is not accidental that women's gatherings in laundries and spinning rooms gave rise to male anxieties about subversions of the social order.[28] When in *The Sleeping Beauty* the king outlaws spindles, he outlaws spinsters as well. Thus, he tries to stop the spinning of stories by wise old women – in other words, to stop the motion of history – and in this way to prevent the curse from coming true.

To be sure, most feminists have not looked at the ballet *The Sleeping Beauty* in formulating their objections to the tale. But some of their arguments are still used by dance writers. Dworkin and the other anti-fairytale feminists may be right about the *plot* of *The Sleeping Beauty*, at least as a literary tale, rather than a danced story. In the literary tale, Beauty is passive; in fact, in typical fairytale fashion neither she, the prince, nor any of the other characters either have much personality or agency. The emphasis is on moving the plot forward, and for that action is required. This counts Beauty, sleeping, out. But the ballet is different, for Vsevolozhsky's libretto changes the plot in significant ways. If the literary plot were the only aspect one considered, one would erroneously conclude that Aurora gets out of bed only to become a catatonic housewife. Yet to look at the ballet *The Sleeping Beauty* is a different matter entirely than reading Perrault's tale, for a number of reasons.[29] First, the female characters created by the ballet turn out to be far more complex than those on the page. As well, the authors of the ballet chose not to include the second part of the Perrault tale, in which Beauty and her children are threatened by her cannibal mother-in-law. (Perhaps, anticipating George Balanchine, Vsevolozhsky *et al.* felt that to portray a mother-in-law in dance was just too complicated.[30]) But the choice to end the ballet with an enormous wedding (a celebration that, strikingly, never happened at all in Perrault's version), instead of Perrault's violent post-honeymoon narrative, is in itself meaningful, even though the final wedding was a standard ballet convention. For the wedding scene emphasizes the intertwining themes of mutual love and dynastic succession that in this context are key to the heroine's life-story (as well as providing a more cheerful ending). Aurora, that is, secures a royal marriage based on mutual affection despite the political demands of aristocratic blood. The ballet foregrounds that triumph over the theme of Beauty's moral forbearance (her 100-year sleep and the apparent loss of her children) and the theme of intergenerational strife (the vanquishing of the mother-in-law so the son's wife may rule the household). In this matter, Aurora exercises extraordinary personal choice in a situation strictly bound by political constraints, and yet she does so graciously, easing the passing of power from the older to the younger generation by choosing the perfect partner.

But most importantly in terms of female agency, when the story of the Sleeping Beauty is staged, especially in dance terms – which *require* action – it becomes difficult, if not impossible, to depict the protagonist as passive and immobile. Even when she sleeps, Princess Aurora dreams – and Prince Désiré sees, in an enchanted vision – that she dances. Now, one could imagine an insipid dancing Aurora. Or even a gentle, ethereal Aurora, on the model of the French Romantic style. But Carlotta Brianza, who first danced the role of Aurora, was one of a new breed of Italian ballerinas who brought to the Russian stage an innovative "steely-toed" technique that stressed physical strength, speed, and force. This bravura technique was terre-à-terre rather than aerial, and it emphasized physicality rather than ethereality. It enabled virtuoso feats – including executing multiple turns and difficult balances, all on pointe – in contrast to the graceful, earlier French style with its softer pointework. That is, both the dancer and the role were virtuoso. It may be partly for this reason that the passiveness, docility, and lassitude that characterize Beauty in the literary version of the tale simply disappear in Petipa's ballet.[31]

Several factors contribute to the image of Aurora as an active woman. Just being a dancing creature already endowed the princess with a certain measure of agency. The original casting choice reinforced that agency by underscoring Aurora's strength and independence. And then the choreography further enhances that agency in very specific ways (which I will discuss). Moreover, the gifts her fairy godmothers give Aurora at her christening turn her into a different kind of woman than Perrault's Beauty, as we will see. Musically, Aurora is associated with the lively energy of the waltz, and her dances are usually in an allegro vivace tempo, signifying a zesty vitality.[32] In fact, Aurora's only passive appearance in the ballet is as a baby in the Prologue. But significantly, there she is represented by a doll, not by a dancer, and the Prologue is only a preface to the action of the ballet. The real beginning of the ballet is in Act I, when Aurora, as a young woman, starts to dance.[33]

But beyond the representation of Aurora, the roles of Carabosse and the Lilac Fairy have been significantly enlarged in the ballet. Indeed, in the transformation of the tale into a ballet, all the female characters – especially the fairies – have been magnified and individualized, given names and personalities. The result of all these elements is that the court of Florestan XIV, Beauty's father, seems to become "a feminine microcosm" (as Arlene Croce described the Prologue and Vision scenes[34]), where women exercise choice and power.

Matrimony is still the glimmering goal, but it is equally so for both Aurora and Prince Désiré, and the structure of their wedding pas de deux seems to promise mutual respect and identical political, as well as domestic power. Of course, it would be anachronistic to expect a female protagonist – especially a princess who

Plate 4 Carlotta Brianza as Aurora in *The Sleeping Beauty*. Courtesy of the Dance Collection, The New York Public Library for the Performing Arts, Astor, Lenox and Tilden Foundations.

is an only child – to be entirely liberated from the expectation of marriage, in either the seventeenth-century literary fairytale or the nineteenth-century ballet (or in the "real" world of the twentieth century, for that matter). But that this marriage is arranged by fate (in the person of the Lilac Fairy), rather than by the bridal pair's parents – most particularly in a royal union, where one would least expect personal feelings to be considered – dramatically underscores the utopian theme of marriage reform pressed by the seventeenth-century French *précieuses*, the authors of literary fairytales, who argued that women should marry for love, not for the sake of their father's political, social, or economic interests.[35]

Choreography: the body of meaning

Boris Asafiev, the Soviet composer and music critic, wrote that the four adagios of *The Sleeping Beauty*'s four sections form not only "the musical points of support for the whole course of action" in the ballet, but also the key moments of Aurora's biography so far: "cradle, girlhood, love, marriage."[36] Examining these adagios and their related dances allows us to see how the authors of *The Sleeping Beauty* created a complex story, in which Aurora is both socially constructed, according to fairytale convention, as the "perfect woman," and simultaneously invested with individuality, agency, and a much more full-bodied character than fairytales normally allow.[37]

The Prologue is Aurora's christening scene. As with each act in the ballet, the scene begins with a ceremonial entrance. Catalabutte, the king's master of ceremonies, has checked to make sure the guest list is in order. Among the guests who arrive for the celebration are the princess' six fairy godmothers. They dance an adagio with their suite, and then, in brief individual variations, present their gifts: Candide represents beauty, but also candor, purity, and tenderness; Fleur de farine (wheat flour), grace and energy; Breadcrumb, abundance, generosity, and fertility; Canary, song, metaphorically symbolizing eloquence; Violente, power, passion, and the ability to command; the Lilac Fairy, wisdom, "which in Russian folklore a child will acquire if it is placed under lilacs."[38] (In the 1994 Royal Ballet production, the attributes are listed as: purity, vitality, generosity, eloquence, passion, and wisdom.)

Several of these fairies' attributes are different from those given to Beauty in Perrault's tale, which were: beauty, good temperament, grace, and the ability to dance, play music, and sing. Petipa's princess has these finishing-school traits, but crucially, she also has intelligence, eloquence, passion, and power. Note, too, that as the Russian choreographer Fedor Lopukhov points out, all the good fairies' variations are performed écarté, effacé, and en dehors – the most open positions in the ballet vocabulary. This he compares to a major key in music, contrasting with Carabosse's inward-turning, en dedans, "minor" movements.[39] Everything about the fairies – and thus, at first, Aurora – is open, positive, clear, and straightforward.

The fairies' variations are similar and closely linked, but their attributes emerge, so to speak, in bas-relief.[40] They are extremely virtuoso, containing runs and jumps on pointe, abrupt shifts in rhythm and tempo, and subtle fluctuations in quality of movement. Several of the variations involve running backwards, forming zigzag patterns, or turning, while the hands pantomime the symbolism of the gift's qualities. But the variety among the variations in rhythm, movement quality, and emotional color also shows distinctions. These are bravura miniature, concise dances, averaging a minute long, and it is partly their expressive economy that makes them so striking. Candide dances first; her hands and arms form gentle cradling and then stroking gestures, and her head tilts sweetly, indicating tenderness. Her steps are the most open of all those belonging to the fairies, as when, in the third section of her variation, she repeatedly turns out her body in sharp écarté. She also introduces the arabesque that will become Aurora's signature.

The second fairy, Fleur de farine, runs backward quickly and then turns, like a mill grinding out flour, but her rhythm is "flowing," not mechanical.[41] Her allegro pace creates a rapid stream of movement, like rushing water, and her image of grace is a vivacious one; her gift is dancing itself. Further, her backwards running steps connote confidence. Then Breadcrumb, symbolizing a typical Russian gift for a newborn – promising that she will never go hungry, or, perhaps, that she will be fertile – dances on pointe in a staccato rhythm, as she mimes scattering crumbs to pizzicato strings. These two fairies, as dance historian David Vaughan points out, add a homely Russian touch to the line-up.[42]

Canary flutters her fingers and executes allegro footwork, suggesting flight but also – especially when she holds those fluttering fingers in front of her mouth – the movement of the voice through the air. This image of eloquence is particularly significant in terms of standard social expectations of women. Violente – who may stand for an electrical storm or lightning – is precise and authoritative. She is completely focused and coordinated as she looks, points, and moves to a single position in space. Her emboîté turns further emphasize her precision. And her series of dismissive gestures is firm but done with a smile. She is a perfectly gracious but no-nonsense executrix. It seems these two fairies are also connected, for one aspect of being commanding is oratorical skill.

Originally a mime role, the Lilac Fairy has, since the early twentieth century, become an active dancer who adds her initial gift to those of the other fairies in pure movement terms. Unlike the other fairies, she does not mime the qualities of the attribute she bestows on Aurora. Rather, she abstractly represents wisdom as the largest, most magisterial and noble of all the gifts. She does this by dancing on a grand scale, with balance, poise, and amplitude. Her wisdom is sensuous – *voluptueuse*, as Petipa described the music he ordered from Tchaikovsky. She commands the entire space with her broadly unfolding arm and leg movements. (Arlene Croce once referred to her as "a five-star general."[43]) Her gestures are as long and stretched as possible while still remaining within the canon of beauty. Her spreading arm movements evoke the scent of lilac flowers perfuming the spring air.

Plate 5 The Fairies and their retinues from *The Sleeping Beauty*, illustration from the Yearbook of the Imperial Theatres (1890–91). Courtesy of the Dance Collection, The New York Public Library for the Performing Arts, Astor, Lenox and Tilden Foundations.

All these gifts come in small packages, but they are crucial to the construction of Aurora's character. Although this first adagio with variations is the only one that does not highlight Aurora as the central dancing figure, it delineates an idea, spread across six bodies, of the Aurora who will become.

Thus the education of Aurora has begun. It is intriguing to note that in the thirty years before the creation of *The Sleeping Beauty*, enormous progress, surpassing that of Western Europe, had been made in the arena of women's secondary and university education in Russia, and, as a result, in the entry of women into the medical, legal, and scientific as well as pedagogical and other intellectual professions. The enlightened gentry and bourgeois women of the mid-nineteenth century, in turn, crusaded for civil and political rights and legal protection for the large Russian population of poverty-stricken peasant and working-class women, and often provided them with medical care. Although *The Sleeping Beauty*'s representation of Aurora does not in any way evoke those nineteenth-century Russian feminists, its first audiences must have been aware that the gains made in education for women in the 1860s and 1870s were deeply eroded in the late 1880s. So a woman's education would have been both topical and controversial.

Overall, not only the fairies but also the courtiers pay homage to Aurora in the most orderly, precise, polite, and symmetrical way. The fairies and the courtiers comport themselves with an aristocratic, elegant mien, with stretched legs and torsos, straight backs, and gracefully rounded arms that open out to frame the face and body like flower petals. They evince composure, balance, and effortlessness – the baroque sense of *complaisance* or eighteenth-century nobility, which becomes the desideratum of Russian nineteenth-century classical ballet as well.[44] And they line up in files and ranks befitting a highly self-conscious aristocratic hierarchy. The courtiers graciously take turns and perform actions in series, and all their dances unfold in a completely balanced order.

But into this blissful image of harmony violently bursts Carabosse, the old, ugly, wicked, hunchbacked fairy, with her train of monsters and rats. She breaks the polite bodily codes of the courtiers. She takes up too much space; her movements are angular, spasmodic, and grotesque. She transgresses the boundary between female power seen as beautiful and good (as in the Lilac Fairy's commanding presence) and female power seen as ugly and evil. Her turns are inward-moving, enclosed – en dedans. Usually played by a man (like Madge in *La Sylphide*, symbolizing her distinctly unfeminine traits and behavior), Carabosse has all the wrong proportions, above all gigantic hands. She is a monster precisely because she is a category error, seemingly violating gender boundaries by combining aspects of male and female.[45] Carabosse hits people and tears out Catalabutte's hair, for he was the master of ceremonies who left her off the invitation list. Unlike the good fairies, who balance confidently on one leg while dancing, she cannot even balance on two legs, for she walks with a cane. And her "gift" to Aurora is a curse – that the princess will someday prick her finger on a spindle and die. The court recoils.

But ugly and wicked as she is, Carabosse is still a fairy, and she is a relative of the other fairies. The Lilac Fairy acknowledges her with a curt bow. Then, with her authoritative, warm, and solicitous gestures, the Lilac Fairy palliates the curse. Aurora, she pronounces, will not die, but will sleep for 100 years, until a prince awakens her with a kiss. With a sweep of her cloak, Carabosse disappears.

Act I concerns the carrying out of the spell. Another celebration is being held in the palace – Aurora's twentieth birthday party.[46] Catalabutte notices some old women, "gossipers . . . knitting stockings," and orders them to be sent to prison.[47] (But clearly these are not just any old women; they must be the three fates of classical mythology, with Carabosse, who is one of them, aspiring to the role of Atropos – she who cuts off the thread of life spun by her sister Clotho.) The king and queen arrive, along with four foreign princes seeking Aurora's hand in marriage. After the king pardons the old women, in the original production an ensemble of forty-eight adult dancers and thirty-two children danced the *valse villageoise*, better known as the Garland Waltz.[48] An elaborate celebration of mating and marriage, the waltz creates the image of a world in which everyone is destined to have a partner. It seems joyously to forecast Aurora's forthcoming marriage, and the garlands the couples hold aloft symbolize the nuptial arches of a church wedding. Even the children dance in pairs, signifying not only that they are the logical result of all these adult couples, but also that they, in turn, will become future couples (and parents) themselves.[49] Aurora's suite – her pages and maids of honor – enters, and then Aurora excitedly runs on stage, making her first appearance in the ballet.

The so-called Rose Adagio begins. Aurora dances with the four princes, repeatedly allowing each one in turn to partner her. But ultimately, she executes her attitudes unsupported – balancing in these most difficult poses steadily and confidently, without a partner.[50] At the end of the twentieth century, this is still the longest and most difficult test in the entire ballet repertoire of balance and aplomb. Jowitt points out that "these balances can poignantly suggest the testing of a young princess's maturity and her ability to be calm, gracious, and balanced in her judgment under stress."[51] But beyond her royal poise, the balances connote Aurora's autonomy.[52] According to the original ballet scenario, Aurora announces to her parents at the beginning of this section that she is loath to choose a husband (this reticence is not in Perrault's tale). "I am still so young," she says. "Let me yet take advantage of my freedom."[53]

After demonstrating her independence both by rejecting all her suitors and – in dance terms – by loosening herself from the support of her cavaliers, Aurora dances a lively solo variation. Here she blends all the steps and qualities bequeathed her by the good fairies at her christening: she does Candide's arabesque, for instance, Fleur de farine's pirouettes, Breadcrumb's piqué steps, and Canary's petit allegro. It is as if she is finally, at her coming-of-age party, growing into these attributes and piecing them together for the first time. The fairies live in her, and she is discovering her powers. She also broadens her domain, for in the Rose Adagio, she danced in a small circle, whereas in her solo variation she signals her joy at being alone by taking up more space. But her variation has shadows in it – she has inherited something from Carabosse, as well, for she executes a series of turns in a wide circle, similar in some versions to those performed by the wicked fairy in the Prologue, but now modified to fall within the canon of feminine beauty.[54]

Petipa, writing in his native French, instructed Tchaikovsky to create music for Aurora's entrance in Act I that would be staccato and "*coquet*," a term that has often been translated as "coquettish," but that can also mean smart, stylish, neat. If Aurora is coquettish, it is in a girlish way, not as a *femme du monde*. But it is more confidence and joy than coquetry that Aurora displays in this part of

Act I. She takes pure, unself-conscious physical pleasure in her powers; she is self-celebratory, proud in the positive, Greek sense. In the language of the late twentieth century, she displays strong self-esteem. It's true that she dances with each partner without committing herself to a single choice. She definitely uses the men (although in a polite, not an exploitative way) to help her achieve movements she cannot do by herself. Her dancing shows that she doesn't mind being courted; it's an important step in her growing up and finding new challenges, as symbolized by the dance steps she can now master. But she does not so much flirt as enjoy the group attention. Clearly she doesn't think courting must lead to settling down with one man, despite her father's assignment. ("Do as you know best," he says, "but remember that the interests of the state demand your marriage, in order that you may bear a successor to the throne."[55])

It is obvious that these suitors are not appropriate marriage partners for Aurora. Since she dances and they do not, they seem to occupy different planes of being. It is as if Aurora spoke a different language and realized that the man she chooses to wed should speak that language too. But Aurora's disinclination to marry, beyond that, is not so much coquetry as a refusal to end adolescence and courtship and enter into marriage and motherhood. It is complicated by the fact that hers is not an ordinary love story, because maintaining the continuity of the aristocratic blood lineage is crucial here. Aurora's story is only partly about marrying and having children; it is also about doing one's duty to the crown – to one's own royal family. Although this detail is not shown in the ballet, in the literary fairytale Beauty herself was the only child of a long infertile couple, a factor that lends special urgency to the threat that the dynastic line might end with her. Her role as a woman is always that of a royal woman, a potential queen and the potential mother of kings and queens. So by refusing to marry, she is putting off a solemn and burdensome responsibility and prolonging the pleasures and joys of youth.

Suddenly Aurora sees an old woman with a spindle (or, in some productions, a bouquet of flowers with a spindle hidden in it). Seizing the spindle, Aurora wields it like a scepter as she dances. But then she pricks her finger and, in a passage reminiscent of the mad scene in *Giselle* (as well as Nikia's death scene in Petipa's *La Bayadère* [1877]), she dances brokenly and finally falls down, unconscious. Carabosse, who had handed her the spindle, reveals herself, then disappears in a cloud of smoke as the court grieves. However, the Lilac Fairy appears, to remind the court that Aurora is not dead, but will sleep for 100 years. The Lilac Fairy waves her wand; the courtiers carry the sleeping princess away, and a thicket of trees and lilacs grows up, completely obscuring the palace. The entire court – symbolizing all of society – goes to sleep as well.

In Act II, 100 years have passed. Prince Désiré is hunting in the forest with his courtiers. Like Aurora in Act I, he should choose a spouse, but cannot bring himself to do so. And, since they perform period social dances, while he dances in the more abstract, elegant style of classical ballet, it seems that like Aurora he is waiting to find someone else of the same order of being – someone who speaks his language.[56] Their compatible dance styles are one signal that Aurora and Désiré are perfectly suited for one another. The Lilac Fairy appears, and she shows him a vision of Aurora, thereby inspiring him to ask the Lilac Fairy to lead him to the sleeping princess. In this adagio and variation, which in many ways resembles the second act of *La Sylphide*, Aurora appears with her companions (or, as they are often referred to, nereids or sea nymphs). They and the Lilac Fairy block the Prince from approaching Aurora, until he declares his love for her. Then, although Aurora occasionally allows Prince Désiré to lift her, she more often runs away from him, slipping out of his reach to lose herself in the formations of the corps de ballet. She then dances a solo variation full of high extensions and *unsupported*, complex turns. It is a metaphor for her articulateness, autonomy, balance, and control, but also for her grief. The entire vision is emotionally stirring and shaded with mystery, due as much to the music as to the choreography of longing.[57] Aurora disappears and, impassioned by this vision, the Prince vows to marry her. He travels with the Lilac Fairy past a fantastic rolling panorama to the castle, awakens Aurora with a kiss, and the entire court comes to life, while the dust and clouds surrounding them magically disappear.

Act III celebrates the wedding of Aurora and Désiré. Various fairytale characters from Perrault's other tales arrive as guests. Since these tales were originally sorted by gender as instructions for either boys or girls, the balance of girls' tales (such as *Red Riding Hood*, *Cinderella*) and boys' tales (such as *Tom Thumb*, *Puss in Boots*) implies that the folk wisdom necessary to educate both sexes will season this relationship.[58] As well, the fairies of precious stones and metals – gold, silver, sapphire, and diamonds – dance a pas de quatre, suggesting that wealth as well as wisdom, love, and beauty will crown the marriage.[59]

As in the Garland Waltz, the dances serve as wedding encomia. And, as in the christening scene in the Prologue, the dances present Aurora (now jointly with Désiré) with more gifts that will mold character. When the Bluebird dances a pas de deux with Princess Florine and the White Cat dances with Puss in Boots, two more literary tales are invoked in which lovers had to persevere through terrible trials to consummate their love – again balanced in terms of male and female gender, for the Bluebird was a prince given animal form by a wicked fairy, while the White Cat was a princess similarly enchanted; both were eventually saved by love. In both the literary versions of "The Bluebird" and "The White Cat," an ongoing, thoroughly satisfying conversation, rather than physical love (an impossibility, given the lovers' different species while the enchantment is in effect), binds the lovers together in mutual affection and respect. Shared conversation, the dances of Act III seem to say (with John Milton), is the only basis for a marriage.[60] When all the fairytale characters have lined up to perform duets that foreshadow the grand pas de deux of Aurora and Désiré, the union of the heroine and her prince is framed as both natural and inevitable.[61]

The grand pas de deux in Act III, which climaxes the plot of the entire ballet as well as the act, sets forth a very specific idea of marriage. On the one hand, as I've just suggested, it is seen as natural and inevitable, the true destiny of both partners.

Musicologist Roland John Wiley has pointed out that, musically, Tchaikovsky created a constantly interrupted tonal progression toward G major in the entire ballet, such that when the wedding act finally reaches that key, stressing it in the pas de deux in particular, the sense of an ultimate destiny long anticipated and finally achieved is overwhelming.[62] But even though marriage is seen as the ultimate goal in a way that in our culture might be seen as negative and identity-draining for a woman, here Aurora is not made to seem inferior or subservient to Désiré in the dance. On the contrary, she retains and even enhances her autonomy and individuality. It's true that in their variations, the dancers have separate vocabularies – she does complex, brilliant petit allegro, while he takes bounding jumps. But there are also steps both dancers share, especially when they come together in the exuberant, bravura coda of the pas de deux.

The pas de deux begins with an adagio in which Désiré leads and supports Aurora in a turn while she stands on pointe in attitude. They separate, but join together again, and he supports her now in arabesques. Twice he lifts her, sets her down to execute two pirouettes, and then carries her forward. They run to the back of the stage, and make their progress forward punctuated by her double pirouettes. Their movement seems to illustrate the turn-taking and sustenance, as well as the adventure, of partnership. Their mutuality allows her to achieve expressiveness and a fuller sense of beauty.

Although they dance together in synchrony with assurance – again, as if they had been fated all their lives to become partners – they also often separate to dance alone, and at times they even compete good-naturedly. That is, of course, the standard structure of the pas de deux as elaborated by Petipa, but here it takes on a specific socio-political meaning with regard to the shape of the marital union. The lovers' pas de deux is a metaphor for a marriage in which both partners need one another but also enjoy their autonomy. They are interdependent, but they can be independent as well.

There are echoes in the bridal pas de deux of the moments in the Rose Adagio when the man moves away and Aurora stands by herself. In some versions, she bows to her bridegroom (as in the 1964 Royal Ballet film). But after that bow, she dramatically rises on pointe while slowly moving her other leg into passé, then arriving in attitude, to stand majestically alone. She also appears, at times, to direct their mutual path, by choosing directions and movements on her own and expecting him to follow in order to catch or hold her. It seems she will be an assertive decision-maker in their marriage. Aurora's use of the suitors' help in the Rose Adagio to perform movements she could not execute on her own is here taken to a higher degree; supported by her prince, she often does quite risky movements, such as fast pirouettes. The bridal pair's partnership allows Aurora to expand her movement vocabulary and, symbolically, her abilities as a person. The relationship pictured here is an empowering, not at all subservient one. Moreover, some of the lifts and the sense of flight serve as metaphors for sexual ecstasy for both partners, clearly asserting a woman's ability to enjoy sexual pleasure. From the Rose Adagio to the grand pas de deux in Act III, one can see in the choreography of *The Sleeping Beauty* a progression from the self-confident but still tentative young girl to a mature, intelligent, authoritative woman who is not only ready to marry, but to rule the kingdom.

Certainly there are moments in the pas de deux when Aurora performs movements that are either deferential, as in Fonteyn's bow, or else coded as traditionally feminine, especially in terms of delicacy. I certainly do not mean, by arguing that she has some degree of agency and independence, to say that Aurora is depicted as a "liberated" woman. She still behaves decorously, according to the mores of her time and temper. She exhibits strength, intellect, and power, but she is still constructed as the perfect aristocratic woman – feminine and graceful, as well as regal. She can be demure and modest. But much more important to the ballet is her ability to command space and to display precision, strength, balance, and control – in short, authority. These, of course, are the gifts the fairies bestowed her at her christening. In her last variation, Aurora demonstrates her mastery of their skills, performing a combination of the same hand gestures, precise footwork, turns, and advancing/retreating paths set forth by her godmothers in the Prologue.

The bridal pas de deux is the climax of the ballet, but the act does not end there. Next the entire ensemble joins in a mazurka and apotheosis. For the couple is not simply a pair of individuals (or an individual pair), but is knitted back into the community whose prosperity, along with that of the realm (according to the reigning views of monarchy), depends on their successful marriage and the continuance of the royal line. This isn't just any loving, happy couple finally being mature enough to get together, nor is the community they are knitted back into democratic. They lead the ensemble, and the other characters are clearly their subjects. Not only is marriage seen as natural and inevitable. The view of monarchy shown here is quite benevolent. According to the ballet's ideology, the world has been set aright, in its correct political as well as emotional order, because these lovers have found their proper partners. And that they will have children to continue the bloodline is promised by the dynastic theme echoed in the final musical motif – taken from a song in tribute to Henry of Navarre, Louis XIV's grandfather and the founder of the Bourbon dynasty in France.

Women in *The Nutcracker* and *Swan Lake*

Far from diminishing women, *The Sleeping Beauty*, the apogee of the Russian Imperial ballet repertoire, makes them its core. They take center stage in ways that affirmatively portray them as powerful and autonomous as well as beautiful.

This is not to say that all Imperial Russian ballets treated women this way. By contrast, the two other Tchaikovsky ballets that, like *The Sleeping Beauty*, have remained cornerstones of the Russian Imperial ballet canon – *The Nutcracker* (1892) and the Petipa–Ivanov *Swan Lake* (1895) – feature more conventional representations of women as fragile and dependent on men, even while the ballets still present alternative visions of female authority.

In *The Nutcracker*, the Sugar Plum Fairy (like the Lilac Fairy) is magisterial, the supreme commander of her realm. But she is also delicate, as her special musical instrument – the celesta, with its ethereal tinkling sounds – indicates. And her empire – Confiturembourg, the sugary, pastel Land of Sweets – is metaphorically coded as feminine, even though many of her subjects are male.[63] The ballet is seen through the eyes of Clara, the adolescent girl who receives the Nutcracker as a Christmas present from her mysterious godfather, Herr Drosselmayer. Clara's age partly caused the problem of how a female protagonist could be portrayed on stage, since there is no single sustained adult female figure; Clara is the heroine of Act I, but does not have the ballerina's power to dominate the stage, while she becomes passive in Act II, in the realm where the Sugar Plum Fairy rules.

Obviously what Clara sees is a bourgeois world in which girls train to be nurturing mothers by playing with dolls and boys learn to be brave soldiers. Even in her fantasy, Clara may throw her shoe at the horrible mouse king, but it is the Nutcracker Prince who uses his sword to deal the villain the final blow. Later, a frightening blizzard is rendered tender and beautiful by anthropomorphic – or rather, gynomorphic – ballerina snowflakes. If Act II is metaphorically Clara's wedding feast, she herself is docile and inactive (the scenario describes her as "dutiful"[64]), not dancing but watching the antics of the various candies and other treats, which are crowned by the grand pas de deux of the Sugar Plum Fairy and her consort. It is not clear whether Clara is only a visitor or will some day be a ruler of the realm, for her potential bridegroom-to-be, the Nutcracker, is a prince of the kingdom of sweets, but the Sugar Plum Fairy still reigns supreme.[65] Still, the second act is Clara's dream, not a man's, and through her visions she has grown in wisdom.

This is a utopian child's-eye view of marriage – as Aurora's too, perhaps, might have been at age 8 or 10 – as a cuddly, idle, hedonistic dream of endless gratification. Indeed, it was probably what the early nineteenth-century *baryshnya* – Russian gentry woman – anticipated marriage would be like. As historian Richard Stites describes her, the *baryshnya* resembled "the Southern Belle of the American plantation – sweet and helpless, child-like, and surrounded by the most capacious crinolines – she awaited her first ball, her first dance, her first taste of life." For her,

> life was still a reverie as she wafted between two worlds that she did not know: beneath her, the servants and the serfs . . . beyond her, the world of men, of wars, of [political] "affairs." . . . Thus suspended between girlhood and womanhood, she was enveloped by a sense of malaise and anticipation. . . . The spell could be broken only by a man.

But, Stites points out, as time went by, and the novelty of running her own home and raising her children wore off, "the languid musings of her youth might give way to a bittersweet nostalgia and to a gnawing awareness that something had passed her by." By 1892, when *The Nutcracker* was made, several generations of Russian feminists and other liberal thinkers had clearly defined that missing "something": it was "life, work, knowledge, freedom, or action."[66] But in the face of thirty years of Russian feminist activism, and at a time when women's advances in education, employment, and other arenas were under attack, *The Nutcracker* restores the dream – or the fantasy – that marriage will be sweet, smooth, and all-fulfilling for women.

In *Swan Lake*, the original libretto states that it was Odette's wicked stepmother, a witch, who cast the spell that changed her into a swan.[67] We never see that stepmother, but there are authoritative women characters on stage – Siegfried's mother and especially Odile, the fraudulent swan. Odile – the most powerful, assertive, and seductive woman in the ballet – is sinister, the daughter of the evil genie von Rothbart, and an impostor whose only purpose is to seduce Siegfried into breaking his vow of fidelity to Odette. Odile's dark costume, as well as her strong, precise movements, her flamboyant virtuosity, and her direct gaze – contrasting with Odette's white costume, soft, feathery steps, lyricism, swooning backbends, and lowered gaze – serve to connote her nefariousness. It is not her feminine aspect that marks Odile as evil; rather, it is her authority, assertiveness, and independence – those consecutive thirty-two fouetté turns on pointe (a step that few ballerinas had then mastered), done entirely without male support – as well as her mechanistic quality that in this context make her mesmerizing and threatening. She is dazzlingly vertical, while Odette's torso swoons and melts. Unlike Carabosse, with her masculine body and her grotesque movements, Odile can be depicted simultaneously as wicked, feminine, and beautiful. She is too direct and assertive – that is what makes us realize (unlike the love-blinded Siegfried) that this is an impostor – but she remains within the canon of female beauty.

Although Odette, the real swan-enchanted woman, ostensibly wishes to free herself from captivity, she also seems submissively resigned to her fate.[68] She clings to Siegfried helplessly in their Act I, scene ii adagio. Unlike Aurora in her grand pas, Odette desperately rushes back into her savior's arms each time they part. And even though the ballerina's dancing in the white swan pas de deux in *Swan Lake* requires every bit as much physical strength as those in Odile's or Aurora's parts, the melting texture of her steps, torso, and pointework – with her footwork constantly broken up by bourrées, changements, and shifts of level – as well as her fluttering arms and volatile, silky style, her self-touching, and her downcast gaze, all create an illusion of feminine fragility (although she does also dance an allegro variation). Odette's vulnerability, indeed her ultimate tragedy, is already inscribed in her first dance. So in *Swan Lake* there is a binary division that sorts women into the categories of wicked and good, expressed in oppositions between active and passive, assertive and yielding, strong and gentle. It is, in many ways, a *fin de siècle* ballet, juxtaposing two technical styles that create two opposite female personalities: a destructive *femme fatale* and a fragile Mélisande. Yet the monster and the angel are wrapped up in a single woman, for one ballerina dances both roles, suggesting an underlying female dualism. Although the binary good and evil is also present in *The Sleeping Beauty*, both principles there are active and assertive.

It is repeatedly argued that in the ballet pas de deux, the woman is manipulated, touched, handled, held, and displayed in ways that symbolize male sexual desire, without granting equal desire or agency to women.[69] However, these charges are often homogenizing and essentializing, viewing all ballet pas de deux as identical, without taking into account the choreographic distinctions among various pas de deux that give rise to expressive difference. Certainly in the Act I, scene ii adagio of *Swan Lake*, the choreography emphasizes Odette's fragility and her dependence on Prince Siegfried. But the choreography in that duet is entirely dissimilar to both *The Sleeping Beauty*'s and *The Nutcracker*'s grand pas de deux, as well as to Odile's part in *Swan Lake*, where the choreography stresses the woman's autonomy and power. For the most part, by the late nineteenth century advances in pointework and therefore in partnering techniques enhanced the woman's dancing role on stage and reduced the male to a porteur. On the one hand, the supported adagio displayed the woman, but, on the other hand, it also allowed her to expand her vocabulary to include difficult, bravura balances and multiple turns.

The question of female agency

It might be argued that Aurora's agency is a modern state of affairs, that late twentieth-century ballerinas willy-nilly supply an interpretation to their roles that invests the nineteenth-century female characters with more power than earlier dancers did. But both the choreography and the historical record would contradict that argument, for not only are Aurora's independence and energy written into the choreography – as we have seen – but also, both Tchaikovsky and the critics specifically praised Brianza in her performance as the original Aurora for her precision and strength, as well as for her grace.[70]

Beyond Aurora's agency, the roles of the two key fairies – Carabosse and the Lilac Fairy – have been greatly expanded from the literary tale, as I've suggested. Although Carabosse might be seen as the stereotypical wicked witch, as the role has come down to us the Lilac Fairy is not simply an angel, all sweetness and light. She is gracious and good, but she is also extremely commanding. And, as dance historian Giannandrea Poesio observes, the yearning quality of her musical *leitmotif* "suggests something other than just the idea of 'good.'"[71] Between these two fairies, one gets a picture of a completely matriarchal world, the likes of which may never have existed historically, either in Russia or in France, but which certainly exists in the utopian, woman-centered world of many fairytales.

It is true that all-female harems, armies, and other communities also peopled Romantic ballets, as well as nineteenth-century pantomimes and burlesque shows, providing a piquant but fantastical view of strong women as a kind of exotic-erotic thrill. Illustrations from the original production of *The Sleeping Beauty* suggest that several of the fairies' pages may have been played by women in travesty, hinting at a spicy leg-show style. The female characters wore tutus with relatively short skirts that revealed much of the dancers' legs. The White Cat is coquettish, and various formations of the female corps use the women as decorative detail. But to argue that *The Sleeping Beauty* simply catered to prurient tastes or to a view of women as merely ornamental would be wrong (the latter partly because the male members of the corps were also used decoratively). For one thing, the framework of state and court sponsorship, as well as the comprehensive Russian system of censorship, emphasized the high moral tone of Imperial ballets (as opposed, for instance, to the presentation of *jolies femmes* in different contexts: either ballets performed on the variety stage or popular entertainment dance genres). Further, both the plot and the choreography of *The Sleeping Beauty* support a complex view of women that consistently combines beauty and power in positive ways, unlike burlesques that showed female strength as a freakish deviation.[72] Ironically, many of the same qualities that make Odile wicked in *Swan Lake* make Aurora noble in *The Sleeping Beauty*. What are we to make of this recognition of female authority, which is never permanently coded as either negative or positive, but changes its value from one ballet to another? And what are we to make of *The Sleeping Beauty*'s encoding of autonomy, intelligence, and control as positive feminine attributes?

Surely *The Sleeping Beauty* is not a feminist ballet, as, for instance, one can confidently argue that Nijinska's *Les Noces* was. (Strikingly, however, the Rose Adagio in certain ways foreshadows the reluctant bride theme of *Les Noces*.[73]) But *The Sleeping Beauty* is certainly a ballet that recognizes female agency beyond the circumscribed sphere available to women at the time. As a ballet about a woman destined to ascend the imperial throne – undoubtedly reminding its audiences of the powerful, assertive, and extremely intelligent Empress Catherine the Great – *The Sleeping Beauty* allotted to its heroine *more* brilliance, *more* independence, and *more* command than the ordinary Russian woman – even an aristocratic woman – of the late nineteenth century possessed. Still, it is worth remembering that the ballerina Mathilde Kshessinska, who in 1890 graduated from the Imperial ballet school into the Maryinsky Theatre ballet company and who was soon to dance the role of Aurora, in 1892 became the mistress of the Tsarevich – the future Tsar Nicholas II – and thus wielded enormous political power.

Given the history of women's status in Russia, this depiction is not necessarily the forward-looking, emancipatory step it might seem to late twentieth-century eyes. For in its "*passé*ism," the ballet looks longingly back to a time when women of the gentry class were at the center of Russian courtly political, social, and intellectual life. Perhaps it even invests the frivolity of 1890s Petersburg salon life with greater nobility. But it simultaneously turns its back on the entirely different situation of Russian women in general in 1890.

By then the fervent debate over "the woman question" that had captured the imagination of the socially engaged intelligentsia in the middle of the century had not only been dampened by repression, but also by the rising revolutionary movements that subsumed women's issues under a larger emancipatory agenda. This was an historical moment when many of the great gains for women won during the 1860s and 1870s, along with other social and political reforms, were rapidly being eroded. Educated women – who were joining revolutionary movements in numbers unprecedented in Western Europe – were now viewed by the government as a dangerous political and social force.[74]

By 1890, it was becoming clear that full legal and economic enfranchisement for various oppressed groups, including women, the peasantry, and the urban working class, would probably be inevitable, though at great cost to the Russian imperial regime. *The Sleeping Beauty* in no way should be viewed as a polemic in the debate on women's rights. But it is timely. How much more pleasant it must have been for the court to turn its back on contemporary feminists and to view, instead, assertive women from an earlier era, from the time of Catherine the Great and Princess Dashkova, head of the Academy of Sciences. In those days, a magical century earlier, Russian women emulated the salon free-thinkers of France.[75]

The course of the nineteenth century had seen shifts in women's status and rights as they, like other social policies, rode the waves of repression and reform. But by 1890, the imperial couple was firmly opposed to female higher education.[76] And the Empress told a visiting delegation of feminists that they would do better to stay home and knit.[77] (In this light, Aurora's ignorance of sewing and knitting takes on new meaning, but surely one of which the authors of *The Sleeping Beauty* were unaware.)

Ironically, the world of ballet, opera, and theater production was one in which the question of a woman's ability to be trained and find work had not been an issue in Russia since the early eighteenth century (however, as in other countries, only rarely did women move through the glass ceiling to appointments of administrative or artistic leadership – although, like Kshessinska, they could manipulate behind the scenes). And although ballet dancers sometimes took rich lovers, the economic situation in the Imperial Theaters created a social system quite different than that at the Paris Opéra. In France after 1830, the ballet dancers were primarily drawn from the working class, and they were employed by a semi-private enterprise that profited by paying low wages to all but the most brilliant stars. As we have seen in Chapter 1, a semi-official system of thinly masked prostitution was practically the only way for a French ballet girl to survive, by supplementing her meager wages with support from a wealthy protector simply for necessities like rent and food. The performance on stage at the Paris Opéra was erotically tinged by the knowledge that the dancers were sexually available after the show. But in the more paternalistic Russian system, once children were accepted into the Imperial Theatrical School, not only was their education and upkeep paid for, but they were guaranteed a government job and then a pension for life.[78] This is not to say that the dancers were never treated like erotic objects by members of the nobility.[79] But the makers of *The Sleeping Beauty*, unlike their peers abroad, lived in a microcosm dominated by women who were economically independent. These were women who sometimes separated from, even divorced their husbands (as did Petipa's first wife). Indeed, Petipa's mother was an actress and one of his sisters was an opera singer. Both of Petipa's wives and four of his five daughters were dancers; his daughter Marie danced the role of the Lilac Fairy in the original production of *The Sleeping Beauty*.[80] Petipa's situation as a son, brother, husband, and father to working women must certainly have molded his views of women's agency.

The Sleeping Beauty engenders a mixed message, riddled with paradoxes, about women. Its ambivalences are connected as much to social class as to gender. Its views of female beauty are double-edged: on the one hand, it speaks of women's beauty as partly consisting of power, intelligence, and agency, while on the other hand, it celebrates the beauty of purely physical feminine display. Unlike Russian literature and drama, which had explicitly begun to treat marriage as problematic and as oppressive to women as early as the 1840s, *The Sleeping Beauty* presents marriage entirely unskeptically.[81] On the one hand, it respects female power. And yet, on the other, it yearns for a time past when female agency was limited to a small group of women who could command intellectual and sexual authority, without threatening the status quo, only in a narrow, hierarchical, hermetic world.

3

EARLY MODERN DANCE

Fire Dance, Lily, Brahms Waltzes, Mother, Revolutionary Étude, Radha

Up until the beginning of the twentieth century, the marriage theme preoccupied ballet choreographers, just as going to see ballet was a social event couples often attended together – whether in or out of wedlock, licitly or illicitly. With the advent of a new century, however, the "woman question" that had emerged in successive waves in Europe and the United States since the French Revolution had made a deep mark on society; it began to raise serious new challenges to the institution of marriage. The new forms of high-art dancing born on the stages of Europe and the United States during this period reflected the new precariousness of an institution that had for centuries been the unquestioned social destiny of both bourgeois and aristocratic women. It did so in two ways. One was in the sudden, abundant appearance of women on stage not only as dancers, but as choreographers – as the producers, as well as objects, of choreography. The second was in the fact that these women appeared on stage alone. As dancer/reconstructor Annabelle Gamson has pointed out, "Women were not only taking center stage; they were taking all of the stage – without any support from men."[1]

But the new modern dance did not only *reflect* changing values surrounding marriage and sexuality. It actually *constructed* new social relations, partly because it produced a new, predominantly female audience. Shifting patterns of spectatorship no longer made going to the dance a courtship activity. (Ruth St. Denis, for instance, performed her early programs at society ladies' reception-teas.) And the images women made on stage and women audiences consumed contributed to a cultural dialogue that deeply problematized marriage relations and brought female sexualities out of the Victorian shadows of the nineteenth century. Thus, modern dance was both a response to and an agent of the changing roles and identities of women in Western, first-world culture.[2]

During the 1992 American elections, politicians declared it "The Year of the Woman." But about 100 years earlier, the coming twentieth century – indeed, the modern era itself – was repeatedly symbolized by the figure of a woman. And modern dance became a unique cultural arena, for throughout the twentieth century it has been the one art form to be almost entirely dominated by women.

The first generation of American modern dancers, including Loïe Fuller, Isadora Duncan, and Ruth St. Denis – often called "forerunners" – referred to their own type of dancing not as modern but as "aesthetic" or "interpretive." These women, along with others of their generation, had been trained in the popular theater and danced in ballet-spectacles (although their autobiographies often frame them as inspired innocents). But, working in an era when American culture began to bifurcate along class strata and to compete with European art, they dared to propose new forms of dancing that would earn "high-art" status and astonish Europe.

In the nineteenth century, ballet went into decline in Western Europe, while reaching a pinnacle of classicism in Russia. The impression the forerunners of modern dance made in Paris, London, and Berlin – and St. Petersburg – changed the shape of dance history, influencing ballet reforms as well as creating a new form of serious dance. These artists also worked at a time when women were demanding dress reform and civil rights. The forerunners of modern dance established a new, more active role for women in the dance world – that of choreographers, as well as dancers. So, unlike nineteenth-century ballet representations of women, the images created on the modern dance stage were not only executed by, but also conceived by women. And the images they created were as complex as the emerging feminist politics of the turn of the century, projecting radical visions of emancipation intertwined with biological determinist notions of "natural" women's spheres, separate and distinct from those of men.

To many, toward the end of the nineteenth century, "the Modern" itself was symbolized by woman. In France, Auguste Villiers de l'Isle-Adam figured modernity as a woman in his novel *The Future Eve* (1886). The German literary critic Eugen Wolff, often credited with inventing the term "the Modern" as a genre label, wrote in 1888 that he imagined that concept "as a woman, a *modern* woman, filled with the modern spirit." Moreover, Wolff declared,

> she is no young virgin, silly and ignorant of her destiny; she is an experienced but pure woman, in rapid movement like the spirit of the age, with fluttering garments and streaming hair, striding forward. . . . That is our new divine image: the Modern.[3]

He could have been describing the three key women who, with so many others, strode onto the dance stage in the 1890s: Fuller, Duncan, and St. Denis.

Since, grammatically speaking, the default or unmarked category in most Western languages has historically been male, it is only logical to mark something utterly new and different as female. Hence the impulse to identify the Modern as Woman. This turn is not, of course, unprecedented; the French Revolutionary concept of La Liberté was visually embodied in female form. But that this notion emerged again in late nineteenth-century imaginings of the future is significant for modern dance. For the three major forerunners of what we now call modern dance, all formed in the twin crucibles of *fin-de-siècle* America and Europe, seemed to be deeply stirred by those icons linking the power of modernity with women. And it is striking that each one consciously created her dancing self as one of three different aspects of this overarching, multi-layered vision: the Fairy Electricity, La Liberté, and Salammbô.

The International Paris Exhibition of 1900, which each of the three forerunners visited (along with Claude Debussy, Serge Diaghilev, and others who would shape the modern arts), displayed a rich fantasia of images of a utopian twentieth-century future, so often molded in the form of woman, to nearly fifty million Parisians and foreign spectators. One of the plans submitted for the show, although never realized, proposed the transformation of the Eiffel Tower into a gigantic woman, 150 meters tall, with eyes made of electric projectors.

Other icons of women did proliferate in the actual exhibition, however. The first to greet a visitor, atop the Porte Binet gateway to the grounds, was *La Parisienne*, three times human height. Sculpted by Paul Moreau-Vautier, she wore clothes designed by the French couturier Jeanne Paquin. It was rumored that Sarah Bernhardt had been the model for this monument, but local residents thought, rather, that the statuesque figure represented "the triumph of prostitution."[4] Perhaps her waist was too tightly corseted, her breasts too uplifted, the palms of her welcoming hands too open, her mien altogether too assertive. Like Manet's *Olympia*, she was inappropriately direct, contemporary, and realistic. Her brand of femininity was not entirely acceptable to society at large. Nor was it impressive to the forerunners of modern dance, who found mythic, more distanced female images of the Fairy Electricity, La Liberté, and Salammbô – also featured at the exhibition – to present on the dance stage. Of course, the representations they discovered there had not been newly invented for the first time. Rather, those images were presented at the exhibition precisely because they consolidated ideas already circulating in the culture.

The Fairy Electricity

Writing about the turn of the century and its cultural expression through this exhibition, Charles Simond described a new industrial force, mysteriously invisible yet able to generate sound, light, and motion; more lightweight and graceful than steam but ten times as powerful.[5] For Paul Morand, electricity had become a new goddess, alluring and beneficent but also dangerous, and the Paris Exhibition was partly her temple:

> A strange, crackling, condensed laughter resounded, the laughter of the Fairy Electricity. She triumphed at the Exhibition; she was born of the heavens, like true kings. The public laughed at the words "Danger of Death" written on the pylons; it knew that Electricity cured everything, even the "neuroses" fashionable at the time. It was progress, the poetry of both rich and poor; it bestowed light in abundance; it was the great Signal; as soon as it was born, it swept acetylene aside.

And, Morand continued, electricity added something unique and unprecedented to this exhibition, something not only technologically new, but also artistically exhilarating:

> At the Exhibition it was used with gay abandon. Women were like the flowers enclosing the electric bulbs, which in turn were like women. It was electricity that enabled the espaliers of fire to climb over the monumental gateway. At night, projectors swept across the Champ de Mars and the Château d'Eau sparkled with cyclamen colours; it was a tumbling mass of greens, orchid-coloured flashes, flaming lilies, orchestrations of liquid fire, a riot of volts and ampères. The Seine was violet, dove-coloured, blood-red. Electricity was accumulated, condensed, transformed, put in jars, stretched along wires, rolled round coils, and then discharged into the water, over the fountains, over the roofs and into the trees. It was the scourge, the religion, of 1900.[6]

He could have been describing Loïe Fuller herself. Although not in the least conventionally attractive, Fuller embodied the "new beauty" of electricity.[7] In fact, she had an Art Nouveau theater at the exhibition, where she performed her marvelous transformations with undulating silks made iridescent by the skillful use of the new theatrical technology of electric lighting and colored gels; atop the building's wave-like facade stood her own billowing form. "Instead of the 'Parisienne,' stiff as a dressmaker's dummy, an effigy of Loie Fuller swirling under the projectors should have crowned the Porte Binet," muses Philippe Jullian, historian of the exhibition.[8]

Fuller, born in rural Illinois, had transformed a standard vaudeville genre – skirtdancing – into a concert dance form whose opalescent colors, organic shapes, and suggestive images were venerated by Symbolist poets and Art Nouveau painters, architects, and craftsmen. She exaggerated the size of the dancer's silk skirts to enormous proportions, manipulating them with rods to make a mobile, sculpted screen on which she projected a constant play of ingenious lighting effects. She used black curtains and rugs, creating a camera obscura effect that seemingly suspended her figure in space and also gave her the means to effect trick disappearances and other optical illusions. Fuller had been a child performer who sang, acted, and gave temperance lectures. As a teenager, she acted and danced in stock companies, where she learned about the technical stagecraft required for the spectacular transformations of the popular theater of her day: dioramas, steam curtains, and magic lantern projections. Her first appearances in Paris in 1892, when she danced her *Serpentine Dance*, *Lily*, and *Butterfly*, were contemporaneous not only with the flowering of Art Nouveau, but also with the birth of cinema and the early use of electricity in the theater. She contributed to these innovations, appearing in films, posters, paintings, and sculptures; advancing several aspects of theatrical lighting as she experimented with carbon arc lights, hand-painted gels, and underlighting; and making several short films.[9]

Plate 6 Loïe Fuller, 1896. Cabinet photograph by Falk. Bequest of Evert Jansen Wendell, Harvard Theatre Collection, The Houghton Library. Courtesy of the Harvard Theatre Collection.

Fuller was an inventor who patented several scenic innovations, experimented with radium (and was friendly with the Curies). Although her effects were partly that of a conjurer, she was also a master technician. As dance historian Deborah Jowitt points out, few contemporaries acknowledged "that it took a small army of sweating electricians to engineer her magic – that because each lamp required its own handler, fourteen men were necessary to create the eerie interplay of red and gold for her *Fire Dance*."[10] But in published interviews and in her autobiography, Fuller was always reminding the public of the scientific, industrial underpinnings of her illusions. And, importantly, she *is* often described on stage more as a scientist – or alchemist – than as a dancing girl.

A representation comprises more than the moving image momentarily seen on stage or captured on film, with all its own experiential richness. The dancing emblem is also produced by surrounding publicity, dancers' and choreographers' conceptions, artistic reproductions in other media, comparisons to other dance works and genres, cultural codes, and other aspects of discourse. Fuller's dancing persona as a woman is difficult to decipher, because different media images disclose contradictory meanings: she is variously depicted and described as a voluptuous temptress, a vision of death, not a woman, not a body, a scientist, a magician. Isadora Duncan described Fuller's work as involving "all the magic of Merlin, the sorcery of light, color, flowing form." Duncan concluded, "What an extraordinary genius!"[11]

Fuller had objected to her first Parisian booking, at the Folies Bergère, not realizing that "girlie shows" were not the only fare offered there or that it was currently the fashion for artists and intellectuals (like the Goncourt brothers and Joris-Karl Huysmans) to frequent the famous variety theater, along with the *demi-monde*. Fuller did not intend her dancing to be sexually titillating – like that of the ordinary skirt or cancan dancer who capitalized on revealing the secret of the female leg (in daily *fin-de-siècle* life fully covered by long skirts and petticoats). She intended it to be serious, high art. Painters and lithographers often represent her body (according to artistic convention) as a scantily veiled and shapely nude, and the poet Stéphane Mallarmé described her dancing as "multiple emanations round a nakedness," but photographs and films show a chunky body, thick around the belly and hips and quite well-draped.[12] Sexual display was obviously not her artistic goal, however much it was the fantasy of many of her artistic admirers.

In Jules Chéret's posters, Fuller's neck arches back and her head tilts flirtatiously, revealing a white expanse of shapely breast and an open, inviting smile. In a portrait by Marie-Félix Hippolyte Lucas (c. 1898), Fuller wears only the most diaphanous drapery (fully revealing her breasts). She cocks her arm akimbo alluringly on a jutting hip and leans against part of her veil for all the world like a courtesan at an open bedroom door. She looks up, as if at a taller, male spectator, with a conventionally pretty face (not at all like her own) wreathed in a wide, pearly smile. The tilted head, the canted figure, the hand on the hip, all denote female sexual charm.

But photographs and films show no such strictly coded feminine wiles, and Toulouse-Lautrec, the one artist who seems to defy the usual artistic gender coding, in his 1893 lithograph of *Fire Dance* shows an erect head atop a shapeless body fully engulfed in a smoky yellow flame. Mallarmé himself described Fuller's figure as "strict, upright." Although Fuller dispensed with the corset commonly worn by dancers and fashionable women of the time, this was not a sign of seduction, but rather, a refusal of the standard icon of feminine sexuality – the tightly laced waist.[13] Instead of sharply defined, uplifted breasts and hips that swelled out invitingly below a cinched waist, Fuller's body provided a desexualized screen on which a spectrum of non-female, even non-human images could literally be projected.

She has been described by historians as exuding a "morbid voluptuousness,"[14] or "erotic danger"[15] but it is often a sense of incorporeal death and decay, rather than sexual desire, that her contemporaries noticed. Mallarmé called her "radiant, cold," and mused that she "is not a woman" – in fact, that she seemed to be "dead, yet flesh and bone." The writer Jean Lorrain stresses this anticorporeal aspect of Fuller's image in his description of *Fire Dance*:

> Modelled in glowing embers, Loïe Fuller does not burn; she oozes brightness, she is flame itself. Standing in a fire of coals, she smiles and her smile is like a grinning mask under the red veil in which she wraps herself, the veil which she waves and causes to ripple like the smoke of a fire over her lava-like nudity: she is Herculaneum buried beneath ashes, she is the Styx and the shores of Hades, she is Vesuvius with its gaping jaws spitting the fire of the earth, and she is Lot's wife transfixed in a statue of salt amid the avenging conflagration of the five accursed cities, this motionless and yet smiling nakedness among the coals with the fire of heaven and hell for a veil.

Writing about *Lily*, too, Lorrain stresses the imagery of death associated with the flower:

> What I have been unable to tell you and could never convey properly (of this I am aware), although I long to do so, is the sublimity, the deathly terror of La Fuller's entrance in the Dance of the Lily. In a sea of shadows a grey, indistinct form floats like a phantom and then, suddenly, under a beam of light, a spectral whiteness, a terrifying apparition. Is this a dead woman who has been crucified, hovering above a charnel-house, her arms still held out under the folds of her shroud, some huge, pale bird of the polar seas, an albatross or a gull, or perhaps a spirit of the dead on its way to the sabbath, a martyr of ancient times or a ghoul of the cemeteries? But how poignant, how superb, how overwhelming and frightening, like a nightmare induced by morphine or ether.[16]

Although Lorrain refers to Fuller's "nakedness," the term seems both metaphoric and desexualized. Only the image of Lot's wife in *Fire Dance* even suggests carnal life. And certainly Lorrain's description of *Lily* undercuts any feminine delicacy associated with flowers. Rather, it reminds us that lilies are funereal. Fuller's visual image in both these dances is connected with death, destruction, and everlasting hellfire. Lorrain does not mention that the musical accompaniment for *Fire Dance* was Richard Wagner's "Ride of the Valkyries," a correlation that adds another layer of meaning: the promise by avenging goddesses of destruction through warfare.

The underlighting Fuller used in both *Fire Dance* and *Lily* gave her audiences the impression of great height (although she was quite short, Mallarmé calls her "statuesque," subverting the female coding of diminutive size).[17] And her costume for *Lily* claimed both vertical and horizontal volume. Mallarmé, somewhat hyperbolically, remarked that she "ecstatically stretched to the extremity of each wing." According to dance historian Sally Sommer,

> the draperies [for *Lily*] could be extended until they seemed to fill the space . . . [The costume] contained 500 yards of gossamer-thin silk and could radiate ten feet from her body in every direction and be thrown up to the surprising height . . . of twenty feet. It was close to 100 yards around the hem.[18]

Not only the above-mentioned backstage electricians, but even Fuller herself worked arduously on stage to create her stage illusions, and this laboriousness itself was part of her public image. She told a newspaper interviewer that, manipulating the huge costume, "I make that lily by sheer will force. . . . [By the end of the dance] I'm so exhausted that I've no physical strength left."[19]

Both the colossal size she blocked out with her extended dancing body and the violence of her imagery contradict the idealized likenesses of her fashioned by Art Nouveau craftsmen. For example, the slender, long-legged butterfly women on the bronze grill designed by René Lalique for Fuller's theater lift their arms seductively over their heads or clasp them flirtatiously at their chins, while their hips swing to one side. Their femininity has a neo-rococo daintiness nowhere evident in photographs and films of Fuller.[20]

Besides the associations of violent death and destruction and the assertive claims on space, other aspects of Fuller's dances militate against conventional (heterosexual) feminine imagery. For instance, in her 1906 film of *Fire Dance*, it is striking that she turns her back to the audience for relatively long stretches of time. And while turning the back can be an erotically teasing move, in this context it has the opposite meaning: it shuns the viewer's gaze. Along with the voluminous costume, it obstructs the presentation of the sexually charged front of the female body. Another important feature is the lack of the marriage theme, love theme, or indeed, any men at all in her dances. These were not narrative works, although both Fuller and her critics referred to her shifting representations of emotions. If her dances could be said to have plots (as when she seemed, in *Fire Dance*, to fight off the flames but ultimately to be consumed and extinguished by them), they did not chart human relationships, but an isolated, ungendered figure – either in nature or as an element of nature. Fuller is characterized as disappearing into her image. She did not elide women and nature, but rather, seemed to cease being a woman on stage in order to assume her transformations.

Despite her formal exploitation of the biologism of late French Art Nouveau – the serpentine line, botanic forms, and nacreous colors – Fuller does not embody what the art historian Deborah Silverman views as Art Nouveau's politically reactionary, anti-feminist embrace of an interiorizing, domestic and decorative organicism. Rather, Fuller represents an earlier stage of artistic development, circa 1889, when Art Nouveau stood for technological advance in the service of democracy, in the form of architecture and other artworks displayed in public spaces.[21]

In many ways, Fuller resembles a witch or sorcerer far more than a seductress. Perhaps partly because she was an openly identified lesbian, she shunned the provocative female representation of enticement so closely identified with "the dancing girl," in favor of an ancient, mythic image of witchcraft and wisdom. But she is not the ugly crone of the Romantic ballet – femininity frustrated and gone sour. She projects a vital, active image of an artificer, a savant, a fabricator of wonders. According to Sommer, the French called her "la Créatrice."[22] In her later works, creating large-scale, nearly abstract naturescapes – storms, the sea – with her all-woman group, or summoning up giant shadows, she seems almost to become a female Prospero. Yet her image as a sorcerer has a modern, futuristic twist – that of the scientist, the inventor. Thus she created a space for women with biological and chemical knowledge to escape the stereotyped image of the folkloric witch and to appear as modern professionals in a field predominantly marked as male. At a time when, for instance, female midwives were being thrust out of the delivery room and obstetrics was becoming a modern medical science dominated by men, Fuller's claim to be a female scientist was daring.

A contemporary of the trick-film director Georges Méliès, Fuller fuses two of his favorite characters. She is like both his prestidigitators who can make dancing women miraculously appear and disappear and his scientists who build a rocket to the moon or fly to the North Pole. Her illusions were magical, but her audiences were always reminded that scientific precision underlay their creation. She prided herself on her election to the French Astronomical Society for her investigations into the properties of light.[23] The Fairy Electricity, Fuller, was, after all, in Mallarmé's words, "an industrial achievement."

La Liberté

Like Fuller, with whom she briefly danced, the Californian Isadora Duncan discarded the dancer's corset, tights, and satin slippers, dancing barefoot in loose clothing. She militated against both the strictures and the decorativeness of ballet, and, inspired equally by her ideas of ancient Greek dance and the rhythms of nature, sought a liberated way of moving that would express a range of emotions. Although her choreography was simple, based on walking, skipping, and running, those steps combined with pantomimic gestures, a highly expressive face, eloquent stillnesses, and personal charisma made an extraordinary impact on the audiences of her day. Her use of emotionally stirring symphonic music (rather than the program music often preferred by ballet choreographers) was controversial. So was her stress on the torso (rather than the arms and legs of ballet) and her use of the floor. Like the theater reformer Gordon Craig, with whom she had an affair and a child, she did away with decorative sets that specified locales; unlike Fuller, she dispensed with the illusion of stage magic. She held the stage as a human-scale figure, and – importantly – as a solo dancer in front of a plain blue curtain.

Duncan was particularly concerned with an alternative physical training method for children, and she established several schools (in Germany, France, and Russia). After the deaths of her own children and the onset of the First World War, her vision darkened and she danced tragic and heroic themes. She created *Marche Slave* (1917) upon hearing that the Russians had overthrown their tsar and later, invited to Moscow to found a school, she trained hundreds of children to dance in patriotic pageants. But her sympathy with early communist ideals and her espousal of free love drew harsh criticism when she toured the U.S. in 1922–23.

The female image Duncan created was as complex as that of Fuller, and it, too, shifted several times over the course of her career. On the one hand, Duncan seemed to be the harbinger of the twentieth century, and she herself envisioned "the dancer of the future." And yet, her own rhetoric and imagery harked back to an older neoclassical intellectual, artistic, and political tradition, with roots in the iconography of the 1789 French Revolution and branches stretching out through the nineteenth century. She was dubbed "the daughter of Prometheus," and she remains an enduring symbol of spiritual, physical, and sexual liberation. But the liberation she advocated was very much a product of her historical moment, and her calls for women's emancipation were tempered by her elision of women's identity with nurture and nature.

I want to analyze three Duncan dances on three themes: *Brahms Waltzes*, on love; *Mother*, on nurture; and *Revolutionary Étude*, on liberation.[24] These three themes intertwine in Duncan's rhetoric and choreography to create a specific emblem of woman: innately procreative, patriotic, and passionate. Her biological destiny does not link her to men through marriage, but through reproduction within the larger social institution of the nation. She is a romantic symbol of revolution that unites nature and political liberation and safeguards the future, in the form of children.[25]

Duncan proclaimed that the *Brahms Waltzes* is about "the many faces of love." The dance is, Gamson explains, "a portrait of a woman in many aspects of her life and of her loving – she is the nurturing mother, the seductive mistress; she's the loving companion."[26] As Gamson has reconstructed this dance, its opening movement embodies a spirited, seemingly artless candor. Her hair flows freely as she skips across the stage, repeating two different phrases. In the first one, she opens her arms out sequentially in a wide, bountiful embrace and then reaches upward. In the second, she reaches up, spins slowly, and opens her palms outward. In the first phrase, as her arms open her body becomes frankly direct and vulnerable. In the second, her final gesture connotes a trusting presentation of the self, gift-like, to the spectator. Her focus alternates self-absorption, spiritual elevation, and a candid, level gaze at the spectator. Her springy step and the directness and strength of her gestures give the impression of confidence. Moving to and fro, turning her back on the spectator, she chastens her straightforwardness with a touch of shyness that is never seductive, but rather virginal. This, combined with the gentle, slightly inquisitive way her head tilts against her shoulder and the innocent vulnerability of her open torso and exposed palms, gives her confidence a sweet, erotic tinge. Here is an image of female sexuality that refuses fragility in favor of that which is lively, tender, and direct. At the end of this section, the music and dancing slows down, adding to the erotic flavor. The dancer goes through the sequence of her first phrase and then draws her arms down across her pelvis before opening her palms outward a final, decisive time. Her gestures seem not only, finally, to present the self to the spectator in a deliberately sexual way, but also to become a sign language narrative linking first earth, then sky, with the female sexual body. Thus the image characterizes female sexuality as fresh and vital, and also graphically joins it to nature.

The second movement moves away from innocence, quietly and deeply celebrating the "natural" female body as sensuous and fertile. The dancer's head drops back and her hands drop, relaxed, as she leans backward in a gesture/posture complex of pleasurable surrender. Her arms lift heavily, resisting gravity at first, then sinking again. Her hands seem to indicate her breasts obliquely and to bestow them on the world. As she opens her arms and gathers them inward, one can almost see her embracing the world, enfolding all its children in her bosom. But she also enjoys her body for its own sake, bending over, reaching to the sky, indulging in self-touching, and relishing the fullness of her arms' upward stretch, her torso's deep bow forward, the textures of her hair, hips, and torso. Every movement, every sensation appears to be savored luxuriously to its fullest, and the section ends with an image of ecstatic flight. Duncan seems to be marking the female body as finding its natural satisfaction in modes of both sexual desire and reproductivity.

The final movement is frolicsome. The dancer takes on the persona of a dancer – flirtatious, sultry, and simultaneously delicate and powerful. To the shifting rhythms of the fandango-flavored music, she skips, places one hand on her hip or her shoulder while she rotates the opposite wrist in a little flourish, and tosses her head back. She bounces her wrists together, as if they were castanets. She lingers as she shifts directions and always casts a knowing backward glance as she moves away from the spectator. While there is a filigreed quality to her dancing, her gestures are full-bodied, and she gradually but steadily increases the amplitude of her steps to claim more stage space. Here, finally, is an image of seduction, but one that is effervescent.

Duncan's dances about motherhood are far from sunny. In *Ave Maria* (c. 1914), she expressed her devastating grief at the death of her two children. In *Mother* (as reconstructed by Gamson), the dancer renders maternity as a combination of pain and compassion, to a somber étude by Alexander Scriabin. Wearing a sack-like long dress gathered at the waist, with her white hair pulled back in a knot, Gamson bears a resemblance to an ascetic pilgrim or penitent. Childrearing takes her on a spiritual journey. She starts standing, looking back at the child she leads

Plate 7 Isadora Duncan, *Ave Maria*, 1916. Photograph by Arnold Genthe. Courtesy of the Dance Collection, Irma Duncan, The New York Public Library for the Performing Arts, Astor, Lenox and Tilden Foundations.

forward and occasionally glancing and reaching toward some goal. She stops to stroke the child, then makes a heavenward gesture, like that from *Ave Maria*, of supplication. She kneels to embrace and rock the child, only to open her arms in surrender – perhaps to the forces of destiny that will eventually take the child from her. She reclines, sitting, on the floor, watching the child with devotion, then kneels to embrace it once again. Finally, she sits again, watching as the child leaves, stretching out a hand, and finally raising that hand in a farewell salute.

The spatial articulation of *Mother* is quite striking. The dancer begins standing and ends up practically lying on the floor. As the child grows up, the mother sinks. She is humbled by her experience of parenthood. Like the Virgin Mary, she is an emblem of renunciation, a "Madonna of Humility."[27] Still, her spine is

phrygian cap in Delacroix's painting, and Marianne wears one in Jules Dalou's group sculpture *The Triumph of the Republic*, in the Place de la Nation in Paris. As the feminist cultural historian Marina Warner explains, the French phrygian cap, a fusion of two kinds of Roman headgear, signified two aspects of liberty: it stood both for the foreigner, marginalized and thus outside the bounds of mainstream society, and also for the slave freed from bondage. For Warner, Liberty's and Marianne's phrygian cap, slipped chiton (revealing the female breast and carrying associations with the mythical Amazons), and bare foot (signifying the wildness of nature) comprise a constantly recycled complex of French Revolutionary symbols that denote liberty, dangerously cast in the form of a woman.[32]

But the breast bared by the slipped chiton is also redolent of the lament of mothers at funeral rituals in the ancient world. And, as Warner puts it, in French political iconography "the oscillation between these two dominant meanings of the breast [the liberty of Amazonian wildness, challenging the state, and maternal nurturance, a function of the custodial state] is constant after the first Revolution . . . , and it reflects swings between accepting woman as an active agent of change or desiring her to remain a passive source of strength."[33]

Turning back to Duncan's two dances to Scriabin, which might at first glance seem antithetical in their themes of Motherhood and Revolution, one can clearly see antecedents – in the iconography of Duncan's adopted country, France – for their yoking together. In these two dances, Duncan enacts the conflict between women's active and passive roles. It is important, too, to recall that France is a Catholic country steeped in the iconography of a significant, ubiquitous grieving Mother – the Virgin Mary. And when one remembers that – although women served as allegories in artworks like Delacroix's painting and Dalou's monument – in both real life and in literature French Revolutionary women were often stigmatized, one can see that in simultaneously celebrating maternity and liberty in the form of nature, Duncan mitigated her political message. That is, even her wild outlaw posture still put her in the realm of pure Nature.[34] Despite her statements that she supported women's emancipation, her view of political liberation was a national, not a gender-oriented one. She railed against marriage, and in neither her dances nor her life did men appear to support her. But still, her feminism was a conservative one, linking sexuality, nature, procreation, and motherhood as women's innate biological and social destiny.

Salammbô

Ruth St. Denis never danced the role of Salammbô, the sensual priestess of ancient Carthage in Flaubert's novel by the same name, but the female representations the dancer created, beginning just after turn of the century, might have emerged from Flaubert's own orientalist reveries after his travels in the Near East over fifty years earlier.[35] Nor, as Jowitt points out, did St. Denis dance the role of Salome in her early career, although that exotic, sadistic image of the dancing woman was ubiquitous on the ballet, modern dance, and popular entertainment stage at the time; St. Denis even worked with the poet Hugo von Hofmannsthal on a never-realized version of the Salome story in 1907.[36]

Perhaps in creating her many images of the "mysterious Orient" St. Denis was inspired, as Morand was, by the colonial pavilions at the 1900 Paris Exhibition that featured the music and dance of Africa, the Near East, and Asia. Wrote Morand,

> The Indo-Chinese theatre adjoined the reproduction of the strange temple which had just been discovered and which was called Angkor. . . . The entire hill was nothing but perfumes, incense, vanilla, the aromatic fumes of the seraglio; one could hear the scraping of the Chinese violins, the sounds of the castanets, the wailing flutes of the Arab bands, the mystical howling of the Aissawas . . . , the cries of the Ouled Naïl with their mobile bellies; I followed this opiate mixture, this perfume of Javanese dancing girls, sherbets and rahat-lakoum.[37]

Not only the heady fantasia of orientalist exoticism and the mystical feminine allure Morand evokes, but even the polyglot mixture of styles and cultures at the colonial pavilions came to characterize St. Denis's choreography. The "Tour of the World" rotunda in Paris, inspired by Jules Verne's novel *Around the World in Eighty Days*, which St. Denis would also have seen, was equally a fanciful *mélange* of architectural traditions. According to Jullian, "a Hindu pagoda, a Chinese temple and a Muslim mosque stood side by side, [and] there were panoramas, jugglers and geishas."[38] This scene, too, is reminiscent of St. Denis, who in her dances joined exotic, esoteric religious symbolism to the imagery of sexual pleasure, via popular entertainment techniques.

St. Denis, who in 1900 was appearing in David Belasco's *Zaza* in London and visited the Paris Exhibition after the tour ended, also brought home profoundly moving memories of performances by the Japanese actress and solo dancer Sada Yacco, who showed her own composites of various forms of Japanese traditional performing arts in Loïe Fuller's theater on the exhibition grounds.[39] According to dance historian Elizabeth Kendall, it was Yacco who inspired St. Denis's own first forays into dance that same year when she created *Madame Butterfly*, a solo in Japanese costume. The dance, of course, was named after the play Belasco mounted in 1900, perhaps himself stirred by Yacco's performances.[40] Although St. Denis's dance probably was never performed publicly, Kendall notes that in imagining this dance, St. Denis expressed new aspirations away from vaudeville skirt dancing and toward serious art dancing that would transcend personality. "What she had made was a genuinely new thing: a dance that was the distillation of a story, a play with the drama taken out, a modest composition, but one saturated with the modern quality of 'atmosphere.'"[41]

In fact, this "atmosphere" was the very quality that would move St. Denis's dancing from the realm of male spectatorship to that of the female-dominated audience. Through the new context of high-art dancing Duncan and St. Denis created, which was patronized by American women of the middle and upper classes (as opposed to the working-class, predominantly male audiences of vaudeville skirt dancing), the display of the female body and St. Denis's orientalist messages of sensuous pleasure took on new meaning.[42] Kendall suggests that what St. Denis saw in Yacco was an unfamiliar sense of dignity in a female dancing spectacle. St. Denis herself remarked that Yacco had an "aura of stillness – so different from our Western acrobatics."[43] Moreover, Yacco's characters were women who acknowledged their sexuality without European or American overlays of Victorian guilt. And this was done in a condensed, abstract form that also distanced the sexuality of female body. "Yacco showed Ruth the possibility of a grand actress-heroine who wasn't a 'bad woman,' one who used ritualistic and rhythmic gestures as her natural mode of expression."[44]

If Europe's fascination with the art of the non-Western world had long been anchored by her colonial interests and imports since the eighteenth century, a new wave of orientalism swept both Europe and the United States around the turn of the twentieth century. Kendall remarks that:

> Orientalism had appeared as 1890s chic in the interiors of the new Waldorf Hotel, 33rd and Fifth, which were Turkish. It took ten or fifteen years for the style to filter down to middle-class wives and daughters, who then designed 'Turkish corners' in their living rooms. . . . Ruth's East Indian skits were perceived as the very spirit of the Turkish corner, expressions of a refined sensuality new to the American palate.[45]

St. Denis's biographer Suzanne Shelton points out that this interest in things Asian was doubly present in American culture at the turn of the century, both at the level of serious intellectual and spiritual concerns (as it had been, for instance, for Ralph Waldo Emerson and the Transcendentalists in the mid-nineteenth century) and at the level of more ephemeral popular-culture entertainments. In part, this turn-of-the-century fascination was an anti-modern gesture of rejecting the industrialized world and turning instead to transcendental solace in the ancient teachings of Asian religions. In part, it was the result of increased commercial contact with the East, not only through trade but through events like the Columbian Exposition of 1893 in Chicago and fairgrounds like that at Coney Island in New York. Shelton observes, "America's new cosmopolites in the early 1900s eagerly bought kimonos . . . , visited the Streets of Cairo at Coney Island, discussed the pros and cons of Buddhism, and sampled Oriental literature," including not only recent translations of the *Bhagavad-Gita* and the *Qur'an*, but mass-market popular books like *Hindu Philosophy in a Nutshell.* Chautauqua and museum lecturers like Ernest Fenellosa also brought Eastern ideas and an appreciation of Asian art to popular, largely female audiences. "Society balls adopted Japanese, Indian, and Chinese motifs, and even the most modest of American homes sported Japanese prints on their walls," Shelton notes.[46]

It was in this milieu that St. Denis, a complex figure who combined the savvy of show business with spiritual aspirations and remarkable physical beauty, created her first success, *Radha* (1906). Born Ruth Dennis in rural New Jersey, St. Denis grew up meeting artists and intellectuals in the bohemian boarding house her mother ran. Mrs. Dennis, who had graduated from medical school and was an ardent dress reformer, feminist, and Christian Scientist, trained her daughter in the methods of François Delsarte, the French music teacher and theorist of the body who created a system of expressive movement that became popular as part of the physical culture movement in the late nineteenth century. From family friends the young St. Denis learned about Hindu thought through theosophy, a mystical doctrine of direct experience of the divine that spread internationally in the 1870s and 80s, with its headquarters in New York.[47]

Like Duncan and Fuller, St. Denis served an apprenticeship on the popular stage. She did acrobatic and skirt dancing at dime museums and roof garden theaters in New York, and she acted in Augustin Daly's stock company and in David Belasco's historically meticulous extravaganzas. However, seeing Genevieve Stebbins turn Delsarte exercises into expressive concert dances in 1892, like Yacco's performances in 1900, was influential in her search for a more serious form of art dancing. Eventually, like the Duncans, the entire Dennis family moved to New York City to support the daughter's performing career, and, like Fuller and Duncan, St. Denis (as Belasco renamed her) found in Europe sympathetic audiences for her experiments in concert dancing. But unlike her two expatriate contemporaries, St. Denis returned to the United States, where between 1909 and 1914 her career as a solo dancer blossomed both on the vaudeville stage and in art theaters.

Before she made *Radha*, St. Denis had been working on an Egyptian dance, based on *The Book of the Dead*, in which she substituted an Egyptian goddess for the mortal who, in the Hall of Judgment myth, appears before a divine jury. St. Denis, rewriting this tale to form her own mythology and thus creating herself as a goddess, recalled that the inspiration for this dance came to her suddenly. She had seen a poster for Egyptian Deities cigarettes, featuring an image of the goddess Isis seated on a throne, in a pharmacy window while on tour with Belasco in Buffalo, New York in 1904. "My destiny as a dancer had sprung alive in that moment. I would become a rhythmic and impersonal instrument of spiritual revelation rather than a personal actress of comedy or tragedy. I had never before known such an inward shock of rapture."[48]

Shelton, however, points out that the roots for *Egypta* had been planted much earlier. Among them were a Stebbins performance that included a pantomime called *The Myth of Isis*, which St. Denis saw in New York in 1892; an outdoor pageant she saw that same year in New Jersey, *Egypt Through Centuries*, that included the sacrifice of a virgin, an Egyptian grand ballet with five hundred performers, and fireworks; her readings in Eastern religions and Christian Science; and her visit to the Paris Exhibition of 1900. Still, the determination to quit Belasco's company and to create her own high-art dances crystallized on that tour in 1904, and so did the template of many of St. Denis's future dances, key to which was the moral trial of a female goddess. Although she immediately copyrighted the scenario for *Egypta*, long before she presented that dance publicly, St. Denis first turned to a new dance based on Indian themes.[49]

Through Edmund Russell, an actor who had been giving readings at high society soirées from *The Light of Asia*, a Buddhist poem by Sir Edwin Arnold, St. Denis became involved in the newly organized Progressive Stage Society, part of the little theater movement that swept Europe and the United States at the turn of the century. In 1905, St. Denis appeared with Russell in an English version of the Sanskrit play *Shakuntala*, by Kalidasa. Shelton speculates that the solo dance St. Denis performed in her role as Sunamati, a nymph, before the fourth scene of the play, may have been an early draft of *Radha*.[50] St. Denis writes that Arnold became her mentor in things Indian: "He told me what books to read; he told me where I would find Indian jewelry and carvings in the Metropolitan Museum. . . . He urged me to complete *Radha* quickly."[51]

Originally planned as a commercial vaudeville venture that would finance the eventual production of *Egypta*, the new dance was based on a patchwork of sources: partly on a Coney Island sideshow (put on by an entire imported "Indian village") that featured native snake charmers and nautch dancers; partly on a character from *The Light of Asia*; and partly on St. Denis's library research into Indian mythology and Hindu belief. The soul's liberation from the bondage of the senses, a phrase she gleaned from A.C. Lyall's essay on Brahmanism in *Great Religions of the World*, became the dance's central theme – more Buddhist than Hindu.[52] According to St. Denis,

> I conceived of [Radha] as an idol in her temple, who for a brief time was infused with life and danced a message for her devotees. Theologically speaking, this was inaccurate, for Radha, although the beloved of Krishna, the god of love, was seldom worshiped on her own account. . . . The beautiful symbology of Radha fascinated me. She was the human soul, forever seeking union with the divine, which was Krishna, and the various poems and legends of Radha showed her sometimes in great ecstasy standing on the same lotus with her beloved and at other times wandering in a night of doubt and pride, far off from him.[53]

This was a high-flown theme for a vaudeville audience, like that at Proctor's Twenty-third Street Theater, where *Radha* was first performed. St. Denis recalls that for several weeks "my act went on between Bob Fitzsimmons, the pugilist, and a group of trained monkeys."[54] According to Caroline and Charles Caffin, when St. Denis performed *Radha* at Proctor's, "the vaudeville audience as a whole did not comprehend her aspirations. At first there was a distinct gasp of amazement, wonderment whether to disapprove of the audacity or to resent the lofty conception."[55] But St. Denis also performed the dance at private high-society parties, one given by Mrs. Stuyvesant Fish and another by the sculptor Rowland Hinton Perry, and eventually Mrs. Orlando Rouland sponsored a matinee performance at the Hudson Theater, funded by twenty-five women from New York's social elite, each of whom invited her friends to the performance. This event launched St. Denis's career as an art dancer. She records in her autobiography: "As this invited audience filed out, Harris [her manager], listening to their comments and feeling the temper of the occasion, knew that we had a great success, a success based upon something which would evade and intrigue audiences for twenty-five years."[56]

The dance is primarily a solo for St. Denis, although it begins with a procession of male priests who serve to frame her dancing and to carry the symbolic props. One of the most striking features of *Radha* – one that must have shocked its vaudeville audiences – is that the dance proper begins with stillness. St. Denis, as the idol Radha, is seated in lotus position, absolutely immobile, on a pedestal. The choreographer describes the opening moments of the performance at the Hudson Theater:

> When the curtain went up a vast temple was shown, incrusted with gold and dim with smoke. On the ground in meditation were the squatting forms of devotees. The wailing music rose as they prostrated themselves before the shrine. Presently, through the incense smoke, the doors of the shrine were seen to open and the impassive form of the goddess was revealed. After a short interval Radha descended from her pedestal and signified to her worshipers that she had taken this human form in order to give them a message. This she would convey through a mystic dance, the meaning of which was that they must not seek permanent happiness in an impermanent world.[57]

Most of the music for *Radha* was taken from the French composer Léo Delibes's 1883 opera *Lakmé*, based on a story by Pierre Loti, which told of the doomed love between a British officer and the daughter of a Brahmin priest in the Indian raj. Surely the music itself evoked imagery of a chorus of French dancers portraying Hindu maidens, dancing sensually on the Paris stage.[58]

The idol awakens, taking several deep breaths, opening her eyes, and forming the shape of a lotus blossom with her hands, and she steps down from her pedestal.[59] She walks over to her priests and takes from one of them two strands of pearls. "The Dance of the Five Senses" began. According to St. Denis,

> [*Radha*] was comprised of three figures, the first being performed in five circles, one within the other, each circle representing one of the five senses. The senses were symbolized by different objects: jewels for sight, bells for hearing, garlands for smell, a bowl of wine for taste, and for touch, kisses on her own hands.[60]

The dance for each sense lasts for only about a minute. In each, St. Denis uses a simple vocabulary of movement: she steps mincingly from side to side, turns, kicks, and strikes some poses, all in strict time to the music. Often, she leans into one hip, curving her body asymmetrically, after the manner of erotic Indian temple sculptures. In the Dance of Sound, she bounces into this pose, while her arms circle in the air, playing the bells in a pizzicato manner. Her bouncing movements seem to embody the music itself (foreshadowing the music visualizations later in her career), and the movements of her arms seem to fill the space with sound. In the Dance of Smell, she sniffs the garlands of flowers as if to illustrate in pantomime the workings of the sense and then crushes them against her body, as if releasing the flowers' heady scent. Swinging the garlands around her, she seems to offer their fragrance to others as she turns. In the Dance of Taste, after drinking, she acts as though intoxicated, whirls, and stops in a deep back bend. Each dance ends in a similar pose of ecstasy, as St. Denis flings her head back and freezes.

For the Dance of Touch, St. Denis kneels, then sits on the floor and arranges her skirt around her. She strokes her arms with her palms and caresses her face with the backs of her hands. She traces the outlines of her breasts, torso, and hips, and leans forward to look at the audience, her hand to her mouth. The sense of touch is made doubly immediate as the dancer feels the physical sensations of her own hands on her skin.

As the music rises to a crescendo, St. Denis stands, places her hands on her hips, and swivels her hips, swirling her skirt, more like a Middle Eastern belly dancer than a nautch girl. Then she begins to spin, first in one direction, then in the other. Finally she falls and twists her body convulsively, then becomes still as the lights dim.

According to St. Denis, that brief section of the dance symbolizes the dead end to which sensual pleasure leads:

> The second figure [of *Radha*] was danced on a square, representing, according to Buddhist theology, the fourfold miseries of life, and was done with writhings and twistings of the body to portray the despair of unfulfillment. At the end of this figure Radha sank to the ground in darkness.[61]

The choreographer describes the final section of the dance, The Renunciation of the Senses, in which Radha rises to return to her throne:

> After a short interval a light disclosed [Radha] in an attitude of prayer and meditation. She now rose and, holding a lotus flower, began the third figure of the dance, which followed the lines of an open lotus flower – the steps leading from the center of the flower to the points of each petal. She danced on the balls of her feet, thus typifying the ecstasy and joy which follow renunciation of the senses and freedom from their illusion. At the close of this figure, which finished the message, Radha

Plate 8 Ruth St. Denis in *Radha*, 1906. Photograph by White Studio. Courtesy of the Dance Collection, the Denishawn Collection, The New York Public Library for the Performing Arts, Astor, Lenox and Tilden Foundations.

> slowly danced backward to the shrine, followed by the priests, and the doors of her shrine were closed.[62]

Semiotically, Radha is portrayed as both powerful and sensual. As the dance opens, she is seated on her pedestal above the priests, and they worship her. And even when she descends, she is still – literally – superior to the men for most of the dance, since she is usually at standing level, while they are seated on the ground. Moreover, they never partner her or make any contact with her, except to hand her the symbolic props. Thus her sensual pleasures do not seem to be outwardly projected in a sexual coupling, for she remains aloof from men throughout. Even in the Dance of Touch, is it self-touching that arouses her.

Although the men never dance with her, it is significant that St. Denis appears with an "ensemble" of men in *Radha.* That is, unlike the ballerina in a nineteenth-century ballet, who (when she is not being partnered by her cavalier) often dances with an ensemble of women, here St. Denis is always the sole woman on stage. In no way is she part of a community of women, but neither is she part of the community of men. This enhances her quality of remoteness. In some ways, it even suggests a gender-role reversal, as if she were a powerful ruler with an all-male harem. While one could argue that, performing for her male priests, she is the quintessential subject of the male gaze and dances for their pleasure, that does not seem to be what happens in the dance. Rather, the dance confirms what St. Denis's verbal account narrates – that the dance constitutes a moral lesson. Thus Radha is the priests' superior in several, linked ways: because she is a goddess and a ruler, but also because she is their teacher. That power relationship cools down the erotic content of her dancing.

Admittedly, the cool quality of the 1941 film of *Radha* could be partly due to St. Denis's age and physical condition; she was 62 when the film was made, and her limbs were stiffened by arthritis. But Shelton, in her observation that *Radha* conveys a mixed message of sensualism and spirituality, quotes contemporary observers as finding it reserved as well. Von Hoffmansthal wrote, "[*Radha*] borders on voluptuousness but it is chaste. It is consecrated to the senses, but it is higher."[63] And Philip Hale somewhat bemusedly remarked in the *Boston Herald*, "Although her body is that of a woman divinely planned, there is no atmosphere of sex about her. Here is a woman who could dance wholly undraped and be the incarnation of unconscious purity. And yet her beauty is not a sexless beauty."[64]

Still, Shelton determines that ultimately *Radha* was a dance of seduction. It was an instance of the female image Shelton believes St. Denis borrowed from David Belasco: "a sanctified vehicle for voyeurism." The Belasco woman, according to Shelton, "allowed the theatregoer a glimpse of evil while reassuring him of the eventual triumph of good."[65] And about *Radha* Shelton concludes,

> As an exercise in eroticism *Radha* was a ritual orgasm, its heroine, the sort of *fin-de-siècle femme fatale* celebrated in the refrain of a popular song: "And you stole my heart/with your cunning heart/And the Egypt in your smile." This aspect of *Radha*, its dark, mysterious force, placed it in a tradition of erotic art which allied the dangerous female, luxury, and the lure of the senses in a powerful allegory.[66]

More recently, Jane Desmond has attempted to characterize *Radha*, with its symbols of racial and cultural Otherness, as a locus of orientalist "scopophilic pleasure" and cultural imperialism. She writes that "the dance . . . unites the goddess/whore duality within the figure of one woman," though she acknowledges that this could permit various readings. She explains:

> One reading reassures the male viewer that even "asexual" women are

> really "women," that is, defined by and reducible to their bodies. Other readings might hold that women themselves are repositories of both relationships to sexuality, indulgence, and control; or that woman's pleasure in her own body is so seductive as to involve a constant struggle between expression and renunciation; or even that the pleasure of the senses is itself a transcendent spiritual experience.[67]

Moreover, Desmond proposes, *Radha* was a work in the "Christian confessional" mode that may have "enabled [St. Denis] to subvert the contemporary standards for 'respectable' women's display of their own sexuality," but that finally merely "reproduced traditional patriarchal designations of that sexuality."[68] Citing Linda Nochlin's discussion of orientalist painting, Desmond characterizes *Radha*'s mixed message of sensuality and spirituality as a "tongue-clicking and lip-smacking response."[69]

However, it seems that Desmond is too quick to dismiss both St. Denis's framing of sensuality as a transcendental experience and St. Denis's radical staging of female sexuality itself. St. Denis's target audience was primarily society women, not vaudeville audiences. For a woman to show other women her enjoyment of her body was a feminist coup in 1906, no matter how that enjoyment was packaged. Also, these were women open to alternative forms of religion and transcendental experience (like the women in Henry James's novel *The Bostonians*), no matter how fashionably diluted. And the way in which female sexuality was represented in *Radha* was unusual, in that it was not performed in relation to a man. Although ostensibly Radha is Krishna's lover, in the dance we never see the male god, so Radha seems to dance only to give pleasure to herself. In this, as in her detachment from and loftiness in relation to the male priests, she seems autonomous and independent. Femininity is represented as both strong and superior, but also as a separate realm.

In fact, I would argue that what at first looks like a mixed message in *Radha* is not a paradox or contradiction, but rather, a new message to Western eyes: that sensuality and spirituality can to some degree be partners, and that sexuality can be enjoyed outside of the marriage plot – and even outside of heterosexual partnering expectations altogether. The yoking together of sensuality and spirituality is a common theme not only of Hindu mythology and poetry, but also of Buddhist tales depicting the lives of sages. Further, *Radha* suggests that a sexual woman might in fact be able elude the "goddess/whore duality" entirely. This fascinated St. Denis in the legend of Radha and Krishna and in Hindu theology generally. (And, of course, it was what nineteenth-century Christian missionaries and colonialists found abhorrent in the temple dancing of India.) It must have been *Radha*'s unusual way of being sensual and holy *simultaneously* – of escaping from the concept of original sin – that was precisely its appeal to its women spectators. *Radha* is not a Christian confessional, because Radha's experiences of the senses are not depicted as sins or as evil. In Buddhist and Hindu philosophy, to transcend the body and the "bondage of the senses" is to move from the material to the spiritual plane, not to rid oneself of sin or evil. Within the narrative frame of *Radha*, instead of seducing men (as, for instance, the sylph did in *La Sylphide*), the goddess uses her sensuality to teach men a spiritual lesson. Although in some ways this theme harks back to the Victorian notion of woman as man's spiritual guardian, educating him not to surrender to fleshly desires, one can equally see it as the opposite: restoring eroticism to the sacred. Finally, Radha exerts agency by choosing to give up the life of the senses in order to achieve a higher plane of existence, rather than "paying" for her sensual pleasures, in the Christian tradition, as James did in *La Sylphide*. For, unlike James, Radha has not died. She has chosen to enter another plane of existence – one marked by the statue, a sign of invulnerability to the demands and desires of the flesh.

In *Radha*, St. Denis releases the body from puritan moralizing and illustrates how the senses may be enjoyed, but at the same time provides the body with an alternative system of spirituality. For this she had to imagine a new female body, one that both was and was not American. Kendall comments,

> The real significance of *Radha* was not its symbology but its rhythms; this was the first time in commercial theater that the body of a dancer had realized its own natural pace and begun to occupy all the space and time on stage that it craved. Ruth Dennis was a big-boned, healthy, even voluptuous American girl; this dance expressed some of the glory of that.[70]

Like the dance, the dancer's body incorporated a *mélange* of styles. In the early versions, St. Denis covered her skin with brown make-up. She used the vocabulary of American popular entertainments (kicks, spins, waltzes, and twirls) but she added a lotus position, angular Asian arm movements, and hands that circled sinuously as she rotated her wrists, as well as the spinning movement of Sufi dervishes, some belly dancing, and poses from erotic Indian temple sculpture. In a way, being an "American girl" gave her the license to invent herself as Other – but not in order to "enhance the audience's right to look sexually at the respectable white middle-class woman on the stage," as Desmond suggests.[71] Rather, it was in order to offer an alternative to a culture she found confining, to bypass the constrictions of the body Americans had inherited from Europe, to find ways of moving and of asserting female agency on stage.[72]

In his day, during an earlier vogue for oriental literature, Ralph Waldo Emerson, who wrote often about the important teachings of the major Hindu scriptures, called Asia "grandsire" to America, and exhorted Americans to "regenerate" Asia.[73] For Emerson, as Frederic Carpenter observes, "Asia is always the land of unity and contemplation – the land where only the elemental questions of life are important."[74] And Emerson connects the acceptance of the salutary spiritual teachings of the Hindu religion, especially in regard to the fundamental unity of all things, with a rejection of European values:

> The Indian teaching through its cloud of legends, has yet a simple and grand religion, like a queenly countenance seen through a rich veil. It teaches to speak the truth, love others as yourself, and to despise trifles. The East is grand, – and makes Europe appear the land of trifles. Identity. Identity! friend and foe are of one stuff.[75]

Importantly for Emerson, evil does not come from original sin, but from the absence of good. In response to Swedenborg, he wrote, "As for 'shunning evils as sins,' I prefer the ethics of the *Vishnu Purana*."[76] In this regard, St. Denis, quoted in the *New York Sun* in an advance story about the Hudson Theater matinee, seems quite consciously to echo Emerson: "'There is nothing new in evil,' explains a pale transcendental young woman, 'therefore to be original you must choose the good.'"[77]

In *Radha*, St. Denis was evoking an idea of India, not attempting to render it with ethnographic precision. Her company of priests included actual Hindus, Muslims, and Buddhists, and Walter Terry points out that she herself often said that *Radha* was a Buddhist theme danced by a Hindu goddess in a Jain temple.[78] *Radha*, and the American idea of Asia, was a composite blend, but then, so was America itself. Kendall points out that in American orientalism, "neither the décors on the stage nor the furnishings in private homes were meant to be faithful copies, but rather visual signals of a realm somewhere on the brink of taste," and she emphasizes that "no exotic strain ever showed up alone; the 'East Indian,' for instance, was always mingled with some of the 'Moorish' or 'Turkish' or 'Hellenic' or 'Byzantine' or even 'Renaissance.'"[79] It was originality – a new way of putting things together – rather than authenticity that mattered, that constituted American identity and American art. Although Asia was old and America was new, the two continents seemed to share something – an imagined simplicity and spiritual wholeness – that Europe lacked. St. Denis writes of the making of *Radha* that "at no time, then or in the future, have I been sufficiently the scholar or sufficiently interested to imitate or try to reproduce any Oriental ritual or actual dance – the mood to me is all, and inevitably manifests its own pattern."[80]

Although Kendall sees orientalism as style, St. Denis, in the Emersonian tradition, saw it as an alternative moral system. Thus her eclectic, cross-cultural borrowing must be seen in a more complex way, historically situated, than facile charges of cultural appropriation can supply. In a way, American national identity was constructed through imagining the Other, bypassing Europe. Somehow the appropriation of Otherness was transformed, in the rhetoric of the times, into constituting a quintessentially American quality. A critic wrote that in her oriental dances St. Denis had "an originality and a spirit that is entirely of this country," and St. Denis herself wrote that Denishawn – the school she later established with her husband Ted Shawn, which offered instruction in nearly every dance style, from Asia to Latin America – was "representative of the spirit of America."[81]

The United States had long lived under the shadow of Western European culture. To try on the trappings of different non-European cultures was itself seen a way of breaking with European art and forging a new, distinctly American culture. To turn to the East was one way to turn one's back on the West. That is, American cultural identity could be asserted not by contrasting with, but by absorbing, Otherness, at least in relation to Euro-American culture. But at the same time, beyond its identity as Europe's Other, Asia had its own salutary aspects. To some, it was seen as primitive (even though Indian civilization, for instance, was ancient and highly advanced), like ancient Greece supplying a way to "get back to basics." For St. Denis, however, Asian culture offered something else: a strategy for challenging the identification of dancing with "dancing girls" – with frivolity and entertainment. Connecting dancing with spirituality was a way to ennoble it, make it a high art, and claim it as a respectable and even refined occupation for a woman. But Christian culture had no apparent models for sacred dancing. Moreover, Hinduism and Buddhism provided the rhetorical framework for transcending the material body. And, unlike Christian iconography, Asian religions offered a variety of lofty images of women in the form of goddesses. Thus the female dancing body could be reclaimed as dignified and spiritual.

Conclusion

Fuller, Duncan, and St. Denis (prior to her partnership with Shawn) used space-assertion and other choreographic strategies literally and metaphorically to sever dependencies from men on stage. Although all three emphatically rejected the marriage theme for dance, each did so in her own way. Fuller revised the old balletic image of the witch as a figure of power, shearing off the negative connotations of frustration and distortion to reconstruct an ancient image of woman as the controller of natural forces – the Creatrix – but in the modern realm of science. Never claiming to be a feminist, Fuller nevertheless asserted a role for women as scientists and savants outside the "natural" sphere dictated by the nineteenth-century view of the biological female body. Indeed, she often seems willingly to destroy the body altogether. Fuller forged a link between a modern, futuristic, protofeminist view of wise women as scientists and an ancient view of wise women as necromancers. But, willy-nilly a product of its times, her vision was still tinged with the imagery of woman as goddess or fairy. Duncan, while insisting on women's emancipation in her writings, remained in thrall choreographically to a determinist conception of female essence, expressed through the anarchic rebellion of the passionate, reproductive body. And St. Denis insisted on the female dancing body as a sensuous container for the spiritual by taking on the role of the Other, a distant goddess who shunned earthly attachments.

Fuller, Duncan, and St. Denis each chose to represent on stage a different cultural idea about femaleness. But those ideas were themselves contradictory amalgams of notions about modernity and progress, on the one hand, and one-dimensional, constraining views of women, on the other. The ways in which each dancer negotiated these contradictions, internalizing them and embodying them, complicated and enriched her chosen image. Fuller feminized science, showing it to be simultaneously constructive and dangerous, life-giving and life-taking, sensuous and impersonal; Duncan manifested the tensions between personal expression and universal meaning; St. Denis revealed the erotic in the transcendent.

4

EARLY MODERN BALLET

Firebird, The Rite of Spring, Les Noces

It is is well known that the Ballets Russes' impact on the course of ballet history was momentous. In the twenty – at times precarious – years of his company's existence from 1909 to 1929, Serge Diaghilev produced the ballets and musical scores that would enter the world's permanent ballet repertory as well as the choreographers and dancers who would continue to shape modern ballet until the twenty-first century. Working with – often discovering and grooming – the most outstanding Russian and French artists and composers, Diaghilev also made ballet a unified Wagnerian *Gesamtkunstwerk*, in which painting, music, and dancing met in a spectacle that was visually, aurally, and kinesthetically brilliant. And, as dance historian Lynn Garafola has pointed out, in many respects his company made men the focal point of the ballet spectacle once again, challenging the ballerina's ascendancy since the nineteenth century.[1]

But what is not widely discussed is the progressive image of women created under Diaghilev's auspices, despite the producer's spotlight on the male dancer and his personal reputation for misogyny. The range of the ballets created for Diaghilev's Ballets Russes enterprise is enormous, and of course the representations of women in those ballets is quite varied. In the first few seasons, especially, several ballets featured representations of sado-erotic *femmes fatales* of the *fin-de-siècle*: *Cléopâtre* (1909), *Schéhérazade* (1910), *Thamar* (1912), *La Tragédie de Salomé* (1913).[2]

However, that feminine image was not a constant theme. Three Ballets Russes works set to Stravinsky scores – *Firebird* (1910), *The Rite of Spring* (1913), and *Les Noces* (1923) – span much of the company's life; a look at these ballets allows us to compare the representations of women created by three different choreographers at three different stages of the history of early modern ballet (although it should be remembered that Diaghilev's company was not the only purveyor of modern ballet in the first third of the twentieth century). I will focus on *Les Noces*, but brief analyses of the other two ballets – as well as a concluding commment on *Apollon Musagète* (1929) – will serve as comparisons and counterpoints.

Firebird

Created for the first season in which Diaghilev presented newly commissioned ballets (rather than works choreographed earlier for other venues, including the Maryinsky Imperial Theatre), *Firebird (L'Oiseau de feu)* was choreographed by Michel Fokine to music by Igor Stravinsky and first performed at the Théâtre National de l'Opéra in Paris on 25 June, 1910, during the second Russian ballet season produced by Diaghilev. *Firebird* is often said to be the earliest truly collaborative project of the Diaghilev "committee," but Fokine is usually credited as author of the libretto.[3] The decor and costumes were designed by Alexander Golovin, with Kostchei's court and castle imagined as a sumptuously orientalist fantasia; Léon Bakst designed the costumes for the Firebird, Ivan Tsarevich, and the beautiful Tsarevna.[4] The libretto was an amalgam of motifs and images taken from various Russian fairytales collected by Alexander Afanaseyev and other sources.[5]

The narrative, as set down in the libretto, involves the conventional fairytale hero Ivan Tsarevich (or Prince Ivan), who captures a magical Firebird. During their struggle, she bargains for her freedom, which she wins in exchange for a magic feather. Ivan then spies twelve dancing princesses, captives of the evil sorcerer-king Kostchei. He falls in love with the beautiful Tsarevna (or Princess Unearthly Beauty), but his presence summons Kostchei with his monsters and court retinue. Just when the sorcerer-king is about to turn Ivan Tsarevich to stone, he uses the magical feather to call on the Firebird. She sets the entire grotesque retinue to dancing until they fall down exhausted, then instructs Ivan to find Kostchei's soul, hidden in an egg. When Ivan breaks the egg, Kostchei meets his death. The final scene celebrates the coronation and wedding of Ivan Tsarevich and his Tsarevna.[6]

At first glance, both the plot and the structure of this ballet seem odd for a number of reasons. The storyline lurches, rather than advancing smoothly.[7] There seems to be an uneasy mixture of styles. Indeed, a complete stylistic shift deliberately marks each section of the ballet: the Firebird dances classical steps with angular, narcissistic, Asiatic arm gestures; the twelve captive maidens walk and skip with Duncanesque simplicity; members of Kostchei's retinue either cavort grotesquely or perform orientalist "ethnic" dances; and in the coronation scene the members of Ivan's court file off in strict formation.[8] Finally, some critics have complained that the love interest is subsumed by the magical element – Ivan's alleged liberation of Kostchei's kingdom by means of the Firebird's feather. In fact, the love between Ivan and the Tsarevna seems rather passionless, while the central pas de deux is not only performed at the beginning of the ballet, rather than the climax, but is, moreover, danced by the *wrong* personages. Instead of Ivan and his love, Ivan and the Firebird form the duet. We shall have to ask, what is the relation of Ivan to the Firebird, such that they are paired in this way?

In analyzing *Firebird*, the paradox that demands attention first is the apparent miscasting of the heroine. Why is the Firebird, rather than the beautiful

Tsarevna, the protagonist of this ballet, and why does the Firebird, rather than the beautiful Tsarevna, dance the crucial pas de deux? Of course, we have seen pas de deux between inhuman love objects and human heroes before; *La Sylphide* is a classic example. But in that ballet, there was no wedding apotheosis. In fact, dancing with the *wrong* love partner sealed James's doom. In *Swan Lake*, Prince Siegfried dances with Odile, another fateful wrong choice of a dancing partner. But his most important pas de deux is with his beloved, the human Odette (only temporarily enchanted in bird form). In ballets that end with marriages, like *The Sleeping Beauty*, the happy couple expresses the perfection of their union in their duet. But *Firebird* ends with a wedding, and yet the happy couple never

Plate 9 Tamara Karsavina as the Firebird and Michel Fokine as Prince Ivan in the pas de deux from *Firebird*. Gift of the Stravinsky–Diaghilev Foundation, Harvard Theatre Collection, The Houghton Library. Courtesy of the Harvard Theatre Collection.

consummates their love in dance terms. And most puzzling is that at first glance, the pas de deux of Ivan and the Firebird seems to be about power – his struggle for domination and hers for freedom – rather than about love.

Ivan captures the Firebird, and they struggle. This in itself is not necessarily new; after all, Siegried captured Odette in much the same way in *Swan Lake*. But this is, perhaps, the first time that a pas de deux is framed as a combat between two equals, without any romantic interest or outcome. For even though the Firebird has been caught, she has already been shown as physically powerful. Later, of course, when she returns to rescue Ivan, we learn just how powerful she is in terms of magic. She is easily capable of subduing Kotschei's entire grotesque retinue, and she repulses the evil sorcerer himself. And yet, her magic cannot protect her from a mere mortal's grasp. This presents a conundrum, until we look more closely at the structure of the pas de deux.

The duet indeed begins with a struggle.[9] But midway through the duet, the music shifts from staccato dissonance to a flowing, melismatic melody in a minor, Middle Eastern-sounding key. The Firebird, forced into a kneeling position with her arms angled around her head, looks seductively at Ivan, then rises on pointe, turns to face him, and does a deep backbend in his embrace. She allows him to support her in a more traditional set of partnering steps. And she strikes a series of deferential poses, ending up on the floor. Each time, she glances at him, as if to make sure the message has sunk in. The pas de deux is indeed manipulative, but after the shift, it is the Firebird who manipulates Ivan, not the other way around.

Given the Firebird's skills and powers in the rest of the ballet, the only way this pas de deux makes sense is to understand it as a benign deception. Like a master spy, the Firebird lets the simple Prince think he has mastered her, in order to send "her man Ivan" as a poison pawn into her enemy Kostchei's court. Although she strikes deferential poses, she is the dominant figure, and Ivan is literally her support. But in a partnering gambit that hints of sado-masochistic eroticism, she creates the fiction that he is dominating her.[10] The Firebird is an extremely powerful female figure, but she is also a designing woman who uses indirect stratagems – culturally identified as Asiatic – to gain political control.

The next section of the ballet – Ivan's meeting with the princesses and his falling in love with the beautiful Tsarevna – underscores the contrast between the two kinds of female figures populating this ballet, partly through Ivan's reaction to them. The Firebird is powerful; Ivan immediately grasps her and struggles with her. The beautiful Tsarevna is demure, and Ivan keeps a civil distance. Indeed, the beautiful Tsarevna is first seen not as an individual but as a kind of clone, part of a group of female figures whose movements are light and contained close to the body. Their heads cant, their hands constantly touch their faces; they bow and strike decorative poses. (In later sections, they weep, they implore, and they pray.) Stravinsky later described them as "insipidly sweet."[11] When Ivan sees the maidens, a folksong motif emerges in the music, evoking nostalgia and comfort – a sense of "coming home" – in counterpoint to the energetic dissonance and oriental mystery of the Firebird's theme. Barefoot, loose-tressed, clothed in long traditional Russian dresses, and dancing Russian folkdances, the princesses appear to remind Ivan of his Russian identity. They are, in this sense, familiar and natural, while the Firebird is strange, exotic, Asiatic, and supernatural.

Although Ivan is immediately attracted to the beautiful Tsarevna and tries to kiss her, he approaches her gently, focusing on her face, rather than her waist. In true fairytale fashion, it takes three attempts before he succeeds in kissing her. The contrast between Ivan's view of the Firebird's sexuality and his view of the Tsarevna's is striking. The first could be termed 'body-sex', while the second is 'person-sex'. He seizes the Firebird's torso intimately, while the Tsarevna merits dignity – he humbly requests her permission to make the first touch. Their love has the blessing of the community, for the other princesses ceremoniously escort Ivan and the Tsarevna toward one another, as if in a preordained ritual betrothal.[12] It is noteworthy that both the Firebird and the Tsarevna try to escape Ivan's touch, yet he allows the Tsarevna to turn away, while he brutally seizes the Firebird.

It could be argued that Ivan treats the Tsarevna with civility because she is human, while his relationship with the Firebird is in some way a non-human encounter, not at all concerned with love. But then one is led to ask, why does the Firebird have to be a woman at all?[13] Nijinsky wanted to dance the role and pointed out to Diaghilev that the Bluebird in *The Sleeping Beauty* had been danced by a man.[14] Perhaps the way to answer this question is to note the several, intertwining levels on which the relationship between Ivan and the Firebird as a female force may be interpreted.

At one level, she is, literally, an animal – a bird – while the Tsarevna is human. At a second level, the Firebird is "non-human" in the sense that she is non-Russian. She is the consummate "other" woman in more ways than one: oriental, sexual, seductive, both powerful and submissive, she is everything desirable the "nice" Russian Tsarevna cannot be. Thus, the Firebird's relationship with Ivan may not be about love (as in love and marriage), but it is erotic. Power is sexy, and the relationship between Ivan and the Firebird is concerned with power in a number of ways. Moreover, her costume emphasizes her voluptuousness, as opposed to the virginal quality indicated by the beautiful Tsarevna's long, loose white gown. The Firebird's incessant self-touching in the form of preening is another marker of her sexual allure. At a third, more metaphoric level, however, although the Firebird is supernatural, she symbolizes nature itself, Mother Earth – and Mother Russia – unattainable and untameable, often benevolent yet mysteriously unpredictable. There is a moment in the "Infernal Dance" when the princesses circle the Firebird as if to worship her, invoking the mythological association among the Firebird, a female sun god, and the *rusalka* (thought to be an early Slavic female deity concerned with fertility, the seasons, and the weather, and worshipped by female cults).[15]

At any level of interpretation, it is not the Firebird but the beautiful Tsarevna whom Ivan must marry, in order that the race (both Russian and human) continue. And yet the Firebird is emphatically his more significant partner. The story ends happily, and we see Ivan Tsarevich together with the beautiful Tsarevna in the final scene. Yet, although they have obviously become partners, this is a coronation rather than a wedding. And even though the beautiful Tsarevna is Ivan's consort, the power behind the the man on the throne is clearly the Firebird, who presides over all in this scene. If she represents nature, then the happy ending of this story is that the natural and political domains have been correctly aligned, and thus the proper monarchy has been established, firmly rooted in a moral, spiritual, and natural order. For the Tsar's dominion is considered part of the natural order. And it is the legitimization of the political order as part and parcel of the natural order that underwrites the relation of Ivan and the Firebird throughout this ballet. Ivan is the agent of the natural order and also its client, for nature – personified by the Firebird, protects him.

In its contrast between the human and inhuman, Russian and oriental female figures, this ballet could be seen, like *La Sylphide*, as a story about marriage – an instruction manual about whom one should marry. But several factors mitigate against that interpretation. It is true that Ivan Tsarevich marries the "right" woman, in that the beautful Tsarevna is both Russian and (therefore?) human. With this gene pool, the Tsarevich can create a dynasty. But Ivan also maintains his relationship with his donor, the Firebird. Given that there is a happy ending in the form of a marriage and that both the human and the inhuman female not only survive, but flourish, this is not so much a cautionary tale against straying from the appropriate marriage class or from the marriage bed, but rather, an endorsement of a more liberal sexual arrangement. This attitude is not surprising, since the ballet was not only created by a group of artists with mixed heterosexual, homosexual, and bisexual orientations and liberal views (or at least behaviors) toward extramarital sex, but was marketed to a sophisticated Parisian audience with similarly liberal mores. Indeed, although the part of the Firebird was originally intended for Anna Pavlova, the love triangle among the characters in the ballet was apparently duplicated by the dancers in the major roles (Karsavina and Fokine had been lovers before his marriage to Vera Fokina).[16] The ballet could also be seen as an advance in the representation of women's agency, for even though the Firebird has all the old markings of an exotic "other" woman (in both senses), she is nevertheless a positive female figure of enormous power. She is Carabosse redeemed, the witch and the Lilac Fairy rolled into one.

However, the final scene is far more coronation than wedding. And the women in *The Firebird* are less gendered beings than political symbols. Ultimately, this ballet is not about sexual politics but about national ideology.[17] It hints at liberal sexual alliances, as well as at a respectful acknowledgment of female power, but its deeper message is a blend of political conservatism, upholding the tsarist policy of colonizing Russia's Eastern borderlands, and an anti-European claim that Russia is at least partly Asian. The beautiful Tsarevna is a "true" Russian maiden, an ideal of racial purity and national superiority. But the Firebird is a more complex, multivalent sign, merging metaphoric images of Mother Russia and Mother Earth with those of the oriental "partner." She is a hybrid creature containing elements of both Russia and the East, embodying Russia's split identity. In many ways, she represents the ancient Russian–Slavic strain. She makes possible, perhaps even engineers Ivan's accession to the throne, and thus she stands for Russian supremacy. In Russian folklore she is associated with at least one pre-Christian Slavic agrarian deity. Yet she is also an exotic outsider, mistress of a distant land, literally framing herself – with her Asiatic arm gestures – as an oriental temptress. She links Russia to nature and the supernatural forces that rule nature, but at the same time, she is a discreet and mighty concubine that makes possible the Russian empire.

The Rite of Spring

The Rite of Spring (Le Sacre du printemps) was first performed at the Théâtre des Champs Elysées in Paris on 29 May 1913. Choreographed by Vaslav Nijinsky to music by Stravinsky, the ballet's libretto was co-authored by Stravinsky and Nicholas Roerich, the Slavophile painter, ethnographer, and archaeologist who had designed *The Polovtsian Dances* presented in Diaghilev's first Russian season of ballet in 1909. Roerich also designed *Rite*, basing the costumes on ancient peasant dress in the ethnographic museum at Talashkino (a folk arts revival colony sponsored by Princess Tenisheva – one of Diaghilev's patrons – that supported the work of many neo-nationalist artists).[18] The role of the Chosen One, originally created on Bronislava Nijinska, the choreographer's sister, was finally danced by Maria Piltz (because Nijinska became pregnant).

While working on *Firebird*, Stravinsky writes, he was already planning another ballet, reaching further back into Russian prehistory. He recalls, "I saw in imagination a solemn pagan rite: sage elders, seated in a circle, watched a young girl dance herself to death. They were sacrificing her to propitiate the god of spring."[19] Upon the departure of Fokine from Diaghilev's company in 1912, Nijinsky – whose eccentric genius had begun to manifest itself with *L'Après-midi d'un faune* (1912) – was entrusted with the choreography. But all three collaborators seem to have contributed to the visual and kinesthetic "score."[20]

As is well known, the opening night of the ballet witnessed pandemonium in the theater. The music, with its unusual sounds, harmonies, polyrhythms, and repetitions, was shocking to Western ears; equally shocking to ballet audiences were the twisting, stunted postures of the dancers, their impassive faces, their angular gestures with jutting elbows, their knock-kneed stances, their turned-in toes, their incessant earth-bound stamping, and their bolting jumps in place. The dancers' movements were awkward, convulsive, and asymmetrical, like the vernal bursting forth of new life, "the total panic ascent of the universal sap"[21] and of sexual energy. They huddled, trembled, flailed, fell down, and appeared to become possessed. This mass of "primitive" bodies seemed to reflect the modern notion that premodern society is marked by a lack of differentiation: religion, law, ethics, and agriculture are all one. But it appeared at the same time to comment on the modern condition: the loss of both individuality and community in the mechanical age – the emergence of mass man. In this meeting of mass man with tribal man, two distinct sorts of nondifferentation became linked.

Roerich and Stravinsky, inspired by ancient ethnographic artifacts and pre-Christian agrarian rituals, had hoped to communicate in this ballet "the secret of our ancestors' close feeling for the earth . . . the closeness between the lives of men and the soil."[22] In reference to the ballet, Roerich wrote to Diaghilev, "I love antiquity, for its sublime happiness, and its deep thoughts."[23] But the spectators of 1913 variously interpreted the dancers' movements as either disturbingly mechanical or driven solely by the energy of a biological imperative. They resembled, in dance historian Lincoln Kirstein's phrase, a "mute mob of throbbing bipeds, responding to the seasons alone [and denying] four centuries of humane art."[24] They were panic-stricken in the face of a terrible god. This was not the exquisite fairytale enchantment of *Firebird*, but a different idea altogether of folklore: a brutal scene of primitive barbarism. It was, wrote Jacques Rivière in his review of the premiere, "absolutely pure . . . completely raw . . . terrifying."[25]

The "choreodrama," as Stravinsky called it, did not have a strictly narrative storyline. Rather, it was subtitled "pictures of pagan Russia in two parts." In the first, the tribe gathers to perform ritual divinations, games, and dances

Plate 10 Six women dancers in *The Rite of Spring*. From *The Sketch Supplement*, 1913.

inaugurating spring, and an ancient sage kisses the earth. In the second, a maiden is selected by lot from the "mystic circles" of virgins. She is honored by the young women, then prepared for sacrifice by the elders of the tribe, who enact the role of the totem ancestors. The Chosen One dances herself to death, thus metaphorically marrying Yarilo, the sun god, ruler of spring.[26]

Although on the surface both the music and the choreography seem completely irregular, *Rite* is based on a series of deeply symmetrical binary structures: day and night, young and old, individual and mass, and male and female. At first glance, the dance simply seems like a formless cacophony of wild movements, done to wild sounds, and indeed, this is how many of its original spectators characterized it. But in fact, it is ordered by a specific sequence of events, named in Stravinsky's score and ultimately discernible in the choreography.[27] The first act, "The Kiss of the Earth," takes place during the day; the second act, "The Sacrifice," takes place at night. In the first act, the games and ceremonies of the groups of nameless, generalized young people – both youths and maidens – are framed by the entrances of two particularized elders, one of each gender: the 300-year-old Woman at the beginning and the male Sage (The Oldest and Wisest One) at the end. It is a scene of balance between age groups and genders. In the second act, there is asymmetry in age and gender: there is one group of young women and one group of male elders, and only one individual – a maiden, the Chosen One. In the first act, there are multiple couples, formed during the "Ritual of Abduction"; in the second act, there is only one couple: the Chosen One and her invisible consort, the sun god. In the first act, the cosmic forces are kept in balance by the act of an old man ritually kissing the earth, followed by "The Dancing Out of the Earth," in which the young people all leap about and embrace the soil; in the second act, the cosmophilic and cosmogonic action of the ritual kiss and its orgiastic aftermath are completed when a young woman consecrates herself to the heavens. Another duality is that between up and down, the earth and the heavens; Roerich wrote that the first part expressed "terrestrial joy," while the second was concerned with "celestial mystery."[28] Perhaps it was this binary division that all the vertical jumps in the ballet, with their complementary collapses into the earth, were meant to resolve.

Robert Craft has written that "choreographically speaking, the music of *The Rite* was conceived in terms of male–female dialogues of action, like any other ballet . . . [and] the musical representation of day and night . . . is also a further dialogue of the sexes, Part Two being essentially female."[29] Although there are definitely male–female action dialogues in *Rite*, this gender contrast in no way resembled that seen previously on the dance stage. In this and so many other respects, *Rite* is hardly "like any other ballet." For one thing, this may be the first time mass rape was ever represented on the ballet stage (albeit as a representation of a representation, that is, the Sabine-style abduction of the women by the men is already a representation within the frame of the ballet, in that it is a ritual miming of such an action – as if the tribe were retelling in dramatic action terms its myth of origin).

But more importantly, although they are often sorted into single-gender groups, the dance movements the young people perform are not, for the most part, gender-coded. Classical ballet crystallized and dramatized the classification of particular steps, gestures, and movement styles by gender. They were coded as belonging to the repertory of either the male or the female dancer. But in *Rite*, both groups shuffle, stamp, jump, shiver, collapse forward at the waist, thrust one arm phallicly in the air, or fall to the ground and pound the earth. Both groups seem to be autochthonic, as if the race were born mythically from the earth when these groups, huddled into mounds resembling the hills in Roerich's landscape, are awakened into action by the old woman. Both groups, as the Russian composer-critic Boris Asafyev puts it, also "[lust] to blend with earth, to become earth itself."[30] And they move with equal strength and directness. Finally, the most crucial gender-coding event of the classical ballet is missing here – for there is no pas de deux. There are couples, but they form only momentarily, and there is no single principal couple taking center stage.

Yet, just as the music sometimes breaks into recognizable melodies, so too the movements take on recognizable shapes and meanings, especially of a gendered nature. For instance, in the "Ritual of Abduction" the men do lift the women (although they hoist them in a cumbersome style diametrically opposed to the graciously airborne partnering conventions of the classical school). In "The Ritual of the Two Rival Tribes," the men show their strength in mock combat, while the women take tiny steps on the sidelines like so many cheerleaders. And at times, as dance historian Shelley Berg points out, the women strike familiar folk dance configurations: they rest their faces on the palms of their hands or tilt their heads onto a loose fist; they put their hands up behind their heads, elbows out, and take stiff steps on three-quarter toe.[31]

At the beginning of the second section, "Mystic Circles of the Young Girls," the young women form a circle in the moonlight. There are echoes here of both *Giselle* and the princesses in *Firebird*.[32] But again, there is a difference. This nocturnal dance, marking out the circle in which the Chosen One will perform her sacrifice, is like a game of "hot potato." After one of the maidens trips for the second time, she freezes; her mistake was deadly, for it is clear that she's "It."[33] That this circle will shortly become a marriage bed for the human and the god is underscored by the music, which quotes traditional wedding *khorovods* (round-dances).[34] In the next section, "The Naming and Honoring of the Chosen One," as Stravinsky describes it, "the other maidens glorify her in a wild, martial dance." (Stravinsky notes that "I was thinking of Amazonians.")[35] But they also teach her her death, previewing the movements that will be the building blocks of the Chosen One's sacrificial dance: a gesture Rivière describes as an "arm raised to heaven and waved straight above her head in a gesture of appeal, threat, and protection,"[36] a vertical jump with the head angled to the side. For now, the Chosen One stands frozen to the spot.

As the ancestors close in, further demonstrating parts of her dance, the Chosen One emerges from her trance and tries to escape. She runs from one side of the circle to another, but there is no way out. She gallops, crouches, trembles, and moves her outstretched arms like a prehistoric bird's powerful wings, ambiguously suggesting both her desire to escape and her aspiration to meet her mate in the heavens.[37] She begins her ordeal, repeatedly striking a pose somewhere between supplication and ecstasy, jumping over and over again without respite, falling to pound the earth, and then rising to whirl and to jump again. Nijinska writes that as she danced the role during the period of its creation, "strong, brusque, spontaneous movements seemed to fight the elements as the Chosen Maiden protected the earth against the menacing heavens."[38] If the earth is female and the heavens male, this suggests a primal struggle between the sexes that mirrors the ritual abduction. Marie Rambert describes the dance of the Chosen One "as being terrifying in focus and ferocity – a dance to be performed by a woman requiring the sinews of a male."[39]

When the Chosen One finally falls, exhausted and lifeless, and the music sighs quietly (according to dance historian Richard Buckle, representing both her last breath and the god's orgasm[40]), the elders lift her up. She has been transfigured. If the first act is concerned with the dividing up of the entire human community into mating couples, standing for procreation on every level – human, animal, and vegetable – the second act is an emblematic wedding that repeats, distills, and abstracts all that has come before.

It is important to note that although it was based on authentic artifacts, *Rite* depicts an imagined ritual. There was no documented practice of human sacrifice among the ancient Slavs. Like the creators of *Firebird*, the authors of this ballet concocted a "purely Russian" vision from a pastiche of sources, not only from different times in Russian history (stone-age, medieval, and nineteenth-century) but from completely foreign cultures, as well. They were fired both by nationalism in the form of Slavophilism and by a universalist primitivist urge they shared with so many other artists, not only Russians, of their generation. Ironically, they sought to delineate their own national customs with ethnographic precision by incorporating elements from disparate, fanciful images of the primordial past, ranging from "Indians trying to put out a prairie fire" to ghost dances "known to virtually all archaic communities."[41] The idea of the human sacrifice may have been based on an Aztec ceremony.[42] But if so, why was the young man of Aztec custom transformed into a young woman?[43]

To speak of the early twentieth-century view of the primitive and the savage is also to invoke a certain view of woman. As women began to demand civil and political rights in Europe and America in the second half of the nineteenth century, a theoretical body of literature grew "proving" that women, whether European or non-European, were mentally and biologically primitive compared to European men.[44] Opposing the tide of feminist demands was the idea of woman as nature itself (as opposed to male culture) and the image of woman as naturally fecund, connected to cyclical changes in nature, and for this reason located outside of time, transhistorically associated with primeval origins. Thus, even within modern "civilization" one could locate the primitive in woman.

Considering the popularity of this view of woman, the distillation in *Rite* of the entire archaic community into the figure of a woman – a woman whose spiritual role in life is to re-fertilize the earth – is not surprising.

As we look further into the role of the Chosen One, it is also useful to ask whether this ballet is about community or about sexuality. To use Rivière's terms in a slightly different way, is *Rite* sociological or biological? Rivière thought that what made the ballet so rich was that it was both, although he conceived of its biologism as far more basic than simply a concern with human sexuality. He writes:

> *Le Sacre du Printemps* is a sociological ballet, an extraordinary vision of an age that until now had to be reconstructed with difficulty, by means of scientific documents, and which here is being set before our imagination. . . . We find ourselves in the presence of man's movements at a time when he did not yet exist as an individual. Living beings still cling to each other; they exist in groups, in colonies, in shoals; they are lost among the horrible indifference of society; they render their devotions to the god they have fashioned together and of which they have not yet been able to rid themselves. Their faces are devoid of any individuality. At no time during the dance does the Chosen Maiden show the personal terror that ought to fill her soul. She carries out a rite; she is absorbed by a social function, and without any sign of comprehension or of interpretation, she moves as dictated by the desires and impulses of a being vaster than herself, a monster filled with ignorance and appetites, with cruelty and darkness.

But on the other hand, Rivière also notes,

> There is still a second meaning in *Le Sacre du Printemps*, something more profound, more secretive, and more hideous. This is a biological ballet. It is not only the dance of man at his most primitive stage; it is the dance that came yet before man. In his article in *Montjoie*, Stravinsky indicated that he intended to represent the coming of spring. But this is not the spring to which the poets have accustomed us, with its quiverings, its music, its tender sky, and its delicate foliage. No, here is nothing but the harshness of budding growth, nothing but the terror and "panic" that accompanies the rise of the sap, nothing but the terrifying labor of the cells. This is spring as seen from the inside; spring in all its striving, its spasm, its partition. One might think of oneself in the presence of a drama acted out under a microscope: the history of mitosis; the profound need of the nucleus to break up and reproduce, the division at the core, the splitting and rejoining of turbulent matter that reaches into its very substance; large revolving masses of protoplasm; germ layers, zones, circles, placentas.[45]

While admiring the artwork, Rivière finds its import horrific, mechanistic. After viewing it, he writes, "for the first time, I saw in the doctrines of evolution a kind of heartbreaking possibility. . . . [*Le Sacre du printemps*] is a rock from the caves from which emerge unknown beasts, engaged in unintelligible tasks that long ago have lost their meaning."[46]

Part of what seems to have horrified the spectators, although it is rarely mentioned explicitly in the reviews, is implicit in Rivière's essay: the biological imperative toward human procreation. And in this aspect, the ballet is simultaneously social and biological. It is a vision of a community, and metaphors for community – including that of Mother Earth – are often sexual metaphors, because community is interrelated to sexuality or sexual processes of reproduction. Certainly there is a great deal in *Rite* about sexual processes. And, echoing Yarilo's possible representation in ancient times as a phallus, there are distinctly phallic movements in the choreography: the arm strongly thrusting upward, the vertical jumps. But ultimately, this does not seem to be a ballet about sexuality in the individual sense – the Freudian "return of the repressed." Through their readings of anthropological writings by figures like Sir Richard Burton, Europeans at the turn of the century became aware of sexual practices in tribal cultures, and they became pruriently interested in learning more about what was repressed in their own culture. One could see *Rite* as an instance of this. In some ways, it does present sexuality in the guise of mock anthropology. It is, after all, sexual energy that is being unleashed in the key moments of the ballet. And polyrhythmic percussion is often linked to sexual expression. The Russian emigré dance critic André Levinson called the music "Hottentot," invoking images of steatopygiac African women circulating in Europe throughout the nineteenth century and thought by Europeans to exemplify "primitive," overabundant sexuality.[47] Levinson also complained about the dancers' syncopation, invoking as well as the newly emergent form of jazz dancing, considered by many whites to express a carnal element.[48] Yet, partly because of *Rite*'s mechanical, impassive quality, partly because of the shapeless long shifts that conceal the women's bodies, partly because of the structure of the Chosen One's dance, partly because the orgiastic behavior of the first act is tied to the larger project of agrarian renewal and ancestor worship, this is not at all a voluptuous ballet. Rather than sexuality, spirituality and its genesis in the social capital of community is its subject.

At the time of its original performances, the issue of the woman's role in *Rite* was almost entirely unremarked. But looking at the ballet in the 1990s, one is struck by the fact that there are two women who stand out from the uniform crowd: the wise woman, or witch, or shaman, who awakens the tribe, teaches it how to perform the rites properly, and predicts the future; and the virgin, the Chosen One, who saves the earth through self-sacrifice. It is true, as several dance scholars have recently commented, that the suffering woman was a favorite theme of nineteenth-century art, including the Romantic ballet. (It is also an enduring motif in twentieth-century art, most deliriously in *King Kong*.)[49]

Garafola comments that this was "a Giselle reimaged through the primitivism of the golden horde." And she concludes, "The Chosen Virgin is, above all, a creation of twentieth-century male sexual anxiety."[50]

These aspects of nineteenth-century romantic and sentimental genres, shading into melodrama, are certainly present in *Rite*, connecting the work more closely with its ballet heritage than is often admitted. But since they are here interwoven tightly with a Slavophile ethic, it seems appropriate to ask – if the ballet is more about spirituality through community than about sexuality – what woman's role is seen to be (other than as sexual/reproductive) in the community in question: the Russian nation.

There is less anxiety in *Rite* about the Chosen One's sexuality than evident sympathy with the figure of woman as victim, woman as sufferer. After all, the Chosen One is performing an important communal and religious function in defending and renewing the earth. This figure of the female martyr is a rich, multi-layered symbol, for it joins in one image several distinct ideas: not only the innocent, invented young pagan girl who dies to propitiate the gods and fertilize the earth, but also generations of peasant brides (whose sorrow Nijinska would solemnly eulogize in *Les Noces*), as well as two renowned long-suffering female figures – Mother Russia and the Virgin Mary – who are extremely potent cultural and religious icons for Russians. Roerich's costume designs for the maidens strikingly underscore the multivalent symbolism, for they seem simultaneously to represent the stance of the Virgin Mary seen in so many icon paintings – with her tilted head and her hands folded at her breast – and the smiling, doe-eyed face of the Matrioshka doll, that emblem of fecund Mother Russia in whose belly generations upon generations are nested.[51]

Decidedly Christian images mix with images of female deities from the pagan past. If the mystic circle of young women calls up images of the Wilis in *Giselle*, it also summons images of the Russian relative to the Slavic original of the legend of the Wilis – certain incarnations of the *rusalki*, pictured as "pale-faced, ethereal beauties, sometimes in white shifts with garlands of flowers in their loose tresses . . . sisterhoods of lovely maidens" who danced khorovods and sang in the moonlight.[52]

The image of woman in *Rite*, in particular that of the Chosen One, is partly socio-political, acknowledging her vulnerable social status, and partly religious, venerating her suffering and self-sacrifice. Marriage, the ballet tells us in no uncertain terms, equals death. And yet, it reminds us, death and suffering can lead to transfiguration. The message is complex and polyvalent. But, ultimately, this is not a conservative work that accepts and subsumes suffering under the rubric of religious faith. For it expresses a deep appreciation of the pre-Christian past, but more drastically, it identifies the Virgin Mary with ancestor worship and orgiastic pagan cults. In its correlation of the mysteries of the adolescent girls (in whom "the strain of nature's growth and vernal renewal can be sensed with particular delicacy and directness"[53]) with the mystery of another virgin who conceived a god at the time of the spring equinox, *Rite*, while nationalistic, unearths aspects of the Russian past – including attitudes toward women, marriage, and sexuality, linked up with spirituality – that were deeply subversive of the official Russian values of its time.

Les Noces

Les Noces (The Wedding) was first performed at the Théâtre de la Gaîté-Lyrique in Paris on 13 June 1923. The ballet was choreographed by Bronislava Nijinska, and its costumes and decor were designed by Natalia Goncharova. The dancers included Felia Dubrovska as the bride and Nicholas Semenov as the bridegroom. A companion piece to *The Rite of Spring* in its close attention to Russian folklore and rituals (even echoing the Nijinsky ballet choreographically in certain ways), *Les Noces* was nevertheless far removed from its older sibling in terms of meaning. Although Stravinsky conceived the music long before *Rite* even had its premiere, the ballet was not choreographed until six years after the Russian Revolution. By then, not only had culture in Russia seemed to change overnight, to its very roots, but the ways in which Russia's past was being constructed – both at home and abroad – had altered drastically, as well.

And most importantly for our purposes, the status of women in Russia had undergone dramatic transformation and with it, the social formations of marriage and the family. This political metamorphosis shaped the representation of the peasant wedding in *Les Noces* in ways far different than had originally been planned. It was not a gaily festive celebration, but a powerful, abstract evocation of the weighty social forces that impinge on individuals in a traditional culture, shaping their destinies and thrusting their mates upon them. Although unlike *Rite* this ballet was set in the not-so-distant past (the nineteenth century), or perhaps even the present, as dance historian Nancy Van Norman Baer has written, *Les Noces* depicts "a primitive ritual where both bride and groom are trapped by fate and repressive social custom."[54]

Stravinsky's idea, in 1912, had been to create "not . . . the dramatization of a wedding or . . . a staged wedding spectacle," but an abstract selection and distillation of the rich socio-religious folk material connected to the Russian peasant wedding.[55] The Russian folklorist P. V. Kireevsky's anthology of folksongs (including 1,043 wedding songs), collected during the nineteenth century, had been published posthumously in 1911. This anthology was Stravinsky's inspiration, providing most of his verbal source material.[56] Although the composer notes that "*Les Noces* is also – perhaps even primarily – a product of the Russian Church," because it makes so many references to the Virgin Mary and to saints, he stylized its ritual content in an extremely modern fashion. In fact, Stravinsky has described his cantata as a Joycean collage of social and religious ritual talk. The composer recalls,

> As a collection of clichés and quotations of typical wedding sayings [*Les Noces*] might be compared to one of those scenes in *Ulysses* in which the

> reader seems to be overhearing scraps of conversation without the connecting thread of discourse. But *Les Noces* might also be compared to *Ulysses* in the larger sense that both works are trying to *present* rather than to *describe*.[57]

Thus, the composer stresses the formal, modern aspects of his work. Yet, although Stravinsky doesn't mention it, Joyce's fragments of "ordinary conversations" certainly include information about social realities and political conflicts.

And so did the abstract collage, a complexly intertwining braid of conventional sayings and imagery, in *Les Noces*. The interest in peasant and folk life that led to the making of *Rite* was laden with political and social meaning for the Russian intelligentsia since the emancipation of the serfs in 1861, heightening in the 1890s and after as the country rapidly industrialized. Then, as the status of women and the institution of marriage became highly charged arenas of social change in revolutionary Russia, the political significance of *Les Noces* emerged much more sharply in 1923 than it would have had it been staged in 1912.

The creation of *Les Noces* was constantly delayed by a number of factors, including financial considerations and the outbreak of the First World War. But that in itself does not account for the many changes its authors made during its gestation. That *Les Noces* was re-imagined so many times by its major collaborators suggests that the artists' interpretation of the material – in fact, the material itself – was rapidly mutating. For, like so many other issues in revolutionary Russia, the very meaning of both marriage and the peasantry had never before been so hotly contested as during this period (and perhaps never would be again).

Between 1912 and 1923, women's social and political status in Russia underwent a massive shift, and, correspondingly, so did the marriage laws. Although not the major rallying cry of the revolutionary movement or the Bolshevik party, "the woman question" had been important to the Russian intelligentsia since the mid-nineteenth century. A liberal feminist movement, composed of middle-class and aristocratic women (of whom Diaghilev's aunt, Anna Filosofova, with whom he lived as a young man in St. Petersburg, was a leading figure) had worked actively in the late nineteenth century to secure educational reforms for women and to establish women's charities. By the turn of the century, a growing number of educated women became artists, writers, teachers, doctors – and revolutionaries. But, as with so many social movements in Russia, feminist activity was embattled in the 1890s and crushed by 1908. It took the overthrow of the tsarist regime for women's rights, tied closely to democratic rights for all, to triumph, and for those rights to be extended to the working and peasant classes.[58] And suddenly, it seemed that the situation of women – although still at times only in theory, not in practice – had totally reversed itself from the benighted times of tsarist oppression.

In its radical rewriting of the social and economic structure of Russia, the Bolshevik Party also re-envisioned the role of the peasant class. Well into the

Soviet period, the vast majority of Russia's population was rural.[59] Continual peasant unrest in response to state interventions, as well as increasingly untenable economic hardships for the peasantry, contributed to the revolutions of 1917 and to the ultimate success of the Bolsheviks. But the peasants did not always agree with the Bolsheviks' agenda. Thus, the peasants were a powerful political force – a repository of traditional values, but a hostile and potentially subversive challenge to any state authority, whether tsarist, socialist, or communist.

By the time *Les Noces* was finally made, the situation of the peasant woman was a particularly vexing social issue for the young Soviet Union. Peasant women, who traditionally bore an enormous burden – working the land, caring for the livestock, bearing and raising children, and running the household, all in a situation of crushing poverty, sometimes coupled with physical and sexual abuse – nevertheless did not rush to embrace the newfound emancipation offered to them by the Bolsheviks.[60] For they had long developed their own protective informal women's networks within the official patriarchy of peasant culture, and their religious and moral views supported the traditional roles and family networks they already knew. Although Zhenotdel, the Women's Department of the Bolshevik Party, worked to organize and educate these women about their rights and their oppression, the tenacious social structures of the old peasant commune did not easily mesh with the new communal structures of the Soviet government. Most peasant women, whose lives had been deeply affected by the disruptions of war, did not see much value in the further social upheaval that female liberation would likely bring to the village. As historian Barbara Clements puts it, "What was it that women were to be emancipated from, but the society of the village, the other men, women, and children on whom they were relying for survival?"[61]

It was against this social landscape that *Les Noces* was created. Understood in this light, the ballet almost seems like an agit-prop theater piece designed to be taken by Zhenotdel to the villages in order to educate peasant women about the social injustices they had long endured, symbolized by the traditional wedding (although, unlike a typical agit-prop piece, the ballet does not offer a solution to the problem). For by accepting the wedding, women also accepted all that the wedding implied about peasant marriage and its place in the village social structure, in which the bride is chosen for her ability as a worker; both sets of parents view the marriage as a business deal, rather than a personal relationship; and women are married off young.

Les Noces took over ten years to create, and the ballet underwent many sea changes during the years preceding and following the First World War. Diaghilev had thought of the choreography first as Nijinsky's assignment, then Léonide Massine's, and only in 1923 as decisively Nijinska's.[62] Stravinsky changed his orchestration plans from an initial idea of a large ensemble to various smaller groupings of instruments to the final version – four pianos, percussion pieces, and a chorus.[63] Goncharova arrived only fitfully at her stark, monochromatic designs, after three sets of more vividly colored studies were rejected by Nijinska, by

Diaghilev, and, it seems, even by the artist herself. Only Nijinska seems to have followed a direct, unbroken path to *Les Noces*.[64]

It was a path, as she writes, toward "utmost simplicity." Like Stravinsky, she saw the wedding as an abstraction through reduction. "To recreate in a ballet the rituals and ceremonies of an actual wedding was, to my mind, the realm of a Theatre other than my own choreographic theatre in which lives and speaks only the movement. Pantomime was alien to me and I had no use for stage props." The choreographer's reductionist approach is exemplified in the conversation she recounts having with Diaghilev about the action. Diaghilev asked Nijinska,

> "Do you remember the first scene? We are in the home of the bride-to-be, she is sitting in a big Russian armchair, at the side of the stage, her friends are combing her hair and dressing her braids . . . "
>
> "No, Serge Pavlovitch," I cut in, "the chair's not necessary, the comb is not necessary and the hair-combing even less so."
>
> "I took up pen and paper and began to sketch a bride with braids which were ten feet long. Her friends, holding the braids, formed a group with her."

Diaghilev then asked,

> "And what happens next? How will the young girls be able to comb such long hair?"
>
> "They won't comb it," I replied. "It will be their dance 'on points' with the bride, that will express the rhythm of braiding."[65]

In fact, the first scene of the ballet, the Blessing of the Bride, is a lament built around the motif of braiding, a motif that symbolizes both the loss of the bride's virginity and the interweaving of two families into a single kinship network.[66] To the words of the soprano singer, "Tress my tress,/O thou fair tress of my hair,/O my little tress," the ballet opens with the bride kneeling in prostration, her face to the floor, while eight women form two descending columns on either side of her, their knees bent to varying degrees to stagger their heights.[67] Because they twist their bodies in different directions, their curved, uplifted arms form a plaited pattern, and the two long rope-like braids link them with the bride and also with one another. It is a literal image of the intimacy and connectedness of the circle of young maidens. The bride's parents stand stiffly off to one side, their hands clenched over their hearts. As the bride rises to standing, the friends drop to the ground in two clusters. As in *Rite*, these women seem to be born of the earth, and the driving percussive beat of the music repeatedly sends them back to it. Garafola writes of this moment, "bodies in huddled clumps bend as if weighted by centuries of toil."[68]

As in *Rite*, too, there is a reference to icon-painting style, here in the elongated Byzantine look Nijinska strove for when she broke with tradition by putting this

Plate 11 The Bride's Chamber scene in *Les Noces*, photographed in rehearsal on the roof of the Casino at Monte Carlo by J. Enrietty, 1923. Courtesy of The Royal Opera House Archives, London.

"character" ballet on pointe – thus invoking the church, the cult of the Virgin Mary, and the saints, without so much as including a priest in the proceedings.[69]

The bride makes various stylized gestures of sorrow and submission: she covers her mouth with her fists; she lifts her hand to her cheek, her chest, her forehead. The friends form a line across the stage, again connected by the braids, with the tall bride in the center. They lift their hands to their brows, duplicating the bride's gesture of sorrow, they sweep their arms in a sowing gestures, and they bow. On pointe, they stamp out a little rhythmic pattern in a series of crossed pas de bourrée: as Nijinska had promised, they "braid" with their feet, while the chorus begins to sing "I comb her tresses, her fair golden tresses, Nastasia's bright hair . . . /I comb and plait it, with ribbon red I twine it."[70] Garafola notes that "the movement's percussiveness conveys pain and violence as well; intercourse, implied by the bedroom to which the bride and groom repair just before the curtain falls, climaxes the day's festivities."[71]

Nijinska did not invent the symbolism of the braiding as representing the loss of virginity, for it is already present in the ritual. Stravinsky explains that "The binding of the bride's tresses with red and blue ribbons was a religio-sexual custom, of course, and so was the tying of the tresses around her head to signify the married state."[72] The turning of the single braid of the maiden into the two braids of the married woman, as a metaphor for sexual violence, is underscored by the ritual greeting the bride traditionally gives her fiancé on the wedding day, when she calls him "a destroyer and ravager" and begs her girlfriends to protect her from him.[73] The imagery in the lyrics chosen by Stravinsky for this section could not be more explicit:

> Cruel, heartless, came the matchmaker,
> Pitiless, pitiless cruel one,
> Pitiless cruel one.
> She tore my tresses, tore my bright golden hair,
> She tore my hair that she might plait it in
> Two plaits,
> O woe is me,
> O alas, poor me.[74]

At the beginning of this song, all the women put their fists to their foreheads. The bride steps in front of the line, and all the women strike a suffering weighted-down pose, with bent waist and angled head, reminiscent of the Virgin Mary as she is represented in icons. The level of the line rises and falls as these semi-crouched women bend and straighten their knees, but in front of them the bride lowers and raises herself in opposition to the group. She performs the same pattern, but she is set apart from them in time. She is, the dance seems to say, indistinguishable from her circle except on this day, her time to be the bride. On the line "She tore my tresses," the bride presses her fists to her mouth, signifying fear of sexual violence, and the women once again form the two plaits of the married woman on either side, and then once again form the single line on pointe, to begin the braiding footwork pattern.

But the girlfriends do not only describe with their feet the painful loss of virginity that lies in store for the bride. At one point, as the chorus sings, "Weep not,/O dear one, weep not,/Let no grief afflict thee," they hand over the braids to the bride and burst into a joyous, bell-like dance, jumping and swinging their bodies like pendulums as the treble music seems to peal.[75] They console the bride, but perhaps they also celebrate their own freedom, in contrast to the bride's loss. Then they begin to jump vigorously, echoing the Amazonian glorification of the Chosen One in *Rite*. But while the lyrics promise "your delight, your happiness," like the Chosen One the bride remains still and somber, awaiting her sacrifice.[76]

The scene ends with the friends forming a pyramid, a single column that widens as it descends, in which the woman in front crouches close to the ground, her head tilted to her right shoulder, the next woman, tilting her head to the left, crouches a bit higher behind her and lays her head on top of that of the first woman, *ad seriatim*. The bride stands contemplatively behind this living braid, resting her chin on top of her hands and her elbows on top of the pillar of inter-leaved heads. The metamorphosis of the bride's plait from one to two is echoed, but in reverse sequence, in the formations of the bridesmaids, which move from two to one. In this way, the violence of rending one braid to make two is

Plate 12 The Bride's Chamber scene in *Les Noces*, photographed in rehearsal on the roof of the Casino at Monte Carlo by J. Enrietty, 1923. Courtesy of The Royal Opera House Archives, London.

tempered slightly by the suggestion that, as a result of the wedding, two people will fuse to form a single family unit. And yet, there is also a grisly tone here, for one is strikingly reminded of the pyramid of skulls in the painter Vasily Vereshchagin's nineteenth-century painting *The Apotheosis of War*. One is also reminded, as Asafyev has put it, that "the Russian wedding rite is virtually a funeral rite" for the woman.[77]

The second scene, the Blessing of the Bridegroom, counterposes the women to the men, whose movements are bolder, harder, higher, brawnier. The men seem more assertive than the women, too, partly because the groom begins standing (in contrast to the bride's submissive opening pose of prostration), and partly because their arms and fists are constantly active (in contrast to the women's demure and constrained hands and arms). The men stamp forcefully, create a variety of group formations, and perform stylized folkdances, in an exultation of virile energy. The groom is blessed first by his father and then his mother, and he sings of his strength: "Bless me, my father, my mother, bless me,/Your child who proudly goes against the strong wall of stone to break it."[78] Then the section ends with the men circling the groom in a driving, percussive sequence of crouched running and jumping. The scene is orgiastic. Both the music and the dancing, as Asafyev puts it, "[celebrate] the invocation and excitation of the male procreative force."[79] Both Asafyev and Slavicist Simon Karlinsky suggest that in this section the emphatic, incantatory command to the Virgin Mary to "come to the wedding, come to the wedding" bears traces of an ancient fertility cult embedded in the Orthodox Christian ritual.[80]

In a choreographic equivalent to a flashback, the brief third scene, The Bride's Departure, opens with the closing tableau of the first scene. We are back in the bride's chamber. Once again the bride's friends comfort her; once more they spread out to form a line and "braid" with their feet. As the chorus sings an invocation to Cosmos and Damian, the wedding saints, the entire line of women kneels and bows, as if at an altar. But then, as the Virgin Mary is invoked, the long rope-braid is gathered up and, in a shocking image, laid around the bride's neck. It is as if she were strangled by this heavy necklace or noose of hair, this symbol of her married state to come. And her friends rub their eyes, as if weeping. The group, which now includes several men, plays games: a man and woman form an arch, under which the entire group passes; they jump and encircle the bride. It is as if the entire community now had arrived to enforce the social imperative toward marriage; the chorus even compares marriage to a natural, agricultural event, implying that it is not only a social, but a biological imperative: "as the hops entwine together,/ So our newly married couple cling together."[81]

Then the stage empties except for the bride's mother, and the scene ends with her bitter farewell to her daughter: she makes patterned gestures of weeping, supplication, and grief, as the singer wails, "My own, my child, dear child of mine./Ah, do not leave me lonely."[82] For the bride is not the only woman who suffers in the peasant marriage. Her mother, an unwilling party to this match, also feels the anguish of losing her daughter.

The final scene is the Wedding Feast. Here, finally, both sides of the village – male and female – coalesce, forming multiple intricate patterns of braids and chains. The lyrics, too, tightly interweave multiple threads. The bridal couple and their two sets of parents sit on a bench on a raised platform upstage. Relegated to the background, they hardly move at all, while the guests dance, crouch, and march in mass architectonic formations in front of them. The corps constructs wedges, lines, and circling spokes, all the while remaining in their gender-sorted groups. At one point, they form two long lines, echoing the bride's braids in the first scene. Their movements are driving, repetitive, fast, and exacting but not showy. They jump, turn, and beat out rhythms with their feet, and although the male and female "blocs" do slightly different movements, their energy and strength are equal. Her intention in this scene, Nijinska writes, was that "all the action would be choreographically delivered by the 'power' of the whole mass of the ensemble."[83] The message is clear: the power and the inexorable movement of the community has obliterated – literally, upstaged – the individuality of the bride and groom. The sudden jumps, without preparation, give the dancing sharp velocity. The shifting, interlocking, repetitive, at times mechanical patterns of the group suggest an inescapable epic movement of historical inevitability. There is no personal agency here, just the implacable pounding trajectory of social and biological compulsion.

A male and female leader emerge, then rejoin the group. As Stravinsky puts it, this was in keeping with his notion of the piece as "ritualistic and non-personal. . . . The choreography was expressed in blocks and masses; individual personalities did not, could not, emerge."[84] The constant theme of the ballet, of individuals separating and reuniting in the overarching social braid of the clan, is especially marked here. The leaders are absorbed back into the group, just as the bride will be absorbed back into the community, and every form of singularity will be subsumed by the whole. This depiction of mass man, driven in every aspect of life by the agrarian form of economic necessity, which erases individuality, echoes that of *Rite*, as well as that embraced by nineteenth-century Russian populist writers.[85] But it is already present, as well, in the standard fixed epithets of the folksong lyrics, in which the bride always has blonde hair and crimson cheeks.[86]

Yet again, the scene is not entirely grim; there is an exciting power in the movement of the group, and there is joy in the dancing of the guests, as well as a touch of humor in the songs. As Nijinska notes, although the bride and groom "are deep in other thoughts . . . the families and guests enjoy themselves. For them, a wedding represents a festivity, a feast, exuberant singing, drinking, and dancing."[87] But this only underscores the pathos of the couple, and especially the woman, who is instructed in this scene, "Let her be submissive, let her be obedient./She who knows how to be obedient, always is happy."[88]

Finally, the bridal families stand, the mothers embrace their children, and then the mothers walk over to open the door, revealing an enormous bed. As the bridal couple enters the nuptial chamber, bells toll, and the corps arranges itself into a double formation: the men produce a phallic shape and the women reform themselves into the pyramidal braid. The rising pitch of action has resolved itself. The marriage has been consummated, and the obligations of maintaining the community have been met. The curtain falls.

As the Russian folklorist Vladimir Propp writes, the folksongs surrounding the wedding ritual express the practical social reality of the peasant marriage. "Here [in the wedding ritual] begins the younger generation's tragedy, which was characteristic of the Russian patriarchal village. For the elders, the marriage of a son was mainly an economic transaction, for into the household entered a female worker who would also increase the family, that is, produce new workers:

> She should have the strength of a beast,
> The power of a horse. . . . [89]

"Such," Propp continues,

> was the ideal bride from the elders' points of view. The choice was also determined by considerations of property; rich brides were preferred. The groom himself was often looking for someone who, above all, could

> help him in his work. "For our brother *mužik* [peasant] a wife is not an icon but a worker." . . . Because the selection was not always based on love, it is understandable that the entrance of a girl into marriage is not portrayed as a happy event in the songs. On the contrary, in wedding songs most verses express the sorrowful lamentations of the bride about her miserable fate.[90]

For instance, one traditional wedding song has the bride ask her aunt how, when she got married, she could bear to leave her family and join a household of strangers. Her aunt replies:

> I will tell you, little dove:
> With difficulty I parted,
> I parted, poor girl
> I left them, bitter!
> I don't remember, a young girl
> Whether by my feet they dragged me out . . .

The aunt recalls how her own mother used to let her sleep late, waking her only to tell her that all the work had already been done. But:

> In that strange land,
> In that cursed, evil place
> With a strange father and mother –
> My strange mother walks . . .
> "Get up, sleepy daughter-in-law,
> You get up, drowsy daughter-in-law!
> I've prepared everything,
> All the work's ready to be done."

As the song concludes, the verb tense shifts to the present, and the character of the aunt and the new bride merge:

> I get up, a young girl
> I wash myself with burning tears.[91]

Propp explains that even if, as sometimes happened, the couple did love one another and were happy about the match, the obligatory laments were still sung. "It is characteristic that for this obligatory ritual there are no happy love songs, but bitter songs about the sad fate of the girl who was entering another family where affection did not await her."[92]

Nijinska echoes Propp in her perspective on the events of the ballet, not only in her choreography but also in her written interpretation of *Les Noces*. She writes:

> I saw a dramatic quality in such wedding ceremonies of those times in the fate of the bride and groom, since the choice is made by parents to whom they owe complete obedience – there is no question of *mutuality of feelings*. The young girl knows nothing at all about her future family nor what lies in store for her. Not only will she be subject to her husband, but also to his parents. It is possible that after being loved and cherished by her own kind, she may be nothing more, in her new, rough family, than a useful extra worker, just another pair of hands. The soul of the innocent is in disarray – she is bidding good-bye to her carefree youth and to her loving mother.[93]

Nijinska agrees with Propp (as well as with the French seventeenth-century *précieuses*) about choosing one's own marriage partner, but she adds a new element. For she also echoes the rhetoric of the new Soviet state and its feminists, like Alexandra Kollontai, who predicted the imminent obsolescence of the family itself and argued that women could only be fully emancipated when relationships were based not on economic relations, but on unfettered love, mutual respect, and sexual freedom. In this light, *Les Noces* serves a mnemonic function, reminding contemporary spectators of the sexual oppression of peasant women in the prerevolutionary past. But in 1923, the traditional peasant wedding was not only a remnant of the past, for clearly the outmoded customs of the countryside had not disappeared overnight, no matter how hard the Bolsheviks pressed their policies.

Goncharova, too, saw the somber side of the peasant wedding, even in her earliest design ideas, in which among the bright hues she placed some characters dressed in dark colors: "beggars and cripples . . . the village priest . . . the landowner . . . who is not rich enough." Goncharova also echoes Propp in her understanding of the wedding's bitter import, and she sees it not simply as a dead archaeological relic of the past, but as a surviving practice. She recalls a wedding she witnessed at age 16:

> Three couples were getting married at the same time. There was no light and the church had a certain gloomy look. . . . The brides were only a little better dressed than on work days . . . they acted very stiffly as though made of wood. . . . They all resembled each other [which was] . . . nothing to be wondered at, as there are villages in which everyone has the same last names . . . [and which] produce a single type . . .
>
> There was no joy, no radiance, no love or tenderness. What kind of wedding was this? Obviously it was a wedding of necessity. Undoubtedly the young men had to leave for the army or they had to go to town in search of employment and it was necessary that someone take their places at their homes in the village. . . . Their wives . . . would be useful to relatives . . . durable. . . . And the old parents had decided everything in place of the young people.[94]

Goncharova (who, it should be mentioned, never married her lifelong partner Larionov), eventually arrived at the same image of the wedding as the choreographer. But it was Nijinska who initiated the drastic change in the conception of the ballet from a joyful, colorful celebration to an austere but powerful depiction of relentless mass social forces sweeping helpless individuals – especially helpless women – along in their wake.

Of course, Nijinska had earlier lived in the West, where she had been exposed to Western European views about women and marriage. Even when she lived in pre-revolutionary Russia, she was a member of the intelligentsia, a class of artists and intellectuals that held liberal and often radical views toward women, gender relations, and the oppressed classes. Her ballet, which underscores peasant women's tragedy without denigrating the Russian peasant, follows in the tradition of Russian populist literature, exemplified by the nineteenth-century writer Gleb Uspensky, whose stories and sketches in the 1860s–1880s took a materialist view of the earthbound peasant's apparent backwardness. Uspensky dignified the peasant without idealizing the miserable conditions of his daily life. Kirstein notes that "*Les Noces* praised the strength and quality of the Slavic peoples for its permanence. It made no decorative reference to a colorful past; it was not nostalgic over the loss of tsardom."[95]

But more important than her knowledge of the populist literary tradition was the fact that Nijinska moved back to Russia and lived there during the years of Revolution and Civil War, finally emigrating to the West only in 1921, the year before she began to think about *Les Noces*. She had seen an entire nation experience tremendous social upheaval on every front, and she had participated in some of its social as well as artistic experiments. In 1919, she opened an experimental ballet studio of her own – the School of Movement – in Kiev. There, inspired by the Russian revolutionary avant-garde arts – in particular the streamlined, abstract functionalism of constructivism – she dedicated herself "to the creation of a new type of ballet artist."[96] She became friendly with the constructivist artist Alexandra Exter, who had opened her own studio in Kiev in 1918, frequently participated in activities at Nijinska's school, and collaborated with the choreographer on several projects. Although Nijinska had certainly not witnessed progress in every stratum of the new society, and indeed had herself suffered permanent hearing loss as a result of the bombardment of Kiev in 1919, she writes that when she worked on *Les Noces* she "was still breathing the air of Russia, a Russia throbbing with excitement and intense feeling. All the vivid images of the harsh realities of the Revolution were still part of me and filled my whole being."[97]

Clearly Nijinska was influenced by the experimental plastic movement studios, machine dances by the Blue Blouse group and Nikolai Foregger, mass spectacles, and constructivist stagings of plays, all of which mushroomed in revolutionary Moscow, Leningrad, Kiev, and Kharkov. Indeed, her own innovations at the School of Movement were part and parcel of this experimental movement.[98] In fact, Levinson called *Les Noces* "Marxist choreography."[99] And he complained that the choreography "reminded one of nothing so much as the athletic stadium or the drill grounds. . . . Or else they were arranged in double files, like the soldiers of a firing squad." Levinson described the final tableau as "a sort of practicable stage property constructed with flesh and blood or an apotheosis of exhibition gymnastics."[100]

Besides these artistic influences, there were personal factors involved in Nijinska's attitude toward marriage. While still in Russia, Nijinska had also separated from her husband and was raising two children and supporting an aged mother on her own while running her school. Her exposure to Soviet avant-garde arts and revolutionary rhetoric, as well as her personal situation, unmistakably shaped both the form and meaning of *Les Noces.*[101]

As we have seen, the traditional peasant wedding ritual already has inscribed within it a dismal picture of the bride's situation; this was by no means Nijinska's invention. The Russian theater historian Vsevolod Vsevolodsky-Gerngross and his State Experimental Theater, mounting their ethnographically detailed *Russian Wedding Ritual* in the Soviet Union in Leningrad in 1923, also created "a maiden's tragedy . . . on a monumental scale" and focused on the bride's ritual lament.[102] But presented in the West, as a new entry into a ballet tradition that had for the most part celebrated marriage as the ultimate desideratum for women, *Les Noces* made a radical statement not only in terms of its abstract form, but especially in terms of its sexual politics. Indeed, these two aspects are related, for it is Nijinska's modernism, akin to James Joyce's or Virginia Woolf's techniques expressing interior consciousness, that distances the bride's point of view from that of the other characters, allowing her gloomy inner life to cast the entire festivity into shadows. *Les Noces* is a watershed work, obdurately shifting the terms of the ballet wedding's significance from the male to the female perspective.

Conclusion

Although *Les Noces* is the most choreographically abstract of the three Stravinsky ballets considered here, it is the most accurate in describing women's real-life situations. Like *Rite*, Nijinska's ballet portrays a ritual, and in many ways it seems to be a continuation of *Rite*'s concerns with the peasant as the embodiment of the Russian nation, right down to the very un-European comportment of the dancers' bodies – their fists, their crouches, their flat-footed stamping, their twisted torsos, their turned-in or parallel legs, their earthbound muscularity.[103] In this way, both ballets depart from *Firebird*'s fairytale aristocratic world of princes and princesses, sorcerers, and magical birds. But in *Les Noces*, Nijinska also seems to break with *Rite*, or even to answer her brother's ballet, by interpolating resistance to the ritual. To be sure, the bride in *Les Noces* is compliant. She goes through with the ceremony. But her recalcitrant consciousness, already implicit in the tradition itself, is heightened in the ballet and brought to center stage.

There is a clear progression in the ways in which women are represented in these three ballets. Female images move, in stages, from idealized to "real" figures (although, as I have indicated, woman's material and political reality in *Les Noces* is constructed in an abstract, non-realistic style). In *Firebird*, the leading female role is that of the Firebird, who is supernatural, an oriental Other, and a ruler. In *Rite*, the key female is the Chosen One. She is human, but the bride of a supernatural creature. She is a victim, but she serves as the intermediary between the reigning god and his subjects. Although she is Russian, she is ancient, an Other – like the Firebird – but chronologically rather than geographically. The female protagonist of *Les Noces*, like those of the two earlier ballets, has no given name. But she differs from them in significant ways. A victim of social tradition, she wields no political power. She is no Other, but a contemporary woman. Not only is she not supernatural, but her relationships take place solely on the human plane.

In both *Firebird* and *Rite*, the female image serves as a metaphor for another political concept – in the former, the monarchy, and in the latter, the nation. In *Les Noces*, the woman stands only for herself and for other women of her age and class. It is striking, as well, that in each ballet the individuated women come in pairs. The Firebird is complemented by the beautiful Tsarevna, who is human, Russian, virginal, and docile. The naive Chosen One's opposite number is the prognosticating witch who begins the ritual activity of the ballet, whose ancient wisdom bespeaks centuries of experience, but who, like the sacrificial victim, is crucial to the success of the rite. The young Bride's binary partner is her weathered mother. In the first two ballets, wisdom and power contrast with youth and innocence. But in *Les Noces*, both women are portrayed as equally powerless in the face of patriarchal custom. In *Firebird*, women are viewed with awe; in *Rite*, they are viewed with sympathy, but they are still exotic. With *Les Noces*, the woman's image finally coincides with her social reality.

In the 1924 ballet *Les Biches*, Nijinska drew a completely disparate social reality – that of Parisian high society, including lesbianism, androgyny, heterosexual seduction, and group sex – in a different, more sophisticated and tongue-in-cheek tone, but with equal lucidity, candor, and acumen.[104] The women in *Les Biches* still have no given names (they are the Hostess, the Girls in Gray, the Girl in Blue), but they no longer fit into binary opposites; they embody a range of ages, temperaments, and sexual proclivities. They are unique individuals who assert their social agency. A London critic wrote of *Les Biches* in 1925 that "feminism [has] at last tinged the ballet."[105] But certainly *Les Noces* had already introduced feminism to the ballet stage, even if the women it portrayed passively submitted to their fate.

In terms of the marriage plot, *Firebird* presents a successful, euphoric outcome, in typical fairytale fashion. Marriage is not only not problematic; monogamy is not an issue either, for Ivan seems to flourish with both wife and mistress. *The Rite of Spring*, however, presents a vexed case. Perhaps this is what makes it truly a modernist work. Its outcome is successful, for the Chosen One is indeed sacrified to the god; although Yarilo never appears, the marriage seems to be consummated. However, whether this is a euphoric or dysphoric marriage is highly ambiguous. From the point of view of the community, it is euphoric, for it propitiates the gods and ensures a successful agrarian cycle. On the other hand, from the point of view of the Chosen One, it is dysphoric, since it signals her death. And thus, since the spectator is uncertain where to place his or her allegiance, the question of the affective value remains an open one. In *Les Noces*, as well, the theme of the reluctant bride makes the successful marriage (for it does take place) ambiguous in terms of its affective value. For the community, it is euphoric. But for the bride, especially, and perhaps to some degree for the bridegroom, this is certainly a dysphoric event. However, unlike the situation in *Rite*, here the affective value for the spectator is not at all ambiguous. The point of view of the ballet's author, and therefore that of the spectator, casts this marriage as a dysphoric one.

Although there is a clear progression in these ballets toward a feminist view of women's issues, especially in regard to the problematizing of marriage and sexuality, this attitude did not necessarily express a company policy of enlightenment, nor was it the final word. After Nijinska left the company, the feminist imagery waned. In 1928, George Balanchine choreographed another major work to music by Stravinsky. In *Apollon Musagète* (later known as *Apollo*), the scene is no longer Russia, but the domicile of the classical gods in the heavens, *à la* eighteenth-century French ballet. A man is the protagonist, and the classical style of ballet technnique returns, although it has expanded to include turned-in legs and jazzy steps.[106] The women – three of the seven Muses – are triply Other: supernatural, ancient (but classically so), and Greek. And, although they are objects of beauty and admiration, even inspiration, the Muses are ruled, instructed, and empowered by the young sun god (a deity altogether different from Yarilo, the primitive sun god in *Rite*).

With Balanchine's *Apollo*, the image of woman in ballet is once again shaped by the male point of view – not in some automatic, essential way (because the choreographer is a man), but because the choreographic structure makes it so. The female dancer is the focal point for much of Balanchine's choreography since the 1920s, as she was on Petipa's stage, and in later Balanchine ballets she assumes a great deal more agency and autonomy (as we will see in Chapter 6). But in *Apollo*, although women are central to the choreography, they play a role subservient to the man. They are muses, demigoddesses, not "real" women – always distant, coolly alluring, and somewhat alien, as the Firebird was in Fokine's *Firebird*. In *Les Noces*, by contrast, the woman – her situation, her point of view, her consciousness – is at the heart of the work.

5

MODERN DANCE

Witch Dance, With My Red Fires, Rites de Passage, Night Journey

As we saw in Chapter 3, the forerunners of modern dance constituted the first generation of women in dance history to rebel as a group against both choreographic traditions and society's gender expectations. Although individual women had certainly done so in the past, the forerunners served as an entire cohort in breaking the rules, both of their art form and of cultural norms for women, by claiming (if not always realizing) liberty for the female dancing body – freedom from corsets and shoes; freedom from the marriage plot; freedom to create new expressive vocabularies of movement. Yet these women, and many other, less famous choreographers of their generation – like the Canadian Maude Allan and the Austrian Wiesenthal sisters – made their innovations in a patriarchal world in which women, though gaining political ground, were still legally second-class citizens. Fuller's assertion of the female self as scientist, Duncan's twin themes of political liberation and the sanctity of motherhood, and St. Denis's appropriation of the exotic Other as an American female identity, all participated, to some extent, in the feminist movements in Europe and America at the turn of the century, as well as in the nascent modern dance movements on both continents.

Although these early forerunners were not politically active feminists and were unaffiliated with any organized groups, they contributed to the growing discourse about women and to the pressure women were applying to society's strictures, whether in the political or cultural sphere. They created an alternative market – and largely female audiences – for dance performances, outside of the male-dominated opera-house ballet stage and popular entertainments. When they put their bodies, their emotions, and their imaginations center stage, these aspects of the particular selves they projected, while not *essentially* female, nevertheless were marked as bodies, emotions, and imaginations of women.

That the next generation of choreographers – both European and American – further promoted the identification of modern dance as a ripe field for female creative artists (choreographers, that is, as opposed to dancers) and effectively relinquished ballet to the male choreographers, suggests two intertwining dynamics. One is that even after the feminist movement of the turn of the century had run its course and women had made progress both politically and culturally in the U.S. and Europe, a gender revolution was far from won. Even in the feminized art form of dance, often women could only find positions of authority in minor or unofficial organizations.[1] The second, related dynamic is that by the 1920s, women dance artists had discovered *en masse* the strategic artistic advantages of secession and alterity. That is, they, too, adopted deliberately marginal, outsider identities, which had, since the mid-nineteenth century, been seized upon by the predominantly male avant-garde in visual art, literature, and theater.

The modern dance was institutionalized by the generation I call "historical modern dance" in a variety of interrelated ways as a set of alternative organizations, in both Europe and the United States. It was an arena in which women could and did play leading roles (in contrast to other art forms, including ballet, where men dominated both practice and pedagogy). On the one hand, these artists saw modern dance as a domain for "high art" innovation, as opposed to dance as popular entertainment. The latter was seen by these choreographers (and also by critics and audiences) as cheap and lower-class. Their ambitions, while often critical of bourgeois taste, were nevertheless frequently bourgeois in their class affiliations or aspirations. Moreover, although the dancers did not state it this way, dance in popular entertainments like burlesque, vaudeville, and cabarets had historically often depended on commodifying women's bodies. On the other hand, these choreographers constructed modern dance as a democratic or communal nationalist art form (contesting what was often seen as the monarchical internationalism that had formed ballet, with its patriarchal views of women).[2]

These modern dancers were then dialectically criticized (whether directly or indirectly) from various directions. Their critics included those who called for a working-class internationalist dance (like members of the Workers Dance League in the United States and communist dancers, such as Jean Weidt, in Germany) and those who felt that dance should be more accessible to mass audiences.[3] From another perspective, their critics also included those (like Merce Cunningham, Anna Halprin, and Alwin Nikolais, as well as the Judson Dance Theater) who sought an even more innovative formal aesthetic. The alternative institutions the modern dancers established were in their turn accused of being as rigid, their dances as bloated, and their themes as outmoded as the "moderns" had found nineteenth-century and early twentieth-century ballet. But, extending the work of the turn-of-the-century forerunners who had preceded them, the historical modern dance choreographers of the 1920s–1940s systematized, streamlined, and criticized both the themes and movement vocabularies of their predecessors. And they often did so through shock techniques.

Indeed, I want to argue that the four choreographers whose works I will analyze in this chapter – Mary Wigman, Doris Humphrey, Katherine Dunham, and Martha Graham – deliberately chose strategies of Otherness and outsiderhood in the characters and narratives of their dances (and often in their personal lives as well). This had the effect, whether intended or not, of criticizing generally the social roles for women that, since the nineteenth century, had been reinforced by theatrical dancing, whether on the lyric stage or the popular stage. That is, the modern dancers found their niche as artists and as women by staking out a flexible space at the fringes of a still uncodified artform. And their often unsettling representations of women frequently took place at the margins of the socially acceptable. It is not so much that the modern dance choreographers chose different roles for women than did the ballet – these modern dances, like so many ballets, also feature witches, mothers, and young lovers, although they abjure sylphs, wilis, fairies, and other supernatural creatures. But, viewing these same roles from the perspective of "the new woman," the moderns rewrote them. A witch could be reclaimed as a positive figure, both frightening and attractive. A mother could be viewed as destructive, rather than nurturing. And the sexual desires of both virgin and older woman could be acknowledged. These were the sides of femininity the "new woman" in dance, like her counterparts in literature and the other arts, explored.

Witch Dance

In the course of her career, Mary Wigman repeatedly returned to themes of death and the demonic. The leading figure of the *Ausdruckstanz* (expressive dance) movement in Germany between the two world wars, Wigman studied eurhythmics with Émile Jaques-Dalcroze and improvisation and movement analysis with Rudolf Laban. The schools she opened in Dresden in 1919 and in New York in 1931 shaped generations of dancers, from Germany and elsewhere, and the impact of her all-female company, which toured widely in the late 1920s and 1930s, was immense in both Europe and the United States. Her rhythmic approach to dance – she often used music that consisted primarily of percussion – stressed the expressivity of the dancer's body by positing an inner motivation for the movement impulse. Her molding of space – what dance historian Susan Manning terms *gestalt im Raum*, or "configuration of energy in space"[4] – through the various modes of spatial harmony she analyzed with Laban created dance images of intense action.

Like many of her contemporaries in the other arts during the Weimar period, especially the German Expressionist painters and filmmakers, Wigman was drawn to apocalyptic and mystical themes. Manning writes that "she conceptualized her body as a medium and her dancing as a channel for subconscious drives and supernatural forces, for ecstatic and demonic energies. . . . Critic after critic wrote about how she . . . [animated] suprapersonal forces beyond her physical self."[5]

Wigman's quest for spiritual transcendence predated her dance studies. In her reminiscences, she recalls that in her early twenties, she "[looked] even toward the Orient for a mystic answer to a wordless riddle."[6] *Monotony (Whirl Dance)* (1926) was a spinning dance in the manner of Sufi dervishes, and several of her dances, like *Seraphic Song* (part of the cycle *Shifting Landscape* [1929]), displayed a beatific otherworldliness. But, more often, Wigman's dances emphasized a different aspect of her spiritual quest – the struggle with evil and the acceptance of death. Her movements – crouching, crawling, or simply lying still – clung close to the earth. The American critic Margaret Lloyd wrote that "Wigman's was largely an ecstasy of gloom, stressing the demonic and macabre, as if to exorcise through movement the secret evils in man's nature."[7]

Wigman's style during the 1920s was closely related to other aspects of German Expressionist art: the intense style of acting developed in the "shriek-plays" of the theater; the telegraphic, percussive poems and dialogues of literature; and the angular, distorted shapes of painting and film. In both style and content, her work, like theirs, pronounced drastic visions of death and evil as well as of spiritual salvation.

The artists working in these separate art forms knew and responded to one another. Wigman writes that in the 1920s, Dresden, an artistic center of the new Weimar Republic,

> was alive and vibrated with the exuberance of its quickened cultural life. I too was on the move, and my pupils with me. It was self-evident that we took passionate interest in everything that was going on in the arts. Harald Kreutzberg danced in Oskar Kokoschka's *Murder, the Hope of Women.* Hanya Holm created the part of the princess in Igor Stravinsky's *A Soldier's Tale*. . . . Art exhibitions presenting for the first time works by Paul Klee, Kandinsky, Feininger, Kirchner, Schmidt-Rottluff, Kokoschka, and many others created enthusiasm as much as shock and fury. . . . Most of these artists I came to know very well.[8]

The artistic cultures Wigman inhabited in Ascona, Switzerland and later in Dresden articulated a sense of apocalyptic despair and revolutionary zeal unleashed in a Germany suffering from war and its aftermath, a nation felt by its younger generation to be rapidly disintegrating (although the members of that generation sought individual answers along utterly divergent political paths, from being totally apolitical to embracing communism or supporting National Socialism). Like other artists of her generation, Wigman was not only pre-occupied with the pressure and threat of implosion in current society, but also expressed hope for a regeneration of humanity. She made dances of death – like *Danse Macabre* (1923), *Dance of Death* (1926), and *Totenmal* (1930) – but she also made dances of life: *Festive Prelude* (1926) and *Celebration* (1928).[9]

It is striking that Wigman returned repeatedly to the theme of the witch. This was the name of her first solo, choreographed in 1914 when she still worked as Laban's assistant. *Witch Dance II* (1926) was part of a cycle entitled *Visions.* A masked dance that begins in a seated position, it seems to owe something of its eerie, powerfully contorted beauty as well as its irregular, percussive rhythms and angular gestures to the ghosts and witches of Japanese Noh dramas and other Asian dance-drama forms. Wigman described this dance as "a rhythmic intoxication."[10] Its resonances are many, for it not only evokes the occult, the forbidden, and the pagan, but it also connects these themes to women.

The costume for *Witch Dance* was a drape of silk brocade and a mask of Wigman's own face, which, modeled after noh masks, gave her a remote, enigmatic aura.[11] According to Wigman, the brocade itself had a mystical connection with the character in the dance. She saw the cloth in a shop window and "[stared] in fascination at this splendor spread out before me: bold designs in metal threads on a copper-red background shimmering in gold and silver traced in black – exciting, wild, barbaric." In fact, Wigman's description of the hold this resplendent fabric took upon her and her "bad conscience" for buying it further amplify the myth of the fabric's mysterious, demonic power. It was too expensive, but she bought it anyway, then hid it from herself in her costume closet. But years later, once she had created the figure of the witch, she says she suddenly remembered – "the piece of brocade! Did it not possess, in its barbaric beauty, in its splendiferous ruthlessness, something that corresponded to the revolting character of the dance?" Then she also remembered a mask of her own face she had made for another dance, a mask "whose features were my own translated into the demonic." Again, Wigman invokes the rhetoric of Otherness when she writes, "I suddenly knew that fabric and mask belonged together and that they had had to wait this long for their return from exile."[12]

Wigman writes of the choreography, as well as the costume, possessing her in a mystical fashion. She reports that her dance ideas kept leading her to "restlessness . . . and some kind of evil greed I felt in my hands, which pressed themselves clawlike into the ground as if they had wanted to take root." Working – crucially – at night in her studio, she felt the character "slowly stirring." But when she tried to create order from her welter of rhythmic ideas, she found "something was opposed to their becoming lucid and orderly, something that forced the body time and again into a sitting or squatting position in which the greedy hands could take possession of the ground."

> When, one night, I returned to my room utterly agitated, I looked into the mirror by chance. What it reflected was the image of one possessed, wild and dissolute, repelling and fascinating. The hair unkempt, the eyes deep in their sockets, the nightgown shifted about, which made the body appear almost shapeless: there she was – the witch – the earth-bound creature with her unrestrained, naked instincts, with her insatiable lust for life, beast and woman at one and the same time.
>
> I shuddered at my own image, at the exposure of this facet of my ego which I had never allowed to emerge in such unashamed nakedness. But, after all, isn't a bit of a witch hidden in every hundred-per-cent female . . . ?[13]

I have dwelt at length here on Wigman's account of the creation and meaning of the dance, neither because I subscribe to her mystical view of choreography

Plate 13 Mary Wigman in *Witch Dance*, 1926. Photograph courtesy of the Stiftung Archiv der Akademie der Künste.

nor because I believe that the artist's mythic narrative of the artwork's origins reveals some essential "truth" of the dance. Rather, what I find interesting here is precisely Wigman's rhetoric, whether she herself believed it, thought she believed it, or simply produced it for public consumption to enhance the dance's mystique. Her account is the myth she constructed about the dance – its origins, feeling-tones, and meaning. Indeed, part of the dance's meaning resides in the choreographer's pronouncements about it – its publicity machine.[14] Not only, Wigman tells us, are we to understand the dance itself as displaying that which is wild, barbaric, evil, greedy, enigmatic, and "burdened with heaviness . . . lurking, animal-like," but we are instructed to understand the role of the artist as that of a vessel, possessed and guided by invisible spirits.[15] The artist, that is, is herself a witch of sorts, or at least a spiritual container for higher powers that create the work through her divine madness.[16]

But surely, despite the evocative rhetoric, the dance did not simply invade Wigman's body from the world of spirits. For one thing, it bears too much resemblance to various Asian dance-drama forms, which could have easily influenced the choreographer, given her fascination with the Orient. In the surviving film fragment of *Witch Dance*, the music is percussion – gong, cymbals, and drum – very similar to the Japanese Noh ensemble (which also includes a flute). Most striking, however, is Wigman's use of poses similar to the *mie* of Japanese kabuki dance-drama. James Brandon describes the *mie* thus: "To perform *mie*, an actor 'winds up' with arms and legs, moves his head in a circular motion, then with a snap of the head, freezes into a dynamic pose. . . . The strongest *mie* are accompanied by the sound of wooden clappers."[17] In *Witch Dance*, Wigman's movements repeatedly increase in intensity, only to culminate with a roll and snap of the head in a frozen, stylized pose, as the percussion pounds out an accelerating rhythm of suspense and climax. While it may be that Wigman never saw kabuki, she would have had the opportunity to do so, and its techniques would have been available to her, for they had been familiar to German theater-goers and practitioners since the late nineteenth century.[18]

For another thing, the dance is masterfully structured. It is no loose outpouring of inspiration, but a tightly designed composition that skillfully creates an image of sinister power. The dance begins with Wigman sitting on the floor facing the spectator, her knees bent, with feet together, flat on the floor in front of her.[19] She claws the air with her hands, stretching her right arm straight up. She rolls her head around and places her hands on her knees. Slowly she pries open her legs like a clamshell. Holding her elbows out from her body and placing her palms on the open knees to form a right angle with her arms, she rolls her head again and then poses, her head facing left, with her hands still on her knees, but with her torso turned to the right, her right arm bent, and her left arm extended. She slowly lifts her right hand to reach out, then to claw the air. Next, she clutches her knees with arms crossed in front of her, then "walks" herself forward, seated, while clutching alternate knees, repeatedly crossing one arm in front of the other. She grasps her ankles and propels herself in a circle, pounding the floor with her bare feet. The film fragment of the dance ends there, but a German critic provides a description of the rest of the dance:

> With a powerful swing the [*Gestalt*] comes to its feet. Now everything happens in rapid, flowing, close succession. A complicated rhythmic movement sets in. . . . Like a giant, the red and gold, phantom-like figure rears up in the space. Now it leaps around in a circle, the right foot is thrown out, the hands of the speeding arms perform a kind of spurting throwing action. . . . The figure leaps out of the circle with fierce increased tempo. . . . Now comes a sudden, wild jump outwards. . . . The forearms cross over each other horizontally, as the fingers open and close . . . it is as if something invisible were being severed with eerie industry, again and again. . . . For a moment the [*Gestalt*] is like a gleaming, enthroned idol, but the body immediately falls over backward, a very powerful swing of both arms throws it forward again, it tumbles back on the ground, the hands support it, the head snaps up, the mask stares toward us in petrified madness. Darkness.[20]

For spectators, *Ausdruckstanz* – deliberately stark, ugly, and wild – presented an entirely different representation of the dancing body, in particular the female dancing body, than the high-art dancing (whether ballet or Duncanesque) or the light entertainments they were used to. Even where critics appreciated Wigman's work, they often could not refrain from pointing out its missing qualities – those associated with essentialized female attributes, most particularly the familiar physical forms of female beauty, but also docile good temper. One critic remarked, "What we admire about Fräulein Wiegmann's performance is her powerful expressivity, supported by her most thorough physical training and directed by her strong imagination. What we miss in her accomplishments is sunniness, happiness, and joy in beauty."[21] Manning suggests that it may have been Wigman's viewing of a 1916 performance by Duncan, which the younger choreographer termed "horrible," that strengthened Wigman's own determination to renounce "'sunniness' in favor of 'expressive power'" and to replace the dancing self with a more objectified, distanced dancing figure.[22]

This was a figure, I want to stress, that was not only distanced, but deliberately constructed as alien. Certainly *Witch Dance* was a paradigm for Wigman's approach. It was "wild," "barbaric," emanating "petrified madness." In this aspiration, of course, Wigman joined other primitivists of her generation, not only in Germany but in Russia, France, the United States, and elsewhere. This was part of modern art's strategy of revitalization – using art from tribal cultures as well as the exotic high art of ancient Asian and African civilizations simultaneously to criticize the rationalism of European Enlightenment values and to find new formal and spiritual components for artistic renewal. Wigman's close friend, the painter Emile Nolde, criticized the rapacious colonialist enterprise, concluding that there was a "primeval vitality," an "intensive, often grotesque expression of energy and life" in tribal art that was vastly preferable to the "over-refined, pallid, decadent" artworks produced by Europeans.[23]

This turn to non-Western art was an example of a panoply of tactics the Russian formalist critic Viktor Shklovsky identified as part of an artistic strategy of innovation and renewal. These included "the knight's move" – an Oedipal gesture that criticized the previous generation's tastes and values by skipping over to those of a generation and a half before, as well as "the canonization of the junior branch" – the introduction of motifs and techniques of previously overlooked or disdained genres.[24] Thus the German Expressionists rejected the pomposity of late nineteenth-century academic art, with its vestiges of neo-classicism, and the dramas that bombastically displayed, in playwright Carl Sternheim's ironic terms, "the heroic life of the bourgeoisie" – a life he criticized as utterly vulgar in its materialism as well as its war-mongering.[25] Even realism in visual art, literature, and theater, a movement that had at least instilled art with social conscience, came under criticism for what was seen by some as its overemphasis on the external world, rather than revealing the internal world of the artistic and social imagination and of psychological depths. As the painter Max Beckmann wrote, "What I want to show in my work is the idea which hides itself behind so-called reality. I am seeking for the bridge which leads from the visible to the invisible, like the famous cabalist who once said: 'If you wish to get hold of the invisible you must penetrate as deeply as possible into the visible.'"[26]

The German Romantic fascination with the repressed, the Other, and the exotic all reappeared in German Expressionism, but with a new, more violent twentieth-century twist – a perspective darkened by the sudden devastation of mass war and the insidiously ongoing ravages of mass industrial capitalism. Like the Romantics before them, the Expressionists also turned to German medieval art, in particular the woodcut, a technique the artists of Die Brücke favored. But equally fascinating to this generation of artists, in the wake of the new science of psychoanalysis, was the art of the insane, which they considered another branch of primitive art.[27] The Romantic fascination with the Enlightenment's repressed – in the form of the supernatural – found a new incarnation in the Expressionists' exploration of bourgeois culture's repressed – the psychological.

Wigman employed all these strategies in her work, adopting what – feminizing Shklovsky's term – we might call "the dame's move," a series of L-shaped trajectories that purloined aspects of Romantic ballet traditions (the grotesque, the folkloric, the witch), German medieval dance (diableries and the *Totentanz*, or Dance of Death), and Asian dance-drama (the mask, the use of percussion, the rhythmic dance climax). And *Witch Dance* shows all these interlocking strategies in operation.

Wigman had already choreographed her first *Witch Dance* in 1914, but her interest in religious mysticism was whetted by a 1917 conference on the occult held on Monte Verità, the bohemians' and artists' community in the Swiss alps where the Laban School had its summer home, and where she stayed on after the outbreak of war.[28] Perhaps the later version of *Witch Dance* was also influenced by the welter of German Expressionist films made between 1910 and the 1920s concerned with the grotesque and demonic as correlated with the psychological – including *The Golem* (various versions directed or co-directed by Paul Wegener, 1914–1920), Robert Wiene's *The Cabinet of Dr. Caligari* (1919), Fritz Lang's *Destiny* (1921), and F. W. Murnau's *Nosferatu/The Vampire* (1921).

Some male artists of the German Expressionist camp self-critically figured themselves as diseased vampires, living off the blood of "real people," as in Klabund's *Der Mann mit der Maske*, in which a writer takes off his mask to reveal his disfigured face to a woman with whom he has just made love; after she kills herself, he uses the event as material for a story.[29] Wigman's fascination with the witch persona creates a specifically female counterpart to this artistic stratagem of antisocial behavior, although she refigures this unnatural being, this social outsider, as positive.

The witch is, moreover, a female role that is strongly rooted in German social, religious, literary, and iconographic history. For although part of Wigman's interest, as I have noted, came from the exoticism of the occult and of Asian theater, there are also sources much closer to home that – although cloaked in barbaric splendor – would create a representation of female resistance. One obvious source from oral folktales and popular literature is the evil witch whose image crystallized in the Grimm brothers' fairytales.[30] She is the paradigm of a bad woman – destructive and powerful in ways that undermine the social order. She may be routed in tale after tale, but, constantly reappearing, she seems to be a perennially enduring, unvanquishable force.

But another source for the witch persona is the history of the European witch hunts and witch trials in the fifteenth century and, more virulently, from 1560–1750, a majority of which occurred in Germany. Although the full history of these events is still being uncovered and analyzed even now, their occurrence was widely known (both at the time and since). The image, definition, alleged actions, and terrible fate of accused witches – most of whom were women – saturated both learned and vernacular German literature and visual art, including plays, sermons, paintings, and popular woodcuts (which later served as inspirations for German Expressionist art). In fact, the emergence of the witch in early modern Europe exactly parallels the emergence of vernacular literature and art, and historian Peter Burke has remarked that "one of the most striking instances of interaction between the learned and popular traditions is that of the witch."[31]

As feminist literary critic Sigrid Brauner has recently written, the "modern witch" – that is, the one hunted down by the witch crazes of the Reformation – was generally a woman. She was most often single, and she was usually an illiterate peasant, while those who tried and executed her were educated men of the upper classes. Brauner notes, "People from disparate backgrounds with clashing ideas about what constituted appropriate behavior for women faced each other in court." She concludes that the rewriting of gender roles during the

Protestant Reformation, as well as "the emergence of a modern society with its money economy, division of labor, and restructuring of human drives" led to the persecution of women who did not fit the newly configured, urbanized cultural conception of women – of women, that is, who refused "the new feminine ideal of the submissive housewife."[32] This ideal, of course, was one against which Wigman revolted in her early works, as well as in her life.

Brauner's conclusion strikingly echoes Wigman's words about the familiarity of the Other in *Witch Dance* – the "bit of a witch hidden in every hundred-per-cent female." Brauner remarks that after the construction of the modern witch in the sixteenth century, "every woman, no matter how seemingly demure – even the most faithful of wives, mothers, or daughters – could suddenly turn into a witch. With her pejorative and frightening connotations, the witch entered the average household as the impulsive spirit and potential troublemaker thought to reside within every woman."[33]

In *Witch Dance*, Wigman reclaims the image of the assertive, untameable woman, fanning the flames of the old conflict between women and bourgeois morality, women and religious authority. Manning interprets the 1914 version of this dance as blurring or refusing gender.[34] Yet it is difficult to believe that Wigman – even if she did not take a special interest in the history of early modern witches and the witch hunts of the Reformation – would not have known, if only in passing, popular representations of witches that typically pictured them as women. One such contemporary popular representation was the 1922 Swedish silent film *Häxan* (Witchcraft Through the Ages), directed by Benjamin Christensen, which based its documentary-style narrative on witch trial records and visual images from the fifteenth to seventeenth centuries; Wigman could easily have seen it in Dresden. Other popular sources included woodcuts from the era of the witch-hunts, which served as a vital iconographic inspiration for visual artists in Die Brücke group. Moreover, Wigman's own account of the dance's creation specifically ties the image of the witch to a female identity. Although Wigman's witch is non-specific in terms of geography or chronology and even, as I have noted, has Asian overtones, the resonance of the word itself is heavily weighted, conjuring up cultural memories of German witchcrazes.

This reclamation of the witch as a positive, resistant female identity – that of a deliberately "bad woman," a social rebel and unregenerate outcast – was also attractive to other women artists of Wigman's generation. For instance, Valeska Gert, the grotesque dancer, film actress, and cabaret performer who first appeared in Berlin in 1916, titled her 1950 autobiography *Ich bin eine Hexe* (I am a Witch), and in it she describes her dance pantomimes as portraits of the outcast. "Because I didn't like solid citizens. I danced those whom they despised – whores, procuresses, down-and-outers, and degenerates." Witches, of course, fell into this category in earlier times. Gert describes her streetwalker's dance, *Canaille*, which, although it is sexually explicit, bears a certain family resemblance to Wigman's *Witch Dance*:

> My white face is almost entirely covered by strands of black hair falling over my forehead. I bow my head deeply. . . . Then I bend my knees slowly, spread my legs wide and sink down. In a sudden spasm, as if bit by a tarantula, I twitch upwards. I sway back and forth. Then my body relaxes, the spasm dissipates, the jerking becomes ever gentler, ever feebler, the intervals longer, the excitement ebbs away, one last twitch, and I'm down to earth again.

And, Gert relates, in Munich in the 1920s there was a discussion of modern dance. "One scrawny girl with a pockmarked face and sharply jutting cheekbones said, 'We want the "outlandish" in dance.' That's what I wanted too. What's outlandish? Birth, love, death. Nobody had previously dared to portray them barefaced and truthfully." Like Wigman, Gert, too, danced death, in a long black dress.[35]

While Wigman's attitude was, as theater historian Laurence Senelick uses the term, "antinomian," striking an oppositional stance against mainstream moral attitudes, unlike Gert and other cabaret performers of the 1920s, Wigman did not gravitate toward satire.[36] And unlike those Weimar artists who savored and borrowed from popular entertainments, she disdained the variety stage and its audiences. She had high-art aspirations and spiritual intentions.[37] During the years of Nazi rule, as Manning points out, Wigman's dances became more closely linked to official values regarding domesticity, family, and the community.[38] But in her formative years in the progressive community of Monte Verità and the experimental period of Weimar culture, she joined the "band of outsiders" who became cultural insiders after the Revolution of 1918.[39]

Wigman grew up in Germany in a period when, as in other European countries, a feminist movement made inroads into gaining advanced educational and career opportunities for women and struggled to win the right for women to vote. This turn-of-the-century women's movement was bifurcated by class and ideology, but both the bourgeois and proletarian wings, while supporting women's suffrage and the right to work, upheld the gender division of "separate spheres" and largely continued to define women's roles as primarily that of wife and mother.[40] Wigman's own girlhood exemplifies the conflicts engendered at the time by women's changing social and political status.[41] Born in 1886 as Mary Wiegmann into a family with a successful business in Hannover, she was groomed to enter the first gymnasium for girls, but her parents rejected this opportunity. Instead, she attended boarding schools abroad, in England and Switzerland, and at age 16 came home, studied social dance and comportment, and spent seven years living with her family. As Manning puts it, she "[struggled] to reconcile her parents' – and the larger society's – expectations that she become a wife and mother with her own sense of wanting more from life."[42]

Wigman had suitors and twice became engaged, but ultimately rejected marriage altogether. She herself characterized that agonizing decision thus: "I had to break away. . . . The entire bourgeois life collapsed on top of me, you might say."[43] In 1910 she joined Émile Jaques-Dalcroze's co-educational eurhythmics institute in Hellerau, a utopian planned community. The community at Monte Verità, which became her home when she joined Laban there in 1913, was co-founded by Ida Hoffmann. Hoffmann wrote pamphlets criticizing state and religious marriage, calling for "marriages of conscience," and she advocated women's equality based on both sexes living closer to nature.[44] Laban himself followed Hoffmann's precept of free love.[45]

In 1918, Wigman suffered a breakdown, a period she herself euphemistically refers to as her "nunlike solitude" (partly because her sanatorium was near a nunnery).[46] The breakdown followed a love affair in which she felt she had to choose between her artistic career and marriage. Manning sees this as a turning-point in Wigman's life, noting that she established an important working relationship and friendship with Berthe Trümpy at this juncture and that Wigman

> built her career from this point around mostly female associates. . . . she turned away from the enabling authority of her male mentor and embraced the enabling atmosphere of female collegiality. . . . The trajectory of Wigman's career after 1918 challenged the (heterosexist) duality of gender and staged a utopian vision of female community.[47]

Nuns and witches, both so fascinating to Wigman in this period, are the polar extremes of sisterhoods cloistered from male intruders. Wigman's group dances in the 1920s and 1930s project these sororal visions.

In *Witch Dance*, the solo form itself seems to serve as a vehicle for expressing otherness. The witch is an alien figure, part human and part animal. Her mode of seated locomotion seems inhuman, and her clawing hands are only one of her animal references. Her intensity, her hieratic gestures, and the rhythmic pulse of her movements all suggest a trance-like state, outside of the flow of everyday life, that opens the body to a flood of inhuman forces. She seems to combine the animal, the supernatural, and the foreign in an inventory of otherness. Although she is marked as female, she contravenes conventional female beauty with her distorted face, her coarse black wig, her angular gestures, and her crude open-legged sitting posture, associating her with the earth. The image of the witch here becomes an extreme paradigm of woman as Other.

Wigman refused the marriage plot for her own life and chose to live in a woman-centered world, creating an all-female company and establishing a school in which the majority of staff and students were women. But perhaps this was only possible because at the same time, she returned to Germany, where the situation for women was undergoing rapid change. The political revolution establishing the Weimar Republic also granted women's suffrage. In Germany a "new woman," exercising a greater degree of professional, intellectual, artistic, and sexual freedom, emerged in the 1920s (as she did in other parts of Europe and the United States). Although the rhetoric of the new woman's emancipation far exceeded the real situation of most women, new opportunities had opened up for women like Wigman who chose to live as artists and intellectuals.

Never an active participant in the feminist movement, but certainly benefitting from it, Wigman made early life and career choices that none the less were predicated on the social crises surrounding women's roles in Wilhelmine and Weimar Germany. Her later artistic choices accommodated themselves to the changing role of women in Nazi ideology.[48] But in Wigman's work in the 1920s, the image of the female as outsider – symbolized as much by the lone witch as by the cloistered female community – was key to the ideal of spiritual and artistic regeneration.

With My Red Fires

When in 1936 the American choreographer Doris Humphrey created *With My Red Fires*, the last section of her symphonic epic *New Dance Trilogy*, she confided to critic Walter Terry that the modern dance establishment – including her own dancers – considered her theme of love and marriage to be hopelessly retrograde.[49] Modern dance, at least that made by Humphrey's generation, had been concerned with what the world saw as larger social and political issues, and Humphrey's interest in portraying romantic love appeared to be overly personal, even trivial – a throwback to the days of Denishawn. But Humphrey's social vision permeated her entire *œuvre*, and *With My Red Fires*, about the conflicting claims of love within the family, proved to be as deeply concerned with the politics of community as Humphrey's other dances and those of her generation.

Of her reasons for creating the entire *New Dance Trilogy*, Humphrey wrote, "There was the whole competitive modern world in upheaval; it must be expressed and commented upon and it was too large a theme for fragments and episodes." *New Dance* (1935), the first piece in the trilogy, was an oblique, optimistic response to the alarming rise of both fascist and communist dictatorships in Europe, Asia, and Latin America in the early 1930s. Humphrey said it had to do with the micro-politics of the dance world, as well. With *New Dance*, Humphrey hoped

> to open up to the best of my ability the world as it could be and should be: a modern brotherhood of man. I would not offer nostrums and I could not offer a detailed answer. It was not time for that, but it was time to affirm the fact that there is a brotherhood of man and that the individual has his place within that group.[50]

Unlike Mary Wigman, Martha Graham, Hanya Holm, and other choreographers of her generation who formed all-female dance groups, Humphrey had consciously chosen to work with a gender-integrated group, co-directed by a male colleague, Charles Weidman.[51]

New Dance was an abstract celebration of a utopian community moving from chaos to enlightened organization that resisted regimentation. Humphrey used rhythmic counterpoint, symmetry, and circular forms to express its complex, at times conflicting socio-political structures. In this imagined society, men and women acknowledge their differences, at first dancing in gender-segregated groups, but ultimately they dance together in a non-hierarchical, democratic, cooperative structure. The ensemble is led initially by two benign leaders – a man and a woman. But they are eventually absorbed back into the group, which all the individuals take turns leading.[52] Although choreographed first, *New Dance* was the conclusion to the trilogy, "the joyous blueprint," as dance historian Marcia B. Siegel puts it, that shaped the trilogy's political agenda.[53]

In the satiric and surrealistic *Theatre Piece* (1936), the second part of the trilogy, Humphrey showed why the utopian vision of *New Dance* was called for. Here, as she states, she "[returned] to the theme of life as it is: in business, in sport, in the theater, and in personal relationships."[54] This chaotic world of capitalist conflict, brutality, and alienation – "a grim business of survival by competition"[55] – begged for an alternative. The business world spawned petty dictators; the commercialization of sports distorted the pleasures of athletic bodies; and theater itself became merely an arena for the egotistic rivalry of stars pandering to the audience. One of the evils Humphrey denounced in the dance was the vicious competition among women for men.[56]

Finally, in *With My Red Fires*, the last section of the trilogy, Humphrey writes, she approached "the theme of love, of the relationship of man to woman."[57] But this is not a simple or unencumbered romance, for, tellingly, elsewhere she writes that the dance "deals with love between man and woman, and between two women."[58] Indeed, it is the difficult love between two women – the Matriarch and the Young Woman – that is central to the work. The dance, which had its premiere at the Bennington School of Dance (where Humphrey choreographed and taught during the summers from 1934 to 1941), depicts the Matriarch's destructive, possessive love far more powerfully than it does the romantic coupling between the Young Man and the Young Woman. Their union is simply the catalyst that sets off the Matriarch's devastating rage. And yet, it is that quiet, hopeful young love – what Humphrey termed "creative love"[59] – that triumphs over senseless hatred in the end.

The dance has two sections: "Ritual" and "Drama." In the original program notes, both parts had epigraphs from Chapter 2 of the long poem *Jerusalem* by William Blake. The title of the dance was taken from Blake's lines introducing "Ritual": "For the Divine appearance is Brotherhood, but I am Love,/Elevate into the Region of Brotherhood with my red fires."[60] In *Jerusalem*, these lines are spoken by Vala, a terrifying figure who, in typical Blakean fashion, fuses multiple identities: female will, mother nature, a dragon woman, Eve, the Whore of Babylon, the dark shadow of Jerusalem, and the negative emanation of Albion, as well as the state and the one who presides over war. Vala is a cosmic seductress, betrayer, and destroyer; a spinner of the veil of illusion and entrapment, and she also seems to be the fate Atropos, of classical Greek mythology, whose job it is to cut off the thread of life. Nevertheless, even in Blake, Vala is not some essential feminine quality, for the poet suggests that she can be saved, and in *Jerusalem* there are many women unlike Vala – most notably, Jerusalem herself. But Vala's power is always framed in feminine imagery: birth, weaving, seduction. In Humphrey's epigraph, clearly Vala's words are identified with the Matriarch in *With My Red Fires*, even though the Matriarch does not appear until the second section of the dance.

"Ritual" shows the emergence of the couple from the group. It begins with a choral dance for an enormous ensemble (for modern dance) of forty-four dancers. Humphrey explained this beginning, in a letter to her husband, as "a hymn to Aphrodite, or Priapus or Venus, anyway to the excitement, the greatness, the rapture, the pain of, frustration that is love."[61] Lloyd describes it as "choreographically gorgeous . . . now serried, now dispersed, in the sudden breaks of arrested action, in the broad sweep of its mass effect, like a collective surge of sexual desire," and she remarks, "It was the people's worship of the god of generation, demanding as for a sacrifice a pair of human lovers to represent, by actual consummation, the age-old ritual of mating."[62]

Both Humphrey and the critics speak of primitive rituals in relation to the dance. Humphrey had in the early 1930s choreographed several dances on ancient Greek themes, as filtered through Nietzschean ideas about tragedy and its birth in Dionysian rites. She had made *Dionysiaques*, inspired by ritual sacrifice in Crete, in 1932 and *Orestes*, based on Aeschylus, in 1931.[63] The percussion in *With My Red Fires*, set against dissonant piano notes, marked the dance as modern-primitivist, along the lines of Wigman's dances or *The Rite of Spring* (in Massine's version of which Martha Graham, a Bennington summer school colleague, had danced at the American premiere in 1930). Also reminiscent of *Rite* was the presentation of sexuality as a social imperative – of a collective surrender to libidinal urges that at the time were labeled primitive, not in the anthropological but in the psychoanalytic sense. But despite all this primitivist rhetoric, in *With My Red Fires* the dancers seem more like members of modern mass society – the men with their repetitive bound gestures like regimented factory workers and the women in their full-sleeved red dresses, with their flexed-foot goose-stepping – than like primitive Greek cult members (although, as we have seen, the conflation of primitive man and mass man was present in *Rite* as well). The movements are so abstract they could represent modern assembly-line work as easily as ancient fertility rites.

As men file in on an upstage platform and women enter in clusters and lines downstage, the music, in a minor key, is foreboding.[64] One of the lines of red-clad female celebrants includes a woman in a grey dress – perhaps an unwilling participant. The group moves slowly and deliberately at first, then the women begin jumping and leaping like bacchae. Forced together at first by the mechanistic propulsion of the group, the couple soon become tender lovers. They reach out to one another as four men hold them aloft. Looking at one another, they create a still center in contrast to the incessant movements of the chorus sweeping around them. The lovers embrace at arm's length, and then, set down on the floor, do a dance of mutual discovery that is based on counter-balancing. All the while clasping one another's hands, they bend their knees and lean backwards so far they kneel, hold each other up, lean back against one another, and balance on one leg, tilting precariously away from one another. They often do symmetrical, identical steps, and there is very little division of labor along gender lines. Their clasp seems to signify a relationship built on trust and companionship, rather than on passion, although at one point they separate to do a stylized clap of joy, and their dance builds excitement in leaps and a slow-motion run. The lovers seem divinely human, liberated by love, in contrast to the others, who appear to be not free agents but bound by group will. This is symbolized by the group's rigid bodies, their shuffling or sliding gait, and their hands, which at one point they hold, palms down, awkwardly bent at right angles to their stiff, straight arms. Finally, the lovers are left alone (or, perhaps, they depart to another place) and they nestle together on the floor.

But a summons calls the young woman back to the house of the Matriarch (originally, the summons came from two figures in red; later, it became a beckoning gesture by the Matriarch herself). The young woman runs back to the box that represents a wall of the house and stands with her hand over her eyes, as if to tell her lover "I'm sorry, but I can't see you any more." According to Humphrey, the Matriarch is a perfectly *modern* mother:

> She says it's late and no time for young girls to be lugging around with unknown young men and goodness knows who he might be or what sort of a family he comes from. Come in this moment, your virtue's at stake, the world will say you're a bad girl. You won't? You will do as I say. Sew the seam, mop the floor, walk like me, talk like me, come away from the window.

And yet, even in Humphrey's description, there is a touch of the fairytale step-mother, an image perhaps of the possessive wicked witch in *Rapunzel* who keeps her stepdaughter prisoner and relentlessly hunts her down when she secretly falls in love and elopes. (In fact, John Martin wrote that in Humphrey's performance, the Matriarch "becomes indeed something of a witch out of the minds of the brothers Grimm raised to a kind of cosmic malevolence."[65])

The young man leaves; the Matriarch kneels, mimes beating her chest and wailing, and she slyly looks sideways to see if her daughter is paying attention. The daughter kneels and joins her, weeping and moving identically to her mother. Pointing at the young woman, the Matriarch castigates her. She steps up on a platform and swings her leg, with its voluminous skirt, above and behind the daughter's head in a gesture of domination. She steps down behind her, places an arm over her chest, and moves her back forcibly to lie down with her.

But soon the young man runs back on stage. Like Rapunzel's lover, he helps his bride down from her window; as he carries her away, she reaches back toward home, but he turns her head forward. When the Matriarch awakens, she discovers that her daughter is gone. She stands on a podium to send out an alarm, looking like a demagogue rousing a mob. She claps, like a town crier, and the chorus runs in. She exhorts them to action, and they do little stamping steps in a circle around her pedestal as she rotates her pelvis and shakes her shoulders. All her expression comes from her body, rather than her face, as if she were a masked Greek tragic actor. She steps down from the pedestal, and the dancers, crouching and clenching their fists, form the spokes of a wheel revolving around her. She seems to control their movements, as she repeatedly freezes, pointing or hunching or whirling, and the music and the chorus freezes along with her. It's like a demonic game of "Mother may I."

The formation carries on the theme of causation found in *New Dance*. It symbolizes nonverbally the idea of matriarchy as control (or causation) by the

Plate 14 Doris Humphrey as the Matriarch in *With My Red Fires*, 1938. Photograph by Barbara Morgan. Courtesy of the Morgan Archives.

mother. It also fittingly illustrates the dance's second epigraph from Blake's *Jerusalem*:

> . . . the Great Selfhood, . . .
> Having a white Dot call'd a Center, from which branches out
> A Circle in continual gyrations; this became a Heart
> From which sprang numerous branches varying their motions,
> Producing many Heads, three or seven or ten, and hands and feet
> Innumerable at will of the unfortunate contemplator
> Who becomes his food: such is the way of the Devouring Power.[66]

For Blake the Great Selfhood was connected to Satan, and it is clear in this section of *With My Red Fires* that the Matriarch is no longer a mother angry with her disobedient child, but a blind force of evil bent on violent destruction. The micro-political story of the family has become a macro-political metaphor for society. This was underscored in the filmed 1972 reconstruction of the dance by the American Dance Festival Repertory Company, where the young man (Raymond Johnson) was black and the young woman (Nina Watt) was white. The interracial coupling created a new level of meaning in terms of the Matriarch's enraged disapproval of the match and the lynch-mob's incitement to murderous frenzy, a meaning entirely consonant with the original choreography.

The mob drags the lovers in; they cling to one another. The Matriarch, possessed, shakes her entire body galvanically and batters the couple apart, advancing between them like a clattering military tank, then rolling off stage. The crowd thrashes the couple mercilessly, deriving a strange, bloodthirsty exhilaration from the brutality. They roll the lovers apart, toss them together, and drag them around like inanimate objects. But when the mob finally leaves the pair for dead, the lovers slowly rise, phoenix-like. Once again embracing at arm's length, they take turns leading one another in a circular ascent, mounting the steps to the upstage platform. There they form a transcendent linked pose: facing one another, they clasp arms and lean backwards with chests open and faces heavenward.

Siegel writes that the end of the dance is "curiously Victorian, a turn of events justified by wishful morality that believes in reward for the suffering righteous." She speculates that "perhaps Doris could not resist making it come out this way because of her own desire for justice and her goal of showing that society could be nobler through a faith in love."[67] Yet there is a precedent for this hopeful ending – both its moral content and its iconography – in Blake's pre-Victorian, visionary poetry and his illustrations.

Although Humphrey claimed that she chose the Blake epigraphs only after she had choreographed *With My Red Fires*, so much in the dance seems inspired by *Jerusalem* that it is hard to believe the correspondences are simply coincidental.[68] For instance, in Blake's poem at one point, Jerusalem personified asks why Vala is dressed in black mourning, saying to Vala: "I hear thy shuttles sing in the sky, and round my limbs/I feel the iron threads of love and jealousy and despair." In Blake's illustration to this page, Vala weaves an iron-tight net around Jerusalem's body. Then Vala expels Jerusalem, calling her a "harlot daughter; daughter of despair." And Vala accuses Jerusalem of being "this cause of these shakings of my towers on Euphrates,"[69] a powerful image easy to connect to the Matriarch's thunderous penultimate movement in *With My Red Fires*. The scene in *Jerusalem* in which Vala's "spindle turnd in blood and fire: loud sound the trumpets/of war" also calls to mind the wrath of Humphrey's Matriarch. And as in *With My Red Fires*, in *Jerusalem* after the cataclysms, the powerful villainess disappears. Jerusalem and Albion are reborn, and a City of Art is built. Moreover, even the triumphant arched-back body and heavenward glance of the lovers in *With My Red Fires* is prefigured in several of Blake's illuminations for *Jerusalem*. One is an autobiographical image of Blake himself, painting the border of the page with his wife Catherine; another is the posture of Jerusalem in her embrace with Jehovah at the very end of the poem, which for Blake symbolized a hermaphroditic recuperation of all the divided men and women named in the narrative.[70]

Besides the Blake references, there are other sources for the character of the Matriarch. Some of Humphrey's associates thought the Matriarch in *With My Red Fires* might be based on the choreographer's own mother, who was living at Bennington the summer the dance was made in order to look after Humphrey's son.[71] The character may have also have been influenced by the choreographer's relationship with her mentor, Ruth St. Denis, who had not taken lightly Humphrey's defection from Denishawn in 1928.[72] Or the role of the Matriarch could have had some basis in the choreographer's relationship with Pauline Lawrence, for many years Humphrey's accompanist, company manager, and roommate. Humphrey, of course, had already depicted a violent female fight to the death shortly after leaving Denishawn, in *Life of the Bee* (1929), inspired by the symbolist writer Maurice Maeterlinck's analogies between the social organization of bees and that of humans.[73]

Whatever Humphrey's source or sources for the character, *With My Red Fires* was above all a devastating portrait of a standard cultural stereotype: the domineering woman whose native strength is twisted into malevolence. Raging at her own impotence, envious of others' happiness, and terrified of being left alone, she can only operate by devious manipulation. The Matriarch's unwillingness to let go of her daughter – the desperate intergenerational possessiveness she engages – marks her fury as a "typically" feminine emotion, according to this cliché. Stereotype though it may be, this image of the possessive mother has some basis in experience, for their powerless situation in patriarchal societies has historically stunted many women's opportunities and turned some of them into just such frustrated, angry domestic tyrants. This female type has deep cultural roots in a well-founded anxiety about growing old and being dispossessed in societies where women can own no property and therefore on the death of a husband become totally reliant on their grown children for their welfare.[74] Yet even in more modern societies where women may own property and have more resources for self-reliance, the stereotype (along with real examples of the type) persists.

In *With My Red Fires* Humphrey seemed to say, along with Maeterlinck in *Life of the Bee*, that the passage of generations – no matter how painful for the old ones – ensures social progress, participating in a teleological, perhaps even a social Darwinian movement toward a better future. "Transition is called for from a precarious, egotistic and incomplete life to a life that shall be fraternal, a little more certain, a little more happy," Maeterlinck wrote.[75] The Old Queen in Humphrey's *Life of the Bee* and the Matriarch in *With My Red Fires* are not simply aged. For Humphrey in these dances, old age stands for social and political reactionism.[76]

In *With My Red Fires*, the Matriarch's image is that of as a nagging mother writ large, but also, her very name connotes political power. She stands not only for destructive maternal love and intergenerational strife among women, but for a demagogue of any gender who can inflame a community with hatred so virulent that the group destroys its own. For in the dance, it was the community that had originally brought the young lovers together; now, lashed into frenzy by the Matriarch's venomous rant, the group abandons its own social rituals to punish the pair for following the rules. The model for the character, then, was clearly not only the old typology of the domineering woman that also generated fairytale stepmothers, but also the very real, contemporary succession of rabble-rousing despots whipping up racist and nationalist violence in Germany, Japan, Italy, and, by the summer of 1936 (when the dance was first made), in Spain. As Deborah Jowitt has pointed out regarding the dynamics of the Matriarch in the community in this dance,

> She's a ruler demented by power. . . . You see [the crowd] as craven, blindly obedient bloodhounds on the track, but as the pattern repeats, you begin also to see a mechanical wheel of destruction that this leader is inexorably winding up, one chillingly analogous to that which Adolf Hitler was setting in motion [at the time the dance was made].[77]

Although Humphrey worried about the "political correctness" of making a dance about heterosexual romance, in her dances of this period relationships were never simply personal, but always located within a dense network of social relations. As in so many ballets about love and marriage, this coupling takes place within – in fact, is first created by – the community. Paul Love writes that Humphrey had read Edward Carpenter's *Love Comes of Age*, "which clarified for her the idea of the place of romantic relationship in society," in a fourfold structure: "desire, personal relationship, personal responsibility and relationship to society."[78] But what is different in *With My Red Fires* from the social web depicted in Romantic and Russian Imperial ballet is that the same community that created the couple later tries to destroy them. And unlike the community in

La Sylphide or *The Sleeping Beauty*, this "brotherhood" is not portrayed as benevolent, but as amoral and mechanical. Driven by biological instinct in "Ritual" and by emotional intoxication in "Drama," the crowd exemplifies unthinking reflex action at its nadir. In this sense, the group in *With My Red Fires* is more like the communities in *The Rite of Spring* and *Les Noces*, although in Humphrey's dance it is the community, rather than the marriage, that is seen as terrifying – precisely because the community opposes a good marriage. That is, their desire to marry one another makes this couple outsiders. This bride is modern, but she is not reluctant.[79]

As I stated earlier, the rhetoric surrounding the dance couches it as "primitive," but this was a model of mob psychology – passive and malleable – in modern automatized mass society that was a common explanation at the time for the rise of fascist and communist dictatorship. Mechanized "mass-man" had been a favorite theme of German Expressionist writers in the 1920s, and both Georg Kaiser's dramatic trilogy *Gas* (1917–20) and Fritz Lang's film *Metropolis* (1927) were prescient warnings of where the toxic compound of mass-man and demagogue could lead. The German Expressionist style, as well as its political and social themes, powerfully influenced many leftist and liberal theater and dance artists in the United States in the 1930s. In *With My Red Fires*, not only the use of the mass chorus and regimented movements, but even the set is reminiscent of this trend, for it quotes the renowned and widely copied *Jessnertreppen* – stairs leading up to a back platform – that were the signature of German director Leopold Jessner.

What is striking about Humphrey's appropriation of the mass-man-cum-dictator theme in *With My Red Fires*, however, is that she makes the dictator a woman.[80] Some critics at the time called the dance's plot "trite" and the Matriarch character "melodramatic," even while praising Humphrey's choreography. And yet, if the plot and the character are taken on the macro-political level – that of dictator, mob, and moral triumph – rather than on the micro-political level of a family squabble, they take their places alongside the plots and characters of much biblical, classical, and modern literature. Was it because the leading characters were female and the surface story domestic that Humphrey's ambitions seemed to some only minor?

Humphrey's Matriarch in *With My Red Fires* is neither essentially female nor essentially evil. She is not a *fin-de-siècle femme fatale*, cast by biological destiny into her role. For Humphrey depicted a wide variety of women in her dances, ranging from leaders to victims, from aspects of nature and abstract qualities to workers. In *New Dance Trilogy*, women are democratic leaders as well. It seems never to have occurred to Humphrey – either in her dances or in her own life – that gender might impose restrictions or limitations. Thus, to cast a dictator as a woman, while it may initially appear to buy into the stereotype of the domineering woman, actually lifts her out of her domestic tyranny into the larger sphere of political tyranny. This may be a dubious victory, but it did enlarge the possibilities for female representations.

Humphrey's own life as a wife and working mother were unconventional for her time. In fact, her own birth announcement, written by her father in 1895, already proudly labels her "a new woman."[81] Devoted to her art and her career, Humphrey refused serious relationships with men until, at the age of 36, she married Charles Woodford, a seaman who was away on duty most of the time. For quite some time after her marriage, she continued to share an apartment with her close friend Pauline Lawrence. Pregnant at 38, Humphrey worked the entire term, and she even induced labor early so as not to miss a concert date. Also, she had at least one abortion. For about eight years, her household included her dance partner Charles Weidman, company members Pauline Lawrence and José Limón, as well as her son and – when he was in town – her husband. She was never inclined toward domesticity, and often her colleagues and even her colleagues' relatives helped care for her child, sometimes taking him on trips while Humphrey worked.[82] Her correspondence with her husband makes it clear that she placed their relationship second to her creative life. Most of the time, Woodford respected his wife's artistic mission, but still he sometimes complained – in a tone traditionally used by women to criticize their workaholic husbands – that he seemed to value their marriage more than she did. As Woodford himself pointed out, the relationship, which was at times seriously threatened by these conflicts, probably only survived because he was frequently absent.[83]

In *With My Red Fires*, as I have noted, Humphrey cast her dictator as a woman, just as, in other Bennington premieres, Hanya Holm danced out "the processes of man's survival" in her all-female *Trend* (1937); Anna Sokolow played a Citizen everyman in her all-female denunciation of Italian fascism, *Façade-Esposizione Italiana* (1937); and Martha Graham represented 100 years of American history, from the Indians and Puritans to Declaration of Independence to the emancipation of the slaves, with a group of twenty-two women and one man in *American Document* (1938). Living in a modern dance world dominated by women, these choreographers did not seem think that in making political statements about war and nationality one had to represent gender literally by casting "gender-true." And yet, perhaps for this very reason, they often seemed unaware that gender itself could be a political issue. While they did not usually choreograph dances specifically about women's political or cultural status, their very assumption that the world of the intellect and of artmaking was as available to them as to men was an important contribution to female emancipation. That is, they assumed agency, and they endowed their female characters with agency as a matter of course.

At least two major figures of this generation of modern dancers – Graham and Humphrey – had been raised in families where women dominated the household. At Bennington itself, the Summer School of the Dance had both male and female faculty, but a female director, Martha Hill. The student body at the School of the Dance, averaging 141 from 1934–1939, had an average male population of five (or 3.5 per cent). Since in 1936 the male enrollment surged to eleven, that meant that most years there were fewer than five men.[84] As in

Germany, in the United States the modern dance world of the 1920s and 1930s was predominantly female. Even beyond Bennington but participating in a network formed there, it depended on women's colleges, women's physical education departments and courses at coeducational schools, and middle-class urban women and girls to form both its audiences and its student constituency.[85]

What gave these women their grit? When many of these choreographers began to organize their all-woman groups and made dances with female protagonists in the 1920s and 1930s, the American women's movement had become dormant after the victory of suffrage in 1920. As I noted earlier, these choreographers and dancers were not politically committed feminists. But they had grown up in what historian Ann Douglas calls a "feminized" culture that had not only won women the vote, but also, during the years of the Progressive Era, moral and cultural suasion. While women remained excluded from political and economic life, from the mid-nineteenth century both white and black middle-class women (but usually in racially segregated groups) became active in moral reform crusades, religious movements, alternative healthcare, social work, and campaigns for suffrage and other women's rights. By the turn of the century, women also came to dominate American literature. And by the First World War, women entered the workforce in record numbers. Douglas argues that the break with the Victorian generation of self-styled "matriarchs," or, as Thomas Beer labeled them in *The Mauve Decade*, "Titanesses," constitutes the emergence of modern American culture in the 1920s.[86] The women who matured in the 1920s not only had an older generation of women as models; they had them to rebel against, as well.

Humphrey and Graham were members of an entire generation of white American artists from middle-class or upwardly mobile families – both men and women – rebelling both in their lives and their art, as Douglas sees it, against the "middle-class piety, racial superiority, and sexual repression" of the Victorian Titanesses.[87] Although in literature much of the "matricide" against the tyrannical mothers of the previous, Victorian generation took place in the works of misogynist male writers like Ernest Hemingway and Sidney Howard, still, as Douglas puts it,

> the daughters of the Titaness were as instrumental in overthrowing her as her sons. The modern American women [artists and intellectuals] . . . were at least as eager as their male peers to seize the liberties of adventurous autonomy, creative and rigorous self-expression, sexual experimentation, and full exposure to ethnic and racial diversity, liberties against which the Victorian matriarch had, as her descendants saw it, ruthlessly campaigned.[88]

Salutary in breaking through the barriers of prudery and blind prejudice the Titaness had come to represent, this extreme matriphobic rebellion nevertheless also overlooked the real social and political gains the suffragists and other female organizers of the period made for women.

Like Sophie Treadwell in her play *Machinal* (1928), and later Lillian Hellmann in *The Little Foxes* (1939), in *With My Red Fires*, Humphrey participated in the intergenerational symbolic matricide – the condemnation of the tyrannical and manipulative Victorian matriarch – that began in the 1920s. Humphrey resembled other women of her generation who discovered the pleasures of smoking like a man, loving like a man, and, most importantly, thinking and working like a man.[89]

The maternal melodrama – in which a long-suffering mother sacrifices all for her children – was a staple of literature, theater, and film in the late nineteenth and early twentieth centuries. But the theme of maternal love – whether in its positive or negative aspect – rarely surfaced as central in dance during that period. Mothers certainly populate the ballet stage, from *La Sylphide* to *Swan Lake* and even *Les Noces*. But they are largely incidental characters (a notable exception is the Widow Simone in the Pre-Romantic ballet *La Fille Mal Gardée*, usually played by a man *en travesti*). And their relationships to their children are not a major emotional focus (although, as we have seen, in *Les Noces* there is a brief, poignant scene of maternal grief at the bride's departure).

But as we have also seen, Duncan introduced a positive maternal theme in her dances, expressing the values of the Victorian matriarchs, whose essentialist ethos held motherhood in sacred regard and in all considered women, as Beer puts it, "the more valuable and important half of the race."[90] When in the 1930s Mary Wigman began to portray motherhood in her dances, it was as a sanctified state, as in *Maternal Dance* (1934), part of the cycle *Women's Dances*. Describing *Maternal Dance* (Mütterlicher Tanz), German dance critic Artur Michel writes of "the kindness willing to embrace everything with love; the humility with which the blessedness of material mission is carried out; the power of complete devotion and sacrifice."[91] Consonant with Hitler's view of women's roles as limited to "Kinder, Küche, und Kirche" (children, kitchen, and church), this perspective was criticized in a 1934 dance by the American leftist Nature Friends Group that took the German phrase ironically as its title. In *With My Red Fires*, Humphrey seems almost dialectically to answer Wigman's *Maternal Dance* with a residue of Wigman's own *Witch Dance*, merging the mother's role with that of the fairytale stepmother and the ballet witch to show that motherhood indeed has a dark side.

The issue of the outsider is complex in *With My Red Fires*, and its intricacy complicates the marriage plot, as well. The lovers are at first insiders, but then, upon the Matriarch's urging, they are cast outside the community. The Matriarch, an insider throughout in terms of her power over the entire community, nevertheless is figured as unnatural – an inhuman presence within the human demos. After the Matriarch performs her shattering final dance of destruction, she rolls off the stage as if permanently extricating herself from the community. Thus she seems ultimately to mark herself as a demonic outsider who had wormed her way inside to carry out her annihilation. But in her role as an insider, the Matriarch provokes the community to persecute the lovers – who had originally been selected to represent the community in "Ritual" – and thereby to turn the couple into outsiders. Thus the values of insider/outsider constantly shift in the dance, for insider status is initially endorsed, only to be revealed as dangerous and inhuman. For the lovers to be cast out of the community is finally to regain their humanity. Certainly, this can be seen as a criticism of the racist Nazi rhetoric of community and the folk in the 1930s. But it can also be seen, in gender terms, as an endorsement of nonconformism to societal expectations for women.

Similarly, the marriage plot in *With My Red Fires* is knotty. The community's attitude toward the marriage mutates from euphoric to dysphoric, while the spectator's point of view is just the opposite. That is, we find the forced pairing in the ritual abhorrent, because it is a violation of individual agency. But when the pair seem eventually to become lovers through free choice, we condone their relationship. The Matriarch's disapproval and the community's violent repudiation of the couple only increases our sympathy for the couple. Thus, the dynamic of euphoria/dysphoria represented in the dance creates a conflict within the community that moves the spectator to take a stand. The marriage plot is hooked so closely to the problematic community that it becomes an issue of moral urgency. For if the marriage plot fails, not only will love be disappointed, but in larger political terms, evil will prevail.

Because there are two levels of politics symbolized in the dance – the macro-political theme of the dictator in the community and the micro-political theme of the mother/daughter conflict – the marriage plot's success against all social odds has a double meaning. The triumph of the lovers stands both for freedom from political tyranny and for the rights of children to reject their parents' preferences and select their own marriage partners. That the lovers survive is a moral victory on both counts. But their future will not be entirely unproblematic, for their unconventional choice has cut them off from family and society. Unlike the couple in *The Sleeping Beauty*, the final scene shows the bride and groom alone, bereft of community.

In presenting the mother figure as a vicious outsider, Humphrey may at first glance appear, like her Oak Park, Illinois neighbor and contemporary Ernest Hemingway, to be a misogynist. But in examining the dance closely, it becomes clear that Humphrey's symbolic matricide staged an emancipation for modern women from the Victorian myths and archetypes of holy, suffering, and suffocating motherhood.

Rites de Passage

Five years after *With My Red Fires*, Katherine Dunham also created a dance based on a fertility rite, with a young central couple and a matriarch. But the "Fertility Ritual" section of Dunham's *Rites de Passage* (1941) was an entirely different approach to staging "primitive" ceremony, and it represented a distinctive, Afrocentric vision both of marriage and of the matriarch.[92] Both *With My Red Fires* and *Rites de Passage* were imagined rituals, not pretending to be either specific to one culture or ethnographically accurate. But these dances expressed two completely different cultural worlds, for one dance was inspired by Western romantic ideas about ancient preclassical Greek rites, while the other was rooted in Western ethnographic analyses of African traditions. Moreover, although both women staged a highly personal vision of a polity, Dunham's anthropological training and her fieldwork in matrifocal societies specifically shaped her choreographic representation of community, while Humphrey had a more imaginary view of lost rituals.[93] If in Humphrey's dance, the young couple defied a tyrannical, manipulative mother and an oppressive group – opting for individual choice over the unethical but socially normative – in Dunham's dance, the community is not only a morally benevolent place, but a sacred one, in which women's power is both significant and benign.

Dunham had studied anthropology, first with Robert Redfield as an undergraduate at the University of Chicago and then as a recipient of a Rosenwald Fellowship to study ritual dance in the Caribbean, under the tutelage of Melville Herskovits at Northwestern University. Her interest in social science had from the beginning centered around the role of dance in culture, and all during the time she studied anthropology she was also active as a dance teacher and concert dancer. She organized a short-lived group in Chicago called Ballet Negre and another called the Negro Dance Group. Even before Dunham visited the Caribbean, she had performed a leading role in Euro-American choreographer Ruth Page's staging of Martinique folklore, *La Guiablesse* (1933).[94]

Dunham notes that her dual training gave her an advantage in doing fieldwork. Unlike many other anthropologists, she was able to penetrate an aspect of culture many had ignored or poorly documented, because her own experience as a dancer allowed her to be an active participant-observer in dance events, both sacred and secular. But beyond her training, her ethnic, gender, national, and class identity also gave her a special perspective. As a woman, she had access to a quite separate female culture that most male ethnographers never witnessed, and as an African American, she had an entirely different relationship to Caribbean culture than the Euro-American anthropologists who had trained her. Moreover, as an outsider to Caribbean society – a middle-class American – she was not (or, perhaps, refused to be) constrained either by the French-derived proprieties that kept middle-class and elite Haitian women, for instance, restricted to a private domestic sphere or by the strict caste system that defined a person's status by his or her fraction of African blood – with the lightest-skinned at the top of the socio-economic pyramid and the darkest at the bottom. She claims she could slip fluidly between the roles of insider and outsider in observing the dynamics of these systems. And one of the aspects of Haitian culture she witnessed was that, in the African-derived vaudun cult of spirit possession, black peasant women were not only the majority of participants; they took charge.[95]

On her return from the Caribbean, Dunham began to create electrifying theatrical spectacles that made creative use of ethnographic material in song, dance, costumes, and decor. Searching for an "authentic" African American dance that had not been either cheapened by minstrel show parody or "whitened" through a segregated but syncretic American culture, she had found sources outside the United States that she felt would better capture the movement history of African Americans.[96] Yet, as anthropologist St. Clair Drake has pointed out, Dunham's quest for authenticity had nothing to do with biological or racial essentialism. Rather, she understood the relatedness of African, Afro-Caribbean, and African American dance in the United States as a cultural and historical formation. Indeed, according to Drake, Dunham "struggled continuously to change the widespread belief that black people inherited the ability to dance through their genes, needing no training; . . . culture, not biology, has shaped the black experience."[97] Dunham added ethnographically authentic social and ritual dances from Africa and the black circum-Atlantic to her training in ballet and Central European dance to synthesize her own influential dance technique.[98]

From the beginning, Dunham's aims in discovering the African roots of black America (connected to Herskovits's pioneering research into African retentions in the Americas) and her deepening appreciation for the emerging international ideology of "negritude" (which she initially learned in Haiti) were tied to an integrationist urge, but not an assimilationist one. Her political and artistic practice was a forerunner of today's multicultural aspiration to appreciate the unique history and qualities of each separate ethnic and cultural strand of American culture while still working toward weaving a unified political whole. She staged the dance culture of the black circum-Atlantic with an at times integrated company for integrated audiences – and where audiences were segregated, she refused to perform until blacks were given seats in the white section.[99]

Without a specifically feminist agenda, in her quest for originary movement sources Dunham also unearthed a distinctive social role for African American women – one that had to do with a tradition, with long roots perhaps traceable back to West Africa, of matrifocal family life that has in the past 400 years systematically invested women with far more power than the dominant Euro-American Protestant kinship structure.[100] As well, in her dances she displayed a frank attitude, based on her anthropological research, toward sexuality as an acknowledged and pleasurable part of both sacred and secular African American life that often came in conflict with the Puritan heritage. At times this led to censorship, but more often it served to attract spectators, just as Margaret Mead's account of sexual life in tribal cultures drew readers.

Rites de Passage, first created as a part of a lecture-demonstration on "An Anthropological Approach to Theater" delivered at Yale University, was later absorbed – without the explanatory lecture – into Dunham's theatrical repertory.[101] Performed as a section of *Tropical Revue* on Broadway in 1943 and then on tour, according to Lloyd this dance, along with *Florida Swamp Shimmy*, *Woman With a Cigar*, and the Melanesian-flavored *Rara Tonga*, "sent the critics thumbing through their thesauruses for synonyms of 'torrid.'" Yet, Lloyd pointed out, even though it was the "solemn, sacred" part of the program, *Rites de Passage* was the only item the censor chose to delete from the revue when it arrived in

Boston, accompanied by advance press from impresario Sol Hurok's office that promised audiences a sensual heat wave. "[*Rites de Passage*] was performed with dignity," Lloyd wrote. "But . . . altogether the outward physicality of the work contributed to the sexational build-up that led to the show's success."[102]

Rites de Passage has four sections in variable order, not all of which were always performed: "Puberty"; "Fertility Ritual"; "Death"; and "Women's Mysteries." The program note, replacing the scholarly apparatus of the original lecture, reads:

> This [dance] can best be characterized as the set of rituals surrounding the transition of an individual or group of individuals from one life crisis to another. The ritual period, often at once both sacred and dangerous, is under the guidance of the elders of the community; the entire community joins in this critical transition so that the individual may, in a changed status, have a complete rejoining with the society.
>
> The rites dealt with here do not concern any specific community nor any authentic series of rituals. They were created to try and capture in abstraction the emotional body of any primitive community and to project this intense, even fearful personal experience under the important change in status and the reaction of the society during this period.[103]

Both the title of the dance and the explanation of the ritual process clearly derive from Arnold van Gennep's influential book *Les Rites de passage*.[104] "Puberty" portrays a male initiation ordeal and ceremony, marking the boy's ritual passage to manhood. "Death" depicts a polygynous society in which the wives of the chief attend his funeral. Life must overcome death, and in this section of the dance, the Matriarch oversees "the life cycle continued in the ceremonial ritual of fecundation."[105]

In "Fertility Ritual," the social crisis is concerned with "marriage or mating."[106] This life passage, too, is presided over by the Matriarch. At first the young women of the village mime harvesting grain, while the men play games. Already we can see that women in this culture are essential to the economic life of the community.[107] In order to build both a sense of fear and trembling in the face of the sacred and a rhythm of fecund erotic heat, Dunham uses the choreographic technique of crescendo. The action starts out at an unhurried, almost glacial pace. Women carrying sheaves of grain enter in a slow processional and pause on their arrival in the village center. A man enters and kneels, making pointing and thrusting gestures with his hands toward a maiden who poses, immobile as a statue, left hand on her hip, on a platform upstage. Her akimbo arm evokes West African poses of authority.[108] The Matriarch slowly traverses the stage and gives a signal for the rite to begin.

Three women walk across the platform, punctuating their cortège with sudden turns and pelvic contractions. They assume the maiden's pose as she descends from the platform to answer the young man's call. The other villagers gather around to witness and to echo the sacred ceremony. This is not simply a personal event, but a communal one. And although the individual maiden and man are singled out in this ritual, that the other women assume the central maiden's pose makes it clear that this is not a unique event; on another occasion, another maiden and man will take their place.

The maiden faces her man and begins rocking her pelvis; he responds in synchrony. The couple – the chosen ones – repeatedly move together and apart. They embrace, fall to the floor, lie back to belly clasped like spoons, rise, and come together again. Now he jumps, falls to the floor, and then pursues her in a large circuit around the stage. He catches her and somersaults her over his shoulder. Increasing their tempo, they face one another as they move from side to side. In another burst of acrobatic virtuosity, he lifts and turns her, and then they separate to whirl on their own. The tempo insistently rises to a peak of excitement, creating an aura of cosmic compulsion. The community divides into gender groups that circle the man and woman, then regroups into couples imitating the actions of the central couple. Finally, the maiden and the young man run up to the rear platform, where he lifts her in a concluding, emphatic phallic formation.

Here was an imagined fertility ritual, in the tradition of *The Rite of Spring*, but one with anthropologically respectable footnotes. Still, audiences, critics, and the Boston censor saw it as risqué. Of *Rites de Passage*, John Martin wrote, "Its movement is markedly uninhibited, and certainly it is nothing to take grandma to see, but it is an excellent piece of work."[109]

As both Lloyd and Drake remind us, the sexual meanings of Dunham's dances varied according to the eye and mind of the beholder. Drake notes that this had a cultural-ethnic component:

> The deep strain of Puritanism in American life that tended to turn sexuality into prurient interest was a constraint that serious black performers had to break through. By means of skilled choreography, Katherine Dunham was able to convey to her audiences that sexuality as expressed in some aspects of African and New World black tradition has symbolic meanings relevant to fertility as well as to sexual satisfaction, and that ostensibly erotic dancing can be cherished for the sheer joy of the bodily movement and display of dancing skill.[110]

Dunham herself repeatedly tried to educate critics and audiences about the social meaning of pelvic movements in African and Caribbean dance. Although Lloyd had written that in *Tropical Revue* "the pelvic girdles . . . [seemed] to be made of melted lastex," she was ultimately convinced, explaining to her readers (albeit in the primitivist rhetoric of the day) that "African movement is pelvic movement, natural and unself-conscious. It becomes erotic on the stages of civilization."[111]

Rites de Passage was often presented as part of a dance evening that included

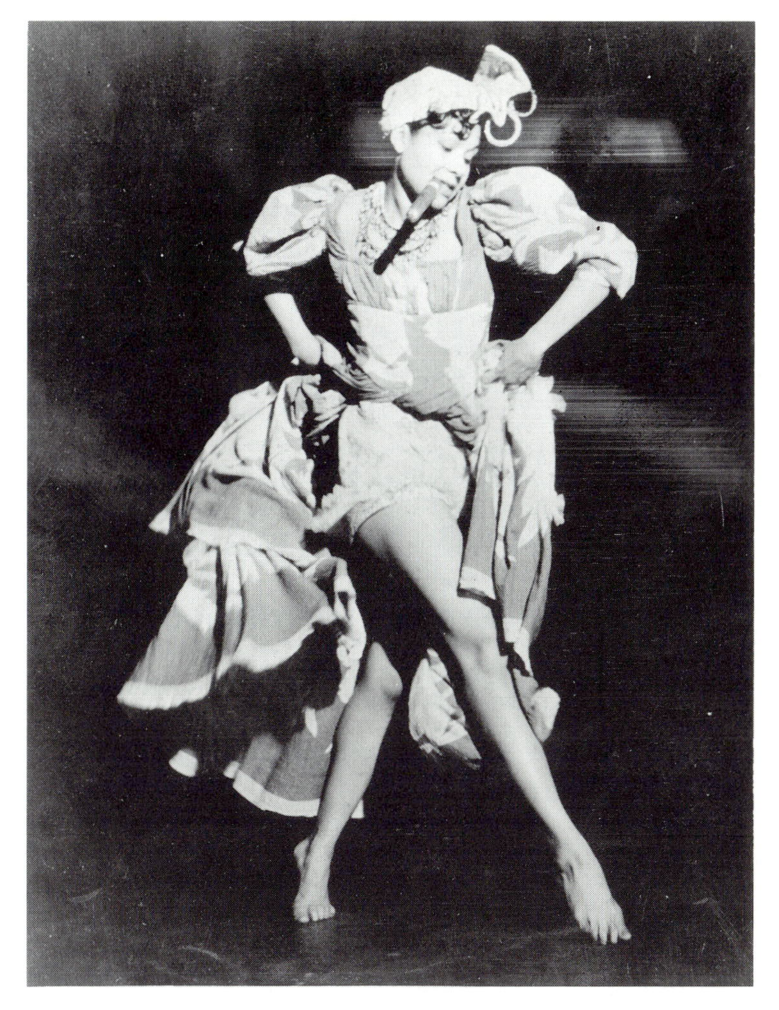

Plate 15 Katherine Dunham as the Woman with the Cigar, from *Tropical Revue*. Courtesy of the Dance Collection, The New York Public Library for the Performing Arts, Astor, Lenox and Tilden Foundations.

Haitian, Cuban, and Brazilian ritual and social dances, as well as southern U.S. plantation dances, bringing an ethnographic kaleidoscope of the choreography of the black circum-Atlantic diaspora to white and black audiences.[112] Like Ruth St. Denis a generation earlier, Dunham flirted with exoticism by presenting sacred and social dance material from other cultures as entertainment on the American popular and concert dance stage. Both Dunham and St. Denis drew on even earlier traditions of staging ethnicity for European and American audiences, from the European international expositions of the nineteenth century to the 1893 Columbian Exposition in Chicago.[113] (In fact, when she attended the University of Chicago, Dunham became part of an avant-garde artists' community housed in buildings on the nearby Midway that had originally been constructed for the Exposition's ethnic pavilions. The Cube Theater Club, a racially integrated student organization through which Dunham met other African American artists, including actor Canada Lee, writer Langston Hughes, and musician W.C. Handy, occupied one of these buildings. Ballet choreographers Ruth Page and Mark Turbyfill, who taught Dunham and encouraged her to choreograph, worked in another.[114]) And Dunham herself staged a dance for seven women at the 1934 Chicago World's Fair.[115]

But despite the spectacular entertainment values of Dunham's performances, as early as the 1940s some critics understood Dunham's work as ethnographic "publication," albeit in a non-book format. James Gray wrote, in the *St. Paul Pioneer Press*, "Katherine Dunham, in her most serious compositions has made skillful and beautiful dramatizations of just such materials as anthropologists like Bronislaw Malinowski and Margaret Mead have analyzed in their sober books."[116] Although Dunham, like Malinowski and Mead, might analyze sexual practices in other cultures, the anthropological lens was meant to provide scientific objectivity. In presenting her dances as a method of anthropological research, Dunham signaled her desire to distance herself from earlier, overtly colonialist forms of staging the "primitive" at fairgrounds and dime museums.[117] And she also distanced herself from "exotic" dancing in the contemporary sense – that is, lascivious dancing in nightclubs. She told dance critic Walter Terry, "I spent almost two years in the West Indies studying and recording the fundamental emotions of primitive people as expressed in their dances. I taught these dances to my company. We have never thought of them as sexy – and in Europe they understand what we are trying to do. We were not regarded [in Europe] as entertainers – but as artists."[118] But she stressed her scholarship as much as her artistry. She told Albert Elias, "In America, where there is a basic national reticence toward sex, you meet some people who do not see how my show can have intellectual content if they also find in it sensuality."[119]

Although she disdained the work of earlier black entertainers in the minstrel show and vaudeville traditions (according to Beckford, Dunham first wanted to show white audiences that blacks had progressed beyond the *Blackbirds* "period of development"), Dunham worked as easily in popular entertainment venues as in concert settings.[120] According to Drake, "Katherine Dunham did not reject those distinctive aspects of black life that have entertainment value when presented on the stage. Rather, through intelligent choreography and careful attention to costume and setting, she transformed every performance into an edifying, anthropological statement as well as an enjoyable, often exciting, experience."[121] Besides presenting her dances in clubs and theaters, she worked in musicals like *Pins and Needles* (1939) and *Cabin in the Sky* (1940, co-choreographed with George Balanchine), and in Hollywood films like *Star Spangled Rhythm* (1942), *Stormy Weather* (1943), and *Casbah* (1948). Her own choreography is featured in the short Warner Brothers film *Carnival of Rhythm* (1939).

In *Carnival of Rhythm*, a Brazilian fruit vendor (Dunham), who is like a magnet for men, falls in love with a dockworker (Archie Savage). The brief narrative frames four songs and dances from the Dunham repertory, some performed as part of her *Brazilian Suite*: *Ciudad Maravillosa*, *Los Indios*, *Batucada*, and *Adeus Terras*.[122] As a single day progresses, the fruitseller and her lover dance several dances of mutual seduction, then he goes off to work with the other men while the women wait at the market. Throughout the film, the beautiful fruitseller, carrying a basket of fruit on her head, bares her shoulders, smiles, switches her hips invitingly, and picks up her voluminous skirts and petticoats to show off her legs. At one point, the man lassoes her with a rope and reels her toward him; they dance together, the rope circling her waist (*Batucada*). After the workers return at sunset, singing a traditional slave lament for the lost homeland of Africa (*Adeus Terras*), there is a general dance. Later, as the rhythms of the day and the dance heat up to the beat of African drums, the fruitseller falls to the floor, arching her back and moving as if possessed – either by African spirits or by passion. Finally, the fruitseller and her man walk off together in the dusk to spend an evening of love.[123]

Although the women Katherine Dunham portrayed on stage and in film might langorously await their men, her own life was quite different – independent and very daring for a woman at the time. She opened a dance studio while still in college. In her twenties, she traveled alone throughout the Caribbean to do her fieldwork, and she never hesitated to attend a ceremony or other event in pursuit of anthropological knowledge, even where there was personal risk involved. Her love life, too, was unconventional. She writes, about her initiation as a *hounci* (which was considered a "marriage" to the loa, or Afro-Haitian god):

> At the time of my wedding to Damballa I was already married, though hardly mature enough of spirit to realize it, to someone who would perhaps rather remain anonymous; I felt myself in love with a dear friend who might also rather remain anonymous; I was smitten with one or more college professors, fascinated by Dumarsais Estimé [a personal friend who later became president of Haiti] and engaged in more ways than one to Fred Alsop [a British car mechanic living in Haiti]. Seen now after time and distance, I realize that this might be considered peculiar, but then, one condition seemed to have nothing to do with the others, and marrying Damballa was an added experience to a life that I have always hoped returned a good part of the richness it received. But I could not take fully into account the significance of this pact believed by some to be more magic than religious. In none of my affections have I been so punished for infidelity as by my Haitian serpent god.[124]

Later, Dunham met and married John Pratt, a Euro-American designer who became the costume and set designer for her company. She ran her own dance company and, from 1945–55, her own school in New York, for which her husband served as Consulting Director. In other words, *he* worked behind the scenes to further *her* public career. She was no fruitseller waiting passively for her man to come home, but more like the Woman with a Cigar she also often portrayed – a woman who was not afraid to take on men's roles in the public sphere.

Yet Dunham seems to have created a deliberately ambivalent public image of herself as simultaneously an intellectual and a sex goddess, as if to be only a scholar might undermine her characters' femininity, but also as if to remind the public that sexual attractiveness and intelligence in a woman are not mutually exclusive. So many writers referred to this split image that one suspects Dunham's own publicity machine may have been the source. For instance, Lloyd remarked, "The brown beauty who could address a Yale graduate class on anthropology in horn-rimmed spectacles, now [in *Rara Tonga*, part of *Tropical Revue*] wore a pearl in her navel."[125] Other articles posed the question as to whether she was "cool scientist or sultry performer?"[126] *Newsweek* traced her trajectory from "torridity to anthropology," and *Ebony* named her "the schoolmarm who glorified leg art."[127] Walter Terry called her the "sexiest anthropologist in the world."[128] But Lloyd concluded that despite the promises of sultry passion, Dunham was "too refined for her milieu. Torrid indeed! . . . This was just a very good looking American girl playing primitive," although some of the company members "made up for it" by dancing up a storm.[129]

The erotic "heat" of Dunham's performances during this period may lead us now to see her representations of women as seductive or "merely" sexual. But given the history of women's expressions of their sexuality in the theatre and the history of representations of African American women on stage, it seems more accurate to see Dunham's women as a complex admixture of qualities, constrained by contemporary attitudes. That a beautiful black woman could be celebrated as a glamorous, sexually attractive person holding center stage, alluring precisely because of her vigor and power, and asserting control in sexual relationships, was a triumph for Dunham's generation, if not for ours. However, Dunham had to go abroad, to the Caribbean and Latin America, for the source material to create these images of glamour and sexual power. Her African American women were rarely women you might meet on the street in New York or Atlanta (at least, at that time), but rather, Afro-Caribbean or Afro-Brazilian women, whose Latin spice was perfectly compatible with the roughly contemporary Hollywood craze for Carmen Miranda and Rita Hayworth.

This was a generation that had grown up in a culture still permeated with minstrel-show stereotypes of the mammy and Jezebel, two widespread popular images of African American women that were equally denigrating and that, as K. Sue Jewell notes, "portray African American women as the antithesis of the American conception of beauty, femininity, and womanhood."[130] Enacted earlier on the minstrel-show stage by men, these character types filtered theatrical images of African American women through the grotesque.

Hollywood added new images of black women as domestic servants. Whether servile or smart-alecky, they were still socially inferior. When white women or women of color expressed their sexuality on stage, in the U.S. it was generally on the burlesque stage for working-class audiences or the cabaret stage for monied spectators (for instance, at the Cotton Club). These performances, usually for a predominantly male audience, tended to take place in economic situations that exploited and objectified the female performer and her sexuality for profit by male entrepreneurs. Moreover, these performances were marked by the dominant culture as tawdry.[131]

But, like Josephine Baker, working in Paris in the 1920s, Dunham portrayed women, and black women in particular, as sexual subjects with individual dignity, rather than as sexual objects. If Dunham often danced the role of a temptress, like St. Denis she drained that role of biblical evil, acknowledging sexuality as part and parcel of biological, social, and ritual life.

And Dunham's women were not only sexual beings. In her portrayals of ritual and social life, they were queens, matriarchs, and religious leaders, as well as ordinary peasants and working women. Even if she had to import her exotic images from those parts of the African diaspora outside the United States, Dunham recuperated the theatrical construction of African American women, presciently declaring by her actions that "black is beautiful."

Night Journey

Martha Graham choreographed *Night Journey* in 1947, during the decade of her most productive years as an artist and some of the most turbulent years in her private life. In the year *Night Journey* was made, it seemed her already rocky relationship with Erick Hawkins might break up over his infidelity and their artistic competition. In 1948, at age 54, Graham finally married Hawkins, her first male dance partner and her lover for over a decade.[132] But although they had lived together for eight years, Graham later wrote, soon after they married their relationship fell apart. "Never try to hold on to anything," she concludes in her autobiography.[133] Hawkins had replaced Louis Horst, ten years Graham's senior, in the choreographer's affections, and although Graham loved many men during her life, Hawkins was the only one she ever married. That the middle-aged, independent Graham – who until the 1940s had always been primarily devoted to her work – was now in love and contemplating marriage to a man fifteen years her junior influenced many of her dances during this period. But her personal situation must especially have shaped her interpretation of the Oedipus myth in *Night Journey*. She created the role of the tortured, remorseful Jocasta for herself and that of Oedipus, Jocasta's husband-son, for Hawkins, her own young husband-to-be.

In *Night Journey*, Graham – creating not only in the gloom of her stormy private life, but, perhaps more importantly, in the shadow of Freud and the Oedipus complex – takes a completely different view of the myth than does

Sophocles in his classic tragedy. To begin with, and perhaps most significantly, Graham retells the myth from the woman's point of view. This enlarges Jocasta's part in the story, but it also changes the content. For what is stressed here about the incestuous relationship between King Oedipus and his wife-mother is their sexual passion. Graham makes space in this dance for something that Freud forgot in his analysis of the Oedipus complex: women's sexual pleasure. That is, what is highlighted in *Night Journey* is not the son's desire, but the mother's.

Moreover, the relationship of both Jocasta and Oedipus to public life and the state, stressed in Sophocles, almost completely disappears in *Night Journey*. This intensely private, erotic perspective modernizes and feminizes the myth just as much as does the new centrality of Jocasta's role in the tragedy. Sophocles describes a world that includes the polis Thebes, populated by its cursed rulers and its suffering citizens; here, a secluded world of intimate feelings – in particular, feelings of sexual love and despair over love's failure – emerges in sharp relief. Graham's is a world of sensibility, of heart-felt secret emotions that in the dominant modern, individualistic WASP culture of the United States in the late 1940s was often considered women's domain.

The dance, as Agnes de Mille has crisply characterized it, exudes "unrelieved misery."[134] Graham called it "an instant of agony."[135] Yet the dance, however bitter, is also a celebration of mature female sexuality. The action of Sophocles' play is rewritten, compressed into thirty minutes, and enacted as an interior drama – a flashback at the moment just before Jocasta's death. The dance opens with Jocasta contemplating a rope.[136] It is a prop that not only serves as her death weapon, but also symbolizes the umbilical cord and therefore, as Graham later wrote, "the symbol of her crime against civilization and life."[137] Also, later in the dance (that is, earlier in the story) the rope stands for the bonds of passion. At this initial moment, Jocasta, holding this rope aloft, sways as if already dangling from its noose. Although by the end of the dance, it becomes clear that at the outset she is still contemplating her death, this motion at the beginning suggests that her fate has long since been sealed.

The set, by Isamu Noguchi, consists of furniture that looks as if it's made from bones: pedestals and a rigid bed comprised of abstract male and female figures. Jowitt describes it as "a torture rack" (popular imagery at the time for the primitive and the barbaric), and de Mille bluntly writes that "Jocasta and Oedipus rolling on top of this couple presented the appearance of stacked cadavers in a concentration camp."[138]

The blind seer Tiresias enters, and, thrusting his oversized stick through the triangle formed by the rope, draws the rope out of Jocasta's hands. Thus the retelling of this tragedy of *eros* begins with a sexual image. Jocasta raises her hand to her face in shame and despair. She falls to the floor, and a chorus of women enters, crouched over in pain. These women – replacing Sophocles' chorus of (male) citizens of Thebes – seem at times to be Jocasta's own thoughts as they make cryptic gestures that imply sorrow and regret, but also solace. That they so often place their hands over their mouths seems to literalize the "unspeakable" nature of this marriage. Graham describes them as "furies, daughters of the night, . . . the terrors we all have. They must be recognized and lived through until they leave your mind."[139] The chorus leader mirrors Jocasta's movements as she turns from side to side, her hand to her forehead, as if desperately trying, while equally intensely fearing, to remember the events of her life. Jocasta lies down, huddled at the foot of the bed, while the chorus implores Tiresias. He is implacable, and finally Jocasta rises to dance her solo of remembrance, as the chorus exits and Tiresias looks on.

In a movement saturated with double meaning, Jocasta kneels and tilts her torso backward, as if surrendering herself both to destiny and to sexual intercourse. She then stands, kicking one leg high above her head. Graham writes, "I call this the vaginal cry; it is the cry from her vagina. It is either the cry for her lover, her husband, or the cry for her children."[140] Jocasta crosses her hands over her groin – a gesture ambiguously suggesting both shame and the recollection of sexual ecstasy. Every time she gestures over her groin, she falls, turning this into *her* tragedy rather than Oedipus', by literalizing the tragic flaw of her sexual error, which led to her downfall. She recoils when she bumps up again the bed, but later crouches over it, performing a kind of physical incantation at what Siegel calls one of the "landmarks of her anguish."[141] She paces through the space, seemingly remembering (as we later see) Oedipus' entry into her life, and she thrice clasps her breasts and groin. She runs to and fro frenziedly, her hand over her mouth in horror. Finally, she returns to the bed and stops. The churning music becomes peaceful. She kisses the male side of the bed, then lies down on the female side, resembling nothing so much as a psychoanalytic patient on the couch, ready to delve into the depths of the unconscious in order to dredge up painful, ancient buried memories. The reference to the popularity of Freudian and Jungian psychoanalysis in the 1940s is unmistakable.

And this is what she remembers: the way Oedipus seduced her, domesticated her, and awakened her to sexual pleasure. He enters, lifts Jocasta from the bed, and carries her like a prize doll on his shoulder to deposit her on a pedestal, while the chorus protests. This is not a marriage the community can condone, and yet Jocasta ignores their signs of disapproval. Oedipus dances for her – a muscle-flexing, heroic celebration of self[142] – while she sits and watches, using two branches he has given her to indicate her own indecision. She wavers between resistance and sexual acquiescence, now holding the branches crossed over her chest, now opening them low at her sides like spread legs. At one point, he stands behind her and possessively hooks one leg over her torso. She tries to stand up, but he pushes her back down with his foot, then leans down to kiss her on the mouth, towering over her as she leans back. Then he resumes his dance. She points the branch at him, and her pelvis contracts in a sexual quiver. Returning to her, he pitches forward until his face is in her lap. He is a completely domineering, even brutal, suitor, and she passively receives him, becoming excited almost despite herself.

Jocasta rises to perform a solo of acquiescence. It is full of deferential bows and sinuous, angular, but ultra-feminine gestures. Her movements with the branches resemble a flirtatious, pseudo-oriental fan-dance, as she keeps her eyes downcast.[143] She dances out her hesitation as well as her surrender. After all, she is a queen taken as a prize by a conqueror. She does a hip-swinging walk, whirls around, then leans toward him until she falls forward, totally prostrating herself at his feet. Here she signals that she belongs entirely to him. Then she gets up, moves the branches and opens her knee teasingly in a game of peekaboo, sits on the pedestal, tilts her head knowingly, and looks at him. Now she seems to say that this is all a game, and that the reins of seduction are in her hands. She stands up, only to fall prostrate again, her face to the floor. Graham quite explicitly writes, of the peekaboo movement of branches and knee, "she is inviting him into the privacy of her body. . . . It is not only a movement, but rather a gesture of invitation for him to come between her legs."[144] But given the alternation of this invitation with the gestures and postures of prostration, Jocasta seems to be seducing Oedipus in the most self-abasing, submissive way imaginable.

Oedipus approaches Jocasta, wraps her in his cape, and helps her to rise. Thus is their marriage sealed. In what seems like a brief wedding ceremony, an exchanging of vows, he takes one of her branches, and they walk toward the bed in a stately, high-kicking lock step, stopping to embellish their walk in a ceremonial way. Once again, she falls, although this time only as far as her knees, and she leans over obsequiously to let him stand over her, one foot on her shoulder, pressing her down into the floor. He seems to be housebreaking her; she is literally brought low by her new husband, as part of the marriage ceremony itself. Graham defines this section "as the marriage procession where the man and the woman acknowledge to the world their great commitment, which is that of the king and the queen."[145] But it also seems clear that both are making a commitment to a particular shape this marriage and consortship will have: the young king's dominance over his aging, yielding queen.

Strikingly, unlike the weddings in nineteenth-century ballet, although there is a community in the dance, they have absented themselves from witnessing the marriage vows. In *Night Journey*, unlike the classical Oedipus myth, one almost begins to feel that incest could happen not because fate had preordained it, but because these people, ignoring the advice of family and society, living in a private world of their own passionate making, chose their own mates. But also unlike *With My Red Fires*, here the rebel couple, defying the community's advice regarding the unsuitability of their marriage, proves to be fatally wrong.

The next section moves the couple from public ceremony (however lacking in witnesses) to private passion. It is surely one of the frankest choreographic expressions of coitus in the Western canon. Oedipus and Jocasta walk toward the bed, but they are overcome by lust. Even before they reach the bed, they begin to make love. She sinks to the floor and lies flat on her back. Apparently Laius, her first husband, favored the missionary position. And it seems, at this point, to be all Jocasta knows. But Oedipus will expand her sexual repertoire. He slowly falls forward on top of her, rises to beat his chest as she weakly reaches an arm up toward him, then returns to fall on top of her again.

But suddenly she stands and, seeming to change her mind, runs away from him in fright. He pursues her, grabbing first one breast, then another, from behind. He picks her up and swings her around, and then she yields, clasping him in a position that is both erotic and suggestive of childbirth. This moment moves her toward more decisiveness and more desire, and she pulls him back down to the floor. They tenderly kiss and lie still for a while, then both stand to do a symmetrical dance of pleasure. In a gesture that seems to be either an unconscious recognition of their blood relationship or a sudden opening up to her own erotic possibilities, Jocasta falls into reverie, touches her own breast, and then takes Oedipus into her arms to cradle him softly, as the music turns from strident dissonance to a gentle melody.

And now their mutual love inspires them. Holding tightly onto Oedipus' hand, Jocasta falls backward – a swoon of passion, and/or the instant of her tragic downfall – but he pulls her back up to standing. She steps onto his thighs to sit facing him, cross-legged, in his lap; their coupling moves into what sex instruction videos of the 1990s would call "advanced lovemaking techniques." In this *Kama Sutra* "lotus-like" position, they nuzzle, and then, still joined to him at the hip, she leans back to hang upside down. He whirls her around, then raises her back up to the lotus-like position once again, as he crouches and she strokes his head. Next he lifts her high up above his head, then he puts her down facing him. As they remain locked in an embrace, he slowly walks forward, guiding her backwards to the bed.

The chorus enters, covering their eyes and rocking forward in pain as Oedipus sees the rope and ties it around Jocasta. It is a multivalent symbol, standing simultaneously for "super-advanced" sex with sado-masochistic overtones, the umbilical cord they once shared, and the inexorable tightening of the web that binds their lives closer together at this new juncture in their tragic destiny. As the music switches once again to a dissonant, anxious theme, the chorus moves agitatedly in the foreground, weeping, jumping, and falling, as the pair moves into different poses, with the rope, on the bed.

Now the narrative rushes to its denouement. As the tension in both the music and the dance of the chorus rises, Oedipus and Jocasta roll off the bed, holding onto the ends of the rope. They separate, moving as far apart from one another as the length of the rope will allow. They swiftly run back together, leaping into their most advanced sexual pose. Finally, they stand frozen, hopelessly enmeshed in the tangled rope. The end comes quickly, as the music reaches to a climax. Tiresias enters and "tells" the truth of the incestuous marriage in a terrifying solo. Moving behind them to stand on the bed, he dramatically touches the rope with his stick, and they let go of it, falling to the ground.

Tiresias exits. Jocasta rises to dash around the space, taking high kicks in a gesture of pain, frustration, and understanding. She lies down on the bed in her

Plate 16 Martha Graham as Jocasta and Erick Hawkins as Oedipus in *Night Journey*. Courtesy of the Dance Collection, The New York Public Library for the Performing Arts, Astor, Lenox and Tilden Foundations.

original position. Oedipus, too, rises, untangles himself from the rope and throws it on the ground, then steps on the bed. He falls along the arms of the chorus to the floor, where he does his own dance of recognition, shielding his eyes both in anticipation of his punishment and in the realization that up to now he has been blind to his own situation. He steps up onto the bed again, falls onto Jocasta as he had when they first made love, and then grasps her brooch, piercing his eyes by fastening it, mask-like, onto them, and stumbles away.

Jocasta stands. The flashback has ended; we have now returned in time to the moment just before the dance began. She passes her hand over the bed, remembering. Then she walks toward the rope, slips off her royal robe to reveal a simple sheath, picks up the rope, and in a single stroke circles and tightens it around her neck. As she falls, she repeats her descent and pelvic rise from the beginning of the dance; it is her death throe as well as her last orgasm. Tiresias passes through like a curtain ending the drama, his stick sounding a death knell.

As I noted earlier, one important change from the Sophocles version is that sexual passion here becomes the crux of the relationship between Oedipus and Jocasta. They have no family life, no children, no relatives, as they do in Sophocles, nor do they share a public life. All they have together is sex – on the floor, in bed, walking, and indeed, wherever and whenever they can. There is a trace of the Sleeping Beauty plot (though certainly not the ballet) in *Night Journey*, for Graham tells the story as one of sexual awakening. Jocasta lies passive and inert in her bed, waiting for Oedipus to rouse her.

In terms of the narrative of the outsider, *Night Journey* is complex. Jocasta is the ultimate insider – she is, after all, Queen of Thebes. But she becomes a rebel in Graham's version of the myth, because she refuses the community's warnings that she should not marry Oedipus. (Sophocles' play, of course, opens long after they have married and implies that the community approved the match.) In *Night Journey*, Jocasta marries for passion, not for "convenience" (with all that entails for a monarch), even at the risk of social ostracism – and, though she could not have known this at the time – her own death. She is also a nonconformist in her sexual adventurousness. But she is not a rebel in one important realm – for she is totally submissive to her husband.

Several commentators have observed that Graham's choreography above all disclosed the conflict between sexual pleasure and puritanical repression. Nowhere in Graham's *œuvre* is this psychological and cultural warfare more poignantly articulated than in *Night Journey*. The heights of Jocasta's sexual ecstasy are matched only by the torment of her guilt. While her incestuous marriage gave her good reason to regret her sexual choice, she is the extreme metaphor for the profound ambivalence that women in Graham dances generally feel toward their sexual desires.

The bride in Graham's earlier *Appalachian Spring* (1944) is more virginal than Jocasta, but she looks forward with both joy and fear – just as Jocasta looks back in combined pleasure and horror – to her first sexual stirring. We see that in the bride's solo, when her closed gestures and mincing steps turn into dreams of flight and openness. Yet, like Oedipus, the Husbandman in *Appalachian Spring* dominates his bride, often encircling her and enclosing her space. Her sexual discovery, it seems, will lead to her domestication, just as she and her husband, pioneering on the land, will tame it. And there are other dangers, as well, that sexual knowledge will bring, for the bride mimes rocking a baby – a sign not only of joy but of life-threatening childbirth and of all the responsibilities and anxieties of motherhood.

In both dances, the woman often becomes passive and immobile when touched by her man. He may lift or carry her, but when he does so, unlike in classical ballet, his support rarely helps her to fly or to take movement risks. Rather, she remains still and rigid, like a doll. Although she desires her man, she seems to fear sexual commitment, for it is when she dances her solos, her interior monologues, that she is most active and alive. That is, she is most open, most luxuriating in space when she dances alone.

Both *Appalachian Spring* and *Night Journey* were choreographed in Graham's mature years. As Siegel points out, these domesticated images of women – brides kowtowing to their men and daring to claim only small, restricted spaces – contrast strongly with Graham's earlier dances for her all-woman group or her own earlier strong solos. "Whether she is dominating space or embracing it, the woman in *Frontier* sees space as her element. . . . She surveys the distance fearlessly," Siegel writes. "To me, *Frontier* is about openness; *Appalachian Spring* is about enclosure." And, she continues, the Bride in *Appalachian Spring* "seems greatly diminished in power and initiative from the women in *Frontier* and *Primitive Mysteries* . . . Graham's central [female] characters seem to have become more dependent."[146]

Was Graham a feminist? Had she become, in these later dances, a feminist who had lapsed, as dance historian Marianne Goldberg suggests regarding Graham's 1984 *Rite of Spring*?[147] Graham had grown up independent-minded in a predominantly female household with a commuting father who treated her like a son. She proudly considered herself "wild," flouted conventional morality by having many love affairs, and was deeply attached to Horst, an older married man, for over thirty years. She also defied her generation's expectations for women by choosing a career over marriage and children, and in the 1930s she created strong images of women, performed by a dance company full of powerful female dancers. Even after she fell in love with Hawkins, took him and then more men into the company, and finally agreed to marry, she insisted on keeping her own name (and she wore a black dress to her own wedding).[148]

Yet Graham herself admits that she became subservient to her husband, despite her better judgement, and de Mille remarks that Graham was in danger of willingly losing her own identity in the relationship with Hawkins.[149] The failure of her short-lived marriage sent Graham into deep despondency and alcoholism. In *Night Journey* she seems to articulate with both wonder and regret her own sense of sexual dependency. Her partnership with Horst, apparently more of an intellectual than a physically passionate love affair, allowed her to prosper as an autonomous individual, even though there was an element of paternalism in their at times student–teacher relationship. The dances she made after falling in love with Hawkins depict a woman struggling against the desire to submerge herself in her lover. Of *Errand into the Maze* (1947), Siegel writes,

> Once again [the protagonist] battles a male who is limiting her freedom to operate, and for Graham I think that threat always implies seduction. It isn't the man's physical strength she fears. . . . What terrifies her is the man's sexual attraction and the knowledge that yielding to it will put her in a subordinate position. The loss of her own power represents an ultimate humiliation to her.[150]

Although she lived her life as if she possessed every right that men enjoyed, and although she made women the subject of her dances, certainly Graham never identified herself as a feminist. An individualist to the last, she writes that she never could understand the need for women's liberation as a political movement, for "I have never felt competition [with other women]. . . . I never had the feeling that I was inferior . . . and I always got whatever I wanted from men without asking."[151] She may never have experienced those feelings personally, but she empathized well, and she created characters who did. The jealous Medea in *Cave of the Heart* (1946), for instance, is the very embodiment of female competition. And Jocasta's pathetic sexual dependency certainly makes her servile. Siegel claims that Graham, in representing a female fear of male sexual domination, "anticipated some of the most radical feminist ideas of a generation later."[152] Yet there are different political as well as apolitical angles from which to express these anxieties, and Graham's perspective, stressing victimization without analyzing it, does not necessarily make her a feminist. One might see her sympathy for Jocasta as an apparent acceptance of the "perennial" conflict between male domination and female acquiescence. "False consciousness," to borrow the Marxist term, could operate here to substitute pity (or even consent) for a desire to change the status quo.

She presents herself as naturally "liberated," without the benefit of political feminism, yet Graham's attitudes toward women in both her writings and her dances often tell a different story. She muses that women are more violent than men. "I know that in a woman, like a lioness, is the urge to kill if she cannot have what she wants. . . . She is more ruthless than any man." And, Graham asserts, there are three basic types present in all women: the virgin, the temptress-prostitute, and the mother.[153] Her stereotypes fall neatly into line with those of patriarchal culture.

In her dances, Graham seems to understand and document the multiple, often contradictory aspects of women's lives – their strength, their dependency, their wisdom, their innocence, their sexual desires, their fears. Even Graham's views of older women are ambivalent. The malevolent Ancestress in *Dark Meadow* (1946) and the kindly Pioneer Woman in *Appalachian Spring* are both based, she writes, on her great-grandmother.[154] So often her strong women are devious, her sexually aware women horribly dependent. Buffeted by their emotional entanglements, her women tend to lose control. They are at their best – their strongest – when, like the woman in *Frontier* (1935), they have no heterosexual relationship. In this way, Graham in her dances turns out to be surprisingly male-identified. That is, her heroines are like addicts where men are concerned – fine as long as there are no men around the house, but hopelessly lost if they show up.

The shift in Graham's female characters from the autonomous females of the 1920s and 1930s to the domesticated women of the late 1940s did not, of course, only have personal origins. It was enmeshed in complex ways in broader cultural shifts, as well. Graham's own view of women was a psychological, not a political one – not surprisingly for a woman who came of age intellectually in New York in the 1920s. The political struggle for women's rights had by then waned, and personal sexual "emancipation," rather than a collective feminist movement, was the order of the day for middle-class women. Graham's generation, armed with psychoanalytic, social scientific, and medical studies, rebelled against Victorian mores partly by asserting women's sexual appetite. As historian Rochelle Gatlin puts it, "'Liberation' for young women [in the 1920s] no longer meant feminism, but rather sexual gratification and personal fulfillment. Movies demonstrated the new priority of attracting men, and girls became anxious about their popularity with the opposite sex."[155] But the acknowledgement of female sexuality that burst into public life in the 1920s had another effect. As the curtains of repression parted and sexuality itself emerged from the locked bedroom, a separate Victorian world of female intimacy was eroded by the "normalization" of heterosexuality and marriage. Quoting Mary Ryan, Gatlin asserts that "the bonds between women were replaced by . . . a 'heterosexual imperative.' This, in turn, 'fostered a degree of distrust and competition between women such as had never been seen before.'"[156]

As women increasingly entered the job market in the 1920s and therefore had less economic need to marry, a new discourse about "companionate marriage" – one that stressed equality and sexual satisfaction for both partners – arose. Under the new ideological regime, the marriage rate swelled, despite middle-class women's rising educational success. A backlash against independent women was the result, as historian Nancy Cott argues, of a fear of deviant female eroticism emerging from the new sexual ideology as well as new economic and social opportunities for women. Both men and women feared "the specter of women on their own, satisfied with and by each other" and experienced "cultural anxiety about the potential for women's escape from men's control."[157] Graham, Humphrey, and their contemporaries – so many of whom ran all-female dance groups and refused conventional marriages – were precisely the kind of independent, successful modern women pursuing careers in the arts, science, sports, and other professions who stirred up this demonizing anxiety about female autonomy.

But by the postwar years, Graham seems to have fallen in step with the "feminine mystique" that celebrated men's return from the war and promised to send women home from the labor force.[158] Gatlin points out that in 1947 (the year *Night Journey* was made), fashion designer Christian Dior inaugurated a "New Look" for women, "replacing the austere androgyny of wartime slacks with an ultra-feminine design shaped like an inverted flower, with a tight waist and flared skirt."[159] Also in the same year, psychologists Ferdinand Lundberg and Marynia Farnham wrote, in *Modern Woman: The Lost Sex*, that an "independent woman" was a "contradiction in terms."[160] These were but two aspects of a conservative postwar gender and sexual ideology, especially prevalent in the United States, that suggested that homosexuals were politically suspect and that feminism as well as state-funded childcare were part of a communist conspiracy to destroy the American family. The rate of women attending universities had fallen considerably since the 1920s. Although after 1945 women actually entered the workforce in greater numbers than ever, their generally lower-paid jobs were increasingly in the service, teaching, and other "feminized" labor sectors, and most women primarily defined themselves in terms of their domestic, rather than career, roles. In other words, "the feminine mystique followed them into the workplace."[161]

Thus, *Night Journey* is a complex product of Graham's sexual politics. It retains traces of her generation's sexual emancipation in the 1920s while buying into the postwar feminine mystique by tying its submissive heroine to a domineering male. Its frank female eroticism is one step forward for womankind – acknowledging women's libidinal desires (including their taboo sexual feelings toward their children) and exalting their amatory education. But nevertheless, the dance also takes two steps backwards, undermining its sexually liberatory aspect with its gender hierarchy and its emotional extremes. And ultimately its message is conservative: Jocasta's erotic enthusiasm was a tragic mistake, for it only signaled her doom.

6

MODERN BALLET

Jardin aux Lilas, A Wedding Bouquet, Rodeo, Agon

Diaghilev died in 1929, Anna Pavlova in 1931. Eschewing Diaghilev's modernism (though she danced in his early seasons) and inspired by Isadora Duncan, the dancer Pavlova opted for a repertoire composed largely of the ballet classics and of short ballets (many by Ivan Clustine) with unexceptional, even sentimental choreography; often they pictured her as a graceful part of nature, like *California Poppy*. Her head often canting flirtatiously, her body snuggling into itself (like the swans with which she was forever associated after dancing Fokine's *Dying Swan* in 1907), she created an image of the ballerina as lyrical, childlike, and ultrafeminine. But the choreography did not survive.

Still, Pavlova's company, like Diaghilev's, had toured throughout the world, building audiences for ballet, recruiting more dancers, and inspiring future dancers, especially female dancers. In the 1930s, the international roster of dancers and choreographers formerly associated with these Russian emigré companies scattered across Europe and America, as those who had passed through these companies had done before them, and these individuals in their turn trained a new generation.

George Balanchine, a Soviet emigré who had joined Diaghilev in 1924, opened the School of American Ballet in 1933 in New York, where with Lincoln Kirstein he ran a series of small companies and eventually built a home base in the New York City Ballet. Two Diaghilev dancers, Marie Rambert (born in Poland) and Ninette de Valois (born in Ireland), created the basis for British ballet with their schools and small companies. Although the choreography of neither of these women survives, their real contributions came in two important ways. First, they mentored other choreographers. Both were involved in the training of Frederick Ashton, and Rambert, who had a gift for discovering choreographic talent, produced the work of Antony Tudor as well as Andrée Howard, Walter Gore, Frank Staff, and others. Second, the companies they founded flourished and formed the basis of contemporary British ballet. Ballet Rambert continues to be the premier experimental ballet and modern dance company in Britain, and de Valois' company became the Royal Ballet, since 1946 the resident company of Covent Garden and an important repository of the classical tradition. The English ballet as it was formed in the 1930s through the efforts of these two women was in many respects a descendant of the Russian ballet. Not only were Rambert and de Valois alumni of Diaghilev's Ballets Russes, but audiences were formed by the regular London seasons of Diaghilev's company and that of Pavlova, who had settled in London in 1912 and formed a company largely of British dancers. Yet, in an assertion of national identity, the new generation of British ballet dancers created a unique style distinguished by its clarity, graciousness, restraint, and gentle wit.

Before the 1930s, ballet in the United States had largely (though not exclusively) consisted of touring European companies and European teachers. Starting in the 1930s, however, American ballet began to define itself in opposition to the dominance of the Ballets Russes and its successor companies. As in Europe, this initiative was framed in terms of national identity. Lincoln Kirstein, one of the patrons and founders of the New York City Ballet, proposed an agenda for building a truly American ballet, but, ironically, it was Kirstein's recruitment of the Russian choreographer George Balanchine that in large part transformed the classical Russian technique into an American style, for American women's bodies. The other first-rank, long-lasting American ballet institution, eventually known as American Ballet Theatre, also had its origins in Russian ballet, but soon established three wings: Russian, British, and American. It hired Agnes de Mille, the sole female choreographer to flourish in modern ballet. De Mille, an American who had studied ballet in California, went to Rambert in London for training and returned to the United States to join the newly-established American Ballet Theatre.

Nijinska formed her own company in 1932 and worked as a peripatetic choreographer in Europe and South America, settling in California in 1938, where she opened a school, and choreographing for various companies, including the Ballet Russe de Monte Carlo and American Ballet Theatre. But her works from this period did not survive.

Thus, unlike in modern dance, which had begun as a women's arena in terms of making dances, the leading choreographers for the ballet stage continued to be men (with the exception of de Mille). And yet, despite Diaghilev's efforts to put men center stage, ballet – not only in the United States and Europe, but internationally – to this day remains an art form culturally identified with women. Young girls flock to ballet classes; boys need to be enticed there with scholarships and break-dancing classes. Women throng to see ballet performances; they drag their husbands along with them.[1] And during the post-Diaghilev period, when ballet became an internationally entrenched art once again (as it had been during the Romantic era), the marriage plot continued to dominate the ballet stage. The modern marriage plot – like that of the Romantic era – brought with it the complications of romantic triangles.

Jardin aux Lilas

Antony Tudor's *Jardin aux Lilas* (known in the U.S. as *Lilac Garden*), originally a chamber ballet choreographed for the tiny stage of the Mercury Theatre and performed by Ballet Rambert in 1936, takes place on the eve of an Edwardian marriage of convenience, in which, as Kirstein puts it, "human emotion is reduced to negotiable commodity."[2] According to Cyril Beaumont, Tudor had originally been inspired by a Finnish story by Aino Kallas, about a peasant couple. They are about to be married when the landowner "announces his intention of exercising his *droit de seigneur.* The bride goes to fulfil the law but armed with a dagger."[3] In translating the theme to an entirely different era, culture, and class, Tudor created a heroine who may be just as passionate as Kallas's, but who ultimately suppresses her resistance, choosing instead to accept the painful status quo. But this narrative transcends the individual story of one woman's acquiescence and suffering. Critic Robert Lawrence writes: "The ballet advances not only the wreckage of two pairs of lives, but the emptiness of a whole social system that demands the marriage of convenience."[4]

At a party for the wedding couple, in a moonlit garden redolent with lilacs (the theater was sprayed with scent just before the opening night performance[5]), four characters – Caroline (the Bride-to-Be), The Man She Loves, The Man She Must Marry, and An Episode in His Past – dance out a fraught web of clandestine meetings, warning glances, stolen embraces, and stifled emotional volleys. Caroline tries to kiss her lover in a final farewell, but is repeatedly interrupted by the passage through the garden of party guests. Her resigned exit on the rigid arm of The Man She Must Marry, as she clutches her memories (in the form of a spray of lilacs her lover has handed her), seals her unhappy fate.

The choreography weaves a tight, knotted story of love repressed. Here, marriage resembles a death sentence, and the choice of a marriage partner, while not explicitly denied to Caroline, is nevertheless unhappily molded by economic necessity in a strict class society where a woman too refined to work must sell herself to a narrow, cold man in order to survive. Dance critic Jack Anderson ruminates on Caroline's situation:

> Affluence restricts, rather than liberates, [the ballet's characters]. Denying affection, Caroline must enter upon a marriage of convenience, probably so that she will have enough money to keep up social appearances. Propriety forbids her from going to the extreme of earning money as a shopgirl or waitress, and she probably lacks the skills necessary for such jobs, even should she decide to assert heself. Similarly, she is probably ill equipped to become a teacher or librarian, even though these are at least genteel occupations. Consequently, she marries a man she does not love.[6]

Why can't she marry her lover? Perhaps he is not well enough established; he seems much younger than Caroline's coldly avuncular fiancé. Or perhaps, as dance critic Clive Barnes suggests, the lover is already married.[7]

Although the ballet's actions are about repressing feelings and keeping up appearances, the music – Chausson's *Poème* – is anything but restrained. It is lushly romantic, ironically underscoring the lovers' losses. Tudor's biographer Judith Chazin-Bennahum calls it "a long-drawn sigh for all things irrecoverable and unobtainable."[8]

The ballet is a keen observation of social protocols and their stultifying effects on human passion. Through gesture, glance, floorplan, and the literalization of movement metaphors (as when the fiancé's aggressive former mistress "throws herself" at him), Tudor layers seemingly formal dance patterns with both social and psychological meaning. Kirstein notes that

> private feelings are submerged in the public decorum of social dancing, although spasms of true emotion momentarily betray tensions below a smooth surface. Conventional custom, the crushing presence of friends smother a show for natural sentiment. . . . Always, in this overscented garden, the exterior world looms – censorious, relentless.[9]

Indeed, the very title – in French, rather than English – accentuates the theme of social artifice.[10] And dance critic Edwin Denby has remarked that Tudor here emphasizes the upper-class carriage of the body, already an element of the traditional ballet posture, in order to signal the characters' excessive, even pathological self-control:

> He purposely exaggerates the constraint of ballet carriage; the dancers dance rigidly, hastily, with dead arms – as beginners might. But the ballet constraint they show portrays the mental constraints of the characters in the story, who rigidly follow an upper-class convention of behavior. Artificial upper-class constraint is the theme and the pathos of *Lilac Garden*.[11]

Of course, choreography in general involves variations among solo, duet, and group formations. But Tudor gives those structures thematic and dramatic significance, as well as formal meaning. When a solo becomes a duet, loneliness has been assuaged and love regained; when a duet becomes a trio, love has to be hidden or a romantic triangle is established; when the entire group is on stage, society has subsumed individual feelings. Thus, even though it might be somewhat tedious to read a blow-by-blow description of the ballet, I think it is worthwhile to examine the entire composition of the ballet, to see how the solos, duets, trios, quartets, and group dances form and dissolve, and to analyze how meaning emerges from these formal designs.

Over and over again, as one or the other pair of furtive lovers finds a moment of intimacy together in the garden, society – in the form of the party guests –

sweeps through and presses them into its unyielding patterns. The first moment of the ballet graphically etches the bleak situation through the use of small, subtle gestures that both reveal psychological detail and serve as literal metaphors for situations: Caroline and her fiancé stand alone in the garden, in a pose that could serve for a wedding portrait of the perfect Edwardian couple. He looms behind her, but there is no physical contact between them. Caroline stands erect with one arm crossing behind her back to grasp her other arm, forming a flesh-and-blood corset – as if to "hold herself together" as silently and discreetly as possible during this impossibly difficult event. But her self-constructed "corset" also suggests the cage this marriage will be for her. Caroline slowly moves her hand down her arm; the gesture reads like a shudder. Simultaneously, her fiancé turns away from her, looking off stage. Thus, the couple-to-be's first movements in fact separate them. The inauspicious nature of this marriage is already imprinted choreographically on the protagonists' bodies.[12]

Her lover enters, and Caroline moves toward him, but signals him to leave. Then, turning back to her fiancé, Caroline holds out her arm. He takes her arm, but closes it across her waist to complete the image of the restricting corset-cage. Next, Caroline takes his arm, promenades on pointe (as if "rising to the occasion"), and gestures supplicatingly to him, but he once again restrains her. Every time she opens her body, metaphorically opening herself emotionally to him, he signals his refusal to respond, literally and bodily putting her in her place. Tudor describes the character thus: "He's a bossy sort of character. If he turns his head, it's almost with a disapproval of everything that's going on around him. And if he looks at her, it's because she belongs to him. And if he takes her, it's a possessive hand."[13] Caroline exits with her fiancé, glancing back longingly at the garden. The opening scene establishes not only the coldness of this relationship, but also how both members of the couple-to-be feel split between two choices. Every change of direction of the head or body comes to symbolize, in concrete physical terms, that internal conflict.

After this initial establishing scene, the rest of the ballet unfolds in a series of brief passages, punctuated by constant, rushed entrances and exits. The community that has gathered to ratify Caroline's marriage begins to appear, filling out the social context. But one character – the husband-to-be's former mistress – fits into the social milieu only uneasily. There is no proper social role for her at this party, just as there is no polite role for her in society; she is neither virgin, nor bride, nor matron. (In contrast, even Caroline's lover has a defined social role: he is a military officer.)

The mistress and Caroline's lover arrive in the garden simultaneously from opposite sides. Both search for their loved ones. The mistress's movements are assertive. Her upstretched arm contrasts strongly with Caroline's arms, which tend to enclose her body softly. Suddenly these two partnerless guests, so intent on those who are absent, notice one another. The mistress offers the lover her hand to kiss, but as he leans over to do so, she makes a primping gesture that simultaneously appears to be a sign of contempt and looks over his shoulder for her own lover. She smiles and nods curtly and turns away; he runs off in the opposite direction, as more women guests pass swiftly through the garden and vanish. Caroline, who has followed the group of women into the garden, innocently greets the mistress. The latter rebuffs her dismissively. The two face one another, as if in a stand-off, and then abruptly the mistress turns and leaves – slowly and ceremoniously, walking on pointe and waving one arm at her side, as if to regain her dignity.

Now Caroline's lover reappears, and the pair dances a private duet, interrupted by signals of secrecy and furtive glances. In a way, the structure of the rest of the ballet is nothing more than this duet – constantly interrupted by the entrances and actions of other characters – persevering in fits and starts throughout the evening. Indeed, the lovers' attempt to continue their duet despite all odds is partly the theme of the ballet. The intimacy of the lovers is literalized in the closeness of their bodies as they dance, as well as the responsive handclasps that Caroline's fiancé had denied her. Unlike the stiff, formal portrait of the bridal couple, the first image of the lovers together consists of an embrace. He, too, stands behind Caroline, but he holds her close to him so that the surfaces of their bodies are touching. At one point in their duet, Caroline raises her arm vertically in a gesture similar to the mistress's, and her lover, in a twist on the earlier "caging" gesture of the fiancé, closes it tenderly across her chest. The two walk a few steps, then dance in close synchrony, warmly touching one another's hands and waists. Caroline rises onto pointe – here an image of ecstasy, in contrast to the stiff, proper pointework with her fiancé – and later runs forward with her head thrown back, one arm stretching back to hold hands with her lover keeping pace behind her. In this impassioned duet, Caroline's backbends – as opposed to the stiffly correct carriage of all the characters, including Caroline, elsewhere in the ballet – signal rapture and "natural" emotion, while the lovers' embraces and easy harmony suggest the depth of their intimacy.

But their duet is interrupted by the entrance of the mistress. Now the three dance together side by side. The stiff unison movement and the hands grasping one another's upper arms here connotes not familiarity, but "keeping in line" with social protocols. It is as if convention has taught them what to do in awkward social situations, and they work hard at remembering. Yet as the trio progresses, with small turns and constant changes of direction, the way the lovers look at one another, touch when the mistress's back is turned, or withdraw upstage, all make this section seems to be two dances in one – a secret duet nested inside a trio. Suddenly two male guests enter and leap through the threesome, taking the mistress and the lover off stage with them.

Caroline is left alone. She continues to turn repeatedly, but now dizzily, on pointe, holding her hand to her forehead as if in a melodramatic swoon. She has let her emotional turmoil come to the surface. And her instability is framed in choreographic terms. She dances a desperate solo, abruptly changing levels as she rises on pointe and comes back to the ground. She moves both head and body to face first one side, then the other, as if torn between her two men even in their absence. Her arms, usually held demurely down at her sides, suddenly become alive, reaching upward and outward as if in search of an answer. Her long party dress swirls around her, literalizing the eddies of emotion that buffet her, and the music rises in volume and speed, signalling her frenzy. Suddenly, both male and female guests run swiftly through the garden, and Caroline moves her hands slowly down her body, as if to restrain her feelings. She dampens her movements, as well. But when the guests rush off, she pirouettes despairingly – dangerously off-center – and, as the wrenching violin solo reaches a climax, her lover runs in just in time – miraculously – to catch her. The perfect timing seems to signal that this pair is "made for each other." He supports her in arabesque and kisses her neck ardently, then, after she checks to make sure no one's coming, he lifts her up high, and they kneel down together. But, hearing guests approaching, they glance quickly in all directions, and Caroline stands up and runs away, hiding her face with her hand.

Now society, in the form of the other guests, re-enters and reincorporates the lovers. They must – literally – take their places in the group dance. Three couples and a woman enter, and the lover joins the single woman to form a fourth couple. The pairs dance in gendered lines, using the movement motifs from the previous solos, duets, and trio. Reconfigured here as components of a formal dance pattern, and repeated by all the couples in unison, those previously charged movements become drained of their prior emotional meaning. So the dancers turn, kneel, extend their arms, and clasp hands and waists, and the women go up on point and arabesque. They also curve their arms to place one hand on top of their heads, a gesture hitherto unseen, that points to a future moment in the dance. It all looks simply like an elegant ballroom dance. Caroline re-enters and dances down the alley formed by the couples; she is unseen by the dancing couples, for the lines of men and women momentarily face away from one another. This dance figure is an inversion of so many ballet wedding dances that celebrate the wedding couple's union with a London Bridge formation of incorporation. Here the other couples turn their backs to the center alley as Caroline rushes through it alone and exits the stage. The backwards pattern symbolizes that Caroline's marriage is all wrong, and her invisibility signals her loneliness and sense of outsiderhood.

The fiancé's mistress enters the garden as the other guests begin to leave. She leaps and turns, preoccupied in her own soliloquy. A young man, also an officer, approaches her, but she aggressively and tauntingly rejects him, advancing on him in a threatening manner until he runs off stage. Now the garden witnesses a duet for the fiancé and his mistress, parallel but dissimilar to that for Caroline and her lover. The Episode in His Past repeatedly throws herself at the fiancé with her arm thrust straight up. It is a phallic gesture, but one that in this ballet stands for a woman's assertive passion. Although he consistently rejects her, she keeps begging him to reconsider. At first she seems happy to be alone with her ex-lover, but as he makes clear his ultimate rebuff, she "puts on an appearance," arranging her face with an artificial, determined smile. He also lifts her and kisses her neck (as Caroline's lover had done to his partner), but coldly, as if against his will. Everything about him seems to be repressed. Maude Lloyd, the first Caroline, remembers Tudor dancing the role of the Man She Must Marry as "stern, knowing exactly this is the moment when I discard my mistress, it's time I had a wife. And he wanted a wife who was obviously pure and unsullied."[14] But he is as rigid with his mistress as he is with his wife-to-be. The mistress coerces him into partnering her, taking the lead in their dance by touching him, forcing him to catch her when she jumps at him, embracing him, and pulling him toward her.

Others enter the garden; once again, society sweeps in to reincorporate those who stray. The dance lays out the roving individuals' social roles, and they are obliged to join the pattern. The dancing pairs form a tight circle, strengthening the image of inclusion and assimilation. Now all four lovers are on stage at once. Caroline must dance with the Man She Must Marry, which only leaves their erstwhile lovers one another for partners. The bridal couple's dancing with their "proper" partners in another sense compels all four protagonists to dance with the "wrong" partners.[15] That is, socially their pairings are correct, but emotionally they are misarranged.

Once again, Caroline and her lover are left alone for a fervent duet. It is as if their earlier duet had never been interrupted; the music's intensity swells, and the lovers' physical passion escalates accordingly. They hold one another close, moving together in absolute synchrony. They turn, sway, repeatedly run apart, then rush together. Their partnering has a strong feeling of mutuality. Her lover holds Caroline tightly and turns her upside down, while she curves her arm over her head to touch her forehead in a symbol of ecstasy. He kneels to kiss Caroline's hand.

But just then, two woman guests enter.[16] One woman smirks with scandal-mongering amusement at the situation, as Caroline shields her face with her hand. Another woman (a character called Caroline's sister in the original production, but later simply a party guest) silences the gossip. The sister figure both restrains Caroline and comforts her. Holding hands, the two become like twins, dipping back and stepping forward in unison with stiff backs. They become as if pressed into a single board, a mechanism for conformity, run by the force of social proprieties. Caroline abruptly breaks from the mold, collapses forward, and lifts her hands to her face, about to sob in an outburst of frustration. Stopping her, her sister takes hold of Caroline's hands and places them back at her sides, as if to remind her to "keep a stiff upper lip." The two women dance in circles around the space, holding out an arm each in a gesture of sympathy.

Her lover enters, and Caroline leaves, but the other women remain, and a third woman joins them. The women surround the man comfortingly. Suddenly, they point to the sky – they seem to notice a shooting star, and all four clasp their hands beseechingly, as if to make a wish upon the star for a better life. The women retreat, forming a circle upstage, as the cadet dances his soliloquy of turns and gestures signifying longing and sadness, ending with a meditative pose reminiscent of Rodin's *Thinker*, or perhaps of a conventional theatrical gesture of deep sorrow.

Soon Caroline returns, the women leave, and the lovers' duet resumes with increased ardor, desperation, and tenderness. They balance together, she in arabesque on pointe, and he in an attitude on demi-pointe. He turns her, lifts her above his head, and lowers her slowly into an embrace. But just as they're about to kiss, the lovers suddenly turn their heads, as if startled by a noise. They rush apart, return, and rush away again, all the while looking longingly at one another. They embrace again, but again look away, alert. They part, clasping hands as they leave one another, as Caroline's fiancé enters; Caroline, putting on a smile, goes to him and they exit, while her lover leaves in the other direction. And now the mistress enters and dances an arm-thrusting, turning, leaping solo reminding us of Caroline's earlier despondent soliloquy. The mistress, too, pirouettes. But no one is there to catch her; she must balance on her own, and she seems in this dance momentarily to accept that fate.

The guests waltz through the garden. At first Caroline and her fiancé dance together, almost tenderly. The correct social pattern seems to have locked into place. But then Caroline dances away, the mistress enters, only to leave again, and the Man is suddenly left alone. It seems he may have lost both women in his life. He searches for them both, while the dance carries on. Now once again, the couples become reconfigured; the "proper" bridal pair has been dissolved, while the "naturally right" partners re-connect. And the "real duet" resumes.

Caroline and her lover enter, seizing a moment when the garden has emptied. They turn, holding their hands to their brows, he lifts her, they leap together agitatedly – as the churning music reflects their turbulence, and they run off stage. The guests dance through, and the mistress once again throws herself again at the fiancé, forcing him to lift her. He does so, but then "puts her behind him." Returning to the fiancé to stand back-to-back with him, the mistress grasps his arms with hers, locking elbows together, then turns around quickly to face him defiantly. They hold hands to join the group dance. As the music reaches a crescendo, the dancers' movements densely criss-cross the stage. Caroline and her lover run back and forth through the garden upstage, in back of all the action. Turning, the fiancé and his mistress glimpse them. Everything now seems to have been revealed. As the mistress confronts the fiancé, Caroline runs to him and throws herself at him with the same desperation the mistress had earlier shown. He lifts her, and she swoons in his arms.

The action of the entire group freezes, as the lushly romantic music plays on. It is as if time had come to a standstill. Caroline alone gradually comes to life, slowly stepping out toward the group, and extends her hand like a sleepwalker or someone in a trance. She reaches toward her lover. Kirstein muses that this moment is the "grand crisis" of the ballet, for Caroline suddenly seems "almost free to act against a choice already made."[17] But then, as if a film were being run in retrograde, she reverses her action, running backwards slowly to resume her swoon. "This is all done, obviously, only in her mind," comments Maude Lloyd.[18] She has made her choice, to go through with the marriage.

Now the whole group comes back to life. The four main characters line up as if for a formal group portrait, forming two couples that are socially correct – Caroline and The Man She Must Marry, and the two publicly "unattached" guests. The other guests leave, pacing off stage. All seems to have been resolved. But desire still lingers. The "proper" couple and the "other" couple – their lovers – dance a pas de quatre. Formed of two couples, the dance keeps threatening to re-form into a different, "natural," emotionally "right" set of pairs, and all four still seem inextricably linked, as the two triangles overlap. When the women, for instance, reach back with their arms while their partners turn them in one direction and then the reverse, first one and then the other seems to be reaching out longingly to her lover to invite him to partner her instead. Both couples do identical steps, but the lack of emotional glue in the partnering leaves each pair lackluster. The glances and the vectors of feeling do not circulate within each couple, but rather, travel across pairs. Both women gesture helplessly, at an impasse.

But then the sister enters, announcing the end of the party. After Caroline's fiancé exits momentarily, her lover thrusts a spray of lilacs into her hands and hurries away. Then the fiancé returns with Caroline's cloak, putting it on her shoulders with a patronizing gesture. Caroline waves goodbye to all the guests (including the mistress, who turns away). Her last, lingering goodbye gesture is to her lover. She reaches out to him, but her fiancé once again closes her arm over her waist, as if locking the cage shut forever. He tucks her hand possessively in the crook of his elbow and they walk away. The lover, left alone, reaches out after them, then forlornly turns his back. The lights dim.

As several commentators have pointed out, this is an "anteroom" ballet, concerned with what might be called the "off stage behavior" of the party guests.[19] If the unseen house is the site for the party's public face of decorum, the garden is the locale for revealing the troubled emotional depths behind deceptively calm social surfaces. And yet, the garden is not entirely a private place, safe for personal revelations. Rather, it is the staging area, where the protagonists move between public and private roles, individualized emotions and social necessities, and where the tensions between those poles poignantly culminate. That is, in a poetic inversion of stage conventions, what is literally off stage in this ballet (the house, the main action of the party) serves metaphorically to represent the masked performance of social conventions, while what is literally on stage (the garden) represents society's backstage dressing room, not precisely a site where masks can be permanently doffed, but rather, where they are removed only to be adjusted or repaired.

There is also a poetic blurring of the usual connotations of indoors and out-of-doors, for the garden may be wilder than the house, a place where "natural" feeling can well up, but it is nevertheless cultivated, perfumed, and claustrophobic. It stands for the secret, extremely interiorized spaces of the heart, as opposed to

Plate 17 Hugh Laing as The Man She Loves, Peggy Van Praagh as An Episode in His Past, Antony Tudor as The Man She Must Marry, and Maude Lloyd as Caroline in *Jardin aux Lilas*. Photograph by Malcolm Dunbar. Courtesy of the Ballet Rambert Archives.

the externalized realm of social behavior in the unseen house. Thus Tudor creates an acute sense of the world being "not as it should be," by deliberately throwing into confusion the social and psychological meanings of inside and outside, private and public. During those moments when the party spills out of the house into the garden, it is as if a second ballet – the one taking place inside the house, about the correct social life of these people – were reaching out into the garden (that is, deep *inside* the psyches of the protagonists) so as to retrieve the errant characters and restore the social order.

Formally speaking, the constant repetition of entrances and exits heightens the metaphor of drama and theatricality. But stylistically, the emotional drama of the situation is understated, even stifled, precisely delineating the repressed social mores of the characters' social class.[20] As critic Peter Williams puts it, "[the] choreography is muted . . . , a nervous whisper; even some of the more violent lifts pass quickly as if they should not have happened."[21]

Barnes has pointed out that the action of the ballet is like a footnote. It takes place after the real story of these people's lives has, in a way, ended.[22] The relationship that is about to begin is barren. The relationships based on love and passion are ending. The party that, celebrating a wedding, should signify fertile new beginnings, is in reality a dull conclusion to a life. And the image of lilacs, heralds of spring, is ironic, for emotionally this is the winter of Caroline's life. The crucial life-bearing symbol of *The Sleeping Beauty* is inverted here.

Performed in Edwardian costume, the ballet is set in the time of the mothers of the original spectators. Agnes de Mille points out that the women in this ballet looked utterly different from the classical ballerinas in tutus whom audiences had come to see as abstract female figures far removed from daily life. Although Diaghilev's company had earlier performed modern-dress ballets, by 1936 British audiences had once again become used to the classics:

> It was Antony Tudor who first put his women in long dresses, the Edwardian dresses his mother wore. . . . The effect was startling and a real shock to the imagination. The audience was called upon to accept the balletic gesture as a form of simple dramatic communication.

But more of a shock, she notes, was the sexual meaning that emerged from the ballet, once it was dressed in the previous generation's clothing:

> [The audience] was also asked to watch women who looked like their mothers and aunts kicking over their heads or wrapping their legs around men's bodies. The beauty of gesture cauterized the connotations at first, it seemed, but soon their full significance became apparent. We had been, we discovered, speaking quite freely in gesture for a long time on subjects that were barred from the language.[23]

What kind of woman is Caroline? George Balanchine and Francis Mason call *Jardin aux Lilas* "a tragedy of manners," remarking that "it does not occur to the girl that her marriage can be put off: that she can escape from its 'convenience.' *Lilac Garden* depicts her mute acceptance in the kind of world where confession of any difficulty would be impossible."[24] Barnes describes her as "a young Edwardian beauty, upper middle-class, ardent, headstrong and unemancipated."[25] Tudor explains, "It's important to me that a woman of this period always remains a lady, no matter what."[26] And Lloyd imagines Caroline as "rather innocent," remarking that "[she] had fallen in love, perhaps for the first time in her life, with a very beautiful ardent young man she had met somewhere. And he was her lover . . . I think very innocently."[27]

Still, it would not take much for the emotionally deadened Caroline to become like her fiancé's mistress – an episode in someone's past. Indeed, the choreography suggests as much. For although Caroline and the Episode are stylistically distinct – the former is both gentle and spirited, while the latter is harshly aggressive – they share many of the same gestures and movements. One can imagine Caroline, bereft of her first love, hardening into just such a desperate creature. And one can even imagine the mistress, in earlier days, loving with Caroline's fresh ardor.

It is striking that there are no mothers in *Jardin aux Lilas*. The community, truly modern, is constituted of a single generation. And community relations are strained at best: the gossip knows the marriage should not take place; the sister keeps the secret of Caroline's love affair. Here is another dysphoric marriage plot, one in which the marriage takes place but to the chagrin of the bride (and the other woman) as well as that of some members of the community – and therefore, to the audience's chagrin as well. But the ballet, with its forced smiles, its repressed emotions, its stunted actions, is all about the community's having to *pretend* the wedding is euphoric.

It may be that there was an autobiographical element in the ballet. Tudor, who was gay, lived for most of his adult life with Hugh Laing, who danced the role of Her Lover in the original production. The ballet could be interpreted, by mixing up the couples a completely different way, as evidence of Tudor's deep regret that he and Laing could not legally form a romantic partnership.[28] Yet this interpretation seems only to be partly true, for although homosexuality was certainly illegal in Britain at the time, the two men were not closeted, but lived together openly and were known in their own circle of friends to be lovers. Nor did Tudor take a wife to conceal his sexual preference, as some gay men of his generation did. Rather, Tudor seems to sympathize with the situation of women and to criticize the marriages of his parents' and his teachers' generation for the ways in which they impinged on and stunted women's lives.

A Wedding Bouquet

At the beginning of his career, Tudor was often compared to Frederick Ashton, a friend and rival at Rambert's studio. Thus, it is intriguing that almost immediately after the success of Tudor's *Jardin aux Lilas*, Ashton also choreographed a ballet about a marriage of convenience – but one in a comic vein. Ashton's ballet, *A Wedding Bouquet* (1937), first performed by de Valois's Vic–Wells Ballet, might even be seen as a parody of *Jardin aux Lilas* in its humorous treatment of *Jardin*'s tragic theme; certainly, in it Ashton parodies other ballets and ballet conventions.[29] Yet *A Wedding Bouquet* did not begin with Ashton. The ballet was initially conceived by Lord Berners (who also supplied the music as well as the scenery and costume designs). The scenario was co-authored by Berners, Ashton, and Constant Lambert, composer and conductor of the Vic–Wells Ballet, and the ballet was set to words by Gertrude Stein, from her play *They Must. Be Wedded. To Their Wife* and other works. At first the text was sung by a chorus but later, during the war, it was spoken by a narrator who sat at a table and drank champagne. That became the recitation mode of choice.[30]

The plot, such as it is, concerns a French wedding party (or is it secretly English? Arlene Croce has pointed out that most of the guests' names sound more British than French, and she complains that the ballet "is as preciously English as the English ever get."[31]). The time is the turn of the century (the same period as *Jardin*). Although Stein's words accompany the ballet, Ashton's biographer David Vaughan reflects that *A Wedding Bouquet*

> is not a narrative ballet, but rather a series of incidents at a provincial wedding . . . , one of those ghastly occasions where everything goes wrong – Julia, one of the guests, who is a little demented, appears to have been seduced by the Bridegroom at some earlier time, and is probably not the only one of his conquests to be present (indeed, if it is not actually a shotgun wedding, it certainly appears to be a *mariage de convenance*).[32]

With her distraught behavior, her dark eyes, and her disheveled hair, Julia bears a certain resemblance to Giselle.[33] But she certainly does not behave like Giselle. Julia clings desperately but shamelessly to the bridegroom's leg as he tries to ignore her, while her dog Pépé also gets underfoot, distracting the Bride. Pépé, based on Stein's and Alice B. Toklas's own male dog, is a female dance role. In *Everybody's Autobiography*, Stein writes,

> Pépé the little Mexican dog is going to be on the stage not in person of course but a little girl to play him but even the littlest little girl is going to be a very large little Mexican. Alice Toklas wanted them to put a little one on wires little like the real Pépé but they said it had to be a little girl.[34]

In her determination to join in the proceedings, Pépé also invokes what was by then a ballet-world cliché – the ambitious little ballet girl who aggressively tries to take center stage at every chance.

Webster, the fastidious maid, opens the ballet. Alone on stage, she holds up a forefinger, not only admonishing in general, but also indicating (as the narrator tells us, too), "This is now scene one."[35] Later, Webster inspects the peasants' hands to see if they've been washed (she slaps a dirty hand), and, still later, she takes a photograph of the wedding party. The guests are announced and described by the narrator as they arrive. Besides the "forlorn" Julia, there is the cheerful Josephine – perhaps already a bit tipsy when she arrives – who drinks so much champagne at the party that she becomes totally and comically inebriated and has to be carted off by the police. The guests also include Paul, John, Violet, Ernest, Thérèse, Guy, Arthur, and four unnamed women.

And then, of course, there is the Bride – who is for the most part blithely oblivious to the goings-on. If in *Jardin* there is one mistress – one episode from the bridgroom's past – in *A Wedding Bouquet* there is an entire multitude of them. "The Bridegroom," writes Dale Harris, "reveals the rakishness of his past in a self-congratulatory tango solo, to which a bevy of his former mistresses (all of them now respectable-looking guests at his wedding) provide a kind of ironic chorus."[36] But the innocent, or perhaps stupid, or perhaps simply determined Bride smiles sunnily at them all.

The Bride changes from her long bridal gown into a short tutu (and a garter) for the nuptial grand pas de deux – in which she somehow keeps ending up being partnered backwards or supported overhanded instead of underneath.[37] "The incompatibility of the bride and groom," Anna Kisselgoff points out, "is signified in a parody of a pas de deux, in which the partners face the 'wrong' direction."[38] This recalls, though in a comically awkward vein, the duets with the "wrong" partners in *Jardin*.

Next, Pépé the dog also puts on a tutu, joins with two male guests in a pas de trois, and then leaps into the foreground of the group to strike a pose for the photo. Kisselgoff aptly notes: "The dog's reclining pose (one leg up) recalls both a similar pose in 'Les Sylphides' and canine connotations."[39] Finally, the ballet ends with the spurned Julia, all alone except for her dog.

The narrator repeatedly remarks that "bitterness is entertained by all"; and many have commented on the bittersweet quality of this comedy. It is in large part the rejected Julia's desolation that brings poignancy to the proceedings. But on the other hand, perhaps there is a British notion of French frivolity when it comes to marriage that leavens this tragedy, making the ballet comic through cultural distance. (Although *Jardin aux Lilas* takes place in an English setting, it too seems to associate loveless marriages with the French, given its French title.)

The decor underscores the cartoon quality of the ballet. Oversized lace curtains frame the goings-on. The drop curtain shows the "happy" bridal couple; in between them stands a bouquet of roses, bigger than a person – perhaps suggesting that the institution of marriage towers over individual needs and desires. As in *Jardin aux Lilas*, however, the picture of marital contentment is soon shattered by the characters' actions, almost immediately after the curtain rises. But all during the ensuing antics, the large backdrop – based on a folk-art

Plate 18 The Sadler's Wells Ballet in *A Wedding Bouquet*. Photograph by Felix Fonteyn. Courtesy of the Dance Collection, The New York Public Library for the Performing Arts, Astor, Lenox and Tilden Foundations.

rug owned by Stein and Toklas – shows a perfect picture of a country house on a placid lake. The decor, as well as the Satie-inspired music based on popular tunes, uses irony to convert the proceedings from domestic tragedy to farce.

In *Jardin aux Lilas*, we sympathize with Caroline, the Bride-to-Be, even if we think she is too passively complying with a social system that has ruined her chances for true happiness. We sympathize, too, with the young Lover who will lose her, and even with the aggressive mistress who has been rejected by Caroline's fiancé, for, unlike Caroline, she is an unwilling, anything but passive victim of the marriage system. Both women are stifled, in their different ways, by the entire socio-political economy linking class, money, and marriage. But in *A Wedding Bouquet*, we laugh at the characters' discomfort, embarrassment, and entirely unpromising futures, the way we laugh at another's slip on a banana peel, no matter how much that fall hurts. Our laughter at the ballet is sparked by many things, especially incongruity and schematism.

The mix of elegant demeanor and popular dancing, high and low culture – a lovely waltz and the groom's debonair tango – is irreverent. The classical ballet steps and the polite gestures of etiquette are done correctly, perhaps too correctly. Then, the bridal pas de deux turns into a series of mistakes, or guests bump into one another. It all has a knowingly ironic, music-hall touch. And of course Stein's words, sometimes "illustrated" by the action and sometimes simply savored without making sense, add to the tone of absurdity.[40]

But, beyond incongruity, *A Wedding Bouquet* trades in the comic mechanism of schematic abstraction. Comic figures often tend to be schematic, like cartoon characters who have only one or two features. For instance, often in comedy alcoholics are treated only as woozy and cheerful. The specifics of why they have become alcoholics aren't given, and so we fail to become emotionally invested in the behavior as problematic. Hence Josephine's comic nature. The more schematic or simplified the figure – that is, the less psychologically detailed – the more distanced that figure is from the audience. And the more distanced the figure, the more comic it becomes. Hence also the difficulty of taking seriously this bride's predicament. But we are touched, momentarily, by the tragic Julia, for – as several critics have noted – despite her extreme behavior, her suffering verges uncomfortably on the real.

Both Tudor and Ashton created dysphoric marriage plots in these ballets of the mid-1930s. It is striking that in neither ballet are the parents of the bridal couple present on stage. And yet, these ballets seem to be all about parents, for the brides and grooms are all members of the generation of the choreographers' parents. That is, whether in a tragic or comic mode, both choreographers seem to look back at the marriage conventions of the older generation, at least of the upper and middle classes, with deep cynicism. Although Tudor's lower-middle-class parents were apparently comfortable in their marriage, Ashton's more upper-middle-class parents were not. Vaughan tells us that "Ashton's family life seems not to have been very happy: his mother and father had little to do with each other and even less with their children." Ashton's mother had married her diplomat husband and gone with him to South America (where Ashton was born) less out of love than a yearning "to get away from Suffolk."[41] Both Ashton and Tudor were gay, and Gertrude Stein, as is well known, was a lesbian. Croce observes that in *A Wedding Bouquet* "[Stein's wit] reveals at its core a Bohemian schoolmistressy hatred and tragic perception of middle-class heterosexual functions."[42] Whether it was due to their bohemianism or their sexual preference, or both, through these ballets these artists harshly criticized the bourgeois marriage plot and questioned the marital values of their parents' generation – especially the idea that marriage, whether it be affectionate or loveless, is a woman's only option in life. For Tudor and Ashton, at least in these ballets, marriage is either a tragedy or a joke.

In both *Jardin aux Lilas* and *A Wedding Bouquet*, we see a variety of negative and positive relationships between women: rivalries as well as sororal feelings are played out. But between men and women there is only the possibility or impossibility of courtship. Perhaps this speaks of the nineteenth-century world of "separate spheres," with its double-edged social consequences. On the one hand, middle-class and upper-class women were isolated from public life and consigned to the domestic realm. And yet, on the other hand, they bonded together in friendship networks and female relationships that were often more intimate and intense than those with their menfolk, even though it was the patriarchal system – those absent menfolk – that structured the women's links with one another. This was a world that by the 1930s seemed antique and faded; yet if the networks had broken down, there was no clear alternative to replace them. Although the brides in these ballets are turn-of-the-century women, they already seem to suffer from that social disintegration. Caroline, facing a lifetime of loneliness, may be consoled neither by her lover nor her sister. And the nameless Bride of *A Wedding Bouquet*, although initially less reluctant to marry, is equally bereft of friends.

Rodeo

Agnes de Mille's heroine in *Rodeo, or the Courting at Burnt Ranch* (1942), as well as her view of marriage, is worlds apart from those of Tudor and Ashton, even though the ballet itself has roots in de Mille's London years, when she became close friends with Tudor and danced in his work. Still, the Cowgirl and her milieu are distinctively, unmistakably American. Of all the Americana ballets and modern dances made during the 1930s and 1940s, such as Ruth Page's *Frankie and Johnny* (1938) and Eugene Loring's *Billy the Kid* (1938) (to which it was often compared), *Rodeo* is by far the one that has stood the test of time to become a classic. De Mille writes,

> The theme of this ballet is basic. It deals with the problem that has confronted all American women, from earliest pioneer times, and which has never ceased to occupy them throughout the history of the building of our country: how to get a suitable man.[43]

It never seems to have occurred to the choreographer – as it does not to the Cowgirl in *Rodeo*, unlike Caroline or the unnamed bride in *A Wedding Bouquet* – that the choice of a marriage partner will not be the heroine's. The impossible cross-class marriages, arranged marriages, and marriages of convenience of European society – whether the Silesian dukedom of *Giselle*, the Russian peasant village of *Les Noces*, or the fading British upper-middle class of *Jardin aux Lilas* – have simply disappeared, as if they were ancient, musty cobwebs dried out by the democratic, self-made American prairie sun. So freedom of choice is simply not an issue. But suddenly, the much more active, even aggressive project of "getting" a man is. This was a new challenge for the ballet heroine, one that at the time perhaps could only have been imagined by an American woman raised on movies and moxie.

In some ways de Mille identified herself as closer to the modern dance movement of her day than to the ballet world, and like the modern choreographers, she portrayed women as outsiders, although in *Rodeo* her focus on the euphoric marriage plot differentiated her work from much modern dance. But her decision to work on the ballet stage produced an unusually plucky heroine for the genre.[44] The issue of marriage as a woman's ultimate goal remains unproblematic in *Rodeo* – although, given the ballet's humor, surely de Mille's comment above is partly tongue-in-cheek – and yet, because her heroine is a feisty nonconformist, at the ballet's end we are convinced that her marriage will be unusual as well.

The ballet takes place in one day on a ranch in the Southwest. During the afternoon, there is a rodeo, and at night, a hoedown in the ranch house. A tomboy Cowgirl wants to ride with the men, and she has a crush on the hunk of a Head Wrangler, but at the dance, after she puts on a dress and wins the Wrangler's attention, she discovers that it's her buddy, the Champion Roper, she really loves.

There is a fairytale aspect to *Rodeo*, which was commissioned by the Ballet Russe de Monte Carlo as a homegrown "novelty," although the fairytale has been modernized and Americanized.[45] The dance critic Claudia Cassidy called *Rodeo* a "tale of an ugly duckling who turns into the most enviable of swans," and its heroine a "cowgirl Cinderella."[46] And indeed, there is a Hollywood – but not quite Disneyfied – bent to its story. But the Cowgirl is ultimately unlike Cinderella, since she decides against marrying the "prince" she has yearned after, and more like the heroine of a Hollywood screwball comedy. In recent years, critics have suggested that the ballet might be anti-feminist and conformist, since the Cowgirl wants to marry and to join the community. But *Rodeo* is more than a romantic story with a happy ending. Simply to recount its plot – even as told by the choreographer – leaves out the features that make this a more complicated tale than it seems to be at first glance. For *Rodeo*'s narrative is one of negotiated – not surrendered – female identity, in which the outsider manages to find a place for herself in the community while still retaining her idiosyncratic character. How she marries and how she joins the community are as important as the fact that she does so.

As de Mille points out (rather defensively, perhaps to show that she had not purloined ideas from *Billy the Kid*) in *Dance to the Piper*, one of her several autobiographies, the 1942 ballet was based on a shorter, all-woman version of *Rodeo* the choreographer had shown in London in 1938.[47] Dance historian Barbara Barker has fully documented that earlier *Rodeo*, showing how it formed the core of the later ballet and also how it, in turn, had developed from *Forty-Niner* (1927), one of de Mille's earliest solo character sketches, first performed in New York in various versions throughout the late 1920s.[48] Barker describes the development of *Rodeo*'s Cowgirl over the course of fourteen years:

> In 1927, the original opportunistic pioneer headed to the California Gold Rush, dressed in calico limp from the sun, introduced herself to the audience with a neighborly salute to her sunbonnet, smartly pushing it back off her forehead with a cocked thumb, and made an awkward approach to an imaginary partner. In later versions she became a participant in a competitive "Hoe Down". . . . In 1938 she became the tossed, tormented rider of an unruly horse, and in 1942 met Rodeo's heroes, the Roper and the Wrangler.[49]

De Mille writes in *Dance to the Piper* that, when making *Forty-Niner*, to a score of cowboy songs by David Guion (which was then reworked as the score for this early *Rodeo*), she recalled her childhood cross-country trip when her family moved from New York to join her uncle, Cecil B. de Mille, in Hollywood. "I had seen the prairies for the first time and recognized the meaning and the love of those large lands."[50] These works invoked her love for the American land, for the prairies, and for the California hills where she grew up.

In London, where she moved in 1933 to study with Marie Rambert and to perform at Rambert's Mercury Theatre, de Mille found herself identified as an "exotic" American and, Barker speculates, made Americana dances not only because she missed the American landscape, but because "in a sense she recreated herself in the image the public devised for her."[51] So, like *The Firebird*, the first version of *Rodeo* was made for export. It was part of an *American Suite* by de Mille that included a group piece to Irish folk tunes, a comic clog-dance solo about a lazy Appalachian, a portrait of a striptease dancer to music by George Gershwin, and *Dust*, a tragic trio about the dust storms of 1936. The suite was created with an eclectic technique that incorporated ballet, acting, modern dance, and various folkdance traditions.[52]

Rodeo was originally atmospheric, rather than narrative. It featured four female soloists with an all-female group; to the musician who arranged the Guion cowboy song score, de Mille described the dancers as "at once horses and horsemen – a sort of American centaur." She explained:

> This dance consists of five arrangements of running and riding rhythms . . . set for 8 figures who appear together only at the climax of the

> "Arkansas Traveler." . . . They run off and on in loose patterns travelling always across the stage, giving the sense of tremendous space and long and formal trails. The movement is vigorous, gay, and for all its violence, dignified – with the exception of the solo figure who is always in trouble, off balance, off beat, frequently progressing backwards or sideways, once on the ground.[53]

Here was the image of "an exuberant cowgirl, thrown but not broken, determined to conquer and compete," as Barker puts it – the prototype for the 1942 Cowgirl.[54] De Mille describes her own 1938 solo as "flashily brilliant, impertinent, and outrageously violent. The dancer suggests a kicking bronco – in spasms of fury – the exit is cocky and under control – but only just."[55] There is, as well, an image of female community and strength in the "steady hard galloping" of the group.[56] Yet this was not planned as feminist dancing; in the early *Rodeo* she wanted to make a dance about cowboys, but no male dancers were available to her.[57] Nevertheless, the dance takes on feminist significance, not only because it shows female strength and female partnership, but also because the women dancers are invested with rambunctious, "male" movement motifs.

In the 1930s in New York, besides her solos, de Mille had also created duets with her partner, Warren Leonard, which often treated comically the troubled relations between the sexes. The 1942 *Rodeo* combines the themes of the duets with the movement material of the solo *Forty-Niner* and the all-female 1938 *Rodeo*. It opens with the centaurian image of the earlier version. But now what is out of place about the de Mille role is that she is a woman among men – although she mimicks their stance and their swagger, her body is immediately recognizable as too small, too delicate, jutting one hip out differently.[58] The cowboys exclude her from the rodeo, even though she begs them to let her take part, but she defiantly cocks her hat, hitches up her pants, swaggers, and mimes riding off on her own and taming a bronco. A group of admiring city girls flounces in, and the men show off for them. Suddenly, the Cowgirl is right in there showing off too, but she falls from her bronco, and the women laugh at her. She thumbs her nose at them, then re-joins the men.

As twilight falls, the riders dismount and go off stage. Some pair up with the women, who whisper among themselves. The Cowgirl looks longingly at the Head Wrangler, but he flirts with the Rancher's Daughter. The Cowgirl tries out a few tap steps in a downcast little solo. Four couples enter to dance a "running set" – a classic square dance with a caller.

In the second scene, the entire community dances inside a ranch house. The cowboys and the women alternate between dancing in pairs and forming one big circle, showing that each individual couple is integrated into the group. All but the Cowgirl, that is, who stands outside the circle forlornly – and the Champion Roper. He tries to console her, and the two pair up to do a slightly awkward clogging variation on a two-step together, contrasting with the more conventional,

Plate 19 Agnes de Mille, Peggy Van Praagh, and Charlotte Bidmead in the 1938 version of *Rodeo*. Gift of Agnes de Mille. Courtesy of the Dance Collection, The New York Public Library for the Performing Arts, Astor, Lenox and Tilden Foundations.

graceful, balletic partnering of the Wrangler and the Rancher's Daughter. (The Roper is no better at courting women than the Cowgirl is at attracting the man she desires; each woman he approaches runs away from him.)

The Cowgirl, too, runs away, but returns in a red dress. She still stands out, since her dress doesn't have the frills of the other women, but nevertheless, the men suddenly notice her, in a classic tomboy story twist. The Cowgirl's spirited entry gets the whole group going in a hoedown, as she dances up a storm with the Roper. Now both the Wrangler and the Roper fight for her attention; she dances with both of them and leans hypnotically toward the Wrangler, but the Roper fascinates her with his virtuoso tap dance. As the Wrangler moves toward her seductively, the Roper intervenes and kisses her on the mouth. The Cowgirl realizes with surprise that he's her man. They dance up another storm together, and the ballet ends.

It is interesting to note that the conversation de Mille reports having with Sergei Denham, the impresario of the Ballet Russe de Monte Carlo, regarding her conception of *Rodeo* is almost identical to that in which Nijinska tried to convince Diaghilev that *Les Noces* should not be simply prettified, imitation folklore, but reach more abstractly and deeply into the meaning of its folk setting. De Mille recalls the exchange: "'Now, Miss de Mille,' Mr. Denham cooed and sighed, 'let us do this thing with lyricism and with beauty.' At the mention of this dangerous word I set my teeth. . . . 'Talk to my lawyer about the aesthetics,' I muttered."[59] And de Mille also had to convince Denham not to either russify her piece of Americana for his largely Russian emigré company or make it a jumble of indistinguishable imaginary folklore from no place in particular. She had a specific idea in mind – "a ranch in the southwest about 1900" – and she wrote, "one must always be conscious of the enormous land on which these people live and of their proud loneliness."[60]

When Denham continued to talk about lyricism, de Mille interrupted him to insist on the consistency and authenticity of her vision, the "homely and ingratiating, lusty and unaffected" quality that critics later noticed in the finished work.[61]

> "Mr. Denham," I interjected, "have you ever seen a running set?"
> "Frankly, no, I have not."
> "Or any native American dance not devised by Leonide Massine?"
> "To tell the truth, no."
> "Then," I said, "relax. You have in mind the Cossack version of our native forms, which differs from the Colorado.". . . .
> Sergei Ivanovitch Denham continued,
> "Let us have a large red barn for the party scene."
> "But, Mr. Denham," I said, "there are no barns in the Southwest. I have a relative who owns eight thousand head of cattle, an average amount. They do not go into a barn at night."
> "But a barn is so interesting, so picturesque. Benois once designed me an enchanting red barn. You cannot imagine what an effect was the deep red behind the dancing."
> "Square dancing."
> "No, *moujiks*, but the reds were incredible."
> "No barn, Mr. Denham."[62]

De Mille recounts that on the bus going home from this meeting, she ran into Martha Graham, who advised her, "They won't respect you unless you're rude." And, de Mille, reports, "I took the pledge. . . . A more opinionated and disagreeable girl [Denham] had never dealt with." She demanded that Denham hire Aaron Copland to compose the music and insisted on a fee of $500.[63]

The anecdotes show us that like Nijinska, de Mille had an abstract vision of the folk-style "essence" she wanted to convey. In her initial notes to Copland, she directs him, "The quieter and gentler and simpler the style the better."[64] But the anecdotes also show us that like her own Cowgirl, she was tough, stood up to the men, and competed with them on their own ground. She writes, with obvious satisfaction, about triumphing in her difficult work convincing the male Ballet Russe ballet dancers – they of the "delicate wrists and the curled fingers of the eighteenth-century dandy" – to perform the roles of the cowboys with effort and power. "For two hours," she recalls, "I rolled on the floor with them, lurched, contorted, jackknifed, hung suspended and ground my teeth. They groaned and strained. I beat them out in impact, resilience and endurance. I broke them to my handling."[65] Clearly de Mille saw herself here once again as the Cowgirl, riding her bronco.

Barker has underscored the irony that de Mille "tried to be the best of wives" and to please her husband in conventional ways even while she was a wealthy, successful Broadway choreographer and "the first woman in America to head a labor union." Moreover, Barker observes, "De Mille, who has an aversion to militant feminism, makes dances that center on classic feminist issues."[66]

In fact, the conflict between marriage and autonomy loomed large in de Mille's own life during the making of *Rodeo*, for at that time she was courting (and in 1943, at the age of 34, married) Walter Prude. Dance critic Joan Acocella points out that not only was de Mille difficult and demanding toward her Broadway employers, and torn between ballet and modern dance, but "added to these troubles was a further conflict: career woman versus 'real' woman. . . . Many of de Mille's friends considered her unfit for marriage. 'She had such drive,' one of her dancers said, 'you couldn't imagine her being sufficiently pliable to fit in with anyone else's life.'" (Comments Acocella, "Imagine this being said of a man.")[67] According to Barker, "at the time of *Rodeo* she was learning about being loved, that she didn't have to work at it, but had to let it happen."[68] Previously, it seems, de Mille had the same idea about how women decided to marry that her sister had had: the day Margaret de Mille met Bernard Fineman at MGM, she announced, "I think I'll marry that man." Six weeks later, she did.[69] The Cowgirl's transformation from the troublesome "cocky," "unconquerable," and "independent" but lonely maverick to the woman who becomes "dizzy," thinks "she has met her master" and is "dead lost" was of great personal interest to the choreographer.[70]

So *Rodeo* is partly a fairytale, partly screwball comedy, and partly autobiographical – after all, de Mille herself was on her way to success in both work and love. But in work, at least, she made it clear that her success would have to be on her own terms, and that she would make no compromises, nor would she conform to the status quo. She *was* her Cowgirl, and the critics always preferred her own rendition of that role to that of other dancers. Cassidy describes her in the role as "a wiry, rangy little dancer with a streak of alkali dust that goes deeper than makeup, and a touch of clairvoyance about a western hoyden who is vulnerable as only a homely girl in love can be."[71]

Barker tells us that at age 29, de Mille, quitting work on her uncle Cecil's film *Cleopatra*, said, "When fifty ladies walk down a golden staircase, all in step, [Cecil] has achieved his object. It is much more interesting to me if one of the ladies is out of step." Barker observes that not only did "de Mille herself [seem] destined to march out of step," then as "a comedienne in serious times, a balletic anomaly in the uncompromising modern dance world of New York," but that her own aesthetic led her to focus on the idiosyncratic, the off-balance, the outsider, as in the character of the Cowgirl.[72] This was what made de Mille identify more closely with Martha Graham than the ballet choreographer Leonide Massine, but ironically, it was also what made Denham turn to her when he wanted an American novelty for his ballet company. Dance historian Marcia B. Siegel writes,

> She must have identified strongly with the wallflower-misfit-Cinderella heroine, because she made *Rodeo* at a time when her life was turning a corner. . . . Too bright not to create, too creative to be accepted in the middle-class world, and too typically American to make the grade with the aristocratic taste that dictated what ballet ought to be, de Mille was like the Cowgirl.[73]

So, like de Mille, who had her share of unhappy love affairs, in *Rodeo*, the Cowgirl is an outsider to both gendered groups – the men and the women. In the first scene, she moves like a man, but the cowboys exclude her from their work. Later, the women shun her, too. In the twilight scene, the Wrangler rejects her in favor of the conventionally feminine Rancher's Daughter, and the Cowgirl remains alone. When the hoedown begins, she stands outside the communal circle of dancers, and when there's a pairing-off dance, she's left partnerless.

Siegel criticizes the ballet for its "pernicious" values of conformism and for "[endorsing] the Hollywood myth." She asserts that "*Rodeo* personifies all the conventional ideas about courting. . . . De Mille hasn't given the Cowgirl any dignity in her independence," and she observes, "the lure of conformism, and the sense that the outsider is not only dangerous to the community but perpetually out of sorts with himself, are very strong in American life." In fact, Siegel argues that "the moral purpose of [de Mille's] ballet is to show the error in being a nonconformist."[74] But even after the Cowgirl's "transformation," she is still not entirely an insider; she hasn't entirely conformed. After all, that her dress is different from the other women's more feminine costumes marks her as still out of step. She has compromised only part way with social niceties. And in terms of resolving the love triangle, as we've seen, she opts not for the princely Wrangler, which is the happy ending one might expect, but for the Roper. And that is precisely because, as Siegel herself observes, "The Champion Roper's tap dance that wins the Cowgirl is the most individual and most persuasive gesture in the ballet."[75] His tap dancing is not unlike her out-of-control adventure with the bucking bronco in the first scene. She chooses him not in order to conform to the neat lines and closed circle of the group, but precisely because he, too, inhabits a world of singularity, excitement, and noisy disorder.

Siegel seems surprised by the Roper's individuality in the midst of what she claims is a suffocating vision of conformity. She sees it as an anomaly, perhaps even as a mistake. Writing in 1979, Siegel wonders "why *Rodeo* hasn't been denounced and picketed by women's liberationists" for its "Cinderella sentiment" and its depiction of the Cowgirl as a "sexual misfit."[76] But if one sees *Rodeo* not as a story about the Cowgirl's learning "to be like everyone else," as Siegel does, but rather, as a narrative of her agency – as the expression of her desires, her aspirations, and her spunkiness – then the power of the tap dance makes utter sense. For the solo tap dance brings it with associations of improvisation, inventiveness, imagination, and singularity. The Roper charms the Cowgirl with that powerful symbol of uniqueness, and he draws her into his dance, showing her the way to live in society but on her own terms. What Siegel misses in her analysis is the ironic humor of this euphoric marriage plot, for the Cowgirl is not at all absorbed tidily into the uniform group, nor is she shown as "[giving] up her peculiar notions."[77] She may find acceptance by the group, but she still dances out of step. Her happy ending is not that she finds love, but that she bucks conformity by choosing a partner on her own terms.

For finally, the dance is less about conformism than about egalitarianism, both in American society and in marriage. Broader themes of social egalitarianism serve here as metaphors for equality in marriage.[78] For instance, the Rancher's Daughter and the Head Wrangler dance together in a balletic style, with elongated, graceful bodies and high lifts – in other words, they are marked as elitist and snobbish – whereas the Roper and the Cowgirl always dance together in an American folk idiom. Thus, the Cowgirl is never really the "ugly duckling who becomes a swan," because she never becomes elegant, never takes on the qualities of that emblematic balletic animal. When the Wrangler makes his last approach to the Cowgirl before the Roper wins her over, he paws the ground with his foot like an excited bull. It signals, in a tongue-in-cheek way, his animal lust for her. But it also brands him as intimidating and manipulative. The Roper, on the other hand, has always been a friend and has accepted her for who she is – including the ways in which she is more masculine than feminine. This, too, puts them on a par, for the Cowgirl is unlike the Rancher's Daughter, a sexually exotic Other to the men. The Roper doesn't dominate the Cowgirl, but wins her with an enthusiastic kiss.

Rodeo is not realistic, and its humor partly derives from the ironic, knowing way in which it enjoys the fantasy of the American Hollywood myth while simultaneously poking fun at it. In fact, Siegel herself responds to that humor. She states, "The values of *Rodeo* seem absurd to me now, even pernicious. Yet I can still have a good time watching the ballet because of its bounce and good humor."[79] Siegel sees the representational frame as transparent, rather than ramified with irony, and so she believes that de Mille wholeheartedly endorses the myth. And yet, given my analysis, it seems that *Rodeo*'s attitude toward both the myth of "getting one's man" and the myth of the tomboy who becomes a woman is complex and ambivalent, in large part because the Cowgirl never relinquishes her idiosyncratic identity.

The theme of female agency is expressed in *Rodeo* in narrative as well as movement dimensions. Taking on male movements shows the Cowgirl's social nature as a tomboy who wants to ride with the men, but it also also signals her spiritedness, assertiveness, and individuality, a development from the 1938 version of *Rodeo*, where the women not only took on male movement but perhaps even in some sense enacted a modern version of travesty dancing, playing the role of cowboys. In George Balanchine's *Agon*, the women also take on movement coded as male. But in *Agon* there is no fleshed-out narrative, nor even the intimations of time and place given by the earlier non-narrative *Rodeo*. The theme of female agency in the abstract ballet *Agon*, as we will see, is expressed in formal movement terms alone.

Agon

Lincoln Kirstein describes George Balanchine's *Agon* (1957) as "an I.B.M. device – but one that thinks and smiles," and Balanchine himself characterizes it as "more tight and precise than usual, as if it were controlled by an electronic brain."[80] These images conjure up many of this storyless ballet's meanings – its imitation of the polyphony, speed, and complexity of modern urban life; its dazzlingly intricate intelligence; its precision; its sense of gamesmanship; and its cool, ironic wit. Balanchine deemed *Agon* the "most perfect work" of his collaborations with Igor Stravinsky; it has been called "a masterpiece of matched artistic intent and purity of vision."[81]

Much of the critical writing about *Agon* has focused on the formal qualities of the ballet and the intricate and imaginative relationship of Balanchine's choreography to Stravinsky's score. For instance, Siegel writes that

> the ballet really has two lines of imagery to follow: the varieties of rhythmic invention – syncopation, suspension, canonic devices, explorations of the dynamic range from percussive to legato – and the constantly shifting arrangements of dancers in the space and of the dancers' body shapes.[82]

In her close analysis of the relationship of the choreography to the music, dance historian Stephanie Jordan concludes, "The excitement of *Agon* is that shifting and volatile musical/choreographic relationships continually enliven our visual/aural awareness. Our perceptions constantly challenged, in *Agon*, the dance virtually begins to sound and music to move."[83]

Yet some critics have made metaphoric interpretations of *Agon*. Croce sees it as a poetic celebration of a very particular city – "the great impersonal bee-swarm of New York."[84] P.W. Manchester pejoratively compares the ballet to "a trapeze performance," while Denby similarly, but enthusiastically, describes it as a series of acts by circus-like "specialty teams."[85] Although Doris Hering notes in her review of the ballet's premiere that "all through *Agon* there was a much more clearly defined contrast between male and female movement than one usually finds in Balanchine's choreography," a great deal more remains to be said about the representations of women in the ballet, as well as its depictions of love and sexuality.[86]

Agon may be a storyless ballet, without characters (either fictional or documentary), but it nevertheless creates meanings regarding human relationships. As Balanchine himself has stated:

> Storyless is not abstract. Two dancers on the stage are enough material for a story; for me, they are already a story in themselves.[87]

Thus even though apparently anonymous men and women dance together (or apart) in *Agon*, headed toward no particular narrative denouement, we can still glean meanings regarding gender and socio-sexual partnering from the ballet's structures. Most striking, on first viewing, is that *Agon* speaks of women as powerful, athletic creatures – skilled, competent, strong, and intelligent. Yet, on closer analysis, clearly it also expresses ambivalent, complex attitudes toward those women: are they to be admired visually (albeit never in a passive mode) and manipulated by men? Or are they understood to be action-makers and free agents? Is marriage (or heterosexual coupling with or without the benefit of lifetime vows) seen as violent and aggressive or as tender and erotic – or as some combination of all those qualities? And is (hetero)sexual partnering seen as monogamous or polygamous – or is no particular preference expressed between those seeming opposites?

Many aspects of *Agon* have been flagged as both modern and modernist, including its serial music, plotless formalism, architectonic use of space and visual design, and distortions of the academic ballet vocabulary, as well as its "mechanical" and "constructed" appearance, fragmented structure, use of cinematic techniques, and stripped-down austerity in regard to theatrical means.[88] But I would argue that beyond these formal aspects, there are further reasons to label it both a modern and a modernist artwork. Like Picasso and his contemporaries, in *Agon* Balanchine specifically borrows from an African-rooted aesthetic, introducing into the classical ballet vocabulary the angular arms, curved torso, percussive footwork, syncopated rhythms, and claps, slaps, and fingersnaps of African American jazz dancing.[89] The music, too, bears traces of jazz influence.[90] The ballet was contemporary and politically progressive in that, during a period of intense struggle in the United States over civil rights, it unabashedly presented an erotic love duet between a black man and a white woman.[91]

In gender terms, and in terms of sexuality generally, not only does the ballet often celebrate strong, independent women and present triangular partnerships dispassionately (marking it as purveying "liberated" modern attitudes toward women and toward non-traditional sexualities). Perhaps more significantly, it is epistemologically modernist, in that its point of view regarding the social and sexual aspects of its own "narrative" is opaque. It is ambiguous, for instance, regarding either the success or failure or the euphoric or dysphoric nature of its marriage plot – or indeed, whether its central pas de deux signals a marriage at all. Moreover, its view of modern love as simultaneously intense and cool exemplifies a staunchly anti-romantic stance. Thus, although it quotes nineteenth-century ballet partnering conventions, it neither remains restricted to them formally nor embraces their implied sexual configurations.

Agon had a long gestation period. On the day after the 1948 premiere of the Stravinsky–Balanchine *Orpheus*, Kirstein suggested to Igor Stravinsky that a third chapter be added to two previous collaborations (*Orpheus* and *Apollo*) between the composer and choreographer, in order to make a classical triptych. Various classical themes were suggested by one or another of the three parties over the next few years – including Apollo Architectons and Nausicaa from the *Odyssey*.[92] But when Kirstein finally commissioned the ballet officially, in 1953, he sent Stravinsky a seventeenth-century dance manual by F. De Lauze. This apparently served as the basis for the music and the groupings, which took the form of a dance suite. In 1954, the composer and choreographer met to plan the ballet. *Agon* eventually had its premiere in December 1957 – delayed by Stravinsky's other commissions, but more seriously by physical tragedies: in October 1956, Stravinsky had a stroke and later that month, Tanaquil Le Clercq, Balanchine's wife and the ballerina who was to dance in the second Pas de Trois, was stricken with polio. Given the history of its making, that *Agon* was ever born is astonishing, but the struggle suggested by its title certainly is not.[93]

Ultimately, according to Balanchine, the "subject" of the ballet was simply dancing. He points out that the ballet's title "was to be the only Greek thing about the ballet, just as the dancing manual, the point of departure, was to be the only French." And he continues,

> In addition to the court dances, we decided to include the traditional classic ballet centerpiece, the *pas de deux*, and other more familiar forms. Neither of us of course imagined that we would be transcribing or duplicating old dances in either musical or dance terms. History was only the takeoff point.[94]

But of course Balanchine is being slightly disingenuous here, for the entire atmosphere of the ballet is an Olympic one of "unwinnable games," as Kirstein has put it, or "ceremonial competitions." And a tongue-in-cheek nod to French courtly gestures and postures threads playfully throughout. One of Balanchine's earliest ideas – "a competition before the [old, tired] gods," still seems to animate the ballet, as the old ballet art is reinvigorated by infusions of contemporary vernacular dancing. As Kirstein explained to Stravinsky, "It is as if time called the tune, and the dances which began quite simply in the sixteenth century took fire in the twentieth and exploded."[95] There is, of course, an element of agonism in the idea of a "contest without competition, a hymn to endless, tireless struggle," as Kirstein puts it. But also, he reminds us, there is another twentieth-century element in the ballet: "*Agon* was by no means 'pure' ballet, 'about' dancing only. It was an existential metaphor for tension and anxiety."[96]

Choreographic structure

According to Kirstein, "There is more concentrated movement in *Agon* than in most nineteenth-century full-length ballets," since "there are no interstitial gaps for parade or decoration."[97] Depending on how one counts it, there are fourteen or nineteen small dances in the twenty-five-minute ballet, grouped into three larger sections. Danced in practice clothes (black leotards and pink tights and toe-shoes for the women; white t-shirts, black tights, and white socks and shoes for the men), the ballet often quotes movements from the two earlier chapters of the Stravinsky–Balanchine dance triptych (*Apollo* and *Orpheus*) – movements that earlier had conveyed symbolic meaning but that now, bereft of their narrative contexts, have become highly abstract.[98]

As with *Jardin aux Lilas*, here it will be necessary to describe the dance in detail in order to explicate the gendered and sexual meanings of the choreography. *Agon* begins with four men standing in a row upstage, their backs to the audience, in a pose strikingly similar to that of Orpheus in the ballet of the same name, but multiplied by four. Their dance repeats Orpheus's large, wiping arm circles and collapsing torso, but this time the movements are drained of the Greek hero's grief. They kick in unison and then in canon, and they stride in formations across the stage.[99]

After this opening Pas de Quatre, there is a Double Pas de Quatre – a dance for eight women. They come out two at a time, kicking their legs high in grands battements, like the Muses in *Apollo*, but at the same time like a squadron of chorus-girls.[100] Compared to the men, with their lunges, their stretched bodies, and their straight arms, these women, with rounded arms, at first look soft and gentle. But they soon turn their limbs into force vectors. In between kicks, they strike contrapposto model's poses. Thus they alternate between icons of super-athletes and of femininity. The music sounds ominous, buzzing in a minor key, as the dancers cluster in various formations. These women, the music and dancing together seem to say, are beautiful, strong, confident, glamorous – and slightly dangerous. Denby describes them as "hang[ing] in the air like a swarm of girl-sized bees."[101] First the pairs, forming two lines as they enter from opposite sides, dance in counterpoint, then – as if each line had become a team – simultaneously, advancing upon one another swiftly like rivals in contest. They repeatedly throw their legs, like so many javelins, out toward their opponents, as they perform ronds de jambe en l'air while whirling back and forth from the side to the center of the stage.

While the men in the Pas de Quatre and the women in the Double Pas de Quatre both frequently move in canon, the delayed repetition seems to differentiate the men as individuals, while it seems to turn the women into an undifferentiated mass. Perhaps this is because the men's intervals are four beats, whereas the intervals between the women's repetitions are much smaller (one beat in the first canon and two beats in the second), which gives us more time to scrutinize each man as he performs his movement. Or perhaps it is because there are eight women, grouped in two vertical lines from downstage to upstage – and so those in front block a clear view of those behind them – and only four men, spread in a row across the stage.

Now two women move to the front of the group to perform a sequence of turns, attitudes, jumps, and grands battements in mirror symmetry, once again rounding their arms. The soloists serve, as Stilwell points out, almost like a melody, while the other six dance and pose behind them, like a musical accompaniment.[102] As in nineteenth-century ballet, the soloists resemble symmetrically faceted gems in a matched setting, and, perhaps recalling older ballet configurations, the music – more melodic than before, with chiming sounds – enhances the jewel-like quality of the duet. Behind the soloists, the diagonal arms and lifted legs of the ensemble form a sunburst pattern reminiscent of that formed by the Muses' legs at the end of *Apollo*. All the women move into various floor-plans (a diamond, then a V-shape) with what is called in the Labanotation score a "peg-walk" – one foot on pointe and the other flat.[103] The peg-walk creates an elegant limping effect – like a woman shod in only one high heel. Perhaps the floor patterns are oblique references to images of women as both elegant and erotic creatures; after all, the Broadway show *Gentlemen Prefer Blondes* had a successful run on Broadway starting in 1949, and the 1953 movie version directed by Howard Hawks featured Marilyn Monroe in the dazzling number "Diamonds Are a Girl's Best Friend." And the V-shape, which reappears not only in a floor pattern in the Triple Pas de Quatre, but more strikingly in a spread-eagled pose by the woman in the Pas de Deux, hints at female private parts.

As the duet ends, all the dancers strike the angular model's pose and, with an air of finality, rotate their bent front legs in and out again. Now they switch to the classical turned-out stance and do a deep plié while circling their arms, and then, moving their legs from this standard balletic turned-out position to a work-aday parallel stance, they all collapse their torsos casually forward over their hips, reaching relaxed arms to the floor. Next, the two soloists do an arabesque penché, each supported by another woman, who is seated on the floor in splits. Letting go of her partner's hands, each soloist then does two more arabesques, unsupported. As the four men from the first Pas de Quatre enter the stage once more, and the women walk to a new formation, first the female soloists and then their female partners nod to one another, and they touch hands as their paths cross. We seem to have witnessed a women's community in which all things are possible without male intervention, including the support of partnering, and in which there are deep, unspoken bonds of quiet affection.

Although it is only one-and-a-half minutes long, the Double Pas de Quatre is a complex dance, full of texture not only in the choreography, but also in its gendered meanings. Women play a multitude of roles, and their relationships to one another are extremely rich. In motion, they can be powerful, precise athletes or graceful dancers, in a myriad of genres. In repose, they are self-possessed models, but they are rarely still. Sometimes they are shown as clumsy, but most of the time they are utterly adroit. And they can be partners or rivals. They can help one another do pointework, or they can perform difficult feats of balance on their own. Sometimes they disappear, undifferentiated, into a faceless mass of other women (as in the communities of inhuman women in the "white acts" of so many Romantic ballets); sometimes they stand out as individuals. Finally, the gentle nod and clasp of sororal friendship mark their connection and mutual respect. Despite the danger signals of the opening moments of the Double Pas de Quatre and the initial view of the women as interchangeable, the dance grows in complexity and women emerge as individuals, and this section ends with a richly multi-layered, exciting view of women and their myriad powers, as well as an image simultaneously strong and tender of female community.

In the next section, the Triple Pas de Deux, the four men join the eight women. They do so, however, in an aggressive way – leaping in a block to part the women, who bolt away, into two groups – that suggests sexual force. The brief impression is that of an invading male army in a surprise attack on a women's village, or perhaps an imagined ancient communal enactment of a sexual ritual, like the Rape of the Sabines. The gender-segregated groups systematically intermingle, then separate again. Then, for the first time in the ballet, they form heterosexual partners. The men stand behind the women to partner them, holding the women steady as they do single, then double pirouettes, ending with their legs hooked back around their partner's waists. But behind the four couples, the four unpartnered women perform the same sequence. Thus the "heterosexual imperative" of ballet partnering is undercut, for it is clearly shown that women do not need men for support to perform this movement. The dancers form a tableau with the men clustered at the center, some dancers kneeling and some standing, but all with one hand on the hip and the other crossed to the opposite shoulder; thus, in stillness, the first section of the ballet ends.

The second section of the ballet consists of two Pas de Trois, based on court dances, and a Pas de Deux loosely based on classical ballet conventions. The first trio, danced by a man and two women, includes a solo Sarabande for the man and a Galliard for the two women, and it begins and ends with a Prelude and Coda for all three. (The music for this Prelude is the same as that for the Interludes introducing the second Pas de Trois and the Pas de Deux. Denby describes it as "a small, circusy fanfare" that begins with a "pushy, go-ahead" flavor and then "keeps sliding without advancing, like seaweed underwater."[104]) The Prelude creates that sense of a team of daredevil acrobats to which the critics refer partly because the three dancers run along the stage, looking down, with their arms held up and out to the sides – for all the world as if they were on a tightrope, saying "now see this!" They quickly run and leap forward and back, as if racing against the others, all doing the same steps. Then, when the music slows down, they do too. The man, who stands between the two women, crosses his wrists and takes the women's opposite hands (the women then take one another's free hand, raising their arms overhead). He supports them in a mirrored arabesque. Then, as he walks around in a circle, he raises his arms to form a "house" around them – echoing a similar formation in *Apollo*. It's as if he were domesticating them. They all bow, and the women run off stage, leaving him alone to perform his "turn." He dances a Sarabande, a hybrid of jazz steps and courtly gestures. Denby writes, "It recalls court dance as much as a cubist still life recalls a pipe or guitar. The boy's timing looks like that of a New York Latin in a leather jacket."[105] Then the male dancer leaves the stage to the two women.

Like the female soloists in the Double Pas de Quatre, the two women dance side by side, mirroring one another's movements, leaning toward one another and back, jumping, lifting their legs through passé to attitude and in grands battements to arabesque, syncopating the rhythms of their movements against the music. They tilt their heads and shoulders and flick their wrists. Those decorative, conventionally feminine touches, added to the twinning function of the mirror image (and the mirror's association with the feminine), the generally low-angled movements of the legs embroidered with the fluttering feet of entrechats quatre, and the rhythmic precision of their movement, makes them look doll-like and demure. Their echappés recall other ballet dolls – in *The Nutcracker*, perhaps – or the automaton in *Coppélia*. At a certain point, they suddenly fall out of mirrored symmetry and into side-by-side unison movement. It suddenly makes both women seem even more doll-like and mechanical, although their choreography changes little. Then they return to mirror symmetry. Oddly, this most conventionally feminine section of the ballet is set to a court dance – the Galliard – that was traditionally reserved for men.

In the Coda to this Pas de Trois, the three dancers again do identical steps, now in canon rather than unison, and as in the Sarabande, they mix and match jazz and ballet steps. They do a soft-shoe, a Susie-Q, and hip-thrusts; they do attitudes, grands battements, and pirouettes. They hunch, touching shoulders. But when the man spins first one woman, then the other, in pirouettes, they don't simply return to classical ballet. One is reminded of a similar movement image in the third theme of *The Four Temperaments*, about which Croce muses, "Could Balanchine have been thinking of the bass fiddle the forties jazz player spins after a chorus of hot licks?"[106]

The second Pas de Trois reverses the gender balance of the first: here there are two men and one woman. It begins with a group Interlude and continues with three bransles: a Bransle Simple for the two men; a Bransle Gay for the solo woman; and a Bransle Double for all three. The Interlude's beginning is even faster and more competitive than that of the Prelude to the previous Pas de Trois, complexified further by its canon form. The dancers run, kick, and turn on zig-zag paths. They, too, form a "house" of intertwined arms in the slow section, this time with the woman in the center, and as they turn her in arabesque, the men sometimes let go and change positions, so that she (like Aurora in the Rose Adagio of *The Sleeping Beauty*) performs difficult feats of balance on her own. Although at times they support her, she is commanding, and they seem to be ruled and domesticated by her. Now she exits, leaving the stage to the two men.

Their Bransle Simple contrasts with the women's duet in the previous Pas de Trois in striking ways. First, it is in canon, where theirs was in unison, once again emphasizing the individuality of the men and the identity of the women. But also, the men's movements are conventionally – almost parodically – virile, where the women's were exaggeratedly feminine. For instance, the men ball up their hands into fists and thrust out their chests as they jump in adversarial poses.

Now the woman reappears. The men move to the back of the stage to clap an accompaniment.[107] Their steady clapping behind her solo, the introduction of castanets into the musical score, and the sinuous play of the dancer's arms against her erect, but constantly deflecting torso, creates a flamenco atmosphere. Weaving a filigreed dance rhythm through the beats and silences of the music, she does increasingly complex footwork – rising up and down on a single pointe with the other leg extended; doing a double developpé while remaining on pointe; making half-turns to do an arabesque in profile first in one direction, then the other; alternating pirouettes with arabesques – all completely unsupported. She also adds to her phrase two "male" steps – a lunge with arms "pushing through" and a pas de chat – that were previously performed in the Sarabande and the Bransle Simple.[108] What is interesting here is that the woman not only appropriates the men's steps, but also performs feats of courage as well as physical skill (involving speed, balance, and the intricate, split-second timing of turns and repeats), that bespeak a motor intelligence often associated with male athleticism (and, in a broader, metaphorical sense, with male heroes). At the same time, she is entirely female – through not always conventionally "feminine," that is, demure or diminutive. Her turned-in leg crosses the pelvis, calling attention to it by momentarily hiding it; she shakes her shoulders in a slow-motion shimmy; she sinks down in a plié, legs drawn together bent, as if in a sexual swoon. But all of this is done not coyly, but in the most cool, detached, dignified manner. (Croce suggests that there is a deep structural relationship between the dance of the woman in the Bransle Gay and Terpischore's variation in *Apollo*.[109]) At times she moves erotically, but her eroticism partly stems from her strength and her authority; it is equally attractive to female and male viewers. The fact that she is a woman (and has different dance qualities than a man, including the use of pointework) neither diminishes her individuality nor glorifies it.

The men join her in the Bransle Double. One lifts her and tosses her to the other, but then all three form a single file, with the woman in front of the men, leading them as they all run, turn, kick, and jump in canon. They lift her while she does a split, then lower her to the ground and lift her once again back to a standing position. Although the men support her, they seem to be moving to her command, assisting her in her feats of agility. Then, as she continues to dance downstage, the men strike poses behind her, forming an ornamental, moving sunburst pattern that recalls both the Double Pas de Quatre and *Apollo*. In a witty gender reversal, the men seem to take on a feminine decorative function, while the woman does the masculine "hard work," which includes the lunges with arms pushing through that were earlier marked as a male movement. Then all three line up in a row to dance in unison, doing low kicks, turns, and soft-shoe patters. The unison movement makes them seem to be equals, while the woman's downstage position makes her a leader among equals. Once again they form the "house" from the Interlude; the woman executes several arabesques, while the men enclose her and circle around her, all three joining hands. Finally, the end of the section circles back to the beginning: as the woman takes a large leap, one man lifts her and hands her to the other. Although at times her positions are unstable (balancing and turning on one leg on pointe) or impossible to do alone (stopping a leap in mid-air), the woman seems to rule and lead this dance. She creates the impression that she can stand, turn, and move alone, but that (again like Aurora, but this time in the Grand Pas de Deux in *The Sleeping Beauty*), she sometimes chooses to enlist help to enlarge her repertoire of risky moves. She seems not less than these men, but *more* than a match for them; it takes two of them, after all, to partner one of her.

The final part of the second section of *Agon* is a pas de deux. It is canonical in structure, but radically unorthodox in style. Balanchine follows the standard pas-de-deux format: entrance, adagio, variations, coda. But the ballet vocabulary is drastically extended, the rules of correct ballet posture broken, and the actions of the dancers sped up or slowed down to extremes. Croce calls the Pas de Deux "revolutionary," a "succession of unthinkable events," "the most astounding the world has ever seen, the pas de deux to end them all."[110]

Jowitt stresses the academic core of the Pas de Deux that anchors it in the classical ballet heritage:

> Although [the male dancer] holds [the female dancer] in intricately knotty ways and handles her with a matter-of-fact intimacy that would have seemed shocking at the end of the last century, his behavior refers to the supported *adagios* of that time. He promenades her in *arabesque* on pointe; only he is lying flat on his back, while she grasps his upraised hand, her leg sweeping above him like a compass needle. It is Petipa inverted, Petipa harried, Petipa atomized, Petipa with more than a nod to a vernacular of American cheerleaders, bred in studios where little girls studied ballettaptoeacrobatics. But Petipa nevertheless.[111]

But Siegel, emphasizing the departures from tradition, notes that the result is a heightened eroticism:

> Without losing track of line and placement, or of the logic that must mold any classical structure, [Balanchine] permits more to happen between the dancers. More parts of their bodies come into contact, their torsos are more articulate, their limbs more twisty. . . . These departures from strict academic form all seem to go in the direction of greater sensuality.[112]

To the now-familiar fanfare of the Interlude, the man and the woman run on stage, kicking high and whirling in canon. This time, as he sprints, kicks, and turns behind her, the action looks less like a race than a chase. The Labanotation score here notes, "Very aggressive, angry."[113] He catches her as she turns, pitches forward, and strikes a high back attitude that angles around his torso – locking his body behind her, inside her raised bent leg. Who has caught whom? To a few measures of courtly music, they step forward and back in a side-by-side pavanne posture, inside hands joined and lifted high. Then, in a duet version of the "house" of both the earlier Pas de Trois, the two clasp both hands, and the woman leads the man in a circle around her. Who is domesticating whom? They face the audience, but stand slightly turned in to face one another as well, holding inside hands, as if to bow – but they don't. It is an oddly courtly moment.

Now the Adagio begins. She leans against him, back to back, and their arms intertwine. Then both twist torsos around to the front and with their free outside hands grasp their own forearms, so that their wrists interlock in an unbreakable chain link. They do an acrobatic series of moves, in which she gives him her weight, doing backbends while he holds her in balance, then a swift, dangerous turn – on pointe and in plié – that ends again with her back leg wrapped around his torso. As if in a tango pose, he walks her backwards. But she slips under his arm and "escapes." He catches her, and as he lifts her, she opens her legs in a wide V. Then he lowers her and she collapses to the floor between his legs, folding up behind him like a jackknife and then opening her legs once again over the top half of her body as she lies on her back.

He helps her rise into an arabesque penché. They join hands and do a simple circling walk. Then a long, fluid sequence begins in which, despite changing levels and extreme bodily contortions, they stay connected, always touching one another's bodies either through handclasps or hand–body contact. The erotic intimacy of this section of the adagio flows both from this continuous touching and from the sense that, despite the extremely difficult, contortionist poses, the entire sequence glides smoothly, as if the two breathed continuously as one. Jordan explains the effect:

> [A] major difference in the Pas de Deux is the breath rhythm, manifest in the long sustained lines of intertwining and stretching motion. The lines are peppered with *staccato* gestures, but these do not override the main *legato* approach. Arthur Mitchell referred to the Adagio as "one long, long, long, long breath." The music too is structured differently

> here: no longer a series of jaggedly contrasting motoric formal cells, but a number of fragile short gestures – some bounded by rests, or passages of a gradual piling up of sound. For the first time, Stravinsky introduces the lyrical qualities of the strings. The effect of the change cannot be overestimated.[114]

The impression of this section of the Pas de Deux is one of imaginative and extreme sexual acrobatics, in an atmosphere of extraordinary mutual trust and sensitivity. For instance, at the beginning, the man kneels and holds the woman's hand as she turns slowly in arabesque. Then she extends her leg forward, grasping both his hands with both of hers, and she places her lifted leg on his shoulder, bending her standing knee. He stands up, stretching both her legs, so that the working leg straightens and the extended leg lifts ever higher, pointing practically to the ceiling, and he walks her around in a circle. Later, kneeling behind her, he takes hold of her foot and swings it forward. She steps into a piqué arabesque, while he supports her from below by holding her calf. Then she swings her working leg into a front attitude, and he grasps her foot with his other hand, moving it into a back attitude and helping her to stretch it toward her head, as she arches her back, to form a "ring." At the end of this part of the Pas de Deux, while she lengthens her working leg into arabesque, he quickly drops to the floor, lying on his back, and turns her and himself by scuttling his feet in a quarter-circle. Then she lowers her leg and pulls him up, and they begin a new series of moves in which, as she changes facings, she repeatedly drops into splits and he pulls her up.

This part of the dance is never obscene, but, as Denby put it, "startles by a grandeur of scale and of sensuousness."[115] It is not only about the sexual act but about the dangers, risks, and pleasures of an intimate relationship. Dance critic Robert Garis has suggested that there is an autobiographical element in the Pas de Deux, which for him "seemed to stem from and reflect, though not quite to imitate, [Balanchine's] work with Le Clercq in physical therapy – not that the dance mimics the movements of physical therapy but that in both cases the man and woman seem required by some urgent necessity to move quietly, cautiously, with all the skill and courage they can muster, and in a mood of held-breath crisis." Garis also notes that beginning with *Agon*, Balanchine presents a new relationship between men and women generally: "an intensely careful, watchful, tender, and grave working together to achieve tense and perilous extensions and balances."[116]

The two separate, for the first time in three-and-a-half minutes (a long time in this densely packed ballet). First he dances his variation – grands battements, jumps with asymmetrical arm and foot gestures, lunges with arms pushing through, a jump, and a leap with flexed feet. Then she dances hers – a few steps with alternate feet raised in retiré, several pirouettes on pointe in plié, some jazzy poses, and a leap. And he answers with a second variation, taking more lunges and small steps away from her, then a big leap and more small steps to join her

Plate 20 Diana Adams and Arthur Mitchell in the Pas de Deux from *Agon*, 1957. Photograph by Martha Swope © Time Inc.

and quietly take her hand. Their variations take up less than a minute – as if they could not bear to be parted – and yet when they rejoin, their duet, like the music, becomes agitated. Several times, she leaps away from him as he holds onto her and stops her flight, in a struggle reminiscent of the Firebird–Prince Ivan pas de deux. Then, not looking at one another, almost as if both were blind, they reach out and slide arms and torsos together to rejoin hands. He kneels and she does a deep arabesque penché behind him. Then she leans over to embrace him and slides forward over his chest as he leans back in a deep arch. She faces him and lifts her leg in a front arabesque; he bends over her foot, as if about to kiss it in a variation of a courtly kiss of a lady's hand. As he holds both hand and foot of his partner, she leans back until her body is horizontal. Then she returns to the vertical, as he pushes her foot through standing to a back arabesque. Slowly, slowly he lies down on the floor and pulls her into a penché. Then she slowly pulls him back up to kneeling. Both raise an arm, and then they collapse into a limp, close embrace.

According to Croce, "After one of the first performances of *Agon*, a well-known New York writer said joyfully, 'If they knew what was going on here, the police would close it down.'"[117] Was that merely because of the erotic nature of the Pas de Deux (especially its suggestion of oral sex), or was it also due to the representation of interracial coupling? Denby writes of the original cast, "The fact that Miss Adams is white and Mr. Mitchell Negro is neither stressed nor hidden; it adds to the interest."[118] Perhaps this was so for the sophisticated New York City Ballet audience, but in a country where in 1957 racial segregation was still practiced, the image must have seemed daring, even startling at the time. According to Kirstein, when the ballet was performed in Moscow in 1962, "attention was drawn to an imagined servility and pathos, as a metaphor of inequality in American society."[119] But this may not have been only imagined. Although Mitchell reports that Balanchine, instructing him in the role, said, "The girl is like a doll, you're manipulating her, you must lead her," in terms of the gender coding of space, the man is often "brought low" – kneeling, lying down, or lunging – in his relationship to his mistress. She changes levels too, but maintains her impression of hauteur, and this is emphasized by her pointework even when in plié.

But overall, to interpret their duet as a metaphor for the man's servility seems as reductive as seeing her as always manipulated. For each takes turns leading, pushing, and pulling. As Stilwell notes, "The implicit balance of power between the two of them constantly shifts. . . . In his attempts to manipulate her, she slips away and forms her own image, seeming to force him to respond to her will."[120] As in *The Firebird*, the relationship is slightly tinged with sado-masochistic role-playing. And here an element of fetishism also emerges in the man's handling of the woman's foot. But all of this is couched in tenderness rather than violence.

The ballet concludes with a brief third section that recapitulates and recombines all the choreographic themes that have come before, to the music of the opening Pas de Quatre. In the Quasi Stretto transition between the Pas de Deux and the Finale, six more dancers enter, striking showy poses of presentation, to join the man and the woman in a circle. All crouch, and then, as partners rise to join hands across the center, the group separates out into four couples. The next section, Four Duos, alternates between classical partnering configurations and separations between genders that momentarily break them apart into the male and female "teams" of the ballet's first part. As the men kneel to support the women in a turn, we see echoes of the Pas de Deux. But to see the four couples lined up in a row across the stage seems to multiply and democratize love beyond the Pas de Deux. Love is not the sole possession of a central "royal couple," this section seems to say, but rather, belongs to everyone.

And love is not simply heterosexual and monogamous, but polymorphous, for soon the four couples are joined by the other four women, to dance the Four

Trios. Reprising many of the choreographic themes and steps of the entire ballet, the four groups of three often move in embedded canon. For instance, the four trios take turns doing a complex move, and as they do so, within each group each set of three dancers kicks or steps in sequence. Moreover, the canon does not always move across the stage, but sometimes radiates from the center outward. As in the first section of the ballet, the women come to the center of the stage to form patterns: first a diamond, then a rectangle, then a V. At one point, the women pair up like twins, reintroducing the mirror image of the Galliard. The men move off to the sides of the stage as the women regroup, then the men sweep through the V as they did in the Triple Pas de Quatre. Once again four trios are formed. Now each trio joins hands to circle around, but in this variation of the "house" formation, in each group one man and one woman share the burden of supporting the central woman in her arabesque promenade.

The groups reconfigure themselves into couples, and the four extra women move away. There are high kicks and turns, a Lindy breakaway, supported pirouettes, and a sudden jazzy flop of the hands. Then the trios regroup, and, though there are only two women per group, they prance exactly like the three Muses in the *Apollo* troika, to music that itself seems to echo the earlier ballet. Now the genders break up into three alternating rows across the stage: women, men, women. They all crouch, in canon, and then the women rise and leave the stage with a final, flourishing leap. The men rise to dance the Coda, striding to the back of the stage, kicking in canon, but this time paired in mirror symmetry, like the women. It seems they have taken on a feminine aspect. Then, with big circular arm gestures, they seem to erase the visual "screen" of the stage, as if to blot out all that had just happened. They turn their backs to the audience, resuming their initial positions, and the curtain falls.[121]

Interpretation

Denby sees *Agon* as "first, an assembling of contestants, then the contest itself, then a dispersal." He writes,

> The first part of the ballet shows the young champions warming up. The long middle part – a series of virtuoso numbers – shows them rivalizing in feats of wit and courage. There is nothing about winning or losing. The little athletic meet is festive – you watch young people competing for fun at the brief height of their power and form.

But he also stresses the contemporaneity of the ballet – its faint echoes of Baroque music and Baroque dancing seen through the filter of the present. It is formal, but full of playful meanings, and its abstractness does not make it dry or recondite. "The 'basic gesture' of *Agon* has a frank, fast thrust like the action of Olympic athletes, and it also has a loose-fingered goofy reach like the grace of our local teenagers."[122]

Indeed, its hybrid, even mongrel nature emerges from *Agon*'s mix not only of historical references, but also cultural strata, dance genres, and even art forms. Stilwell points out that *Agon* includes aspects of court dance, classical ballet, demi-caractère, modern dance, Broadway show dancing, and vernacular social dancing. She also sees cinematic techniques, such as reverse movement and freeze-frame, operating in the choreography.[123] Importantly, the dance mixes not only a black and a white dancer in the Pas de Deux, but black and white dance traditions.

In some ways, the dance is mathematically rigorous, although not, as Kirstein points out, "mechanistic." He writes,

> Group numbers assume the well-oiled synchronism of electrical time-keepers, achieved by humane teamwork rather than mechanics in automata. Blocks of units in triads and quartets shift like chess pieces or players in musical chairs. Dancers are manipulated as irreplaceable spare parts, substituting or alternating on strict beats. . . . Imperson-alization of arms and legs into geometrical arrows (all systems "go") accentuates dynamics in a field of force; dancers are magnetized by invisible commands according to logical but arcane formulas.[124]

Stilwell points out that the alternations between binary and tertiary structure in both music and dancing contributes to Agon's "symmetrical asymmetries."[125] There is a pervasive sense that dancers are interchanged digitally (as in the gender-switching in the Triple Pas de Quatre and the two Pas de Trois).[126] Siegel speculates that in fact, the movement between balance and instability – what Denby in part refers to as "acuteness of rhythmic risk" – humanizes the ballet. "The tension between symmetricality and asymmetricality, between propriety and unorthodoxy, is a primary source of *Agon*'s energy," she asserts.[127]

But, as I have noted throughout, there are gender references galore in the ballet, and I would argue that this stress on gender differences also softens the rigor of the ballet, setting its mathematical contrasts in human terms and recasting the "abstract" ballet into a social narrative – though one whose meaning is not always precise. Even the ostensibly abstract music codes the ballet in terms of sexual difference. Stilwell remarks:

> Certain timbres connote gender in *Agon*, as in the older ballet repertoire: brass are associated with male dancers (the trumpets in the Pas-de-Quatre and the Bransle Simple, the trombones in the Saraband-Step, the horns in the male variation of the Pas-de-Deux); flutes are associated with female dancers (the Galliarde, the Bransle Gay, the female variation of the Pas-de-Deux).[128]

So the divisions between genders, the pairings and quartets within genders, and also the comings-together in gender-mixed couples and trios, all speak of familiar social interactions. They speak – though obliquely – of men's and women's separate spheres in terms of both the segregation of the sexes and the bonding that takes place within single-gender groups; they speak – again, obliquely – of courting or married couples and romantic triangles. Although in a modernist vein, the narrative questions and their resolutions may not be entirely clear-cut, the general topics – women's community and the marriage plot – are those familiar to us from the ballet canon at least since *La Sylphide.*

One theme of the ballet, momentarily forgotten in the second Pas de Trois and the long Pas de Deux, is a recipe for male ecstasy once succinctly worded by the Beach Boys: "Two girls for every boy." The opening and closing sections of the ballet, as well as the first Pas de Trois, with their 2:1 proportion of women to men, seem to say that Balanchine subscribes to that motto. The most ecstatic and erotic moments of the ballet come in the Pas de Deux, and of course there is a Pas de Trois in which the proportion is reversed: two men for one woman. But, since the ballet begins and ends with two women for every man, in terms of (hetero)sexual relationships, Balanchine seems to take an open view – one woman is good, but two might be just as good. He doesn't seem to state a preference between monogamy and polygamy. Given the serial polygamy of his own life – he married four of his ballerinas and had a marriage-like relationship with at least one other – this view, too, might be autobiographical. Yet, the reverse proportion of the second Pas de Trois undermines whatever female exploitation that Beach Boy motto might entail, for it seems to state that not only can men be polygamous; women can be happily polyandrous, as well. There may be a vague narrative of sexual coupling here: at first the sexes live in separate communities; the men arrive at the women's "house," and they court in various non-monogamous configurations; one couple settles down and marries. But marriage in this ballet doesn't last forever, and other configurations re-emerge, including the women's abandoning the men altogether.

What is the view of women Balanchine presents in *Agon*? Ann Daly has complained that although the ballerina is omnipresent in Balanchine's choreography, his women are not dominant, but rather are passive and submissive, consistently manipulated, displayed, and tamed for male voyeuristic pleasure. Taking as her example the third theme of *The Four Temperaments*, Daly argues that in the Balanchine canon, "Woman as the to-be-looked-at-Other remains the norm." And she concludes that ballet, both of the Balanchinian and classical varieties, and even current modern dance should be shunned, for all these genres contribute to the exploitation of women in daily life. "A totally new way of dancing and choreographic form – if that is possible to imagine within the framework of patriarchy – is needed in order to encode a gender-multiple dance."[129]

But as Daly herself admits, her criticism is rests on one small section of one ballet, "but a few minutes in the many hours of Balanchine's repertory."[130] By generalizing from this example to the many hundreds of hours of the Balanchine *œuvre*, Daly cannot help but oversimplify Balanchine's representation of women. Thus she is surprised, for instance, to find that in a performance of *Symphony in*

C, Merrill Ashley "literally and figuratively left her partner behind."[131] But this happens as often in Balanchine as a glamour-girl pose or a male manipulation. For Balanchine shows us so many facets of so many women, one can never say with confidence that he has a singular, univocal view of a stereotyped, one-dimensional Woman. In *Agon* alone, women are manipulated and displayed, but they are also powerful agents who live happily in a world without men and who, when they have male partners, share an equal footing with them and sometimes even dominate them. In "Free and More than Equal," Croce remarks that "[Balanchine's] women do not always live for love, and their destinies are seldom defined by the men they lean on." Moreover, she points out that "sexual complicity in conflict with individual freedom is a central theme of the Balanchine pas de deux, and more often than not it is dramatized from the woman's point of view. The man's role is usually that of fascinated observer and *would-be* manipulator – the artist who seeks to possess his subject and finds that he may only explore it."[132] In the Pas de Deux in *Agon*, the man at times attempts to manipulate the woman, but she slips free of his grasp, just as in *Diamonds*, as Croce explains,

> [Suzanne Farrell's] confidence in moments of great risk gives her the leeway to suggest . . . that she can sustain herself, that she can go it alone. . . . In the finale, her partner . . . is only there to stop her. She slips like a fish through his hands. She doesn't stop, doesn't wait, doesn't depend, and she can't fall. . . . *Diamonds* [is] a riveting spectacle about the freest woman alive.[133]

There is a connection between Balanchine's multifaceted, contemporary image of women in *Agon* and the notion of "agon" as a peculiarly modern idea of artistic creation. "True agonism," Kirstein quotes Renato Poggioli (an early theorist of the modernist avant-garde) as saying, "strives to transform the catastrophe into a miracle."[134] This idea connects *Agon* thematically with the earlier parts of the Stravinsky–Balanchine triptych, for both *Apollo* and *Orpheus* also treat the birth and the making of art. But the part women play in the making of art in *Agon* is far more full-bodied and active than in the earlier two Balanchine ballets. For one thing, there are more leading women in *Agon* – they dominate by numbers alone – but also, their image is richer and more complex, and it involves far greater agency. In *Apollo*, the Muses are at first Apollo's teachers and inspiration, but by the end of the ballet, they become his followers and, in the chariot or "troika" image, he becomes their "driver." In both the myth and in Balanchine's ballet, Eurydice is also Orpheus' inspiration, the motive for his making music, but she unwittingly destroys his art when she persuades him to break the rules by looking at her. The Furies are lulled by his music, while the Bacchantes eradicate it by killing him. But in *Agon*, the women are dynamic makers of art, driving forces and social agents as much as if not more than the men, not only through their technical prowess (which the Muses, Eurydice, the

Furies, and the Bacchantes also display), but through the meaning of the choreography itself – for example, their appropriation of male-coded steps and their autonomous, unsupported virtuosic motion.

Rather than reinforcing ideologies of male manipulation, in *Agon* Balanchine's choreography presents the modern woman's dilemma as she negotiates among various, not necessarily mutually exclusive options: male domination in a patriarchal world, freely given and equally shared love, female friendship, and personal autonomy.

Conclusion

What I have been doing throughout this book in considering the marriage plot may be organized according to the following grid:

	Ballet	*Succeed/fail*	*Affect* (i)	*Affect* (e)
1	*La Sylphide*	F (×2)	–	–
2	*Giselle*	F (×2)	–	–
3	*Coppélia*	S	+	+
4	*The Sleeping Beauty*	S	+	+
5	*Swan Lake*	F	–	–
6	*The Nutcracker*	S	+	+
7	Forerunners	(no marriage plot)		
8	*Firebird*	S	+	+
9	*The Rite of Spring*	S (?)	–/+	?
10	*Les Noces*	S	–/+	–
11	*Witch Dance*	(no marriage plot)		
12	*With My Red Fires*	S	+/–	+
13	*Rites de Passage*	S	+	+
14	*Night Journey*	S	–/–	–
15	*Jardin aux Lilas*	S	–/+	–
16	*A Wedding Bouquet*	S	–/+	–
17	*Rodeo*	S	+	+
18	*Agon*	?	+	+

Note: Where under internal affect there are two signs separated by a slash, the first refers to the bride's affect and the second to the community's affect.

It is interesting to note that in the works of the dance canon I have examined here, the marriage plot fails only rarely, and that the preponderance of failures take place in nineteenth-century ballets – *La Sylphide*, *Giselle*, and *Swan Lake*. Moreover, the marriage plot fails twice in each of the first two of those ballets. But, also notably, these ballets in which the marriage plot fails are not marginal to the dance canon. Rather, they are the staples and classics of the ballet repertory. In a sense, their view of marriage is sentimental – wringing out pathos for marriages that should have happened, based on affection rather than economic or social interests, but could not, given the current status of the marriage institution. These ballets indicate that marriages of love seem simply to be doomed.

I have pointed out that the early modern dancers, or forerunners of modern dance, partly proclaimed their independence from men simply by excluding the marriage plot from their dances altogether. So at the turn of the century, the marriage plot disappeared from the modern dance stage, and that in itself became a structuring absence. In a metaphorical sense, although technically these works fall outside the marriage grid altogether, one could see this entire genre as a group disavowal of marriage – that is, as euphorically greeting a failed marriage plot just by refusing to install such a plot in the dance at all.

Other than the works of those early modern dancers and Wigman, who is a transitional figure between early modern dance and historical modern dance, the marriage plot succeeds in all the twentieth-century works analyzed here, whether they are categorized as ballet or modern dance. Thus it is impossible, for instance, to make genre distinctions between ballet and modern dance along the lines of whether the marriage plot fails or succeeds, since it does succeed in both genres throughout much of the twentieth-century dance canon. However, despite the persistent success of the marriage plot, what is striking is that the affect attached to all those marriages varies widely (but it still does not vary along genre lines).

As I suggested in Chapter 4, one significant break in the marriage grid may signal the beginning of modernism in dance. Up until *The Rite of Spring*, when the marriage plot failed (*La Sylphide*, *Giselle*, *Swan Lake*), the affect was consistently dysphoric, both internally and externally. When the marriage plot succeeded (*Coppélia*, *The Sleeping Beauty*, *The Nutcracker*), the affect was consistently euphoric. But in *Rite*, the value attached to the marriage is, for the first time, extremely complex. The marriage plot may be euphoric to the community, which will be saved by the sacrifice, but it is probably dysphoric to the bride – the Chosen One, the sacrifical maiden. Moreover, there is a further dichotomy between internal and external values. That is, as we have seen, the plot is euphoric to some characters in the ballet, but dysphoric to at least one other. But what the audience is supposed to feel – based on the authorial viewpoint of the choreographer – is almost impossible to discern. It is not clear what the author's viewpoint is or which character's affect the audience should sympathize with. And finally, by the ballet's end, it is not entirely apparent that the marriage plot – the union of the Chosen One and the god – has taken place at all.

In *Les Noces*, the affect is also mixed, although it is not as ambiguous as that in *Rite*. The internal affect is split between the reluctant bride, to whom the marriage plot is clearly dysphoric, and the community, to which the successful marriage is euphoric. However, the external affect is unambiguously negative, since the audience shares the choreographer's point of view, which is identical to and sympathetic with the bride's. In *Les Noces* for the first time there is an obvious disjunction between the success of the marriage plot and both a character's and the audience's affect. And this anti-marriage attitude (or, at least, the disapproval of this kind of marriage) marks the ballet as a feminist statement.

With My Red Fires is almost a reverse image of *Les Noces*, in that the community disapproves of the marriage, while the bride sees it as euphoric. But again, the audience (through the choreographer) identifies with the bride's positive evaluation. In this context, *Rites de Passages* offers an alternative view of marriage, euphoric in large part because it takes place in a tribal culture (albeit an imagined one) where the marriage institution (between two humans) is still a ritual mystery – an integral, unquestioned, sacred part of the social fabric. *Rodeo*'s consistently positive affect also places it in the mythic realm.

Jardin aux Lilas and *A Wedding Bouquet* both offer dismal views of the marriage plot as a cruel byproduct of the European class and economic system. Although both represent marriages that do, indeed, take place (i.e., the marriage plot succeeds), the affect is (like that in *Les Noces*), entirely mixed – negative for the bride (and in the later ballets, for the mistresses as well), but probably positive for the community. Still, in each ballet, the authorial and spectatorial affect is dysphoric, in line with the reluctant bride's point of view.

Night Journey is perhaps the most bitter portrayal of marriage in the works of the dance canon I examine here. Although the marriage plot succeeds, that success is utterly disastrous in every respect and is assigned a negative value by the protagonists, the community (as embodied in the chorus), the choreographer, and the audience alike.

With *Agon* we once again encounter – as in *The Rite of Spring* – confusions regarding the success or failure of the nuptial plot. All of the groupings in the ballet appear to be euphoric, both internally and externally. But first of all, it is not clear whether the central pas de deux leads to marriage at all. And second, the majority of the "marriages" in the ballet are three-way propositions. So it is not clear that marriage is taking place here. But if it is, this is not your mother's marriage. In a way, Balanchine's modernist ballet prefigures the sexual revolution of the 1960s.

I might note that there is another Balanchine ballet, one I have not analyzed here, that presents another conundrum regarding the marriage plot. So far in my examples, we have seen successful marriage plots with both positive and negative affects. We have also seen failed marriage plots with a negative affect. However, we have not seen a failed marriage plot with a euphoric affect. Although Giselle's failed earthly marriage to Albrecht may have pleased two characters (Hilarion and Bathilde), it was tragic to the protagonists and, therefore, one presumes, to the author and the audience. But there is a striking example in the dance canon of a failed euphoric marriage. In Balanchine's ballet *A Midsummer Night's Dream* (1962), based on the Shakespeare play, there are, of course, several marriages. The play itself is an exemplary comedy, in that two threatened courtships and one frayed marriage are renewed and restored and, in the end, form happy nuptial unions. This gave Balanchine an excuse to stage an entire wedding act, *à la* Petipa. But Balanchine ends this wedding act with a pas de deux between two anonymous dancers who are not characters in the play, as if to celebrate the surfeit of happy couples by adding yet another, entirely superfluous one.

That final pas de deux perhaps democratizes marriage by presenting it as superabundant and accessible to all.[135] There is also, in *A Midsummer Night's Dream*, a rare example of a euphoric failed marriage plot. For after all, Titania and Bottom – transformed into an ass – have a night's dalliance but do not marry. And for that, not only the protagonists, but the choreographer and spectators must all be thankful.

ENVOI

Recent developments

The year 1963 saw the publication of Betty Friedan's book *The Feminine Mystique*; that same year the Judson Dance Theater was at its most prolific, cooperatively producing ten group concerts and three "one-person shows." Thus, one might say that the roots of the second wave of the American feminist movement were utterly contemporaneous with the blossoming of early postmodern dance.

Was this a coincidence? I think not. Although the events were unconnected, the publication of *The Feminine Mystique* and the rise of American postmodern dance both participated in a growing consciousness in the 1960s that women had not yet gained full rights and opportunities. Friedan's book – a critique of the stunted opportunities and frustrations of predominantly white middle-class suburban women in the United States – did not call for immediate political action. Rather, it described a social problem, revealing deep dissatisfactions that in less than a decade would rise to a crescendo in a militant women's movement. And although the choreographers of the Judson Dance Theater certainly did not set out to create consciously "feminist dances" – to claim that would be anachronistic – works by both men and women in the group reveal a protofeminist sensitivity to gender roles. As well, women choreographers of the Judson generation carved out a niche for themselves as artists in a way that even their female predecessors in modern dance had not.

The American feminist movement of the 1970s and after hatched neither instantaneously nor fully formed. An outpouring of feminist discourse and political action – and the channeling of that action into a social movement – grew, in disparate cultural arenas, out of just such local analyses and changes of consciousness as Friedan's book and the rise of postmodern dance.

Of course, as we have seen, modern dance had been a feminized field since its founding at the turn of the century, by a generation of "foremothers" (the early modern dancers, including Isadora Duncan, Loïe Fuller, and Ruth St. Denis), and its systematization by a second generation of predominantly female teachers and choreographers (including Mary Wigman, Doris Humphrey, Katherine Dunham, and Martha Graham). So the women choreographers of the 1960s needed no special dispensation to enter the field. And yet, ironically, after two generations of female domination, American modern dance in the Fifties had been led by men – Alwin Nikolais, José Limón, Merce Cunningham, Erick Hawkins, Alvin Ailey, and Paul Taylor. These men specifically departed from the precepts of the modern dance colossi. That is, often they were the rebellious sons of the domineering mothers (aesthetically speaking).

For several of those men, it was dance's concern with emotion that needed change. That, to some, was a deeply feminine concern. Nikolais, for instance, explained that "the early modern dance explored the psyche," but that the time had come to move on. He proclaimed,

> the male is far more inclined toward the abstract, and the field of dance is overpoweringly female and matriarchal. I hope fervently for the time when the socio-dynamic climate will re-establish the male in a more just position in the modern dance world.[1]

But just then, a new generation of women choreographers was coming to the fore, often making dances that put gender in the foreground. And they questioned whether emotion should be the primary concern either of dance or of women choreographers. Both men and women participated in the Judson events. In that sense, the group was egalitarian and gender-integrated. But several of the dominant figures in the group – like Yvonne Rainer, Judith Dunn, Elaine Summers, Lucinda Childs, Deborah Hay, Trisha Brown, and Carolee Schneemann – as well as Simone Forti (never a member of the Judson group) refeminized dance in a new key by claiming it as open territory for serious women artists.

Merce Cunningham's choreography in the the 1950s and 1960s often gave dancers similar tasks to perform, whether they were male or female. His dancers, working with pure movement in an abstract, non-narrative form, at times became completely androgynous figures in an environment where the dancing "task" required no gendered image.[2] Both men and women took large leaps and executed detailed, brilliant footwork. But in his use of partnering, Cunningham could not, or would not, escape the heritage of classical ballet. For all his radical reworkings of choreography and movement, men usually still supported and lifted women in his pas de deux in quite traditional ways. Men did not partner men, nor did women lift or support women.[3]

But the cohort that followed Cunningham questioned these conventions, reimagining women's identity and gender relations on stage with gusto, in much the same way that their generation refashioned them in life. Not simply a reflection of political life, these developments in dance kept pace with changes in the feminist movement and feminist theory.

The early 1960s: criticisms of the status quo

Several dances of the early Sixties operated like *The Feminine Mystique* to present a criticism of the status quo in terms of gender relations. Although at the time they were not presented as feminist polemics, in retrospect it is clear that they challenged gender expectations – in ways that were shocking to contemporary sensibilities – both in the dance tradition (even the avant-garde tradition) and in the larger arena of socio-cultural conventions. Indeed, their aggressive treatment of gender issues may be part of what defines them as postmodern.

Steve Paxton off-handedly introduced his critique of partnering when in *Proxy* (1961), among other activites, Lucinda Childs lifted Robert Rauschenberg. This was not the point of his dance, which also involved walking, eating, drinking, and getting into poses taken from photographs. But this taboo act cast into question the convention, in both ballet and modern dance, that the only possibility for lifts was that men hoisted women aloft, and not vice versa. So entrenched was this convention that Paxton's break with it alone could not change it. When, among others, Senta Driver in the 1970s and Mark Morris in the 1980s refused to follow the rules, audiences still muttered and giggled uncomfortably.

Lucinda Childs's *Carnation* (1964) is a different kind of critique. In it, a woman metaphorically struggles against a revolt of ordinary household objects. She sits at a table handling various mundane things (sponges, plastic curler, and a colander), folds a sheet, and interacts with a plastic garbage bag. All these would be part of a housewife's typical workday. But the dance becomes comic, surrealistic, and critical of domestic oppression in the surprising way Childs uses the items. For instance, she places the curlers carefully, one at a time, on the prongs of the collapsible colander (placed on her head like a beautician's implement), then methodically takes them off to make "hot dog sandwiches" from the curlers and sponges. These she stacks and places in her mouth, distorting it grotesquely, as if her role as household cook and nurturer has turned into an eating disorder. Then she spits the whole mouthful into the plastic bag – the cook as bulimic. Rising, she reveals that the plastic bag also encases her foot, like a manacle on a prisoner in a chain gang. She limps (hampered by her clutching the bag) to a stage flat, against which she does a handstand, releasing a large sheet from the bag and, at the same time, "vomiting" the sponges and curlers from the bag. One corner of the sheet is attached to her sock, and she pulls on a second sock attached to another corner. She appears to be in bed, only upside down. But she rights herself, folds up the sheet, and "detaches" it from her body by taking off the socks. Next, she becomes "threatened" by the empty bag. In the next section she begins by walking on a diagonal, then steps on the bag. It makes her cry, so she tries out different approaches to it, including an indifferent glance, a surprise attack, and a somersault.[4] The somersault, turning the world upside down, seems like a gesture of liberation – like the handstand that initially frees her from the plastic bag encasing her foot.

Although Childs has said that she was interested in handling objects and in the contrasts between their different qualities – heavy and rigid, soft and flexible – the acerbic commentary on housework in *Carnation* is unmistakable. In a series of surrealistic images, Childs seemed to consume the objects, to take them into her body, her very identity, only to cast them out again and to be attacked and imprisoned by them. The character's obsession with beauty aids, her compulsive sandwich-making, and her need to fold her linens perfectly – as well as her battle with a garbage bag – constitute a small domestic tragedy. She is a woman overcome by the mechanical repetitiveness of housework. The objects seem to her to rise in revolt. But ultimately she quells the recalcitrant garbage bag, signaling her critique of housework, her resistance to the petty tyranny of domesticity.

Yvonne Rainer has succinctly described her *Three Seascapes* (1962) as follows:

> Solo in three parts: 1) Running around the periphery of the space in a black overcoat during the last movement of Rachmaninoff's *Second Piano Concerto*. 2) Traveling with slow-motion undulations on an upstage-to-downstage diagonal during La Monte Young's *Poem for Tables, Chairs, Benches*. 3) Screaming fit downstage right in a pile of white gauze and black overcoat.[5]

Later, the critic Jill Johnston wrote that she thought *Three Seascapes* "was a spoof on romance, or Rachmaninoff, or the whole past idea of romantic music wedded to romantic dancing." But, she says, Rainer meant to focus on the dance movement as a single, simple event – in contrast to the complexity and emotional quality of the music.[6] In this way, *Three Seascapes* may be seen as a critique of hysteria – that is, of the female dancer's image as gripped by out-of-control emotion. Al Giese's photo of the dance shows Rainer, in leotard and tights, legs spread, knees bent, arms gracelessly angled and hands flopping at shoulder height. She stands practically in the laps of the audience, seated on the Judson Church gym floor. Rainer later described her performance as "like a goofy, sexy, crippled, possessed, audience-be-damned, nothing-to-lose, shameless, female critter."[7] This "in your face" quality of Rainer's dance underscored her critique, as did her joining together references from various forms, high and low, of theatrical dancing – modern, ballet, and burlesque.[8] Rainer's exuberant "agony" in the white gauze and black overcoat forced the audience to recognize that much of what they were used to seeing in ballet and modern dance, and even in burlesque, was a polite representation of woman flailing about, in thrall to her emotions.

Dispensing with politeness and detaching the music – whether Rachmaninoff, Young, or the dancer's screams – from the movement drove her point home. In the first section, Rainer contrasted the emotionally laden, grandiose music with the dancer's matter-of-fact actions; in the second section, she undulated her pelvis, a movement that often stands as an erotic sign, but to the distinctly unpleasurable screeches of tables and chairs dragged across the floor. This separation of the meaning of the music from dancing taught the audience to decouple the dancer's screams from her actions in the third section. Thus Rainer disrupted the final image of a dancing woman indulging in hysterics, asking, so to speak, "What is wrong with this picture?"

The late 1960s and the 1970s: the intelligent female body

If in the early 1960s, choreographers (albeit sometimes unwittingly) commented on and criticized the condition of women, gender relations, and images of women in dance itself, by the end of the decade a new representational direction had emerged. Choreographers presented alternatives to what they perceived as the over-emotionalized female roles in the dance tradition. And an important alternative was the intelligent body, sometimes signified by the talking body.

In the late 1960s or early 1970s, the choreographer Yvonne Rainer wrote an essay about Jill Johnston, the dance critic for the *Village Voice*. In the course of dredging up memories about Johnston, Rainer recalled going to dance concerts in the early 1960s at the 92nd Street YHMA, one of the most important modern dance venues in New York City, where an audience of "cranky old ladies in Mexican jewelry and sagging boots with wizened faces not getting old with good grace" watched "crazy ladies on the stage eking out their private agonies, fantasies, and deprivations in the name of all that is or was holy and aesthetic." Rainer continues, "Their raptures, ecstasies and agonies even then or maybe especially then turned me off or turned me on to my own holy mission."[9]

I will say more about Rainer's "own holy mission" later. But her point about her (and her generation's) dissatisfaction is an important one in this context. Modern dance had once been engaged in formal experimentation, but it had also always been closely linked with emotional expression. John Martin, the *New York Times* dance critic and leading apologist for modern dance in America, stated categorically in 1933 that "emotional experience can express itself through movement directly," and that, through "metakinesis" and "muscular sympathy," modern dance had reinstated the ancient Greek tragic mode of conveying through the dancing body "the 'inexpressible residue of emotion' which mere rationality – words and pantomime – could not convey."[10]

But by the postwar years, modern dance had become for many a pompously over-inflated, histrionic artform. Agonies and ecstasies were indeed the reigning emotional registers, and usually the feeling states represented – jealousy, anger, fear, and sometimes even joy – were the tortured passions of love. *The Moor's Pavane* (1949), José Limón's distillation of Shakespeare's *Othello* and one of the major works of the modern dance canon, is a perfect example. So is Martha Graham's *Cave of the Heart* (1946), based on the Greek myth of Medea. Anna Sokolow's *Rooms* (1955), about the angst and alienation of contemporary society, did not deal specifically with love, but still portrayed the tortured sensibilities of the inner life of individuals.

Despite Martin's dismissal of ballet as concerned only with design and abstract lyricism, even the modern ballet of the postwar period – such as *The Cage* (1951) by Jerome Robbins, Birgit Cullberg's *Medea* (1950) (which entered the New York City Ballet repertory in 1958), and especially various works by Antony Tudor and Roland Petit – rendered the extremes of amorous fervor and anguish. In these modern dances and ballets, emotions were usually expressed as dramatic functions of a character or a narrative situation. Thus, Cunningham's *Suite by Chance* (1953), which through the use of aleatory techniques subverted any emotional or representational unity, was a radical statement.

In early postmodern dance, the performers often expressed a spontaneous *joie de vivre* that had to do with the immediate exhilaration of moving. They did not "perform" or represent emotion in terms of character, narrative, or even abstraction. For instance, in Simone Forti's early pieces, based on children's games and play, the performers displayed an infantile, joyous high energy. In *Rollers* (1960), two performers sang while seated in unstable boxes, while six other performers pulled them by means of three ropes attached to each of the two wagons. Forti describes the situation:

> The three ropes fastened to the boxes seem to create a situation of instability, and in no time the boxes are careening wildly. For the singers in the boxes, this produces an excitement bordering on fear, which automatically becomes an element in their performance.[11]

In permitting this sort of spontaneous and "authentic" expression to flood the performance, the postmodern choreographers were unusual, for even Cunningham's dancers at the time usually wore a tightly controlled facial mask, complete with glazed eyes.

Yet the postmodern choreographers did not only introduce unexpected emotions on stage. They also calculatedly rejected passion precisely where one might ordinarily expect to find it. In the "love" section of "Play" in Rainer's *Terrain* (1963), for example, Rainer and William Davis performed a series of erotic poses based on Indian Kama Kala sculpture, but the choreographer deliberately undercut the romantic intensity and intimacy of the movement content. While miming ardent lovemaking, the two simultaneously engaged in a flat, deadpan dialogue of hackneyed phrases about love.

People like Rainer, Steve Paxton, and others tried to make dancing bodies into "neutral 'doer[s],'" rather than agents of affect.[12] Perhaps influenced by Bertolt Brecht, they attempted to drain the emotional catharsis of drama from their performances. Rainer was deeply influenced by the film comedian Buster Keaton, "the great stone face," – in particular, his impassive visage and his close attention to performing specific tasks. For the most part, the postmodern dancers did not act or represent characters, but sought to *present* movement for its own sake. Rainer wrote:

> The artifice of performance has been reevaluated in that action, or what one does, is more interesting and important than the exhibition of character and attitude, and that action can best be focused on through the submerging of the personality.[13]

In this respect, the postmodern choreographers followed the trail blazed by Cunningham and even Nikolais, but they took the denial of expressivity to new heights. Further, they rejected technical virtuosity as well. Thus they revelled in the matter-of-factness of ordinary movement found in the performance of tasks and other everyday activities, using casual situations and actions to undermine and subvert a drama of temperament. But postmodern dance shifted the long-standing debate in dance theory about whether dance should be an art of expression or of technical virtuosity to a new key, because it valued neither. Instead, it opted for the dance as a frame to scrutinize movement – action – as material.

When the postmoderns performed emotion, they did so in ways that were distanced and framed, as in a Brechtian *Verfremdungseffekt.* In this regard, they used similar strategies to those of the Pop Artists who were their contemporaries. Roy Lichtenstein, for instance, ironized emotion by monumentalizing it beyond proportion, blowing up frames from romance comics to underscore just how exaggerated they made the melodramatic passions of love appear. Through repetition, Andy Warhol flattened emotion, reducing the horror of an event like a car crash to a banal monotone. Surely the choreographers were also influenced by filmmakers of the French New Wave, like Jean-Luc Godard in *Breathless*, who (directly influenced by Brecht) also distanced emotions and ironized them through exaggeration and allusion.

Trisha Brown remembers that in Robert Dunn's fall 1961 composition class (which led to the first Judson Dance Theater concert), one of the assignments was to make a three-minute dance. She recalls:

> Dick Levine taught himself to cry and did so for the full time period while I held a stopwatch instructed by him to shout just before the time elapsed, "Stop it! Stop it! Cut it out!" both of us ending at exactly three minutes.[14]

The ability of the dancer to stop and start crying voluntarily – an action that is normally the involuntary result or sign of intense feeling – was surprising, because it indicated an unexpected emotional detachment. In other words, it showed that even the kind of extreme emotion that causes crying was not necessarily spontaneous or authentic, but rather, could be performed at will.

Another example of calculated emotional detachment was the first section of Lucinda Childs's dance *Geranium* (1965), performed to the sounds of a taped broadcast of a football game. Childs, dressed in overcoat and sunglasses, indicated with a pole the level of excitement of the spectators (which was audible on the tape). Her cool, impersonal, Warholesque appearance contrasted starkly and pointedly with the crowd's heated enthusiasm.

Sometimes the postmodern choreographers deliberately dealt with emotions that might be called the low-grade-temperature end of the feeling spectrum. In

Brown's *Inside* (1966), the choreographer "read" the interior of her loft (hardware, woodwork, etc.) as instructions for movement and then performed the dance in another space (the Judson Church), with the audience seated in a rectangle. She moved around the very edge of the space directly in front of the spectators' knees, looking them straight in the eye. Brown remarks:

> Up until that time dancers in dance companies were doing rigorous technical steps and one of the mannerisms was to glaze over the eyes and kick up a storm in there behind your eyes. Many people used that device to hide from their audience; we all knew about it and talked about it. So I decided to confront my audience straight ahead. As I traveled right along the edge of their knees in this dance, I looked at each person. It wasn't dramatic or confrontational, just the way you look when you're riding on a bus and notice everything.[15]

Brown's frankness was not a histrionic passion that could ignite a modern-dance drama or a ballet epic. But it did connote a low-key feeling state of vulnerability or openness.

The postmodern dancers explored a range of alternative emotional expressions in the 1960s. But as the 1960s moved into the 1970s, postmodern choreographers became more and more interested in blotting out emotion altogether. In Deborah Hay's *No. 3* (1966), three assistants toppled and dragged three stacks of bricks while Hay ran evenly in circles. Rainer wrote an essay about the dance, in which she stated that its importance lay in the dancer's neutrality (in contrast to balletic "glamour, apotheosis, or accentuated vagaries of the prima donna, prima ballerina, and prima starrinarosa").[16] What was crucial to Rainer was that in *No. 3* the emphasis was on the movement, rather than the mover. Being moved, emotionally, was replaced by movement *qua* physical action. Whereas modern dance had emphasized emotional movings through physical movement, post-modern dance attempted to examine movement as such. In Hay's dance, Rainer thought, personality and expression had been erased. The task-like quality of the movement was impersonal and inexpressive, and the dancing was equal to – no less and no more important – than the actual task of brick-moving. In Rainer's own *New Untitled Partially Improvised Solo with Pink T-Shirt, Blue Bloomers, Red Ball, and Bach's Toccata and Fugue in D Minor* (1965), the choreographer tried to eliminate personal projection by painting her face black.

The same year, Rainer and her group performed *Parts of Some Sextets*. Shortly after, describing the process of the dance's creation, Rainer wrote her well-known manifesto:

> NO to spectacle no to virtuosity no to transformations and magic and make-believe no to the glamour and transcendency of the star image no to the heroic no to the anti-heroic no to trash imagery no to involvement of performer or spectator no to style no to camp no to seduction

> of spectator by the wiles of the performer no to eccentricity *no to moving or being moved.*[17]

Some have interpreted the last six words in Rainer's statement as a denial of physical movement altogether – a call for a dance of stasis. Fifteen years later, Rainer commented that she herself did not understand what she meant by that phrase.[18] But in the context of the next paragraph of the manifesto, the meaning becomes crystal clear: Rainer was discussing not dance movement, but psychological expressivity and manipulation – "no to moving or being moved" *emotionally*. Her manifesto is a refusal to participate in that particular aspect of historical modern dance. For the next sentence reads:

> The challenge might be defined as how to move in the spaces between theatrical bloat with its burden of dramatic psychological "meaning" – and – the imagery and atmospheric effects of the non-dramatic, non-verbal theater (i.e., dancing and some "happenings") – and – theater of spectator participation and/or assault.[19]

Some considered Rainer "the dullest in [her] relenting defiance of everything conventional in theater and dance," charging that she offered nothing more than "utter boredom" and "non-dance."[20] But what Rainer offered, rather than the drama of psychological anguish, was intellectual complexity, something that had hitherto not been considered modern dance's – or women artists' – domain. Rainer's *Trio A* (1966) was also known as *The Mind is a Muscle, Part I.* It later became the nucleus for the evening-length work *The Mind is a Muscle* (1968) and appeared in many other works by Rainer, as well as in performances of the improvisational group The Grand Union. *Trio A* was not by any means created as a feminist dance – in the final version of *Mind*, the trio was danced by three men as well as in a solo version by Rainer. Nevertheless, when danced by a woman, *Trio A*'s messages about the economy and skill of the human body become a vision of the intelligence, competency, and strength of the female body in contrast to the way the female body was generally regarded in the culture at the time – as feminine, delicate, dainty, weak, and an object rather than an actor on the intellectual stage. The title itself implies a whack at Cartesian dualities that divide mind/body, thinker/dancer. But the dance actually proposes, instead, a new split – one that divorces the body from the emotions – thereby suggesting an alternative category of representation in which the dancing body might be engaged.

In making *Trio A*, one of Rainer's aims was to translate the theoretical concerns of minimalist sculpture to dance and choreography. The intellectual rigor of her essay on this dance, "A Quasi Survey of Some 'Minimalist' Tendencies in the Quantitatively Minimal Dance Activity Midst the Plethora, or an Analysis of *Trio A*," which was published in Gregory Battcock's anthology *Minimal Art*, shows that she could hold her own as a thinker in artworld discourse – an arena that was historically dominated by male artists (especially those, like Robert Morris and Donald Judd, who published manifestos and criticism) and art critics. And that, in itself, was a blow against the traditional identification of women with nonverbal, emotional expression. Noël Carroll has pointed out that by the time Rainer was making films in the 1970s, she used "the disembodied female voice, especially a disembodied female voice discoursing on theory," in order to claim power and parity for women. According to Carroll, "the choice of the disembodied voice . . . undercut what was perceived to be a presiding homology that body/mind : : spectacle/discourse : : female/male." Thus, to refuse to show the female speaker's body through spectacle and to present woman as a bodiless mind through discourse meant that the representation of the female body as sex object "was subverted and replaced with the voice of theory and reflection." Through this strategy, Rainer and other feminist filmmakers asserted the equality of women "as thinkers and speakers with equal access to authority and equal claims to seriousness."[21] To Carroll's homologies one could append the additional binary emotion/intellect.

Long before she began making films, and indeed, long before there was a second-wave feminist movement, Rainer was already installing the female discursive intellect in her dances. However, in her choreography – as distinct from the films – she looked for ways not to disembody the female mind, but rather, to foreground it in and unite it with the female body, while simultaneously excising emotional expression from that body. There are disembodied voices – one male and one female – in the spoken, non-dance interludes of the longer version of *The Mind is a Muscle.* They discuss a movie, its characters' psychological states, and their own emotional relationship. But what is distinctive is that these discussions of affect are forcibly separated from the dancing. But the body is still important. In her program note to the full-length work, Rainer wrote:

> If my rage at the impoverishment of ideas, narcissism, and disguised sexual exhibitionism of most dancing can be considered puritan moralizing, it is also true that I love the body – its actual weight, mass, and unenhanced physicality. . . . My body remains the enduring reality.[22]

In her essay, Rainer describes how she made *Trio A* super-intricate, because "dance is hard to see. It must either be made less fancy, or the fact of that intrinsic difficulty must be emphasized to the point that it becomes almost impossible to see."[23] In *Trio A*, Rainer chose the latter course, making movement that "by dint of its continual and unremitting revelation of gestural detail that did *not* repeat itself, thereby [focused] on the fact that the material could not easily be encompassed."[24] The dance is equally exacting for the spectator to see and for the dancer to remember, for – besides the fact that there are no repetitions – it seems to have neither phrasing nor logical sequence. It refuses rhythm, variety, and virtuosity, as well as climax.[25] And, most importantly for our purposes, it rejects "the exhibition of character and attitude," and therefore the passions modern dance traditionally attached to character.[26] *Trio A* substitutes for those emotional storms the complexities of bodily intelligence, indicated partly by the leading of the body by one or another body part and partly by the cross-rhythms created by disparate actions taking place simultaneously in different parts of the body.

In *Trio A*, the dancer's gaze never engages that of the audience. The head is often either in motion or facing away from the audience, and when the head does face front, the dancer looks down or to the side. Roger Copeland has suggested that in both *Trio A* and her "No" manifesto, Rainer was perhaps refusing the male, voyeuristic gaze of the spectator (as later theorized in cinema by Laura Mulvey) and participating in a "critique of the visual" that was meant to short-circuit erotic exhibitionism. But as he later, correctly, points out, Mulvey's arguments regarding film spectatorship do not easily translate into dance-viewing practices. Moreover, the refusal of the gaze in *Trio A* is a Brechtian distancing technique, a tactic to solve Rainer's concern "that the *spectator* will be seduced by the wiles of the performer, not that the performers will fall victim to a predatory gaze."[27] When Rainer said "no to seduction of spectator by the wiles of the performer," she was not speaking of sexual seduction, but rather of the intense emotional, metakinetic identification that, according to Martin and the modern dance establishment, formed the bedrock of modern dance.

In much the same way that Rainer substitutes analytic intelligence for emotional inspiration and manipulation, Brown shows in her solo *Accumulation with Talking Plus Water Motor* (1979) that dancing can be an act of intelligence rather than an arena where, as Copeland puts it, "women are reduced to (and equated with) their bodies."[28] In *Ordinary Dance* (1962), Rainer had shocked spectators by talking while dancing – by restoring the speaking voice to the dancer, who had once been banished to a world of silence. Brown took the issues of envoicement and of the intelligent dancing body to new heights in *Accumulation with Talking Plus Water Motor*. In this dance, Brown splices together two earlier dances – *Accumulation* (1971), a series of repeating straightforward gestures strung together according to a complex mathematical progression, and *Water Motor* (1978), a fluid, syncopated, sensual strand of off-balance movements like falling and diving. As in Rainer's *Trio A*, in *Water Motor* Brown's body often seems to move in two different directions at once, but here the energy is explosive rather than smooth. In addition to intercutting between these two quite different dances, Brown also tells two distinct, alternating autobiographical stories, one of which concerns the making of the dance. Thus, while concentrating on the dance sequences and using enormous physical effort to execute them, she must also keep the narrative flow going and find the breath to talk. At every juncture, she must keep track of four end-points – one for each dance and one for each story.

Brown introduces the dance by telling how it was made and showing its structure. She began, she explains, by splicing together the two dances while talking. However, she continues,

> as time would have it, I became too good at talking and dancing, and so I had to add yet another element. A: Mr. Prebble called from Aberdeen. . . . B: Corky met me at the airport, and on the way into town. . . . A: to ask if I would accept the distinguished alumni award at my high school.[29]

In other words, the mental ante had to be upped. In *Accumulation with Talking Plus Water Motor*, Brown does not refuse the sensuality of dancing. The silkiness of *Water Motor* as well as the insistence of some of the repeated gestures (a small hip thrust, for instance) in *Accumulation* savor the body's physical sensations. But she does refuse the harnessing of that physicality to emotionalism. Instead, she polishes physicality – specifically, female physicality – with intelligence. The sheer mental – as well as muscular – complexity of Brown's task, spiced with her dry wit, is enormously impressive. Without overt feminist rhetoric, she easily stakes out a space for women as intellectual artists on a par with men.

Both Rainer and Brown, as well as other women choreographer/dancers of their generation, grew up in an American culture in which, according to mainstream values, women were men's silent, intuitive, emotional partners. Copeland has suggested that "dance has often been regarded as a 'mute' art of pure physical presence in which women are reduced to (and equated with) their bodies."[30] But to speak on stage symbolically liberated these women from their silence, and from being defined only as bodies. One could have it all – one could be sensual at the same time that one could be dazzlingly smart.[31]

So complete was the postmodern division between dancing and the passions by the early Seventies that when Rainer became interested in exploring emotion in her art, she forsook dance in favor of cinema. She wrote, in 1973, that "dancing could no longer encompass or 'express' the new content in my work, i.e., the emotions." And, she continued, completely contravening the canonical modern-dance view of metakinesis and muscular sympathy,

> Dance is ipso facto about *me* . . . ; whereas the area of the emotions must necessarily concern both of us. . . . [T]he more I get into it the more I see how such things as rage, terror, desire, conflict, *et al.*, are not unique to my experience the way my body and its functioning are.[32]

Rainer, Brown, and others also entered an artworld in which men became visual artists and theorists, while women were relegated to the "minor" art of dance. Yet their generation began to rewrite these gender divisions. Beginning in the early 1960s, male visual artists and composers were drawn to participate in the community created by the dancers at the Judson, and art critics and institutions began to take seriously the dancers' intellectual work, both as choreographers and as writers. Rainer, in particular, became a role model for other women artists, not only in dance, but also in performance art and film. Women like Rainer and Brown were actually carrying out on the dance floor the liberal feminist project of establishing gender equality. Their work was not simply a reflection of feminist theory or political action, but a real site of political transformation in the artworld itself.

Modern dance had historically been a field for emotional expression, often attached to female bodies. One of the most important breaks between it and the analytic postmodern dance of the late 1960s and 1970s was the latter's refusal of emotion – especially the passions associated with love – as primary subject matter for a dance. The postmodern choreographers used a number of strategies, from exaggeration to irony to the separation of emotion from the body, to challenge the canonical view of emotion as the subject best suited for dancing. Often, they substituted ratiocination as a preferable subject-matter. In doing so, they not only changed the terms of dance theory, but also participated in a feminist debate about women's bodies and women's art, challenging the traditional link between mind-intellect-male and body-emotion-female.

The 1970s to the 1990s: the politics of identity

Rainer, Brown, and others claimed equal rights for women in the 1970s by creating dance images of women as intellectual powerhouses. In this respect, their work parallels that of "liberal feminism," which sought equal opportunities for women in the workplace, at home, and under the law. But several choreographers took a different path, paralleling the cultural feminist movement of the 1970s and after, which emphasizes women's putatively essential, biological differences from men and builds female communities.

Meredith Monk's *Education of the Girlchild* (1973) is an important early example of this trend. An "opera" with narrative shape but poetically vague meaning, its first section presents a tribe or family or fellowship of women – all distinctive individuals, of different sizes, shapes, ages, and ethnicities. They sit at a round table and chat silently, travel together on a pilgrimage, perform rituals, harvest and raise a girlchild, and finally meet their deaths. The second section of *Girlchild* is a solo for Monk, who through voice and gesture travels backwards through an individual's biography, moving from an old woman, whose scratchy song emanates from a hunched, shuffling body; through a hale and hearty middle-aged figure; to a young girl whose breathy, bell-like, expectant voice reverberates through a light, strong frame. *Education* pictures a rich world entirely populated by women; it also participated in a growing interest in women's biographies in the 1970s, part of a feminist rediscovery of female role models in the arts, letters, and sciences.

A number of dances in the 1970s were concerned with pregnancy and parenting. Most striking was a piece that could not be realized live, but only on film – Jane Comfort's *For the Spider Woman* (1980, directed by Neelon Crawford), a recording of a brief, energetic solo, repeated six times during the course of her pregnancy. As her body changed, the phrase did too – certain movements becoming slower and ungainly as her shape altered and her weight and bulk increased. In the postpartum moment of the film, she danced the phrase with her

Plate 21 Meredith Monk in *Education of the Girlchild*. Photograph by Lorenzo Cappellini. Courtesy of The House Foundation for the Arts.

new baby in her arms. Comfort's film asserted that a pregnant woman's body is worth watching, and that the dancing body need not only be lithe and virginal. Indeed, this cycle of mother's dances with children present on stage continued into the 1980s with Johanna Boyce's *The Tree Isn't Far From Where the Acorn Falls* (1987), which included the choreographer's infant daughter in the cast.

Blondell Cummings made *Cycle*, a multimedia piece about menstruation, in 1978 and then embarked on a series of dances about food and its relation to gender. In *Chicken Soup* (1982) she was a universal mother figure, cooking soup and scrubbing the floor. When she performed the piece at the Dance Black America Festival in 1983, its meaning changed; she became more specifically an African American mother, forced to do domestic work but still reveling in African-rooted rhythms and hip swings as she prepared the chicken in her frying pan.

The issue of difference within gender – the diversity of women in terms of class, race, and ethnicity – came to the fore in the women's movement in the 1980s and 1990s. Concurrently, in both American dance and performance art, women staged the politics of complex identities inscribed on, in, and by the body. Jawole Willa Jo Zollar and the Urban Bush Women, a group of African American women who combine speech, song, and dance, often work with folklore of the African diaspora, from African village women's songs and dances of bitterness to girl groups of 1960s rock and roll, to drill teams in contemporary black urban centers. Zollar's *Bones and Ash: A Gilda Story* (1995), based on a novel by Jewelle Gomez, spins a fantasy chronicle of benevolent lesbian vampires, connected to Afro-Brazilian spirit powers, who survive slavery and live on into the era of the civil rights movement, migrating north from a bordello in nineteenth-century New Orleans to a beauty parlor in 1950s Boston. It offers a utopian vision, in which strong women magically save the world, but it is also a celebration of the real communities that have enabled black women's survival.

Similarly, Latina women, such as Merián Soto and Viveca Vázquez, and Asian-American women, such as Li Chiao-Ping, Peggy Choy, and Avanthi Meduri, have made pieces exploring their identities as women within a specific American subculture. In the videotape *Yellow River (Hwang Ho)* (1992, directed by Douglas Rosenberg), Li uses materials from her past, both painful and beautiful – including schoolmates' racist remarks about "yellow skin" and "slanty eyes"; a lover's or friend's contrasting characterization of her as pretty and smart and Chinese; culturally eclectic bits of folklore and superstition ("Step on a crack, break your mother's back." "If you eat every single grain of rice in your bowl, you'll bear many children."); silk robes; references to bound feet; and a pile of raw rice spread, through her dancing, in new designs around the floor – to create a poetic autobiography about moving from the past into the future, acknowledging one's cultural heritage as part of creating one's own identity.

Just as the liberal feminists of dance actually installed gender equality in their dances, choreographers whose interests paralleled the cultural/biological feminist project did not necessarily *reflect* in their art what feminists were doing in "the real world." Rather, they were involved in a *Realpolitik* in which women's communities were created both in the images on stage and together with women spectators.

The 1980s and 1990s: bad girls

The exploration of gender identity as a social, rather than biological, construction in the 1980s collided with political resistance and an avant-garde urge to shock the bourgeoisie, as women artists in the 1980s and 1990s began to use parody to both flaunt and criticize notions of femininity. To be "bad" was seen as a way to cast off all the shackles society has traditionally used to "keep women in their place." Deliberately transgressing the rules of polite discourse about female bodies, joyously espousing bad manners and bad taste, these artists use a blend of humor and aggression to push questions about gender in the arts and in society to the outer limit. Madonna's parodic hyper-sexuality is only the mainstream tip of the iceberg of this school, which embraces Karen Finley, Holly Hughes, and Annie Sprinkle in performance art, Joan Braderman in video, and Cindy Sherman and the Guerrilla Girls in the visual arts. In Europe, Pina Bausch's dance-theater is a leading example of this genre. Many of these artists are involved in a materialist feminist project that emphasizes the social construction of women. To adopt the persona of the "bad girl" is seen as a salutary way to resist the bonds of social construction.[33]

Karole Armitage was an early pioneer of the "bad girl" aesthetic in the 1980s. In *The Watteau Duets* (1985), she exposed the erotically sadomasochistic subtext of many ballet pas de deux, dancing in a leather miniskirt and spike heels that functioned like pointe shoes, as David Linton's high-volume art-punk-rock music assaulted the spectators' ears. More dance "bad girls" include the group Kinematic, with its fractured fairytales; Dancenoise (Anne Iobst and Lucy Sexton), whose *Half a Brain* (1988) was an antic, gloriously outrageous mess of raw fish, fake blood, and TV-inspired violence committed by frustrated, chain-smoking housewives; and Diane Martel, whose scatological pieces of the mid-1980s involved women pointedly displayed both as sex objects and as helpless objects of male anger.

More recently, young choreographers do not merely resist social constructs, but are also concerned to represent the psychological toll that the imposition of certain limited social roles on women exacts. For example, in *Bridle: A Trilogy*, Asimina Chremos harks back to Rainer's critique of dance conventions in the 1960s, but with a more explicitly feminist agenda, as well as to the nineteenth-century ballet tradition of the marriage plot and the wedding celebration. Each of *Bridle*'s three sections is introduced by two "flower girls," women dressed as little girls in pigtails, braids, and short skirts, who cavort in ways that unmask ballet's coy display of female crotches. In the first solo section, "The Bachelor Bride," the flower girls peek inside the front of the giant, dark pink dress that forms the set. They part the front panels, forming a shape suggestive of a vulva, and Chremos, in bridal dress and veil, emerges to the sounds of bells. It is as if the flower girls visualize their own future. The bride lifts her veil, grimaces, and then raises her enormous skirt to reveal a veritable chef's rack of pots, pans, and dolls suspended from her hoops, recalling Childs's imagery of women tyrannized by household objects. One realizes that it was their sound, not wedding bells, that made her musical accompaniment. She rises on pointe and cooks up a baby in a saucepan. Then, still on pointe, she leans over to pick up various objects on the floor and put them in her pot. Cleaning up and cooking all at once, her posture is transformed into that of a crone, recalling another recurrent female image in canonical dance. As in the surrealist artist Meret Oppenheim's mysterious objects of the 1930s – such as her *Ma Gouvernante-my nurse-mein Kindermädchen* or her *Fur-Covered Cup, Saucer, and Spoon* – Chremos condenses images of the erotic, the reproductive, and the culinary. She also seems to comment on the nineteenth-century wedding ballet, specifically by staging what is left unsaid in it about the future the happy bride faces. "The Bachelor Bride" is a Cinderella tale in reverse, imagining bitterly that after the wedding, the wife merely becomes a kitchen drudge.

In the second section, "The Little Velvet Theater," the gigantic dress becomes more explicitly vaginal, and Chremos, in a swirling pink dress, repeatedly stretches a pink cap high above her head, turns, and runs full speed ahead until she is swallowed up by the red velvet folds. The image is unmistakably phallic, as sounds of sexual pleasure are heard within. And there is a result – she emerges in a bathrobe, squats, and pulls out, with great effort, a baby doll. She then disappears behind the curtains, which now become a puppet theater, where, like so many mothers, she "invisibly" manipulates her child. In a complex, multilayered, even contradictory image, she condenses the image of mother-as-manipulator with the suggestion that women's work as nurturers has traditionally been relegated off the stage of history.

In the third section, "Teapot," Chremos emerges once again and sings the nursery rhyme, "I'm a little teapot, short and stout . . . " Dressed in provocative clothing that reveals her navel, she sings slowly but soon becomes enraged and possessed by the song's implications. "I'm a little teapot, sugar bowl, honey pot, sugar tit, daughter, bitch, kitchen witch," she screams, gesturing lewdly and slapping herself, implying both the social construction of women and the maddening tensions it can provoke. She rants and pantomimes a myriad of female roles – martyr, battered wife, abusive mother – and finally melts, like the Wicked Witch of the West from *The Wizard of Oz*, into a pile of clothes, insinuating the unstable nature of the imposition of various social roles and the ways in which they may give rise psychologically to degradation, deterioration, and dissolution.

If in the last three decades, feminism in the United States has explored a range of options – including liberal feminism, cultural feminism, and materialist feminism – then one can see a parallel, related, and not simply reflectionist evolution in the concerns of postmodern choreographers. Focusing alternatively on gender equality, the specificity of women's experience, and the limitations of patriarchal constructions of female identity, postmodern choreographers have offered us what may seem to some to be contradictory visions of feminism. But I would argue that these are not contradictory; rather, they are intimately related parts of an evolving vision – stages or steps toward a comprehensive, complex and rounded view of the past, the present, and the future of women's emergence from patriarchy, not only in dance, but in the culture at large.

NOTES

INTRODUCTION

1 Erving Goffman, *Gender Advertisements* (New York: Harper and Row, 1979).

2 Christy Adair, *Women and Dance: Sylphs and Sirens* (New York: New York University Press, 1992); Ann Daly, "The Balanchine Woman: Of Hummingbirds and Channel Swimmers," *The Drama Review*, Vol. 31, no. 1 (Spring 1987; T113): 8–21. Although Daly later renounced her position, it has nevertheless been influential in feminist dance studies. In "Isadora Duncan and the Male Gaze," Daly writes, "The male gaze theory forces the feminist dance scholar into a no-win situation that turns on an exceedingly unproductive 'succeed or fail' criterion" (in Laurence Senelick, ed., *Gender in Performance: The Presentation of Difference in the Performing Arts* [Hanover, NH: Tufts University/University Press of New England, 1992], p. 243).

3 For a criticism of Mulvey's male gaze theory as applied to cinema, see Noël Carroll, "The Image of Women in Film: A Defense of a Paradigm," *Journal of Aesthetics and Art Criticism*, Vol. 48, no. 4 (Fall 1990): 349–360, reprinted in Noël Carroll, *Theorizing the Moving Image* (Cambridge: Cambridge University Press, 1996), pp. 260–274.

4 Arlette Farge, "Method and Effects of Women's History," in Michelle Perrot, ed., *Writing Women's History* (Oxford: Basil Blackwell, 1992), p. 15.

5 Susan Leigh Foster, "The Ballerina's Phallic Pointe," in Susan Leigh Foster, ed., *Corporealities: Dancing Knowledge, Culture and Power* (London: Routledge, 1996), pp. 1–24.

6 Susan Manning, "The Female Dancer and the Male Gaze: Feminist Critiques of Early Modern Dance," in Jane Desmond, ed., *Meaning and Motion: New Cultural Studies in Dance* (Durham, NC: Duke University Press, 1997), p. 163.

7 On the shaping of artistic practices, see Noël Carroll, "Art, Practice, and Narrative," *The Monist*, Vol. 71, no. 2 (April 1988): 140–156.

8 Erik Aschengreen, "The Beautiful Danger: Facets of the Romantic Ballet," trans. Patricia N. McAndrew, *Dance Perspectives*, 58 (Summer 1974): 7–11.

9 See Jill Dolan, *The Feminist Spectator as Critic* (Ann Arbor, MI: UMI Research Press, 1988), p. 63. Dolan cites Adrienne Rich, "Compulsory Heterosexuality and Lesbian Existence," *Signs*, Vol. 5, no. 4 (Summer 1980) and Gayle Rubin, "The Traffic in Women: Notes on the 'Political Economy' of Sex," in Rayna Reiter, ed., *Towards an Anthropology of Women* (New York: Monthly Review Press, 1978).

10 See Lincoln Kirstein, *Dance: A Short History of Classic Theatrical Dancing* (New York: G.P. Putnam's Sons, 1935); Roy Strong, *Splendor at Court: Renaissance Spectacle and the Theater of Power* (Boston: Houghton Mifflin, 1973).

11 Arlene Croce uses the term "feminine microcosm" in discussing the Prologue and Vision scenes of *The Sleeping Beauty* (in "From a Far Country," *The New Yorker*, 22 May 1978, reprinted in *Going to the Dance* [New York: Knopf, 1982], p. 88).

12 Louis Menand, "What Jane Austen Doesn't Tell Us," *New York Review of Books*, 1 February 1996, p. 15.

13 Antony Tudor's *Judgment of Paris* (1938), featuring three squalid café dancers and set to music by Kurt Weill (from *The Threepenny Opera*), is one of the few exceptions. (For a description of the dance, see Judith Chazin-Bennahum, *The Ballets of Antony Tudor: Studies in Psyche and Satire* [New York: Oxford University Press, 1994], pp. 83–86.) Another is Ruth Page's *Frankie and Johnny*. (See Marcia B. Siegel, *The Shapes of Change: Images of American Dance* [Boston: Houghton Mifflin, 1979], pp. 109–113.)

14 See Northrop Frye, *Anatomy of Criticism* (Princeton: Princeton University Press, 1957).

15 "A Tudor Evening with American Ballet Theatre," prod. Judy Kinberg and Thomas Grimm, dir. Thomas Grimm and Judy Kinberg, *Dance in America*, exec. prod. Jac Venza, a co-production of WNET/Thirteen, New York, and Danmarks Radio, Great Performances, PBS, WNET/Thirteen, New York, 13 April 1990.

16 Carolyn Abbate, *Unsung Voices: Opera and Musical Narrative in the Nineteenth Century* (Princeton: Princeton University Press, 1991), p. ix.

17 Abbate, *Unsung Voices*, p. x; emphasis in original.

18 Carolyn Abbate, "Opera; or, the Envoicing of Women," in Ruth A. Solie, ed., *Musicology and Difference: Gender and Sexuality in Music Scholarship* (Berkeley: University of California Press, 1993), p. 254.

19 However, in discussing the gendered employment hierarchies of ballet, Lynn Garafola has shown that there were more women ballet choreographers in Paris in the nineteenth century, for instance, than has been documented previously, although they usually worked on the popular stage or in second-rank theaters ("Where Are Ballet's Women Choreographers?," University Lecture, University of Wisconsin-Madison, 10 November 1995).

20 On dancers' interpolations into choreography, see Selma Jeanne Cohen, *Next Week, Swan Lake: Reflections on Dance and Dances* (Middletown, CT: Wesleyan University Press, 1982), p. 10.

21 As I pointed out earlier, my choices for this book were partly dictated by what was available for close study on film and video; indeed, those recordings have themselves contributed to these dances' survival and canonization.

1 THE ROMANTIC BALLET

1 Ivor Guest, *The Romantic Ballet in Paris*, 2nd ed. (London: Dance Books, 1980), pp. 114, 5.

2 Théophile Gautier, "Farewell Performance of Marie Taglioni," in *The Romantic Ballet as Seen by Théophile Gautier*, trans. Cyril W. Beaumont (New York: Dance Horizons, 1973; reprint of 1947 ed.), p. 73.

3 See Guest, *The Romantic Ballet in Paris*, pp. 4, 22, 30, 105–108.

4 On Taglioni's life and career, see André Levinson, *Marie Taglioni*, trans. Cyril W. Beaumont (London: Dance Books, 1977; reprint of 1930 ed.); Leandre Vaillat, *La Taglioni, ou la Vie d'une danseuse* (Paris: A. Michel, 1942).

5 Théophile Gautier, "Revival of 'La Sylphide' [1844]," in *The Romantic Ballet/Gautier*, p. 70.

6 Quoted in Selma Jeanne Cohen, ed., *Dance as a Theatre Art*, 2nd ed., (Princeton, NJ: Princeton Book Company, 1992), p. 67.

7 An English translation has recently been published: Charles Nodier, *Smarra and Trilby*, trans. Judith Landry (Sawtry, Cambs: Dedalus, 1993).

8 Erik Aschengreen, however, compares *La Sylphide* to *Trilby* and argues that the similarities between the two should be examined. One example he gives is that both Jeannie (the heroine of *Trilby*) and James (in *La Sylphide*) first meet their supernatural

loves in a half-waking state at the hearth, while dreaming or fantasizing about unattainable erotic desires ("The Beautiful Danger: Facets of the Romantic Ballet," trans. Patricia N. McAndrew, *Dance Perspectives*, 58 [Summer 1974], p. 13).

9 See Nancy Moore Goslee, "Witch or Pawn: Women in Scott's Narrative Poetry," in Anne K. Mellor, ed., *Romanticism and Feminism* (Bloomington: Indiana University Press, 1988), pp. 115–136. Gautier notes that in the part of the Sylphide, Marie Taglioni "resembled unmistakably those fairies of Scotland of whom Walter Scott speaks, who roam in the moonlight near the mysterious fountain, with a necklace of dewdrops and a golden thread for girdle" ("Revival of 'La Sylphide' [1838]," in *The Romantic Ballet/Gautier*, p. 27).

10 In *Ballet and Modern Dance* (New York: Thames and Hudson, 1988), Susan Au remarks that *La Sylphide* "might be interpreted as a cautionary tale" (p. 51). But her interpretation differs from mine, in that she finds the Sylphide "such an appealing figure" that the cautionary aspect is undermined.

11 The forest is a crucial symbolic site in which various psychological transformations – including falling in love and coming to maturity – take place, not only in fairytales like *Red Riding Hood* but in other literary genres (including several Shakespeare plays).

12 The hearth is also a multivalent image that is internal to *La Sylphide* itself; I will discuss it further below, in note 14.

13 According to Guest (*The Romantic Ballet in Paris*, p. 113) and Cyril W. Beaumont (in *Complete Book of Ballets* [London: Putnam, 1937], p. 95), the ballet takes place on James and Effie's wedding day. However, according to the Bournonville scenario (in Cohen, *Dance as a Theatre Art*, p. 79), it is their betrothal day.

14 It should be noted here that in many fairytales, the fireplace or hearth is the dwelling place of fairies or spirits. The fairies conjure with the embers, often in ways that prove troublesome for humans. (See, for instance, "My Own Self," an English fairytale retold by Joseph Jacobs, in *The Book of Virtues: A Treasury of Great Moral Stories*, ed. William J. Bennett [New York: Simon and Schuster, 1993], pp. 30–32.) But at the same time, the hearth is first and foremost a symbol of comfort and domesticity. Perhaps this perfectly contradictory signification has to do with the liminal status of the hearth – its indeterminate status as a threshold (*limen*) between inside and outside the home, a symbolically charged space in terms of the ritual and social process. (See Arnold Van Gennep, *The Rites of Passage* [Chicago: University of Chicago Press, 1960], pp. 20–21.) I will discuss the use of liminal spaces in the choreography of *La Sylphide* below.

15 The formal analysis of the ballet here follows the Bournonville version, since the original Taglioni choreography has been lost. My analysis is based on the 1988 made-for-TV film, directed by Thomas Grimm and produced by the National Video Corporation in association with Danmarks Radio, of a performance of *La Sylphide* by the Royal Danish Ballet at the Royal Theatre in Copenhagen. The cast includes: Lis Jeppesen (The Sylph), Nikolaj Hübbe (James), and Sorella Englund (Madge).

16 See, for instance, Guest, *The Romantic Ballet in Paris*, p. 114; Aschengreen, "Danger," p. 9.

17 Aschengreen points out that it is James's erotic contact with the Sylphide in Act II that causes her death (and, eventually, his). This is not only symbolized by his wrapping her in the scarf, but also (in Bournonville's scenario) directly stated: "In his outburst of joy [James] gives her a thousand caresses." Aschengreen notes that "the harmony and happiness James has experienced in the woods are shattered the moment the sensuous and sensual are admitted" ("Danger," p. 9).

18 Gautier wrote that "the theme of this very poetic *pas* [in which the Sylphide loses her wings] is almost certainly borrowed from the natural history of insects. Virgin ants shed their wings after the love-flight" ("Revival of 'La Sylphide' [1844]," p. 70).

19 Aschengreen, "Danger," pp. 7, 11.

20 I am grateful to Cathryn Harding for this insight.

21 Effie's solo was an interpolation added to Bournonville's original choreography by Hans Brenaa. Nevertheless, I include it in my analysis because it is perfectly in tune with the rest of the choreography and with Effie's character in the ballet. I am grateful to Erik Aschengreen for this information.

22 In this respect, of course, the Bournonville ballet may differ from the Taglioni version. For Bournonville, a strong dancer himself, often created more technically demanding, powerful male roles in his ballets than was the current practice in France, where men were seen as unwelcome interlopers into a graceful, distinctively female province. However, since the Taglioni version has been lost, we do not know how complex a role Taglioni père created for Paul Taglioni, Marie's brother, who originally danced the part of James.

23 See Erving Goffman, *Relations in Public: Microstudies of the Public Order* (New York: Basic Books, 1971), Chapter 2; Nancy M. Henley, *Body Politics: Power, Sex, and Nonverbal Communication* (Englewood Cliffs, NJ: Prentice-Hall, 1977), Chapter 2.

24 Originally, like many old-woman roles in ballet, Madge was danced by a man, and in some companies that perform the Bournonville ballet today, she still is. But in Copenhagen, the tradition changed when Henning Kronstam became artistic director of the Royal Danish Ballet in 1979, since – as in the version I analyze here – he preferred to cast a woman in the role of Madge. Once again, I thank Erik Aschengreen for this information.

25 When, for instance, Thomasine Heiberg (later known as a writer under the name Thomasine Gyllembourg, having taken her second husband's surname) asked her husband for a divorce in 1800 because she was in love with another man, it was a scandal that still reverberated in the 1830s. For a time, Gyllembourg was deprived of the custody of her son. That son, Johan Ludvig Heiberg, became one of the most important thinkers of the Golden Age in Denmark. He was a poet, playwright, literary critic and theorist, university professor, and public lecturer in philosophy, as well as a theater director, and he married the leading actress of the Danish stage, Johanne Luise Pätges. Gyllembourg lived with her son and daughter-in-law until her death in 1856, and they hosted the most influential salon in Copenhagen in the 1830s and 1840s, receiving visitors such as Hans Christian Andersen and Søren Kierkegaard. See Mette Winge, "With Greetings from Rosenvænget: Johanne Luise Heiberg and Other Authoresses of the Golden Age," in *The Golden Age in Denmark: Art and Culture 1800–1850*, ed. Bente Scavenius, trans. Barbara Haveland (Copenhagen: Gyldendal, 1994), pp. 68–73; Bruce H. Kirmmse, *Kierkegaard in Golden Age Denmark* (Bloomington: Indiana University Press, 1990), pp. 138–139. I thank Erik Aschengreen for drawing Thomasine Gyllembourg's story to my attention.

26 Aschengreen notes that in general, Bournonville did not approve of this kind of gratification. He points out that Bournonville was criticized by the Danish Naturalist critic Edvard Brandes for *discouraging* eroticism in his female dancers and for "fear[ing] the passionate," and he quotes Bournonville's own statement regarding the goal of ballet: "[To] intensify thought, to uplift the spirit, and to refresh the senses." In looking at the choreographer's entire *œuvre*, Aschengreen concludes that ultimately Bournonville upheld the *biedermeier* ethos, which, he states, differed from French Romanticism in that it "was willing to delight and to refresh, but never by toying with the provocation of the senses." According to Aschengreen, Bournonville strongly held "the deep and, at that time, common concept that eroticism could endanger man's peace of mind," and therefore the choreographer deliberately softened the original French production's eroticism, as well as its demonic qualities. However, Aschengreen's assessment of Bournonville's general point of view does not undermine my argument, since Aschengreen still considers *La Sylphide* – as an

expression of spiritual dissonance, eroticism, and thus anti-*biedermeier* sentiments – a completely anomalous ballet in the Bournonville canon ("Danger," pp. 36, 48).

27 *Les Noces de Pélée et de Thétis* (1654), though danced by French courtiers, is an early example of this trend.

28 Guest, *The Romantic Ballet in Paris*, p. 215.

29 Evan Alderson, "Ballet as Ideology: *Giselle*, Act II," *Dance Chronicle*, Vol. 10, no. 3 (1987): 296–297.

30 See Joellen Meglin, "Representations and Realities: Analyzing Gender Symbols in the Romantic Ballet" (Ed.D. diss., Temple University, 1995) for a thorough discussion of the changing social role of women, as well as of changing views toward sexuality and marriage in the 1830s and 1840s. Meglin focuses her discussion on the expression of these sociopolitical shifts in three ballets: *La Sylphide*, *La Révolte des Femmes* (also known as *La Révolte au sérail*), and *Le Diable boiteux*.

31 See James H. Johnson, *Listening in Paris: A Cultural History* (Berkeley: University of California Press, 1995), pp. 279–280.

32 See Guest, *The Romantic Ballet in Paris*, p. 28.

33 Johnson, *Listening in Paris*, pp. 239–246.

34 Johnson, *Listening in Paris*, p. 245.

35 See Cyril W. Beaumont, *The Ballet Called Giselle* (London: Dance Books, 1988; reprint of 1969 ed.); Guest, *The Romantic Ballet in Paris*, pp. 186–216.

36 Théophile Gautier, "Fanny Elssler in 'La Tempête'," in *The Romantic Ballet/Gautier*, p. 16. See also Gautier, "Revival of 'La Sylphide' [1838]," p. 27.

37 As is well known, the version of *Giselle* that survives today was heavily revised by Marius Petipa in the 1880s. I have based my choreographic analysis on my live viewings of productions of *Giselle* by American Ballet Theatre, Boston Ballet, the Ballet Nacional de Cuba, and the Bolshoi Ballet, as well as the following video-recordings of the ballet: "*Giselle*," prod. John Goberman, dir. Robert Schwarz, *Live from Lincoln Center*, PBS, WNET-TV, New York, 2 June 1977, with Natalia Makarova, Mikhail Baryshnikov, and American Ballet Theatre, staged by David Blair; *Giselle*, dir. Hugo Niebeling and David Blair, with Carla Fracci, Erik Bruhn, and American Ballet Theatre, staged by David Blair, Unitel and TVE, 1969; *The Bolshoi Ballet*, dir. Paul Czinner, with Galina Ulanova, Nikolai Fadeyechev, and the Bolshoi Ballet, staged by Leonid Lavrovsky (in an abridged version), 1956. My analysis also draws from Beaumont, *The Ballet Called Giselle* and from Gautier's scenario, set forth in his "Giselle," in *The Romantic Ballet/Gautier*, pp. 50–59. For an excellent, insightful choreographic analysis of *Giselle*, see Giannandrea Poesio, "*Giselle*: Part II," *The Dancing Times*, Vol. 84 (March 1994): 563–573.

38 See Poesio, "*Giselle*: Part II," pp. 567–569, for a discussion about the controversy regarding the cause of Giselle's death.

39 "*Giselle*," *Live from Lincoln Center*.

40 Johnson, *Listening in Paris*, p. 255.

41 Preface to *Giselle*, in Théophile Gautier, *Théâtre, Mystère, Comédies et Ballets* (Paris: Charpentier, 1872), p. 366, quoted in Guest, *The Romantic Ballet in Paris*, p. 205. Guest notes that Amani was a dancer from India who performed in Paris in 1838.

42 Two twentieth-century French writers – Jean Giraudoux and Jean-Paul Sartre – represent the Furies as flies. F. C. St. Aubyn and R. G. Marshall write that in referring to the Furies as flies, both authors "were giving to the Erinyes what was probably their original form" (Introduction, in Jean-Paul Sartre, *Les Mouches*, ed. F. C. St. Aubyn and R. G. Marshall [New York: Harper and Row, 1963], p. 10).

43 Aeschylus, *The Oresteia*, trans. David Grene and Wendy Doniger O'Flaherty (Chicago: University of Chicago Press, 1989), pp. 145–146, 171.

44 See Claire Goldberg Moses, *French Feminism in the Nineteenth Century* (Albany: State

University of New York Press, 1984), pp. 11–14. Also see Meglin, "Representations and Realities," pp. 85, 87, 107, 109.

45 See Meglin, "Representations and Realities," pp. 85–87.

46 Meglin, "Representations and Realities," p. 110.

47 Aeschylus, *The Oresteia*, pp. 169–170.

48 See Darline Gay Levy and Harriet Branson Applewhite, "Women and Political Revolution in Paris," in Renate Bridenthal, Claudia Koonz, and Susan Stuard, eds., *Becoming Visible: Women in European History*, 2nd ed. (Boston: Houghton Mifflin, 1987), pp. 279–306; Moses, *French Feminism*, pp. 1–15, 39, 41.

49 Meglin, "Representations and Realities," p. 113.

50 *Revue des deux mondes*, 29 November 1831, quoted in Johnson, *Listening in Paris*, p. 250.

51 *Mrs. Longefellow: Selected Letters*, pp. 27–28 (letter dated 15 January 1836), quoted in Guest, *The Romantic Ballet in Paris*, p. 112.

52 Gautier, "Giselle," pp. 55–56.

53 Moses, *French Feminism*, pp. 32–36.

54 Quoted in Moses, *French Feminism*, p. 33.

55 See Moses, *French Feminism*, pp. 24–31.

56 A-J.-B. Parent-Duchâtelet, *De la prostitution dans la ville de Paris*, 2 vols. (Paris: Chez Baillière, 1836), 1:32, quoted in Moses, *French Feminism*, pp. 29–30.

57 See Moses, *French Feminism*, p. 30–31.

58 See Michelle Perrot, ed., *A History of Private Life, Vol. IV: From the Fires of Revolution to the Great War*, trans. Arthur Goldhammer (Cambridge, MA: Belknap/Harvard University Press, 1987), pp. 180–187.

59 See Moses, *French Feminism*; also, see Perrot, *A History of Private Life*, pp. 162–165, 180–187.

60 Alderson, "Ballet as Ideology," pp. 295, 297.

61 Giannandrea Poesio discusses *Coppélia*, including its relation to operetta, in "A Controversial Ballet: Reflections on *Coppélia*," *The Dancing Times*, Vol. 83 (June 1993): 889–893.

62 S. Kracauer, *Orpheus in Paris: Offenbach and the Paris of his Time*, trans. Gwenda David and Eric Mosbacher (New York: Vienna House, 1972), p. 249.

63 Divorce had been legalized in France in 1792 and modified by the Napoleonic Code of 1804, but then prohibited in 1816. It was reestablished by the Naquet Law of 1884. (See Moses, *French Feminism*, pp. 19, 209.)

64 I have based my description and interpretation of *Coppélia* on the following sources: Ivor Guest, *The Ballet of the Second Empire* (London: Pitman; Middletown, CT: Wesleyan University Press, 1974), pp. 238–247; Nancy Reynolds and Susan Reimer-Torn, *Dance Classics* (Chicago: Chicago Review Press, A Cappella books, 1991), pp. 67–73; and the video-recording *Coppélia*, with Lisa Pavane, Greg Horsman, and the Australian Ballet, with revised choreography by Marius Petipa and Enrico Cecchetti, reproduced by Peggy Van Praagh, devised and dir. George Ogilvie (n.d.). Most versions performed today are based on the revised choreography by Marius Petipa. The original third act was lost before Petipa's revision.

65 For an excellent account of how Swanilda's character is only gradually revealed through her dancing – as opposed, for instance, to the "characteristic" entrances of other female ballet heroines like Giselle and Aurora (in *The Sleeping Beauty*) – see Poesio, "*Coppélia*," p. 890.

66 Quoted in Guest, *The Ballet of the Second Empire*, p. 14.

67 Quoted in Guest, *The Ballet of the Second Empire*, p. 17.

68 Quoted in Guest, *The Ballet of the Second Empire*, p. 20.

69 Lynn Garafola, "The Travesty Dancer in Nineteenth-Century Ballet," *Dance Research Journal*, Vol. 17, no. 2 and Vol. 18, no. 1 (1985–86): 36, 38.

70 See Guest, *The Ballet of the Second Empire*, pp. 14–20.

71 Guest, *The Ballet of the Second Empire*, p. 3.
72 Garafola, "The Travesty Dancer," p. 35.
73 Guest, *The Ballet of the Second Empire*, p. 3.
74 Garafola, "The Travesty Dancer," p. 35.
75 Guest, *The Ballet of the Second Empire*, p. 21.

2 THE RUSSIAN IMPERIAL BALLET

1 See Giannandrea Poesio, "The Awakened Beauty," *The Dancing Times*, Vol. 84 [October 1993]: 41–43 for an enumeration of the ways in which *The Sleeping Beauty* summarizes the ballet traditions of the entire nineteenth century.
2 See James Billington, *The Icon and the Axe: An Interpretive History of Russian Culture* (New York: Random House, Vintage Books, 1970), pp. 210–219.
3 See Ivor Guest, "An Earlier 'Sleeping Beauty': 'La Belle au Bois Dormant' in the Eighteen Thirties," *Ballet*, Vol. 12, no. 4 (April 1952): 36–42. Marie Taglioni was praised for her dancing in the role of the principal naiad in the third act. Also, see Gennady Smakov, "Marius Petipa and the Creation of *The Sleeping Beauty*," in Nancy Van Norman Baer, ed., *100 Years of Russian Ballet: 1830–1930* (New York: Eduard Nakhamkin Fine Arts, 1989), p. 18, who points out the resemblance of the gifts of the fairies scene to the plot of Jules Perrot's ballet *La Filleule des fées* (1849).
4 Several contemporary critics found *The Sleeping Beauty* nothing more than a trifle (see Tim Scholl, *From Petipa to Balanchine: Classical Revival and the Modernization of Ballet* [London and New York: Routledge, 1994], pp. 32–33). The critic of the *Peterburgskaya gazeta* (4 January 1890) wrote, "Don't even look for meaning!" (quoted in Scholl, *From Petipa*, p. 33).
5 Scholl, *From Petipa*, pp. 36, 39. Roland John Wiley, in *Tchaikovsky's Ballets: Swan Lake, Sleeping Beauty, Nutcracker* (Oxford: Oxford University Press, 1985), argues that although the ballet glorified the monarch in many ways, it also showed an inept Master of Ceremonies and an inefficient secret police. "The Tsar . . . may well have thought that if *Sleeping Beauty* were somehow an allegory of his realm it was uncomplimentary, if not wholly undeserved" (p. 149).
6 Petr Il'ich Chaikovskii, *Dnevniki P. I. Chaikovskogo 1873–1891* [The Diaries of P. I. Tchaikovsky, 1873–1891] (Moscow and Petrograd, 1923), p. 249, quoted in Wiley, *Tchaikovsky's Ballets*, p. 164. On the Tsar's cultural nationalism, see Wiley, *Tchaikovsky's Ballets*, p. 95.
7 See Richard Pipes, "Towards the Police State," *Russia Under the Old Regime* (New York: Charles Scribner's Sons, 1974), pp. 281–318.
8 Jack Zipes, *Fairy Tales and the Art of Subversion: The Classical Genre for Children and the Process of Civilization* (New York: Wildman Press, 1983), pp. 3, 19–23. In discussing "the civilizing process" in which the literary fairytales of seventeenth-century France participated, Zipes often refers to Norbert Elias's seminal work *The Civilizing Process* (New York: Urizen, 1978).
9 See Richard S. Wortman, *Scenarios of Power: Myth and Ceremony in Russian Monarchy*, Vol. 1 (Princeton: Princeton University Press, 1995), who, borrowing from Marshall Sahlins's analysis of Polynesian kingship myths, argues that the Russian court adopted foreign images of sovereignty (including the use of a foreign language – French) to create a "heroic history" that symbolically identified monarchs as "strange and powerful outsiders" and thus "affirmed the permanence and inevitability of their separation from the population they ruled" (p. 5). However, Wortman points out that although there are similarities between the royal ceremonies of Louis XIV and the eighteenth-century Russian court, the disparity between the two political systems generated entirely different meanings. It is striking that *The Sleeping Beauty* follows the older mythos of foreign elite images, celebrating the Russian dynasty in thoroughly

French terms, at a historical juncture when the Tsar himself and some strata of the elite struggled to reject foreign cultural influence, thus attempting to shift the terms of the "theater of power," albeit in ways quite distinct from the intelligentsia's populist embrace of Russian roots.

10 Deborah Jowitt, *Time and the Dancing Image* (New York: Morrow, 1988), p. 243.

11 Jowitt notes that there are royal courts on stage in all the surviving works of the Petipa era: *The Nutcracker*, *Swan Lake*, *Sleeping Beauty* and *La Bayadère* (*Time*, p. 244).

12 Anna Federovna Tiutcheva, *Pri dvore dvukh imperatorov. Vospominaniia, Dnevnik, 1853–1882* [At the Court of Two Emperors. Reminiscences, Diary, 1853–1882] (Moscow, 1928–1929), 1:36, quoted in Wortman, *Scenarios of Power*, 1:3.

13 Larosh [Laroche], German Avgustovich, *Izbrannye stat'i* [Selected Articles], 5 vols. (Leningrad, 1974–), quoted in Wiley, *Tchaikovsky's Ballets*, p. 191.

14 Charles Perrault, Preface to *Contes en Vers* (1695), in *Contes de Perrault*, ed. Gilbert Rouger (Paris: Garnier, 1967), p. 3, quoted in Zipes, *Subversion*, p. 16.

15 Indeed, Marina Warner, in *From the Beast to the Blonde: On Fairy Tales and Their Tellers* (New York: Farrar, Straus, and Giroux, 1995), argues that "The Sleeping Beauty's enchanted sleep . . . may not represent the slow incubation of selfhood, of consciousness of the Other and eventual sexual fulfillment. Rather, it may stand for the dark time that can follow the first encounter between the older woman and her new daughter-in-law, the period when the young woman can do nothing, take charge of nothing, but suffer the sorcery and the authority – and perhaps the hostility – of the woman whose house she has entered, whose daughter she has become," i.e., her mother-in-law (pp. 219–220). Although it seems to me that Warner has to dig far too deeply into the tale to elicit this meaning convincingly, in general, her materialist feminist analysis of the social and historical meaning of fairy tales is enlightening and valuable. Although I reject as too extreme this specific interpretation of this tale – that Beauty's sleep symbolizes her relationship with her mother-in-law – for, after all, Beauty doesn't even meet her mother-in-law until years after she wakes up, my own analysis is not incompatible with Warner's point, for the intergenerational struggle between bride and mother-in-law is certainly part of the coming-of-age story.

16 Leo Tolstoy's novels of the 1860s and 1870s, of course, include memorable female characters. *War and Peace* tells about the maturation of Natasha Rostov, a young woman whose personality in some ways reminds us of Aurora, but she is a secondary character compared to her fiancé Andrei Bolkonsky and her eventual husband, Pierre Bezukhov.

17 See Zipes, *Subversion*, p. 7.

18 The story is similar to one, titled "Sun, Moon and Talia," in Basile's *Lo Cunto de li cunti* [The Story of Stories], first published (in Neapolitan dialect) in 1634–36. In Basile's version, which seems to be the earliest published European variant of the Sleeping Beauty theme, the heroine, Talia, seemingly dies when she gets a sliver of flax in her finger. A king who is out hunting discovers her and rapes her ("gathers the fruits of her love") while she sleeps; comatose, Talia gives birth to twins nine months later. Two fairies help the babies nurse, but when one of the children sucks his mother's finger instead of her breast, he sucks the sliver out and she wakes up. Some time passes, and the king returns to discover that he has a family; he and Talia become acquainted. But his wife finds out about his affair, sends for the children, and orders the cook to prepare them as a meal for her adulterous husband. The cook, of course, substitutes two kids. The queen then sends for Talia and orders her thrown into a fire. But Talia outsmarts the queen, stalling for time and shouting until the king comes to help her. He orders the queen thrown into the fire instead of Talia, and they all live happily ever after (*The Pentamerone of Giambattista Basile*, trans. from the Italian of Benedetto Croce, ed. N.M. Penzer [London: John Lane at the Bodley Head, 1932], Vol. II, pp. 129–132).

19 Zipes, *Subversion*, p. 25.
20 *Introduction aux Contes de Grimm et de Perrault* (Paris: Minard, 1978), p. 40, quoted in Zipes, *Subversion*, p. 25. However, Warner points out that although Perrault may have extolled ignorance in women, he still spoke out against misogynists like Boileau in favor of women; he defended marriages based on love, and he was definitively a partisan of women's literature, in the form of the fairytale genre (p. 169).
21 Andrea Dworkin, *Woman Hating* (New York: Dutton, 1974), pp. 32–33, quoted in Jack Zipes, *Don't Bet on the Prince: Contemporary Feminist Fairy Tales in North America and England* (New York: Methuen, 1986), p. 5; emphasis in original.
22 Madonna Kolbenschlag, *Kiss Sleeping Beauty Good-Bye: Breaking the Spell of Feminine Myths and Models* (New York: Doubleday, 1979).
23 Sandra M. Gilbert and Susan Gubar, "The Queen's Looking Glass," in *The Madwoman in the Attic: The Woman Writer and the Nineteenth-Century Imagination* (New Haven: Yale University Press, 1979), excerpted in Zipes, *Prince*, p. 201.
24 See Zipes, *Prince*, p. 5.
25 See Warner, *Beast*.
26 Warner, *Beast*, pp. 409–418. Also, see Jack Zipes, *Breaking the Magic Spell: Radical Theories of Folk and Fairy Tales* (New York: Methuen, 1984), pp. 1–19.
27 Warner, *Beast*, pp. 22–23.
28 Warner, *Beast*, pp. 33–35.
29 As I noted in the Introduction, musicologist Carolyn Abbate makes a similar argument in regard to women in opera. See my discussion of the disparity between plot and performance in the Introduction of this book.
30 Poesio suggests that in writing the scenario, Vsevolozhsky may have referred to Ivan Turgenev's 1864 Russian translation of Perrault's tales, which ends the tale with the wedding, as did the Grimm Brothers' *Dornröschen* ("Beauty," p. 37).
31 I am grateful to Frida Eriksson for pointing out the importance of casting Brianza in this role to the representation of Aurora as an autonomous agent.
32 See John Warrack, *Tchaikovsky Ballet Music* (London: British Broadcasting Corporation, 1979), pp. 39, 43, 47.
33 I am grateful to Lynn Garafola for making this point.
34 Arlene Croce, "From a Far Country," *The New Yorker*, 22 May 1978, reprinted in *Going to the Dance* (New York: Knopf, 1982), p. 88.
35 See Warner, who views the seventeenth-century tales as "the fiery protest of a whole generation of French noblewomen against the serfdom of dynastic matrimony and mental inanition – and the two were bound together, as education was clearly unnecessary to the life of a *châtelaine*" (*Beast*, p. 169).
36 Boris Asafiev, "Annals of 'The Sleeping Beauty': II. The Music," *Ballet Review*, Vol. 5, no. 4 (1975–76): 43.
37 My analysis is built on a composite "text," including scholarship, criticism, and performance. My scholarly and critical sources are: John Wiley's detailed description of the first production (itself a composite, taken from the musical scores, the choreographic notation, and the published libretto, as well as from contemporary reviews and from Yuri Slominsky's description in his book *P.I. Tchaikovsky and the Ballet Theatre of His Time*) (Wiley, *Tchaikovsky's Ballets*, pp. 165–188); M. Konstantinova, *Spyashchaya Krasavitsa* [*The Sleeping Beauty*] (Moscow: Iskusstvo, 1990); Vera Krasovskaia, *Russkii baletnyi teatr vtoroi poloviny XIX veka* [Russian Ballet Theater of the Second Half of the Nineteenth Century] (Leningrad: Iskusstvo, 1963); Vera Krassovskaya, "Marius Petipa and the 'Sleeping Beauty,'" trans. Cynthia Read, *Dance Perspectives*, 49 (Spring 1972); Lincoln Kirstein, *Four Centuries of Ballet: Fifty Masterworks* (New York: Dover, 1984), pp. 174–177; Arlene Croce, "Annals of 'The Sleeping Beauty': The Royal Ballet in New York," *Ballet Review*, Vol. 3, no. 4 (1970), reprinted in Arlene Croce, *Afterimages* (New York: Knopf, 1977), pp. 360–374; David Vaughan, "Annals of 'The

Sleeping Beauty': Aurora Awakened," *Ballet Review*, Vol. 6, no. 4 (1977–78): 78–86; Robert Greskovic, "*The Sleeping Beauty*, the British, and Ballet," *Ballet Review*, Vol. 13, no. 4 (Winter 1986): 60–72; Alastair Macaulay, "*The Sleeping Beauty* – A Hundred Years of 'Beauty,'" *Dance Gazette*, no. 204 (June 1990): 14–16. My performance sources are: Marius Petipa, *Six Fairy Variations: from the Prologue of the Ballet* The Sleeping Beauty *by Tschaikovsky*, reconstructed by Mary Skeaping, Labanotation by Ann Hutchinson Guest (New York: M. Witmark and Sons, 1961); the American Ballet Theatre production of the reconstruction by Mary Skeaping of the Petipa choreography, which I viewed in New York in the late 1970s; the Boston Ballet version, staged in 1993 by Ann-Marie Holmes, with additional staging by Natalia Dudinskaya; and several film and videotape versions of the ballet: the 1965 Kirov film, directed by A. Dudko and Konstantin Sergeyev, with Alla Sizova as Aurora; the 1946 Royal Ballet Nicholas Sergeyev-Ashton-de Valois version, filmed in 1964 by Anthony Asquith and Havelock Allan, with Margot Fonteyn as Aurora; "*The Sleeping Beauty*," narr. Mikhail Baryshnikov, prod. Doris Bergman, dir. Andrea Reiter, exec. prod. Paul Noble, Metromedia Television, Channel 5, in cooperation with the BBC, WNEW-TV, 16 December 1978, with choreography by Kenneth MacMillan after Marius Petipa based on the version by Frederick Ashton and Nikolai Sergeev, with Merle Park as Aurora.

38 Warrack, *Tchaikovsky Ballet Music*, p. 40; Petipa, *Six Fairy Variations*; Kirstein, *Four Centuries of Ballet*, p. 175.

39 Fyodor Lopukhov, "Annals of 'The Sleeping Beauty': I. The Choreography," *Ballet Review*, Vol. 5, no. 4 (1975–76): 27, 30.

40 See Poesio, "Beauty," pp. 38–39 for an excellent analysis of the fairies' attributes and movement.

41 Wiley, *Tchaikovsky's Ballets*, p. 128, describes the musical devices that create a sense of both flow and pivot.

42 Vaughan, "Aurora Awakened," p. 80.

43 Croce, "The Royal Ballet," p. 371.

44 See Shirley Wynne, "Complaisance, An Eighteenth-Century Cool," *Dance Scope*, Vol. 5, no. 1 (Fall 1970): 22–35.

45 Noël Carroll, in *The Philosophy of Horror: Paradoxes of the Heart* (New York: Routledge, 1990), defines monsters in what he calls art-horror as category errors, a status that elicits our revulsion: both living and dead (vampires), both human and animal (werewolves).

46 Several dance writers refer to this as Aurora's sixteenth birthday party, but according to both the original scenario (written, but not signed, by Vsevolozhsky) and Petipa's balletmaster's plan, Aurora is 20 in Act I of the ballet. In Perrault's tale, Beauty is "fifteen or sixteen" when, visiting with her royal parents one of their many country houses, she wanders into a tower where an old woman sits spinning, sees a spindle for the first time, and pricks her finger. There is no scene with suitors in the original Perrault tale, nor is the old woman with the spindle the wicked fairy, for she, "greatly embarrassed . . . called for help" (*Beauties, Beasts and Enchantment: Classic French Fairy Tales*, translated and with an introduction by Jack Zipes [New York: Penguin/New American Library, 1989], p. 45).

47 Wiley, *Tchaikovsky's Ballets*, p. 172, quotes from the choreographic notation of *The Sleeping Beauty* in the Harvard Theatre Collection, which includes prose "translations" of mime passages, diagrams of floor plans, and symbols for body movements according to the system devised by the dancer Vladimir Stepanov. Note the traditional connection of the terms "gossipers" and "knitting."

48 Wiley, *Tchaikovsky's Ballets*, p. 173.

49 In the Disney film, set to Tchaikovsky's music, the Garland Waltz is Americanized, reduced to just one individual couple – Aurora and Désiré – sans human community.

But Aurora, dressed like a peasant girl (because her fairy godmothers are raising her incognito in a cottage in the woods), nevertheless harks back to the villagers of Petipa's ballet.

50 Alastair Macaulay notes that it was Margot Fonteyn who introduced the sustained unsupported balances on pointe, in attitude ("A Hundred Years" p. 15). But I would submit that this late addition is entirely in keeping with the original choreography, in which Aurora maintained perfect equilibrium while shifting her hold from one partner's hand to that of the next. Fonteyn merely accentuated and prolonged that unsupported moment. Also, Aurora often balances on pointe, unsupported, in her variations.

51 Jowitt, *Time*, p. 251.

52 My own feminist interpretation, acknowledging the strength displayed by both the dancer and the character in this section, differs from that of the anti-ballet feminists, for instance, Christy Adair, who writes, "The Rose Adagio, in which the princess dances with each of her suitors in turn, is an excellent example of the woman on display. She balances on pointe whilst they take turns to revolve her slowly on the spot. . . . [The dance] emphasises the woman as object" (*Women and Dance: Sylphs and Sirens* [New York: New York University Press, 1992], pp. 104–105).

53 Wiley, *Tchaikovsky's Ballets*, p. 329.

54 See Lopukhov, "Choreography," p. 29.

55 Wiley, *Tchaikovsky's Ballets*, p. 329.

56 It should be noted, however, that Pavel Gerdt, the original Désiré, wore heeled shoes.

57 John Warrack points out that the andante cantabile at the beginning of the adagio resembles the second theme of the slow movement in Tchaikovsky's Fifth Symphony, which the composer apparently wrote as a declaration of love (*Tchaikovsky Ballet Music*, pp. 46–47).

58 Krasovskaia suggests that the various fairytales correspond to different life stages ("Petipa and 'Beauty,'" pp. 46–47).

59 According to Wiley, the *pas de quatre* finally consisted of a trio for Gold, Silver, and Sapphire (to the music originally intended for Silver's variation), a solo for Diamond, and a coda for all four (*Tchaikovsky's Ballets*, p. 184). The music originally intended for Gold was used for Aurora's variation in Act II, the vision scene, and the solo variation for Sapphire was cut entirely (p. 153).

60 See John Milton, "The Doctrine and Discipline of Divorce," in *Complete Poetry and Selected Prose of Milton* (New York: Modern Library, 1950), pp. 615–662.

61 In the Disney film, Aurora communes with all the animals in the forest to show what a loving person, in touch with nature, she is, and there is a bluebird in her sylvan menagerie.

62 Wiley, *Tchaikovsky's Ballet*, pp. 132, 146.

63 I am following the spelling (Confiturembourg, Drosselmayer) and name usage (Clara rather than E.T.A. Hoffmann's Marie) given by Wiley in his translations of the libretto (*Tchaikovsky's Ballets*, pp. 333–337) and of Petipa's instructions to Tchaikovsky (pp. 371–376) and in his transcription of Petipa's balletmaster's plan (pp. 376–382).

64 Wiley, *Tchaikovsky's Ballets*, p. 336.

65 My sources for *The Nutcracker* include: Wiley, *Tchaikovsky's Ballets*, pp. 193–241, 333–337, 371–382; Jack Anderson, *The Nutcracker Ballet* (New York: Mayflower, 1979); George Balanchine's production (first choreographed in 1954 and revised in 1964). Although Balanchine's version does not pretend to be an exact restoration of the original, which was choreographed by Lev Ivanov according to Marius Petipa's plans (Petipa fell ill before he could compose the dances), Balanchine danced in the St. Petersburg version as a child and a young man. In much of the ballet – especially the group dances – Balanchine followed Ivanov's style, and often he quoted the exact steps of the original. (See Nancy Reynolds, *Repertory in Review: 40 Years of the New York*

City Ballet [New York: Dial, 1977], pp. 153–158.) Balanchine's New York City Ballet production, staged by Peter Martins, was directed for film by Emile Ardolino in 1993, with a cast that includes Darci Kistler as the Sugar Plum Fairy, Damian Woetzel as the Cavalier, Kyra Nichols as Dewdrop, Bart Robinson Cook as Herr Drosselmeier, Jessica Lynn Cohen as Marie, and Macaulay Caulkin as Drosselmeier's Nephew (the Nutcracker Prince). The film is available on videotape.

66 Richard Stites, *The Women's Liberation Movement in Russia: Feminism, Nihilism, and Bolshevism, 1860–1930* (Princeton: Princeton University Press, 1991), pp. 10–11.

67 My sources for *Swan Lake* include the following scholarly and critical texts: Wiley, *Tchaikovsky's Ballets*, pp. 25–91, 321–327, 411–413; Cyril W. Beaumont, *The Ballet Called Swan Lake* (New York: Dance Horizons, 1982); Yuri Slonimsky, *"Lebedinoe Ozero" P. Chaikovskogo* [P. Tchaikovsky's "Swan Lake"] (Leningrad: State Musical Publishing House, 1962); A. Demidov, *Lebedinoe Ozero* ["Swan Lake"] (Moscow: Iskusstvo, 1985); Janice Ross and Stephen Cobbett Steinberg, eds., "Why a Swan?," *San Francisco Performing Arts Library and Museum Journal*, 1 (Spring 1989); Arlene Croce, "Swans," *The New Yorker*, 27 August 1973, reprinted in *Afterimages*, pp. 8–12. My performance sources include viewings of many versions by myriad ballet companies, especially David Blair's 1967 staging for American Ballet Theatre, which is available on videotape, dir. Kirk Browning, with Natalia Makarova and Ivan Nagy dancing the lead roles.

68 Arlene Croce writes, of Makarova's performance, "Odette appeared isolated, inviolable, already free in her totally passive acceptance of her fate. It was the fate of a slave. Until the last act she did not protest" ("Swans," p. 10).

69 See, for instance, Susan Leigh Foster, "The Ballerina's Phallic Pointe," in Susan Leigh Foster, ed., *Corporealities: Dancing Knowledge, Culture and Power* (London: Routledge, 1996), pp. 1–24. Cynthia Novack refers sweepingly to balletic "stereotypes of gender which perpetuate representations of women as fragile creatures supported by powerful men" ("Ballet, Gender, and Cultural Power," in Helen Thomas, ed., *Dance, Gender and Culture* [London: Macmillan, 1995], p. 39).

70 Wiley, *Tchaikovsky's Ballets*, pp. 188–189.

71 Poesio, "Beauty," p. 41.

72 See Robert C. Allen, *Horrible Prettiness: Burlesque and American Culture* (Chapel Hill, NC: University of North Carolina Press, 1991).

73 Warner associates the reluctant bride motif to the Beauty and the Beast tale (*Beast*, pp. 273–297).

74 Attention to women's issues was crushed just when, in the last two decades of the century, rapid industrialization, urbanization, and the decline of the aristocracy created new problems that deeply affected a new female proletariat (one that also involved unmarried gentry women), including wretched working and living conditions, wife and child abuse, and a rise in prostitution, venereal disease, and sex crimes against women (see Stites, *The Women's Liberation Movement*).

75 Stites informs us that "scores of well-read, witty, polyglot, literary-minded women appeared in both the capitals. . . . Their ready erudition became so renowned that foreign visitors were willing to testify, at the end of the [eighteenth] century, that women in Russian high society tended to be better read and generally more cultivated than men." Beyond that, these women were appreciated for their sexual sophistication (pp. 14–15).

76 That same year, the Ministry of Education closed down women's university courses (they were seen as hotbeds of anarchism), and attacks were made even on girls' secondary education (*The Women's Liberation Movement*, p. 168).

77 Stites, *The Women's Liberation Movement*, p. 168.

78 Bronislava Nijinska describes her brother's situation on the eve of his momentous audition for the School in 1898: "Once accepted, there would be no more uncertainty

or financial anxiety about his education. He would become an Artist of the Imperial Theatres, a permanent government position. If, God willing, he should advance to the rank of *premier danseur*, and Mother had no doubt that he would, then he would be assured not only of a large salary but also of a distinguished and honorable position in the Imperial Theatres and, at age thirty-six, a life pension almost equal to his salary." (Bronislava Nijinska, *Early Memoirs*, trans. and ed. Irina Nijinska and Jean Rawlinson, intro. and in consultation with Anna Kisselgoff [Durham, NC: Duke University Press, 1992], pp. 74–75.) Also, see Lynn Garafola, *Diaghilev's Ballets Russes* (New York: Oxford University Press, 1989), pp. 189–190.

79 Reportedly, during her 1911 American tour, Anna Pavlova told a reporter, "How would you feel toward a country where it is possible for a Grand Duke to come backstage and order the *maitre de ballet* to line up the ballet corps for his inspection? Then, as he strolls down the lie, he points with his cane. 'There. That one! Put her in my carriage. I will take that one for tonight'" (Keith Money, *Anna Pavlova: Her Life and Art* [New York: Knopf, 1982], p. 140n, quoted in Garafola, *Ballets Russes*, p. 446 n. 41).

80 On Petipa's family, see *The Diaries of Marius Petipa*, trans., ed., and intro. Lynn Garafola, *Studies in Dance History*, Vol. 3, no. 1 (Spring 1992): xxv.

81 Turgenev's play *A Month in the Country* (1850) directly addresses a woman's unhappiness in marriage, and Tolstoy's *Anna Karenina* (1877) treats the marriage theme and adultery tragically. Alexander Herzen's novel *Who Is to Blame?* (1846) and Nikolai Chernyshevsky's novel *What Is to Be Done?* (1863) both treat gendered domestic hierarchies as metaphors for larger social structures of domination, and both indict marriage in ways that were enormously influential for the nineteenth-century Russian feminist movement. However, these debates do not enter into the world of *The Sleeping Beauty* in the slightest. On the ideology of sexuality in late imperial Russia, see Laura Engelstein, *The Keys to Happiness: Sex and the Search for Modernity in Fin-de-Siècle Russia* (Ithaca, NY: Cornell University Press, 1992).

3 EARLY MODERN DANCE

1 *Annabelle Gamson: On Dancing Isadora's Dances*, dir. Scott Morris, 1988.

2 For a cultural history of early modern dance, see Elizabeth Kendall, *Where She Danced* (New York: Knopf, 1979).

3 Eugen Wolff, "Die Moderne," reprinted in Erich Ruprecht, ed., *Literarische Manifeste des Naturalismus, 1880–1892* (Stuttgart, 1962), pp. 138–141. Quoted in Malcolm Bradbury and James McFarlane, "The Name and Nature of Modernism," in Malcolm Bradbury and James McFarlane, eds., *Modernism* (Harmondsworth: Penguin, 1976), pp. 41–42.

4 Philippe Jullian, *The Triumph of Art Nouveau: Paris Exhibition 1900* (London: Phaidon, 1974), pp. 38, 42.

5 Jullian, *Art Nouveau*, p. 94.

6 Quoted in Jullian, *Art Nouveau*, pp. 94–95.

7 Jullian, *Art Nouveau*, p. 85.

8 Jullian, *Art Nouveau*, p. 90.

9 On Fuller's life and career, see Loïe Fuller, *Fifteen Years of a Dancer's Life* (Boston: Small, Maynard, and Co., 1913; reprint ed., Brooklyn: Dance Horizons, n.d.); Margaret Haile Harris, *Loïe Fuller: Magician of Light* (Richmond: The Viriginia Museum, 1979); Sally R. Sommer, "Loïe Fuller," *The Drama Review*, Vol. 19, no. 1 (March 1975; T-65): 53–67; and Sally R. Sommer, "The Stage Apprenticeship of Loïe Fuller," *Dance Scope*, Vol. 12, no. 1 (Fall/Winter 1977–78): 23–34.

10 Deborah Jowitt, *Time and the Dancing Image* (New York: William Morrow, 1988), p. 345.

11 Isadora Duncan, *My Life* (Garden City, New York: Star Books, 1927), p. 95.

12 Quoted in Frank Kermode, "Poet and Dancer Before Diaghilev," *Puzzles and Epiphanies* (New York: Chilmark Press, 1962), p. 24. All the quotes from Mallarmé following this one are also taken from the Kermode article.
13 See Valerie Steele, *Fashion and Eroticism: Ideals of Feminine Beauty from the Victorian Era to the Jazz Age* (New York: Oxford University Press, 1985), pp. 174–177.
14 Jean Lorrain, quoted in Jullian, *Art Nouveau*, p. 89.
15 Jowitt, *Time*, p. 347.
16 Quoted in Jullian, *Art Nouveau*, pp. 89–90.
17 Jowitt notes that Roger Marx, writing about *Lily* in 1905, remarks on precisely this effect of the underlighting (*Time*, p. 344).
18 Sommer, "Loïe Fuller," p. 61.
19 New York *Blade*, 11 April 1896, quoted in Sommer, "Loïe Fuller," p. 61.
20 The Lalique grill is reproduced in Jullian, *Art Nouveau*, p. 89.
21 Deborah L. Silverman, *Art Nouveau in Fin-de-Siècle France: Politics, Psychology, and Style* (Berkeley: University of California Press, 1989).
22 Sommer, "Stage Apprenticeship," p. 24.
23 Sommer, "Loïe Fuller," p. 63.
24 In analyzing these dances, I have relied on reconstructions by Annabelle Gamson. *Mother* and *Revolutionary Etude* appear in two video versions: *On Dancing Isadora's Dances* and "Trailblazers of Modern Dance," narr. Michael Tolan, prod. Merrill Brockway, dir. Emile Ardolino, *Dance in America*, PBS, WNET/Thirteen, New York, 4 January 1978. *Brahms Waltzes* appears in *On Dancing Isadora's Dances*.
25 In *Ecstasy and the Demon: Feminism and Nationalism in the Dances of Mary Wigman* (Berkeley: University of California Press, 1993), pp. 34–40, Susan Manning discusses the essentialism or, as she terms it, the cultural feminism, of Duncan's views on gender and nationality. She points out that Duncan's rhetoric was both liberatory and potentially racist, linked as her views of physical culture were with to a notion of eugenics. In *Done Into Dance: Isadora Duncan in America* (Bloomington: University of Indiana Press, 1995), pp. 178–204, Ann Daly points out how skillfully Duncan wove together themes of nationalism and motherhood to project powerful images of patriotic fervor during her American tour in 1916 and especially 1917, as the U.S. prepared to enter the First World War. Daly, however, argues that Duncan's feminism – and in particular her championing of motherhood – was not biological essentialism, but rather, influenced by various American and European movements for women's emancipation, was an iconoclastic, liberationist refusal to subjugate women's sexuality to the state (pp. 162–166). Daly tantalizingly speculates that Duncan was sympathetic to the German *Mutterschutz* movement, which advocated legal rights for women, welfare for unmarried mothers, and abortion rights. But while Duncan frequently advocated the right to motherhood outside of wedlock, it is not at all clear that she supported abortion rights, and she certainly disparaged the suffragist demand for the vote.
26 Gamson quotes Duncan in her own characterization of the dance in *On Dancing Isadora's Dances*.
27 Marina Warner, *Monuments and Maidens: The Allegory of the Female Form* (New York: Atheneum, 1985), p. 283.
28 See Denys Haynes, *Greek Art and the Idea of Freedom* (London: Thames and Hudson, 1981), plates 39–41.
29 Haynes, *Greek Art*, p. 84.
30 Isadora Duncan, *Isadora Speaks*, ed. and intro. Franklin Rosemont (San Francisco: City Lights Books, 1981), p. 49.
31 Daly, *Done into Dance*, p. 289.
32 Warner, *Monuments*, pp. 267–293. See my Chapter 1 on the dangerous potential for violence and disorder seen in French women after the Revolution.
33 Warner, *Monuments*, p. 282.

34 See Warner, *Monuments*, pp. 292–293. She writes, "Otherness is a source of potential and power; but it cannot occupy the center" (p. 293).

35 I use the terms "orientalist" and "orientalism" here to mean artistic constructions and representations of the East, in particular of the Middle East, Central Asia, and South Asia. As John M. Mackenzie points out, the term "orientalism" has a long and complex history, ranging from its politically oppressive use in British imperial policy in eighteenth-century India to its descriptive use of Asian motifs in Western art history (*Orientalism: History, Theory, and the Arts* [Manchester: Manchester University Press, 1995], pp. xii–xviii). In the literature on ballet and modern dance, the term has often been used without political resonance – simply to refer to the use of Eastern motifs in the West. My use of the term has been influenced by Edward Said's pioneering work on the subject, most notably in *Orientalism* (New York: Pantheon, 1978). However, I depart somewhat from Said's view that orientalism is nothing but a negative term in a discourse of European (and in this case, Euro-American) domination, since I will argue that St. Denis used orientalism as a positive framework for understanding national identity as well as gender identity.

36 Jowitt, *Time*, pp. 126–127. Jowitt does point out, however, that in 1931, St. Denis did finally dance the role of Salome and also acted the role in Oscar Wilde's play. For a thorough discussion of the Salome theme in American high and popular culture, see Kendall, *Where She Danced*, pp. 74–90.

37 Quoted in Jullian, *Art Nouveau*, p. 159.

38 Jullian, *Art Nouveau*, p. 169.

39 See Shelley C. Berg, "Sada Yacco in London and Paris, 1900: le rêve realisé," *Dance Chronicle*, Vol. 18, no. 3 (1995): 343–404.

40 Suzanne Shelton has documented through St. Denis's letters that she asked Belasco if she could perform her own Japanese dance, called *Madame Butterfly*, inbetween the performance of the short play *Madame Butterfly* and another play (Suzanne Shelton, *Divine Dancer: A Biography of Ruth St. Denis* [Garden City, NY: Doubleday, 1981], p. 41). But according to Shelton, the Japanese dance never materialized. This would have taken place in London, before St. Denis's visit to the Paris Exhibition. But both Belasco and St. Denis might have already seen Sada Yacco, who made an American tour in 1899–1900, or might have known about her work through newspaper reviews. (See Shelley C. Berg, "Sada Yacco: The American Tour, 1899–1900," *Dance Chronicle*, Vol. 16, no. 2 [1993]: 147–196.)

41 Kendall, *Where She Danced*, p. 47.

42 In calling St. Denis's *Radha* a "scopophilic" performance, for instance, Jane Desmond neglects the social context of audience reception for the dance ("Dancing Out the Difference: Cultural Imperialism and Ruth St. Denis's 'Radha' of 1906," *Signs*, Vol. 17, no. 1 [Autumn 1991]: 28–49).

43 Quoted in Kendall, *Where She Danced*, p. 48.

44 Kendall, *Where She Danced*, p. 48.

45 Kendall, *Where She Danced*, p. 78.

46 Shelton, *Divine Dancer*, p. 55.

47 On St. Denis's biography, see Shelton, *Divine Dancer* and Jowitt, *Time*.

48 Ruth St. Denis, *An Unfinished Life* (New York: Harper and Brothers, 1939), p. 52.

49 See Shelton, *Divine Dancer*, pp. 46–49.

50 Shelton, *Divine Dancer*, pp. 49–50.

51 St. Denis, *An Unfinished Life*, pp. 59–60.

52 Shelton, *Divine Dancer*, pp. 50–51.

53 St. Denis, *An Unfinished Life*, p. 57.

54 St. Denis, *An Unfinished Life*, p. 66.

55 Caroline and Charles Caffin, *Dancing and Dancers Today* (New York: Dodd, Mead, 1912), quoted in St. Denis, *An Unfinished Life*, p. 66.

56 St. Denis, *An Unfinished Life*, p. 71.
57 St. Denis, *An Unfinished Life*, p. 70.
58 See, for instance, the engraving of the dancing chorus in *Lakmé*, dressed in quasi-Indian costume but kicking up a cancan, reproduced in Roger Parker, ed., *The Oxford Illustrated History of Opera* (Oxford: Oxford University Press, 1994), p. 164.
59 As Suzanne Shelton points out, St. Denis constantly changed the choreography of *Radha* over the many years she performed it. My description is taken both from my viewings of Dwight Godwin's 1941 film and from Shelton's account. The latter is a synthesis of several sources, including St. Denis's unpublished scenario; see Shelton, *Divine Dancer*, p. 279.
60 St. Denis, *An Unfinished Life*, p. 70. In Godwin's film, the objects have apparently changed slightly; the jewels represent touch, the flowers smell, cymbals sound, and a bowl taste (although she takes the prop, the Dance of Taste was not filmed). However, there may be a mistake in the film's subtitles, because in the film there is no Dance of Sight at all, and also because there is a later section in which St. Denis touches herself, but, according to the film's subtitles, that is part of the Delirium of the Senses. In other words, I suspect that the proper sequence of titles for the film *should* be: Dance of Sight, Dance of Smell, Dance of Sound, Dance of Taste, Dance of Touch.
61 St. Denis, *An Unfinished Life*, p. 70.
62 St. Denis, *An Unfinished Life*, p. 70.
63 Hugo von Hofmannsthal, "Her Extraordinary Immediacy," p. 38, quoted in Shelton, *Divine Dancer*, p. 64.
64 Philip Hale, *Boston Herald*, quoted in St. Denis, *An Unfinished Life*, p. 135.
65 Shelton, *Divine Dancer*, p. 39.
66 Shelton, *Divine Dancer*, p. 65.
67 Desmond, "Dancing out the Difference," p. 44.
68 Desmond, "Dancing out the Difference," p. 45.
69 Linda Nochlin, "The Imaginary Orient," *Art in America*, Vol. 71, no. 5 (May 1983): 125, quoted in Desmond, "Dancing out the Difference," p. 45.
70 Kendall, *Where She Danced*, p. 51.
71 Desmond, "Dancing out the Difference," p. 46.
72 Although Desmond spends the bulk of her article criticizing St. Denis for her politics of cultural appropriation, she does acknowledge in her conclusion that performance "[unsettles] the binarisms of the ideologies that undergird racism, sexism, and orientalism." However, she concludes that "the element of mastery . . . , implied by the right to represent the 'other,' remains" ("Dancing out the Difference," p. 47).
73 Ralph Waldo Emerson, *Journals*, I, 342, quoted in Frederic Ives Carpenter, *Emerson and Asia* (Cambridge, MA: Harvard University Press, 1930), p. 8.
74 Carpenter, *Emerson and Asia*, p. 32.
75 *The Journals and Miscellaneous Notebooks of Ralph Waldo Emerson, Vol. IX, 1843–1847*, ed. Ralph H. Orth and Alfred R. Ferguson (Cambridge, MA: Belknap Press/Harvard University Press, 1971), p. 322.
76 *Journals of Ralph Waldo Emerson*, IX: 315.
77 Quoted in St. Denis, *An Unfinished Life*, p. 68.
78 *Radha*, film by Godwin.
79 Kendall, *Where She Danced*, p. 78.
80 St. Denis, *An Unfinished Life*, p. 57.
81 Quoted in Shelton, *Divine Dancer*, p. 132.

4 EARLY MODERN BALLET

1 Lynn Garafola, "Beautiful Boys (and the Girls): Reconfiguring the Sexes in Diaghilev's Ballets Russes," in Lynn Garafola and Nancy Van Norman Baer, eds., *The Ballets Russes and Its World* (New Haven, CT: Yale University Press, 1998).

2 See Joan Acocella, "The Reception of Diaghilev's Ballets Russes by Artists and Intellectuals in Paris and London, 1909–1914" (Ph.D. diss., Rutgers University, 1984), pp. 225–238.

3 Alexandre Benois, who perhaps initiated the idea of a new Russian fairytale ballet (to supersede *The Little Humpbacked Horse*), remembers, "The working out of these elements [of the libretto] was undertaken by a sort of conference in which Tcherepnine (who was supposed to be writing the music), Fokine, the painters Steletzky, Golovine, and I took part" (*Reminiscences of the Russian Ballet* [London: Putnam, 1941; reprint ed. New York: Da Capo, 1977], p. 304). However, according to Stravinsky, even more changes took place in the scenario after he received the music commission: "Fokine is usually credited as the librettist of *The Firebird*, but I remember that all of us, and especially Bakst, who was Diaghilev's principal adviser, contributed ideas to the plan of the scenario" (Igor Stravinsky and Robert Craft, *Expositions and Developments* [Garden City, NY: Doubleday, 1962], p. 146). The symbolist writer Aleksei Remizov, known for his grotesque, comic diableries based on pagan Russian rites, was called in to consult on Kostchei's retinue and other aspects of Russian folklore. (See Prince Peter Lieven, *The Birth of the Ballets-Russes* [London: Allen and Unwin, 1936; reprint edition, New York: Dover, 1973], pp. 106–107, and Michael Green, ed. and trans., *The Russian Symbolist Theatre* [Ann Arbor: Ardis, 1986], pp. 311–312. Also see Richard Taruskin, *Stravinsky and the Russian Traditions*, Vol. I [Berkeley: University of California Press, 1996], p. 558.)

4 In 1926, the ballet was restaged with new costumes and decor by Natalia Goncharova.

5 See Cyril W. Beaumont, *Complete Book of Ballets* (London: Putnam, 1937), p. 712, who mentions "The Tale of Ivan Tsarevich," "The Bird of Light and the Grey Wolf" and a story about Kostchei. Also see Simon Karlinsky, "A Cultural Educator of Genius," in Nancy Van Norman Baer, ed., *The Art of Enchantment: Diaghilev's Ballets Russes 1909–1929* (San Francisco: Fine Arts Museums/Universe Books, 1988), p. 21; Lynn Garafola, *Diaghilev's Ballets Russes* (New York: Oxford, 1989), p. 29; Richard Taruskin, "From *Firebird* to *The Rite*: Folk Elements in Stravinsky's Scores," *Ballet Review*, Vol. 10, no. 2 (Summer 1982): 74; and Taruskin, *Stravinsky*, pp. 556–558.

6 I have based my analysis of *Firebird* on the written sources in note 5 and on my viewings of the American Ballet Theatre version, as well as on the version danced by the Royal Ballet in *The Royal Ballet* (dir. Paul Czinner, 1959), featuring Margot Fonteyn as the Firebird. This version, with costumes and decor by Goncharova, unfortunately omits the dance of the maidens with the golden apples.

7 Lieven writes, "The ballet was jumbled together from rags of various classical Russian fairy tales. The resulting patchwork, although colourful, was not convincing for a Russian. It was as if Alice of *Alice in Wonderland* were partnered with Falstaff in a Scotch jig" (*Birth of the Ballets Russes*, p. 107). And the critic André Levinson considered the pas de deux "annoyingly silly," and while complimenting the design, he complains that the ballet "has nothing in common with real folk art and even the plot of the folk tale was presented in the scenario in an insipid, confused way." (*Ballet Old and New*, trans. Susan Cook Summer [New York: Dance Horizons, 1982], pp. 14, 16).

8 Fokine himself notes: "In the composition of the dances I used three methods vastly different both in character and technique. The evil kingdom was built on movements at times grotesque, angular and ugly, and at times comical. . . . The princesses

danced barefoot with natural, graceful, soft movements and some accent of the Russian folk dance. The dance of the Firebird I staged on toe . . . [It] was highly technical" (*Fokine: Memoirs of a Ballet Master*, trans. Vitale Fokine and ed. Anatole Chujoy [Boston: Little, Brown, 1961], p. 167.)

9 Garafola describes it thus: "Ivan Tsarevich stands behind his prey, clutching her with the arrogance of a cad; she twists, bends, turns, reaching for his hands, aspiring to the distancing clasp that will return each of them to their separate spheres" (*Ballets Russes*, p. 36).

10 Although Levinson simply disparages the pas de deux, without seeing in it an alternative interpretation of the sort I am advancing (on the contrary, he thinks there is a mistake), he hints that there is a conflict between the plot and the performance: "She wants to break loose, fly off, but his strong hand holds her fast. Whether it was a difficulty with the musical rhythm or the technical inadequacy of the *danseuse*, the impression created was just the opposite, and was annoyingly silly. It looked as though Ivan Tsarevich were attempting in vain to hoist the Firebird into the air, to force her to leave the ground and fly while she, meanwhile, was foiling his plan" (*Ballet Old and New*, p. 14).

11 Igor Stravinsky and Robert Craft, *Memories and Commentaries* (London: Faber and Faber, 1960), p. 33.

12 See Nancy Reynolds and Susan Reimer-Torn, *Dance Classics: A Viewer's Guide to the Best-Loved Ballets and Modern Dances* (Pennington, NJ: A Cappella Books, 1991), p. 98. Taruskin points out that the princesses' khorovod (round-dance) "is not really a khorovod but rather a wedding song – more specifically, a song to be sung at a *devichnik*, the wedding eve bridal shower at which the bride's girlfriends plait her hair" (*Stravinsky*, p. 627). Thus, Ivan has arrived just in time to become the Tsarevna's awaited bridegroom.

13 In Maurice Béjart's 1970 version of the ballet, the Firebird is a male figure.

14 Boris Kochno, *Diaghilev and the Ballets Russes*, trans. Adrienne Foulke (New York: Harper and Row, 1970), p. 53.

15 See Joanna Hubbs, *Mother Russia: The Feminine Myth in Russian Culture* (Bloomington: Indiana University Press, 1988), pp. 27–34.

16 Richard Buckle, *Diaghilev* (New York: Atheneum, 1979), p. 121.

17 I have written about this in more detail in "*Firebird*, the Asian Bloodline, and the Russian Body Politic," in Garafola and Baer, eds., *The Ballets Russes and Its World*.

18 On Roerich, see Kenneth Archer, "Nicholas Roerich and His Theatrical Designs: A Research Survey," *Dance Research Journal*, Vol. 18, no. 2 (Winter 1986–87): 3–6.

19 Igor Stravinsky, *An Autobiography* (New York: M. and J. Steuer, 1958), p. 31. Stravinsky recalls that he immediately recounted his vision to Nicholas Roerich, who then became his collaborator. But Millicent Hodson, in "Nijinsky's Choreographic Method: Visual Sources from Roerich for *Le Sacre du printemps*," *Dance Research Journal*, Vol. 18, no. 2 (Winter 1986–87): 7, refutes this, pointing out that Roerich had already written a scenario for a ballet on this theme before Stravinsky first suggested the collaboration. She cites Bronislava Nijinska (*Early Memoirs*, trans. and ed. Irina Nijinska and Jean Rawlinson [New York: Holt, Rinehart, and Winston, 1981], p. 448), who in turn cites an August 1910 interview with Roerich in the *St. Petersburg Gazette*. According to the interview, Roerich had by then written the scenario. However, this chronology does not preclude Stravinsky's version of events, since he would have told Roerich about his idea sometime before the premiere of *Firebird*, which took place in June 1910.

20 See Hodson, "Nijinsky's Choreographic Method," pp. 7–15.

21 Igor Stravinsky (interviewed by R. Canudo), "Ce que j'ai voulu exprimer dans Le Sacre du printemps," *Montjoie*, 29 May 1913, quoted in Jann Pasler, "Music and

Spectacle in *Petrushka* and *The Rite of Spring*," in Jann Passler, ed., *Confronting Stravinsky: Man, Musician, and Modernist* (Berkeley: University of California Press, 1986), p. 69.

22 Igor Stravinsky, Letter to N.F. Findeizen, 15 December 1912, in Igor Stravinsky, *The Rite of Spring: Sketches, 1911–1913* (London: Boosey and Hawkes, 1969), Appendix, pp. 32–33.

23 The letter is quoted in Serge Lifar, *Serge Diaghilev: His Life, His Work, His Legend* (New York: G. P. Putnam's Sons, 1940), p. 200.

24 Lincoln Kirstein, *Four Centuries of Ballet: Fifty Masterworks* (New York: Dover, 1984), p. 206.

25 "From 'Le Sacre du Printemps' by Jacques Rivière: November, 1913," trans. Miriam Lassman, in Lincoln Kirstein, *Nijinsky Dancing* (New York: Knopf, 1975), pp. 164, 168.

26 See Stravinsky, *The Rite*; Kirstein, *Four Centuries*, pp. 206–209; Hodson, "Nijinsky's Choreographic Method."

27 The original Nijinsky choreography was lost after the season the ballet was created, when it was performed only seven (or, as some historians speculate, nine) times, although many other choreographers have created dances to Stravinsky's music. In 1989, Millicent Hodson and Kenneth Archer created the choreography and design for a reconstructed version of the original production. Performed by the Joffrey Ballet, it was documented in "The Search for Nijinsky's *Rite of Spring*" (narr. Kathryn Walker, prod. Judy Kinberg and Thomas Grimm, dir. Thomas Grimm and Judy Kinberg, co-production of WNET/NY and Danmarks Radio in association with Czechoslovak Television and BBC, La Sept, NOS Television, *Dance in America*, exec. prod. Rhoda Grauer, Great Performances, PBS, WNET, New York, 24 November 1989). Although the Hodson/Archer reconstruction is surely not the same as the original, the extensive research this team carried out and their considered speculation has produced something as close to the original as we can hope to get, and therefore I base my analysis on their production, which I have viewed both live and on videotape. For a criticism of this reconstruction, see Joan Acocella, "Nijinsky/Nijinska Revivals: The Rite Stuff," *Art in America* (October 1991): 128–171.

28 Letter to Diaghilev, quoted in Lifar, *Serge Diaghilev*, p. 200.

29 Robert Craft, "'The Rite of Spring': Genesis of a Masterpiece," in Stravinsky, *The Rite of Spring*, p. xxi.

30 Boris Vladimirovich Asaf'yev, *A Book About Stravinsky*, trans. Richard F. French, intro. Robert Craft, Studies in Russian Music No. 5 (Ann Arbor, MI: UMI Research Press, 1982), p. 39.

31 Shelley C. Berg, *"Le Sacre du printemps": Seven Productions from Nijinsky to Martha Graham* (Ann Arbor: UMI Research Press, 1988), p. 52.

32 Richard Buckle notes that one of the melodies in this section is "reminiscent of the 'Firebird' princesses" (*Nijinsky* [Harmondsworth: Penguin, 1980], p. 351).

33 This is the method of "choice by lot" Millicent Hodson discovered in Marie Rambert's rehearsal notes from 1913. For an account of Hodson's work on the Chosen One's role, see Millicent Hodson, "*Sacre*: Searching for Nijinsky's Chosen One," *Ballet Review*, Vol. 15, no. 3 (Fall 1987): 53–66.

34 See Taruskin, "From *Firebird* to *The Rite*," p. 82.

35 Stravinsky, Letter to N.F. Findeizen, p. 33.

36 "From 'Le Sacre du Printemps,'" p. 167.

37 Millicent Hodson discusses the bird imagery in "*Sacre*: Searching for Nijinsky's Chosen One," pp. 63–65. The Russian folklorist Vladimir Propp points out the importance of bird imagery in traditional folk rituals on the spring equinox. "In spring the birds would come, and the peasants thought the birds had brought spring with them. The invocations of spring have the form of an address to the birds. . . . The children baked pastry in the form of birds . . . and tossed them up in the air. . . . All

this was to portray (and consequently, also summon) the arrival of the birds and the arrival of spring. . . . On this day birds were let out of their cages – a custom celebrated in verse by Pushkin." (V. Ja. Propp, "The Russian Folk Lyric," *Down Along the Mother Volga*, trans. and ed. Roberta Reeder [Philadelphia: University of Pennsylvania Press, 1975], p. 6.)

38 Nijinska, *Early Memoirs*, p. 450.

39 Kirstein, *Nijinsky Dancing*, p. 145.

40 Buckle, *Nijinsky*, p. 353.

41 The quote about Indians (referring to the action in "The Dancing Out of the Earth") and the characterization of the ghost dance (referring to "The Ritual Action of the Ancestors") are Stravinsky's, related by Craft, "The Rite of Spring," pp. xxi–xxii.

42 Hodson cites not only Simon Karlinsky, "Preliterate Russian Theatre," unpublished manuscript, and Cyril Beaumont, *Vaslav Nijinsky* (London: Beaumont, 1932), p. 10, but also an essay by Nicolas Roerich, "The Stone Age," *Adamant* (Paris: Franco-Russe, 1923; New York: Coruna Mundi, 1924), pp. 125–139, in which he connects archaic Slavic, Scandinavian, and Mexican ritual practices (Hodson, "Nijinsky's Choreographic Method," pp. 9–10).

43 Garafola attributes female sacrifice to the Aztecs (*Ballets Russes*, p. 72), citing both the 1900 and the 1913 editions of James Frazer, *The Golden Bough: A Study in Magic and Religion* (London: Macmillan). However, she notes that none of the authors of the ballet mentioned Mexican rituals as a source or influence.

44 See Colin Rhodes, *Primitivism and Modern Art* (London: Thames and Hudson, 1994), p. 62, who cites Hermann Ploss, *Woman* (1885) and Havelock Ellis, *Studies in the Psychology of Sex* (1903). One might also refer to Sigmund Freud, *Three Essays on Sexuality* (1905).

45 Rivière, "From 'Le Sacre de Printemps,'" p. 168.

46 Rivière, "From 'Le Sacre de Printemps,'" p. 168.

47 André Levinson, "Nijinsky's Ballets: *Le Sacre du Printemps, Jeux*," in *Ballet Old and New*, p. 54. On the sexualized stereotype of black women, and especially the Hottentot, see Sander L. Gilman, *Difference and Pathology: Stereotypes of Sexuality, Race, and Madness* (Ithaca, NY: Cornell University Press, 1985), pp. 76–93.

48 Levinson, "Nijinsky's Ballets," p. 55.

49 Hodson speculates whether Roerich chose to cast the sacrificial victim as a woman in order to reconcile "the desire to use an archaic subject with what he considered an appropriate way to end a ballet," for, as she points out, the "death of a young woman, or apotheosis of her spirit, is, after all, the crux of Romantic ballet" ("Nijinsky's Choreographic Method," p. 11). Joan Acocella, Lynn Garafola, and Jonnie Greene note that "female sacrifice, in its more lyrical manifestations, had been an obsession of the nineteenth century. As Edgar Allan Poe put it, 'the death . . . of a beautiful woman is, unquestionably, the most poetical topic in the world.'" But, they continue, "here there is no pretext: no poisoned scarf, no madness. The girl is forthrightly sent to her death in order to benefit the community. The situation could hardly be more horrible" (Joan Acocella, Lynn Garafola, and Jonnie Greene, "*The Rite of Spring* Considered as a Nineteenth Century Ballet," *Ballet Review*, Vol. 20, no. 2 [Summer 1992]: 68–71). And Garafola elsewhere points out that this sacrifical victim has been "shorn of . . . subversive sexuality, [assuming] the 'safe' guise of a young girl, ballet's traditional instrument of redemption" (*Ballets Russes*, p. 72).

50 Garafola, *Ballets Russes*, p. 72.

51 The intensity of the cult of the Virgin Mary, and her association with Mother Russia and Mother Earth, on the one hand, and individual human mothers, on the other hand, has been crucial to Russian folk and popular culture both in medieval and modern times. Indeed, both the Virgin herself and her image in icon paintings were

thought to serve an intercessory role with God in saving medieval Russian cities from invasion from the East. The Vladimir Mother of God, as an important twelfth-century icon is known, became, according to historian James H. Billington, "a symbol of national unity long before such unity became a political fact. She was the supreme mother image of old Russia: at peace with God, yet compassionately inclined toward her infant son." Mary's inclination toward her son was literal, for in many icons, "the Virgin bends her neck down beyond the point of anatomical possibility to embrace the Christ child" (*The Icon and the Axe: An Interpretive History of Russian Culture* [New York: Random House, Vintage Books, 1970], pp. 32–33).

52 Linda J. Ivanits, *Russian Folk Belief* (Armonk, NY: M. E. Sharpe, 1989), pp. 75–76. The *rusalki* could also take the form of monstrously ugly old women, however.

53 Asaf'yev, *A Book about Stravinsky*, p. 40.

54 Nancy Van Norman Baer, *Bronislava Nijinska: A Dancer's Legacy* (San Francisco: The Fine Arts Museums of San Francisco, 1986), p. 32.

55 Stravinsky and Craft, *Expositions*, p. 130.

56 See Roberta Reeder, "The Kireevsky Collection and the Neo-Russian Movement," *Dance Research Journal*, Vol. 18, no. 2 (Winter 1986–87): 32–36. Stravinsky credits Kireevsky in *Expositions*, p. 130.

57 Stravinsky and Craft, *Expositions*, pp. 130–131.

58 In July 1917, under the Provisional Government, women gained the right to vote (predating women's suffrage in the United States and most of Western Europe). After the October Revolution, full emancipation for women became a national goal for the first time in Russian history. The Bolsheviks advocated equal legal and political rights for women, protection from sexual harrassment, equal access to education and employment, pregnancy and maternity leave, and relief from the domestic burdens of housework and childcare. The Family Code of 1918 secularized marriage, recognized common-law marriage, and legalized divorce. The Women's Department of the Party (Zhenotdel) organized local discussion groups, sponsored education and job training for working-class and peasant women, and held national women's congresses. In 1920, abortion was legalized. See Barbara Evans Clements, *Daughters of Revolution: A History of Women in the U.S.S.R.* (Arlington Heights, IL: Harlan Davidson, 1994); Wendy Z. Goldman, *Women, the State, and Revolution: Soviet Family Policy and Social Life, 1917–1936* (Cambridge: Cambridge University Press, 1993); and Richard Stites, *The Women's Liberation Movement in Russia: Feminism, Nihilism, and Bolshevism, 1860–1930* (Princeton: Princeton University Press, 1991).

59 Emancipated from serfdom only in 1861, the peasants constituted more than four-fifths of Russia's population by 1917, and they had long had an adversarial relationship with the state that had exploded in massive uprisings and state retaliation in the 1905 revolution. Efforts to speed up industrialization since the 1890s included regular attempts to undermine the peasant commune and the rural economy.

60 See Vladimir Andrle, *A Social History of Twentieth-Century Russia* (London: Edward Arnold, 1994), pp. 46–47, on the patriarchal structure of the peasant household, the woman's sphere within that household, and the special oppression of young wives within the peasant family, including sexual abuse by fathers-in-law.

61 Clements, *Daughters of Revolution*, pp. 45–46.

62 Diaghilev assigned the ballet to Nijinska in 1922, but after their disagreement over the original Goncharova designs, he apparently withdrew the commission until April 1923. According to Buckle, the withdrawal "was bluff. If he did mean it for a moment, he did not mean it for long," and Buckle assumes that Nijinska began work on the ballet in 1922 (*Diaghilev*, pp. 400–401). But Nijinska remembers the situation differently: "The subject was dropped. . . . For a whole year, in our conversations, neither Diaghilev nor Stravinsky made any mention to me of *Les Noces*. Not until the spring of 1923 . . . " ("Creation of 'Les Noces': Bronislava Nijinska," trans. and intro.

Jean M. Serafetinides and Irina Nijinska, *Dance Magazine*, Vol. 48, no. 12 [December 1974]: 59). Thus, when Diaghilev said to her in April 1923, "Are you ready to begin rehearsals and choreograph this ballet?," Buckle assumes that she had been working on the ballet for a year, but Nijinska implies that she had not given it any thought at all, and that this was when the commission was finally settled.

63 Stravinsky writes, "No work of mine has undergone so many instrumental metamorphoses" (*Expositions*, p. 134).

64 Nijinska claims that it was she who categorically rejected the brightly colored designs, in the style of *Le Coq d'or*, first presented by Goncharova, as too operatic (although "admirably drawn"), too "Russo-Boyar." She recalls just as clearly that upon hearing the music, "I saw the picture of *Les Noces* and my choreographic line for this ballet" ("Creation," p. 59). Boris Kochno claims that it was Diaghilev who was displeased with both the vivid "folkloristic" and the pastel and silver versions, and that it was the impresario who suggested a "Russianized" version of the dancers' practice clothes, including the choice of colors (*Diaghilev and the Ballets Russes*, p. 189). But Stephen Weinstock points out that Goncharova herself later traced her own changing ideas about the subject of the ballet and expressed dissatisfaction with her designs ("The Evolution of *Les Noces*," *Dance Magazine*, Vol. 55, no. 4 [April 1981]: 70–75). Stravinsky, too, approved of the final design choices, as well as the choreography, although he does not give Nijinska any credit for changing Goncharova's designs. He writes, "[Nijinska's] conception of *Noces* in blocks and masses . . . coincided with my ideas, as well as with the real – not realistic – décors. The set of *Noces* was a bees-wax yellow and the costumes were brown peasant costumes, instead of the hideously un-Russian reds, greens and blues one usually sees in foreign stagings of Russian plays" (Stravinsky and Craft, *Memories*, p. 40).

65 Nijinska, "Creation," p. 59.

66 My description of the ballet is based on my viewings of the choreography in performances by the Royal Ballet (London), the Oakland Ballet, the SUNY-Purchase Dance Corps, and the Maly Ballet (St. Petersburg), as well as a study of the videotape of the Oakland Ballet's performance (*Les Noces*, prod. Frederick J. Maroth, dir. Jerome Schnur, Educational Media Associates, 1981), with Johanna Breyer as the Bride and Philip Sharper as the Groom.

67 The lyrics are taken from Igor Stravinsky, *Les Noces/The Wedding/Die Hochzeit: Ballet with Soli and Chorus*, English trans. D. Millar Craig, German trans. K. Gutheim and H. Kruger (London: J.W. Chester, 1922), p. 1.

68 Garafola, *Ballets Russes*, p. 128.

69 Kochno reports that Nijinska told Diaghilev, "*Noces* is a ballet that must be danced on point. That will elongate the dancers' silhouettes and make them resemble the saints in Byzantine mosaics" (*Diaghilev and the Ballets Russes*, p. 189).

70 Stravinsky, *Les Noces*, p. 3.

71 Garafola, *Ballets Russes*, p. 127.

72 Stravinsky and Craft, *Expositions*, p. 131.

73 Propp, "The Russian Folk Lyric," p. 23.

74 Stravinsky, *Les Noces*, pp. 5–7.

75 Stravinsky, *Les Noces*, p. 10.

76 Stravinsky, *Les Noces*, p. 15.

77 Asaf'yev, *A Book about Stravinsky*, p. 130.

78 Stravinsky, *Les Noces*, p. 48.

79 Asaf'yev, *A Book about Stravinsky*, p. 130.

80 Asaf'yev writes, "The deity is commanded, persistently and repeatedly: 'Pod' na svad'bu.' One has the impression that Stravinsky has laid bare the ancient heathen roots of orthodox ritual and its primitive incantatory signification (the cult of fertility and the propagation of the race)" (*A Book about Stravinsky*, p. 138), and Simon

Karlinsky points out, "When the Virgin Mary is commanded to bless the wedding and help comb the bridegroom's hair and then is given a direct order by the divided bassos (*Pod' na svad'bu*, which is roughly 'Off to the wedding with you!'), we realize that the mother of the Savior is here replacing some ancient fertility goddess. In monotheistic religions, divinities do not get ordered about" ("Igor Stravinsky and Russian Preliterate Theater," in Jann Pasler, ed., *Confronting Stravinsky: Man, Musician, and Modernist* [Berkeley: University of California Press, 1986], p. 9). And Stravinsky himself points out that the wedding saints Cosmos and Damian, who are invoked in this section, "were recognized as wedding saints in Russia, and they were popularly worshiped as deities of a fertility cult. (I have read that in southern Italian churches, peasant-made phallic objects are still found by images of Cosmos and Damian.)" (Stravinsky and Craft, *Expositions*, p. 131).

81 Stravinsky, *Les Noces*, pp. 84–85.
82 Stravinsky, *Les Noces*, pp. 87–88.
83 Nijinska, "Creation," p. 59.
84 Stravinsky and Craft, *Expositions*, p. 133.
85 Andrle points out that the nineteenth-century Russian journalist and sketch-writer Gleb Uspensky, working just after the emancipation of the serfs, argued that he could not develop individual characters in his narratives, because (in Andrle's words), "they live in a mass of humanity whose thought and will is embedded in the imperatives of their environment" (*A Social History*, p. 30).
86 See Reeder, "The Kireevsky Collection," p. 35.
87 Nijinska, "Creation," p. 59.
88 Stravinsky, *Les Noces*, pp. 151–153.
89 Propp, "The Russian Folk Lyric," p. 17.
90 Propp, "The Russian Folk Lyric," p. 17.
91 *Down Along the Mother Volga*, pp. 160–162.
92 Propp, "The Russian Folk Lyric," pp. 17–18.
93 Nijinska, "Creation," p. 59; emphasis in original.
94 Natalia Goncharova, "The Metamorphosis of *Les Noces*," quoted in Weinstock, "Evolution," p. 74.
95 Kirstein, *Four Centuries*, p. 222.
96 Nijinska, "Creation," p. 59.
97 Nijinska, "Creation," p. 59.
98 Garafola points out that "Nijinska herself preferred blue – the color of worker denims [worn by the Blue Blouse troupes] – to brown for the costumes [in *Les Noces*], but acceded to Gontcharova's wishes. Brown, the painter felt, stressed the proximity of the ballet's community to the earth" (*Ballets Russes*, p. 126). Garafola (*Ballets Russes*, p. 126), Baer (*Nijinska*, p. 35), and Marianne Moore ("Modern Art and Dance," *Art and Dance* [Boston: Institute of Contemporary Art, 1983], p. 43) have all pointed out the similarity of Nijinska's architectonic mass groupings to early Soviet constructivist theater.
99 Quoted in Joan Acocella and Lynn Garafola, Introduction, Joan Acocella and Lynn Garafola, eds., *André Levinson on Dance* (Hanover, NH: Wesleyan University Press/University Press of New England, 1991), p. 21.
100 Acocella and Garafola, *Levinson on Dance*, p. 41.
101 On Nijinska's years in Russia, see Baer, *Nijinska*, pp. 18–22 and Garafola, *Ballets Russes*, pp. 122–123.
102 Olga Vsevolodskaya-Golushkevich, "Vsevolod Vsevolodsky-Gerngross and the Dance," in Elizabeth Souritz and Sally Banes, eds., *Experimental Dance in the Soviet Union in the 1920s* (London: Gordon and Breach, forthcoming).
103 See Baer, *Nijinska*, p. 35.
104 On *Les Biches*, see Garafola, *Ballets Russes*, pp. 129–132; Baer, *Nijinska*, pp. 38–40.

105 Edith Shackleton, review in the *Evening Standard*, 26 May 1925, quoted in Baer, *Nijinska*, p. 40.
106 See Nancy Reynolds, *Repertory in Review: 40 Years of the New York City Ballet* (New York: Dial, 1977), pp. 46–50.

5 MODERN DANCE

1 In "Where Are Ballet's Women Choreographers?" (university lecture, University of Wisconsin-Madison, 10 November 1995), Lynn Garafola unearths the names of many forgotten women ballet choreographers working at the turn of the twentieth century. She argues that these women have disappeared from dance history for a complex of reasons: in an era before "choreographer" was a standard program credit, they were not always publicly identified as the creator of their dances; they usually worked in less than prestigious venues (often, popular stages); they frequently created dances that were not at the time considered "ballets" (for instance, dances in operas and féeries). Garafola notes that by the 1930s, women ballet choreographers (for instance, Marie Rambert and Ninette de Valois in England) had developed a way of creating dances according to models much like that of modern dance – by forming alternative, unofficial, female-headed organizations.
2 I address the nationalism of American modern dance in "Twentieth Century Dance," *The Great Ideas Today* (Chicago: Encyclopedia Britannica, 1991), pp. 84–101. Susan A. Manning, in *Ecstasy and the Demon: Feminism and Nationalism in the Dances of Mary Wigman* (Berkeley: University of California Press, 1993) discusses the nationalist implications of German modern dance.
3 Manning characterizes the American debate about whether dance should be an arena for left-political content as a struggle between a "leftist" wing of the modern dance movement and the "humanist" wing – consolidated, in her view, as the Bennington "consensus." Since much of this debate has little to do with representations of women, I will not engage with it here. Valuable as Manning's account of this struggle is, I would argue that the historical evidence shows that the Bennington "consensus" was not as politically homogeneous as she suggests. For instance, in 1935 members of the New Dance League (a later incarnation of the Workers' Dance League), including Anna Sokolow, Miriam Blecher, Sophie Maslow, Merle Hirsh, Jane Dudley, Lily Mehlman, Marie Marchowsky, and Lil Liandre, presented "An Evening of Revolutionary Dance," and in 1936, members of the New Dance League gave a concert of dances by Anna Sokolow, Bill Matons, Edith Orcutt, and Eva Desca. The 1937 season featured dance premieres on the subjects of the Spanish Civil War, the rise of fascism in Italy, and the imminence of war in Europe (See Sali Ann Kriegsman, *Modern Dance in America: The Bennington Years* [Boston: G. K. Hall, 1981]). On the Workers' Dance League, see my "Red Shoes: The Workers' Dance League of the 1930s," *Village Voice*, 24 April 1984 (reprinted in my *Writing Dancing in the Age of Postmodernism* [Hanover, NH: Wesleyan University Press/University Press of New England, 1994], pp. 199–204); Stacey Prickett, "From Workers' Dance to New Dance," *Dance Research*, Vol. 7, no. 1 (Spring 1989): 47–64; Stacey Prickett, "Dance and the Workers' Struggle," *Dance Research*, Vol. 8, no. 1 (Spring 1990): 47–61; Ellen Graff, *Stepping Left: Dance and Politics in New York City, 1928–1942* (Durham, NC: Duke University Press, 1997); "Of, By, and For the People: Dancing on the Left in the 1930s," ed. Lynn Garafola, *Studies in Dance History*, Vol. 5, no. 1, Spring 1994.
4 Manning, *Ecstasy and the Demon*, p. 41.
5 Manning, *Ecstasy and the Demon*, p. 43.
6 Walter Sorell, ed., *The Mary Wigman Book* (Middletown, CT: Wesleyan University Press, 1975), p. 28.

7 Margaret Lloyd, *The Borzoi Book of Modern Dance* (New York: Dance Horizons, n.d.; reprint of 1949 ed.), p. 12.
8 Sorell, *Mary Wigman Book*, p. 55.
9 For a chronology of Wigman's works in English, see Mary Wigman, *The Language of Dance*, trans. Walter Sorell (Middletown, CT: Wesleyan University Press, 1966), pp. 113–118.
10 Wigman, *Language*, p. 40.
11 Wigman writes of the mask, which was originally created for an earlier dance, *Ceremonial Figure*, that it was made by "a young mask-maker who, in the circle of my students, experimented with Japanese No masks. . . . The mask he brought was an almost demonic translation of my face." She also discusses her intention that the mask depersonalize her dancing persona (*Language*, p. 34).
12 Wigman, *Language*, pp. 40–41.
13 Wigman, *Language*, pp. 40–41.
14 See Boris Tomaševskij, who argues that, beginning with the Romantic era, authors often construct autobiographical legends as part of their creative work. He writes, "The legends are a premise which the author himself took into account during the creative process. . . . The poet considers as a premise to his creations not his actual curriculum vitae, but his ideal biographical legend" ("Literature and Biography," trans. Herbert Eagle, in Vassilis Lambropoulos and David Neal Miller, eds., *Twentieth-Century Literary Theory* [Albany, NY: State University of New York Press, 1987], pp. 120–121. The essay was first published in Russian as "Literatura i biografija," *Kniga i revoljucija*, 4 [1923]: 6–9).
15 Wigman, *Language*, p. 42.
16 Plato expounded this view of art's creation in *Ion*.
17 James R. Brandon, "Form in Kabuki Acting," in James R. Brandon, William P. Malm, and Donald H. Shively, *Studies in Kabuki: Its Acting, Music, and Historical Context* (Honolulu: University of Hawaii Press, an East–West Center Book, 1978), p. 84.
18 See Erika Fischer-Lichte, "Inszenierung des Fremden. Zur (De-) Konstruktion semiotischer Systeme," (Staging the Other: Toward a (De-)Construction of a Semiotic System) in Erika Fischer-Lichte, ed., *TheaterAvantgarde: Wahrnehmung-Körper-Sprache* (Avant Garde Theater: Perception – Body – Speech) (Tübingen and Basel: Francke, 1995), 156–241. I am grateful to Marc Silberman for this reference.
19 My description is based on the film *Mary Wigman: Four Solos* (1929; director unknown), a short sound film that, besides an incomplete *Witch Dance*, also includes three solos from the *Shifting Landscape* cycle. These four solos have been incorporated into the documentary videotape *When the Fire Dances Between Two Poles: Mary Wigman, 1886–1973*, prod. and dir. Allegra Fuller Snyder, 1982.
20 Rudolph Bach, *Das Mary Wigman Werk* (Dresden: Carl Reissner, 1933), pp. 29–31. English translation provided by the Dance Film Archive, University of Rochester, quoted in Manning, p. 129.
21 Rudolf Lämmel, *Der moderne Tanz* (Berlin: Oestergaard, 1928), p. 110, quoted in Manning, *Ecstasy and the Demon*, p. 61.
22 Manning, *Ecstasy and the Demon*, pp. 61–62.
23 Emile Nolde, *Jahre der Kämpfe, 1902–1914* (Years of Struggle, 1902–1914) (Berlin, 1934), quoted in Victor H. Meisel, ed., *Voices of German Expressionism* (Englewood Cliffs, NJ: Prentice-Hall, 1970), p. 35.
24 "According to the law which, as far as I know, I was the first to formulate, in the history of art the legacy is transmitted not from father to son, but from uncle to nephew," Shklovsky wrote. And, further, "When the 'canonized' art forms reach an impasse, the way is paved for the infiltration of the elements of non-canonized art, which by this time have managed to evolve new artistic devices" (Viktor Shklovsky, *Literatura i kinematograf* [Literature and Cinema] [Berlin, 1923], pp. 27, 29, cited in

Victor Erlich, *Russian Formalism: History-Doctrine*, 3rd ed. [New Haven and London: Yale University Press, 1981], pp. 259–260).

Also, Noël Carroll discusses the dynamic of artistic repudiation, which, he points out, "stays in a structured relation with the tradition insofar as it proposes itself as contrary to prevailing practices" ("Art, Practice, and Narrative," *The Monist*, Vol. 71, no. 2 [April 1988]: 148).

25 Quoted in Peter Gay, *Weimar Culture: The Outsider as Insider* (New York: Harper and Row, 1968), p. 5.

26 Max Beckmann, *On My Painting* (New York: Buchholz Gallery, 1941), quoted in Bernard S. Myers, *The German Expressionists: A Generation in Revolt* (New York: McGraw-Hill, 1966), p. 254.

27 See John M. MacGregor, *The Discovery of the Art of the Insane* (Princeton, NJ: Princeton University Press, 1989), especially Chapter 14, "Expressionism and the Art of the Insane."

28 Manning, *Ecstasy and the Demon*, p. 62.

29 See Walter Sokel, *The Writer in Extremis* (Stanford, CA: Stanford University Press, 1959), pp. 126–132, for a discussion of the Expressionist artist as a self-figured vampire.

30 I thank Laurence Senelick for this observation.

31 Peter Burke, *Popular Culture in Early Modern Europe* (New York: Harper and Row, 1978), p. 62, quoted in Sigrid Brauner, *Fearless Wives and Frightened Shrews: The Construction of the Witch in Early Modern Germany*, ed. and intro. Robert H. Brown (Amherst: University of Massachusetts Press, 1995), p. 11.

32 Brauner, *Fearless Wives*, pp. 113, 116. Anne Llewellyn Barstow, *Witchcraze: A New History of the European Witch Hunts* (San Francisco and London: Pandora/Harper-Collins, 1994), offers an account of the persecution based in widespread gynophobia. Gerhild Scholz Williams, in *Defining Dominion: The Discourses of Magic and Witchcraft in Early Modern France and Germany* (Ann Arbor: University of Michigan Press, 1995), argues that women accused as witches were marginalized and associated with other outsiders as a response to epistemological changes brought about by increasing religious diversity in Europe and the discoveries of the new world.

33 Brauner, *Fearless Wives*, p. 119.

34 Manning, *Ecstasy and the Demon*, p. 41.

35 Valeska Gert, "My Dance Pantomimes (from *Ich bin eine Hexe*, 1950)," in *Cabaret Performance, Volume II: Europe 1920–1940. Sketches, Songs, Monologues, Memoirs*, ed. and trans. Laurence Senelick (Baltimore: Johns Hopkins University Press, 1993), pp. 14–16.

36 *Cabaret Performance, Volume I: Europe 1890–1920. Songs, Sketches, Monologues, Memoirs*, ed. and trans. Laurence Senelick (New York: PAJ Publications, 1989), p. 9. Senelick cites Petra-Maria Einsporn's use of the term in this context.

37 In 1925, Wigman wrote: "One does not discriminate between crudeness and sensitivity. How would contemporary musicians of rank react to having their performances evaluated on the level of skillfully performed dinner music? Wouldn't a first-rate orchestra be infuriated when, led by a great conductor, it would be named in the same breath with a sophisticated jazz band? These mistakes are still made daily as far as the dance is concerned. . . . To experience an artistic dance creation means absorbing it through the eye and feeling it kinesthetically. One needs gifted eyes for it" ("We Are Standing at the Beginning," in Paul Stefan, ed., *Dance in Our Time* [Vienna: Universal Edition, 1925], reprinted in *Mary Wigman Book*, p. 82).

38 To discuss Wigman's politics during the Nazi period is not germane to my project here. Although for many years various narratives – including her own memoirs and dance history books – had constructed her as a virtual prisoner of the Nazis, condemned as a "degenerate artist," in recent years evidence has come to light that

she continued to work under the Nazi regime and was not unfavorable to it. Hedwig Müller, in *Mary Wigman: Leben und Werk der grossen Tänzerin* [Life and Work of the Great Dancer] (Berlin: Quadriga, 1986), revealed this aspect of Wigman's career, and Manning analyzes her later choreography in light of it.

39 See Gay, *Weimar Culture*, p. 4.

40 See "Introduction," in Renate Bridenthal, Atina Grossmann, and Marion Kaplan, eds., *When Biology Became Destiny: Women in Weimar and Nazi Germany* (New York: Monthly Review Press, 1984), pp. 1–7.

41 My account of Wigman's biography relies on Manning, pp. 49–59, which in turn relies on Müller's biography.

42 Manning, *Ecstasy and the Demon*, p. 50.

43 Gerhard Schumann, "Gespräche und Fragen: Mary Wigman," in *Arbeitshefte*, 36 (Berlin: Akademie der Künste der DDR, 1982), p. 39, quoted in Manning, *Ecstasy and the Demon*, p. 50.

44 See Manning, *Ecstasy and the Demon*, p. 57; and Martin Green, *Mountain of Truth* (Hanover, NH: University Press of New England, 1986).

45 Manning, *Ecstasy and the Demon*, p. 57.

46 Sorell, *The Mary Wigman Book*, pp. 50–51; Müller, *Mary Wigman*, p. 64, cited in Manning, *Ecstasy and the Demon*, p. 59.

47 Manning, *Ecstasy and the Demon*, p. 59.

48 See Manning, *Ecstasy and the Demon*, pp. 170–202.

49 Kriegsman, *Modern Dance in America*, pp. 140–141.

50 Doris Humphrey, "New Dance," in Kriegsman, *Modern Dance in America*, p. 284.

51 See Marcia B. Siegel, *Days on Earth: The Dance of Doris Humphrey* (New Haven: Yale University Press, 1987), pp. 75–76.

52 In a discussion of what he calls cinematic "ampliation," Noël Carroll analyzes how matched movement can create the impression of causation. This sort of strategy seems to operate often in *New Dance* ("Causation, the Ampliation of Movement and Avant-Garde Film," *Millennium Film Journal*, nos. 10/11 [Fall–Winter 1981–82]: 61–82). For descriptions of *New Dance*, see Lloyd, *Borzoi Book*, pp. 95–96; and Marcia B. Siegel, *The Shapes of Change: Images of American Dance* (Boston: Houghton Mifflin, 1979), pp. 81–89.

53 Siegel, *Days*, p. 157.

54 Humphrey, "New Dance," p. 284.

55 Selma Jeanne Cohen, *Doris Humphrey: An Artist First* (Middletown, CT: Wesleyan University Press, 1972), p. 238.

56 For a description of *Theatre Piece*, see Lloyd, *Borzoi Book*, pp. 96–97; and Siegel, *Days*, pp. 158–160.

57 Kriegsman, p. 284.

58 Doris Humphrey, "New Dance," in Cohen, *Humphrey*, p. 239. This is a different variant of the essay reprinted in Kriegsman.

59 Kriegsman, *Modern Dance in America*, p. 141.

60 Kriegsman, *Modern Dance in America*, p. 139.

61 Kriegsman, *Modern Dance in America*, p. 140.

62 Lloyd, *Borzoi Book*, p. 98–99.

63 See Siegel, *Days*, pp. 134–135.

64 My description and analysis of the dance are based on my viewing of the 1972 film (now available on videotape) produced by Ted Steeg Productions, of a performance by the American Dance Festival Repertory Company, with Nina Watt and Raymond Johnson as the Lovers and Dalienne Majors as the Matriarch. The performance was staged by Christine Clark from the Labanotation score.

65 Cohen, *Humphrey*, p. 141; John Martin, *New York Times*, 14 August 1936, quoted in Kriegsman, *Modern Dance in America*, p. 144.

66 Kriegsman, *Modern Dance in America*, p. 139.

67 Siegel, *Days*, p. 165.

68 According to Kriegsman, Humphrey read Blake after she had completed the choreography for the dance, which had been provisionally titled *Romantic Tragedy*. Kriegsman cites Eugene C. Howe, whose article "The Modern Dance and William Blake" quotes Humphrey as saying, in a letter to the author, "I was looking for a title for 'Red Fires' when I came across the passage in *Jerusalem II*, and I immediately seized on this and its context as a word illumination for what I had been doing" (*Journal of Health and Physical Education*, Vol. 9, no. 1 [January 1938]: 8, quoted in Kriegsman, *Modern Dance in America*, p. 140).

69 *The Illuminated Blake*, annot. David V. Erdman (Garden City, NY: Anchor Books, 1974), p. 324.

70 See *The Illuminated Blake*, plates 36 and 99 (pp. 315 and 378). Also, see *Milton* in the same volume, plates 32 and 37 (pp. 248 and 253), in which first William Blake and then his brother Robert are pictured in the same pose, but facing one another in mirror-image. The occasion is Blake's reception of Milton's "falling star," after Satan (earlier seen in flames) has gone up in smoke.

71 Siegel, *Days*, pp. 164–165.

72 Afterwards, Humphrey wrote to her parents, "The Shawns are very bitter – and listen to all sorts of lies and slander – and have convinced a number of people that I am most unethical in every way. . . . I am dishonest, I am grasping and greedy and selfish, ungrateful, and no loyal Denishawner is allowed to take lessons of me on pain of dismissal" (24 September 1928, quoted in Cohen, *Humphrey*, p. 86).

73 See Siegel, *Days*, pp. 77–80; and Cohen, *Humphrey*, pp. 85–86.

74 See Marina Warner, *From the Beast to the Blonde: On Fairy Tales and Their Tellers* (New York: Farrar, Straus, and Giroux, 1995), pp. 227–229.

75 Maurice Maeterlinck, *The Life of the Bee* (1901), trans. Alfred Sutro (New York: Dodd, Mead), p. 394, quoted in Siegel, *Days*, p. 78.

76 Siegel notes that in the earliest versions of *Life of the Bee*, the struggle was not necessarily between the old and young queens, for the older bee had left the hive before the younger one was born; rather, the young queen had to fight to protect her "throne" from an intruder who ultimately triumphed. Only in 1941 did Humphrey designate an Old Queen and a Young Queen, with the Young Queen winning the battle between the two (*Days*, p. 79).

77 Jowitt, *Time*, pp. 196–197.

78 Paul Love, "The Adventure of Doris Humphrey," *Dance*, Vol. 1, no. 6 (1937): 9, 30, quoted in Kriegsman, p. 140.

79 Siegel argues that the "Ritual" section of *With My Red Fires* is conceptually similar to *Les Noces* and suggests that Humphrey may have seen Nijinska's ballet, which had been given its American premiere by Colonel de Basil's Ballet Russe in New York in April 1935, when Humphrey was preparing to work on *With My Red Fires* (*Days*, pp. 162–163).

80 In *Metropolis*, the demagogue is a robot in the form of a young woman. But she is merely the pawn of the real demagogue – the millionaire who opposes his son's love for a working-class girl.

81 Cohen, *Humphrey*, p. 2.

82 See Cohen, *Humphrey*, and Siegel, *Days*, for details of Humphrey's personal life.

83 Much of their correspondence is quoted in Cohen, *Humphrey*.

84 Kriegsman, *Modern Dance in America*, pp. 22–23.

85 See Kriegsman, *Modern Dance in America*, pp. 15, 28–29; and Siegel, *Days*, pp. 146–147.

86 See Ann Douglas, *Terrible Honesty: Mongrel Manhattan in the 1920s* (New York: Farrar, Straus, and Giroux, 1995), especially Chapter 6, "The 'Dark Legend' of Matricide."

Douglas quotes Beer on p. 241 and makes reference to Elizabeth Cady Stanton's essay "The Matriarchate" (1891) on p. 242. Also, see Ann Douglas, *The Feminization of American Culture* (New York: Knopf, 1977). Douglas cautions that although apparently "white middle-class women had seized the reins of national culture in the mid- and late-Victorian era," nevertheless "the situation was not so simple or straightforward as the moderns' matricidal declarations and acts [in literature] would have us believe. For starters, the Victorian matriarch was less powerful and less privileged than her attackers took her to be. The moderns were fiercely astute about her failings, but many of these failings can be attributed to her lack of real political and economic power, to her efforts to compensate in terms of moral and cultural influence for the responsibilities and rights she was denied in the economic and political realms." And Douglas continues, "One might argue that the apparent ascendancy of the matriarch in the high Victorian period and her subsequent demolition in the early twentieth century constitute nothing but a crisis in a firmly patriarchal or male-dominated culture; women getting a little power in a society that preferred them to have none were perceived as monstrous usurpers and punished within an inch of their lives" (*Honesty*, pp. 6–7). I should note that although I do not endorse Douglas's psychoanalytic interpretations of culture in this book, I find many of her historical and political points, including that in the quote above, quite apt.

87 Douglas, *Honesty*, p. 8.

88 Douglas, *Honesty*, p. 247.

89 On both smoking and thinking like a man, see Douglas, *Honesty*, p. 247. Humphrey was proud enough when she began smoking to write home to her parents about it, and, shortly after, she wrote that she had acquired a new lover, but had no intention of marrying him. "Don't believe in it," she said. However, this new lover was Charles Woodford, whom she did eventually marry. (Cohen, *Humphrey*, pp. 99–100.)

90 Beer, *The Mauve Decade*, quoted in Douglas, *Honesty*, p. 242. On the importance of motherhood and domesticity as an ideology even to single feminists (some of whom may have been lesbians) and reformers of the Victorian matriarchate, like Clara Barton (founder of the Red Cross), Carrie Chapman Catt (president of the National American Women's Suffrage Association), and Frances E. Willard (founder of the Women's Christian Temperance Union), see Douglas, *Honesty*, p. 243.

91 "The Development of the New German Dance," in Virginia Stewart and Merle Armitage, eds., *The Modern Dance* (New York: E. Weyhe, 1935), pp. 12–13, quoted in Manning, *Ecstasy and the Demon*, p. 179.

92 I am putting the term "primitive" in quotes to mark my understanding that this is a contested, often vague term, now considered colonialist at best, that has been used, understood, and valued differently in various scholarly and vernacular contexts at least since the nineteenth century. Anthropologists have used it to mean societies with simple agrarian economies; art historians have used it to refer not only to art from tribal cultures and art from early historical periods, but also deliberately naive art made by first-world artists; psychoanalysts have used it to refer to primal sexual instincts; in religion it can refer to an early form of a faith; in logic and mathematics it means that which is irreducible. The popular use of the term connotes wildness, barbarity, and "uncivilized" behavior, often with sexual overtones – qualities whose social and artistic value has historically oscillated between positive and negative.

93 For a definition and analysis of matrifocality, see Nancie L. González, "Toward a Definition of Matrifocality," in Norman E. Whitten, Jr. and John F. Szwed, eds., *Afro-American Anthropology: Contemporary Perspectives* (New York: Free Press, 1970), pp. 231–244. Matrifocality differs from matriarchy in that it refers to woman-centered authority in the domestic unit and in what González calls the "supra-domestic" realm (institutions outside the home that directly touch on domestic life, such as schools, neighborhood organizations, consumer groups, and so on, as well as

relations between households), without suggesting that political and jural authority in the society at large (i.e., at levels above the supra-domestic) is held by women.

94 See Ruth Beckford, *Katherine Dunham: A Biography* (New York: Marcel Dekker, 1979), pp. 23–27, and Joyce Aschenbrenner, *Katherine Dunham: Reflections on the Social and Political Contexts of Afro-American Dance*, Dance Research Annual XII (New York: CORD, 1980), p. 11.

95 Beckford, *Katherine Dunham: Biography*, p. 31; Katherine Dunham, *Island Possessed* (New York: Doubleday, 1969; reprint ed. Chicago: University of Chicago Press, 1994), pp. 11–13, 23. On Dunham's initiation as a vaudun *hounci*, see *Island Possessed*, Chapters 4–7.

96 In 1938, Dunham wrote: "Realizing that the amalgamation of the Negro into white America has in a large measure brought about a complete lack of contact with those things which were racially his, I have recently begun an intensive study of the Negro under other less absorbing cultural contacts; in the West Indies the French, Spanish and English influence have been of far less importance than that of the American in this country. In the recreational and ceremonial dances of the island peasantry are preserved the dance forms which are truly Negro." ("The Future of the Negro in Dance," *Dance Herald* [March 1938]: 5, quoted in Aschenbrenner, *Katherine Dunham: Reflections*, p. 45).

97 St. Clair Drake, Foreword, in Aschenbrenner, *Katherine Dunham: Reflections*, p. xi.

98 Ludmilla Speranzeva, one of Dunham's early teachers in Chicago, had studied with Mary Wigman and taught Wigman-style modern dance (Lloyd, *Borzoi Book*, p. 250). According to Lloyd, Speranzeva had also danced with the Russian emigré group La Chauve-Souris, which may have been a folklore-spectacle model for Dunham.

99 See Beckford, *Katherine Dunham: Biography*, p. 69.

100 Although the causes and history of matrifocality in Afro-Caribbean and African American culture are contested, there is widespread (but not universal) agreement among social scientists that it is a striking feature of social organization in these communities.

101 Don McDonagh, *The Complete Guide to Modern Dance* (Garden City, NY: Doubleday, 1976), p. 165.

102 Lloyd, *Borzoi Book*, p. 245.

103 Program for a performance at the Masonic Temple Auditorium on 19 April, 1943, in Spokane, reprinted in its entirety in Beckford, *Katherine Dunham: Biography*, following p. 78.

104 Arnold van Gennep, *Les Rites de passage* (Paris: E. Nourry, 1909). The book was published in English as *The Rites of Passage*, trans. Monika B. Vizedom and Gabrielle Caffee, intro. Solon T. Kimball (Chicago: University of Chicago Press, 1960).

105 Program note, 19 April 1943.

106 Program note, 19 April 1943.

107 My analysis is based upon my viewing of *Rites de Passage* at a performance at Carnegie Hall in 1979 and on the video *Divine Drumbeats: Katherine Dunham and Her People*, which includes a reconstruction of "Puberty," "Fertility Ritual," and "Death," narr. James Earl Jones, prod. Merrill Brockway and Catherine Tatge, dir, Merrill Brockway, *Dance in America*, PBS, WNET-TV, New York, 16 April 1980. Apparently, the choreography for "Women's Mysteries" has been lost.

108 See Robert Farris Thompson and Joseph Cornet, *The Four Moments of the Sun: Kongo Art in Two Worlds* (Washington, DC: National Gallery of Art, 1981), pp. 31, 234.

109 John Martin, "The Dance: 'Tropical Revue,'" *New York Times*, 26 September 1943, Section II, 2.

110 Drake, Foreword, p. xii.

111 Lloyd, *Borzoi Book*, pp. 245, 247.

112 For instance, see program note, 19 April 1943.

113 On the 1893 Columbian Exposition, see R. Reid Badger, *The Great American Fair: The World's Columbian Exposition and American Culture* (Chicago: Nelson-Hall, 1979).
114 Beckford, *Katherine Dunham: Biography*, pp. 25–27.
115 Beckford, *Katherine Dunham: Biography*, p. 41.
116 James Gray, Review, *St. Paul Pioneer Press*, 2 October 1944, quoted in Aschenbrenner, *Katherine Dunham: Reflections*, p. 57.
117 Of course, anthropologists of Malinowski's and Mead's generation have recently come under criticism themselves for participating in a quasi-imperialist enterprise.
118 Walter Terry, "Interview with Katherine Dunham," *New York Herald Tribune*, 9 May 1950, quoted in Aschenbrenner, *Katherine Dunham: Reflections*, p. 57.
119 Albert L. Elias, "Conversation with Katherine Dunham," *Dance Magazine*, Vol. 30, no. 2 (February 1956): 17, quoted in Aschenbrenner, *Katherine Dunham: Reflections*, p. 57.
120 Beckford, *Katherine Dunham: Biography*, p. 42.
121 Drake, Foreword, p. xi.
122 Program note, 19 April 1943; Beckford, *Katherine Dunham: Biography*, pp. 131–136.
123 *Carnival of Rhythm*, produced by Warner Brothers in 1939, was written and directed by Stanley Martin.
124 Dunham, *Island Possessed*, p. 111.
125 Lloyd, *Borzoi Book*, p. 245.
126 Dorathi Bock Pierre, "Cool Scientist or Sultry Performer?," *Dance Magazine*, Vol. 21, no. 5 (May 1947): 11–13.
127 "Torridity to Anthropology," *Newsweek*, 27 January 1941, p. 62; "The School Marm Who Glorified Leg Art," *Ebony* (January 1947): 14.
128 Walter Terry, Interview with Alvin Ailey, Phonotape, Dance Collection, New York Public Library for the Performing Arts, quoted in Aschenbrenner, *Katherine Dunham: Reflections*, p. 57.
129 Lloyd, *Borzoi Book*, p. 245.
130 K. Sue Jewell, *From Mammy to Miss America and Beyond: Cultural Images and the Shaping of US Social Policy* (London: Routledge, 1993), p. 36.
131 See Robert C. Allen, *Horrible Prettiness: Burlesque and American Culture* (Chapel Hill, NC: University of North Carolina Press, 1991).
132 See Agnes de Mille, *Martha: The Life and Work of Martha Graham* (New York: Random House, 1991), for details about Graham's personal relationships.
133 Martha Graham, *Blood Memory* (New York: Doubleday, 1991), p. 174.
134 De Mille, *Martha*, p. 281.
135 Program note, *Night Journey*, quoted in Ernestine Stodelle, *Deep Song: The Dance Story of Martha Graham* (New York: Schirmer Books, 1984), p. 148.
136 I am basing my description on the film of *Night Journey*, dir. Alexander Hammid (1961), with Martha Graham as Jocasta, Bertram Ross as Oedipus, Paul Taylor as Tiresias, and Helen McGehee as the leader of the chorus. There are excellent descriptive analyses of the dance in: Graham, *Memory*, pp. 212–218; Jowitt, *Time*, pp. 215–218; John Mueller, *Films on Ballet and Modern Dance* (New York: American Dance Guild, 1974), pp. 45–55; Siegel, *Shapes*, pp. 202–209; and Stodelle, *Deep Song*, pp. 146–150.
137 Graham, *Memory*, p. 213.
138 Jowitt, *Time*, p. 216; de Mille, *Martha*, p. 281.
139 Graham, *Memory*, p. 213.
140 Graham, *Memory*, p. 214.
141 Siegel, *Shapes*, p. 203.
142 Jowitt points out that the extremely phallic solo in the film was not part of the original choreography, but was created with Bertram Ross after 1950, when Hawkins left the company (*Time*, p. 216).

143 Graham herself describes her solo as having "2 Bali turns" and "Javanese foot movement" (Martha Graham, *The Notebooks of Martha Graham*, intro. Nancy Wilson Ross [New York: Harcourt Brace Jovanovich, 1973], p. 158).
144 Graham, *Memory*, pp. 214–215.
145 Graham, *Memory*, p. 215.
146 Siegel, *Shapes*, pp. 144, 150.
147 Marianne Goldberg writes, "Graham, who in the 1930s created some of the most feminist dances this country has seen . . . has in *Rite of Spring* trapped women within a male-dominated world that destroys any possibility of their own assertion" ("She Who Is Possessed No Longer Exists Outside: Martha Graham's *Rite of Spring*," *Women and Performance*, Vol. 3, no. 1 [1986; #5]: 17). But the same could have been said as early as *Night Journey*.
148 Graham, *Memory*, pp. 171, 174.
149 Graham, *Memory*, p. 181; de Mille, *Martha*, pp. 281–282.
150 Siegel, *Shapes*, p. 201.
151 Graham, *Memory*, p. 25.
152 Siegel, *Shapes*, p. 202.
153 Graham, *Memory*, p. 26.
154 Graham, *Memory*, p. 232.
155 Rochelle Gatlin, *American Women Since 1945* (Jackson, MS: University Press of Mississippi, 1987), p. 12.
156 Gatlin, *American Women*, p. 12. Her quote is from Mary P. Ryan, *Womanhood in America: From Colonial Times to the Present*, second edition (New York and London: New Viewpoints/Franklin Watts, 1979), p. 173.
157 Nancy Cott, "The Modern Woman of the 1920s, American Style," in Françoise Thébaud, ed., *A History of Women in the West. V. Toward a Cultural Identity in the Twentieth Century* (Cambridge, MA: Belknap Press/Harvard University Press, 1994), pp. 79–82.
158 Betty Friedan published her critique of this pervasive post-war affliction of the middle-class in *The Feminine Mystique* (New York: Norton, 1963).
159 Gatlin, *American Women*, p. 7.
160 Ferdinand Lundberg and Marynia F. Farnham, MD, *Modern Woman: The Lost Sex* (New York and London: Harper, 1947), p. 319, quoted in Gatlin, *American Women*, p. 12.
161 Gatlin, *American Women*, pp. 8–24.

6 MODERN BALLET

1 Of course, ballet, like opera, is also an object of cultural appreciation by a gay male subculture.
2 Lincoln Kirstein, *Four Centuries of Ballet: Fifty Masterworks* (New York: Dover, 1984), p. 230.
3 Cyril W. Beaumont, *Complete Book of Ballets* (London: Putnam, 1937), p. 1013.
4 Robert Lawrence, "The Ballet: The Tudor Style," *New York Herald Tribune*, 4 May 1943.
5 Hugh Laing, Interview by Marilyn Hunt, 9 May 1986, quoted in Judith Chazin-Bennahum, *The Ballets of Antony Tudor: Studies in Psyche and Satire* (New York: Oxford, 1994), p. 61.
6 Jack Anderson, "The View from the House Opposite: Some Aspects of Tudor," *Ballet Review*, Vol. 4, no. 6 (1974): 17.
7 Clive Barnes, "Ballet Perspectives 11: *Jardin aux Lilas*," *Dance and Dancers*, Vol. 10, no. 6 (June 1959): 19.
8 Chazin-Bennahum, *Antony Tudor*, p. 65.

9 Kirstein, *Four Centuries*, p. 231.
10 Dance critic and historian Alastair Macaulay has pointed out that there were many English ballets of the period that had French titles, including Ashton's *Les Masques*, *Les Rendezvous*, *Le Baiser de la Fée*, and *Les Patineurs*, and he speculates that it was more the cachet of the French title than artifice that mattered to the British choreographers. "The French *sounded* better," he muses (personal communication).
11 Edwin Denby, "Tudor and Pantomime," *New York Herald Tribune*, 11 July 1943, reprinted in Edwin Denby, *Dance Writings*, ed. Robert Cornfield and William McKay (New York: Knopf, 1986), p. 130.
12 For this analysis, I have based my description of the dance on my viewings of American Ballet Theatre's production and on "A Tudor Evening with American Ballet Theatre," prod. Judy Kinberg and Thomas Grimm, dir. Thomas Grimm and Judy Kinberg, *Dance in America*, exec. prod. Jac Venza, a co-production of WNET/Thirteen, New York, and Danmarks Radio, Great Performances, PBS, WNET/Thirteen, New York, 13 April 1990. In this version, Caroline is danced by Leslie Browne; Her Lover by Ricardo Bustamonte; The Man She Must Marry by Michael Owen; and An Episode in His Past by Martine Van Hamel. I have also relied on the various texts in the notes to this section.
13 "A Tudor Evening."
14 Maude Lloyd, Interview, WNET/Thirteen, Typescript, Dance Collection, New York Public Library for the Performing Arts, p. 27.
15 Barnes writes that "a constantly recurring note of yearning is struck as [the two pairs of lovers] are parted and forced to dance with the 'wrong' partner" ("*Jardin*," p. 28).
16 In earlier versions, only two women guests appeared in this scene, although in current versions a third woman joins them.
17 Kirstein, *Four Centuries*, p. 231.
18 "A Tudor Evening."
19 See Barnes, "Jardin," p. 28; Peter Williams, "*Lilac Garden*: Landscape Gardening," *Dance and Dancers*, Vol. 20, no. 1 (January 1969): 35.
20 Williams notes that this understated drama, rejecting ostentatious display, was an important innovation. "What was so remarkable about the work at the time was the lack of dramatic emphasis, especially at a time when dramatic ballets meant the broader histrionics, some might call it 'ham,' of the *Schéhérazade* school" ("*Lilac Garden*," p. 35).
21 Williams, "*Lilac Garden*," p. 35.
22 Barnes, "*Jardin*," p. 19.
23 Agnes de Mille, *Dance to the Piper* (Boston: Little, Brown, 1952), p. 65.
24 George Balanchine and Francis Mason, *101 Stories of the Great Ballets* (New York: Doubleday, Anchor Books, 1975), p. 241.
25 Barnes, "*Jardin*," p. 19.
26 Antony Tudor, Interview with Judith Chazin-Bennahum, April 1986, New York City, quoted in Chazin-Bennahum, *Antony Tudor*, p. 63.
27 Lloyd, Interview, p. 26.
28 See, for instance, Donna Perlmutter, *Shadowplay: The Life of Antony Tudor* (New York: Viking, 1991), who writes: "Antony deeply understood the silent anguish of the ballet's heroine, Caroline. He had been there. He know that she could not act on her desire – marry the man she loved – for her family had chosen another bridegroom, one who could benefit its fortunes. Nor could *he* 'marry' Hugh, who would remain forbidden to him, both by society and the law. . . . Not to be taken lightly, either, is Antony's role as the spoiler; the husband-to-be robs Hugh of Caroline, his great heterosexual hope. . . . There would apparently be instances where he thought that, but for him, Hugh might opt for the so-called straight path. It's little wonder, given these elements, that *Jardin* sprang so powerfully from his imagination" (pp. 64–65).

29 Although several other commentators have noted the parodies of *Les Sylphides* and the obligatory nineteenth-century bridal *pas de deux*, Arlene Croce seems to be the only one to have made the connection to *Jardin* in print. She reports that at the time of the ballet's premiere, some viewers thought that *A Wedding Bouquet* was a satire of either *Les Noces* or *Jardin* (Arlene Croce, "The Spoken Word," *The New Yorker*, 6 November 1978, reprinted in Arlene Croce, *Going to the Dance* [New York: Knopf, 1982], p. 128).

30 David Vaughan, *Frederick Ashton and His Ballets* (New York: Knopf, 1977), pp. 152–153. My descriptions of *A Wedding Bouquet* are based on several sources, including my viewings of the Joffrey Ballet's 1978 revival of the ballet and two filmed excerpts: [Sadler's Wells Ballet and others], filmed by Ann Barzel, with Moira Shearer as Julia (1941?–1959); and *Celebration*, dir. Jolyon Wimhurst, with historical footage of Margot Fonteyn as Julia, Independent Film Production Associates in association with the Royal Opera House, Covent Garden; Sadler's Wells Theatre; and Jaras Entertainments, 1981. Also: Vaughan's account of the making of the ballet and his analysis in *Ashton*, pp. 149–154; Clive Barnes, "Ballet Perspectives: 10: *A Wedding Bouquet*," *Dance and Dancers*, 10 (April 1959): 20–21, 34; Mary Clarke, "The First Wedding Bouquet," *Dancing Times*, 60 (November 1969): 69; Croce, "The Spoken Word," pp. 127–129; Dale Harris, "Dance: The Joffrey Institution," *Keynote: A Magazine for the Arts* (January 1979): 28–29; and Anna Kisselgoff, "A Ballet is a Ballet is a Masterpiece," *New York Times*, 26 November 1989, pp. 12, 44.

31 Croce, "The Spoken Word," pp. 129, 128.

32 Vaughan, *Ashton*, p. 150.

33 David Vaughan notes that Margot Fonteyn, the original Julia, actually danced both roles – Giselle and Julia – in a single matinee, on 8 May 1937 (Vaughan, *Ashton*, p. 152n.).

34 Gertrude Stein, *Everybody's Autobiography* (New York: Random House, 1937), p. 194.

35 See Vaughan, *Ashton*, p. 152.

36 Harris, "Dance," p. 29.

37 Three moments from this duet of errors, danced by the original Bride and Bridegroom, Mary Honer and Robert Helpmann, are reproduced in Vaughan, *Ashton*, pp. 150–151.

38 Kisselgoff, "A Ballet is a Ballet," p. 12.

39 Kisselgoff, "A Ballet is a Ballet," p. 12.

40 Croce objects that "what we see is a series of bustling, giddy, and broadly comic dances and characterizations that are not at all related to the deadpan, taciturn style of Gertrude Stein" ("The Royal Ballet in New York," *Ballet Review*, Vol. 3, no. 4 [Summer 1970], reprinted in Arlene Croce, *Afterimages* [New York: Knopf, 1977], p. 376).

41 Vaughan, *Ashton*, pp. 1–2.

42 Croce, "The Royal Ballet," pp. 176–177.

43 Quoted in "Rodeo: Dorati Conducts Four Dance Episodes from Copland Ballet," *RCA Victor Record Review* (July 1948): 8.

44 While it's true that Frankie, in Page's 1938 ballet, also has grit – after all, as in the song, she shoots Johnny for "doin' her wrong" – she is a cartoon figure whose nerve has no redeeming qualities.

45 Agnes de Mille, *Dance to the Piper* (New York: Bantam Books, 1954), p. 252.

46 Claudia Cassidy, "Ballet Russe's 'Rodeo' Dance Wins Acclaim," *Chicago Tribune*, 26 December 1942.

47 De Mille, *Piper*, p. 226.

48 Barbara Barker, "Agnes de Mille, Liberated Expatriate, and *The American Suite*, 1938," *Dance Chronicle*, Vol. 19, no. 2 (1996): 113–150. De Mille refers to the dance by two different titles: *'49* and *Forty-Niner*. I have chosen to follow Barker in consistently referring to it as *Forty-Niner*.

49 Barker, "Expatriate," p. 118.
50 De Mille, *Piper*, p. 100.
51 Barker, "Expatriate," p. 123.
52 Barker, "Expatriate," pp. 124–135.
53 *Rodeo*, MS Choreographic Notes and Original Score, 1938, (s) *MGZMD 37 Box 33. Agnes de Mille Collection, New York Public Library for the Performing Arts, Dance Collection, quoted in Barker, p. 136.
54 Barker, "Expatriate," p. 141.
55 *Rodeo*, Original Score, quoted in Barker, "Expatriate," p. 138.
56 *Rodeo*, Original Score, quoted in Barker, "Expatriate," p. 138.
57 Barbara Barker, "The Development of Narrative in de Mille's *Rodeo*, 1942," Perspectives on Movement Conference, City University of New York, November 1994.
58 I have based my descriptions of *Rodeo* on my live viewings of the American Ballet Theatre production and on the version of the first scene in "American Ballet Theatre: A Close-Up in Time," prod. Jac Venza, dir. Jerome Schnur, PBS, WNET/13-TV, New York, 8 October 1973, with Christine Sarry as the Cowgirl, Terry Orr as the Champion Wrestler, and Marcos Paredes as the Head Wrangler.
59 De Mille, *Piper*, p. 258.
60 Agnes de Mille, Choreographic Notes, *Rodeo* (s) *MGZMD 37, New York Public Library for the Performing Arts, Dance Collection. I am grateful to Barbara Barker for calling my attention to these notes, which constituted the scenario written to instruct the composer, Aaron Copland.
61 Irving Kolodin, "'Rodeo' Is Real American Ballet," *New York Sun*, 17 October 1942.
62 De Mille, *Piper*, pp. 258–259.
63 De Mille, *Piper*, pp. 257, 259–260, 263.
64 De Mille, Choreographic Notes [to Copland], *Rodeo*.
65 De Mille, *Piper*, p. 270.
66 Barbara Barker, "Agnes de Mille's Heroines of the Forties," in *Proceedings of the Twelfth Annual Conference of the Society of Dance History Scholars* (Riverside, CA: Society of Dance History Scholars, 1989), pp. 140–141.
67 Joan Acocella, "She Made Them Dance," Review of *No Intermissions: The Life of Agnes de Mille* by Carol Easton, *New York Times Book Review*, 11 February 1996, p. 6.
68 Barker, "Heroines," p. 143.
69 De Mille, *Piper*, p. 133.
70 De Mille, Choreographic Notes [to Copland], *Rodeo*.
71 Claudia Cassidy, "Crowd Enters into Spirit of 'Rodeo' Ballet," *Chicago Tribune*, 1 January 1943.
72 "Agnes de Mille and Uncle Cecil," unidentified clipping, de Mille Clipping Scrapbooks. *ZMD 429, V. III. New York Public Library for the Performing Arts, Dance Collection, quoted in Barker, "Expatriate," p. 113.
73 Marcia B. Siegel, *The Shapes of Change: Images of American Dance* (Boston: Houghton Mifflin, 1979), p. 131.
74 Siegel, *Shapes*, pp. 126, 131, 128–30.
75 Siegel, *Shapes*, p. 130.
76 Siegel, *Shapes*, pp. 127–128, 131.
77 Siegel, *Shapes*, p. 128.
78 Here the dance works in just the opposite way from the Russian novels by Herzen and Chernyshevsky cited in Chapter 2, note 81, where domestic equality served as a coded metaphor for larger socio-political equity, which in nineteenth-century Russia could not be written about openly.
79 Siegel, *Shapes*, p. 126.
80 Kirstein, *Four Centuries*, p. 242; Olivier Merlin, et al., *Stravinsky* (Paris: Hachette, 1968),

quoted in Nancy Reynolds, *Repertory in Review: 40 Years of the New York City Ballet* (New York: Dial, 1977), p. 182.

81 Paul Hodgins, *Relationships between Score and Choreography in Twentieth-Century Dance: Music, Movement and Metaphor* (Lewiston, NY: The Edwin Mellen Press, 1992), p. 131.

82 Siegel, *Shapes*, pp. 228–229.

83 Stephanie Jordan, "*Agon*: A Musical/Choreographic Analysis," *Dance Research Journal* Vol. 25, no. 2 (Fall 1993): 11.

84 Arlene Croce, "Balanchine's Girls: The Making of a Style," *Harper's Magazine* (April 1971), reprinted in *Afterimages*, p. 417. And in "The Spelling of Agon," Croce writes: "I have always thought that 'Agon' drew its personality from the city it was made in, New York, and its sensibility from the men who made it. The blare and heat in the music, the crazy timing, the disconcerting eruptions in the choreography . . . match the hectic behavior of city streets. The ballet's interior life, though, is quiet and purposeful. . . . This is the public and private life of the city as seen, as lived, by foreigners. But we are all foreigners in New York" (*The New Yorker*, 12 July 1993, p. 84).

85 *Dance News* (January 1958), quoted in Reynolds, *Repertory*, p. 184; Edwin Denby, "Three Sides of 'Agon,'" *Evergreen Review* (Winter 1959), reprinted in Denby, *Dance Writings*, p. 462.

86 Doris Hering, Review of New York City Ballet, *Dance Magazine*, Vol. 32, no. 1 (January 1958): 24.

87 George Balanchine, "Marginal Notes on the Dance," in Walter Sorell, ed., *The Dance Has Many Faces*, second ed. (New York: Columbia University Press, 1966), p. 99.

88 See, for instance, Margaret Thompson Drewal, "Constructionist Concepts in Balanchine's Choreography," *Ballet Review*, Vol. 13, no. 3 (Fall 1985): 42–47 and Reynolds, *Repertory*, pp. 182–186.

89 On Balanchine's persistent use of the African American aesthetic, see my "Balanchine and Black Dance," *Choreography and Dance*, Vol. 3, no. 3 (1993); reprinted in my *Writing Dancing in the Age of Postmodernism* (Hanover, NH and London: Wesleyan University Press/University Press of New England, 1994), pp. 53–69. Also see Brenda Dixon Gottschild, *Digging the Africanist Presence in American Performance: Dance and Other Contexts*, Contributions in Afro-American and African Studies no. 179 (Westport, CT: Greenwood Press, 1996), pp. 59–79.

Denby writes that in *Agon*, "The dancers have been 'cool' in the jazz sense – no buildup, inventions that did not try to get anywhere, right after a climax an inconsequence like the archness of high comedy" ("Three Sides," p. 463). Robynn J. Stilwell, in "Stravinsky and Balanchine: A Musico-Choreographic Analysis of *Agon*" (Ph.D. diss., University of Michigan, 1994), pp. 116–117, notes the use in *Agon* of what she calls "show dancing," including a soft-shoe step, as well as vernacular dancing, such as the Lindy and the Jitterbug. She remarks that a section marked "cha-cha" in the Labanotated score looks closer to the Twist, although "*Agon* was choreographed in 1957, and the popular dance, the Twist, did not appear until 1960" (p. 168 n. 100). Of course, the dance craze called the Twist in the 1960s had far-reaching antecedents in black dance, including the Suzie-Q and the Mess Around. (See Marshall and Jean Stearns, *Jazz Dance: The Story of American Vernacular Dance* [New York: Macmillan, 1968].)

90 Stravinsky himself notes the influence of blues and boogie-woogie on two sections from *Agon* (the Bransle Double [de Poitou] and the Bransle Simple), in Igor Stravinsky and Robert Craft, *Dialogues and a Diary* (Garden City, NY: Doubleday, 1963), p. 87.

91 This was not necessarily a conscious political gesture on Balanchine's part, although surely he must have been aware of its racially sensitive (to some even shocking) implications. In *Agon*, Balanchine seems only to have been interested in the formal, visual

aspects of contrasting skin colors, although initially when Balanchine came to the United States, either he or Kirstein had hoped to establish a fully racially integrated ballet company. Kirstein, writing in 1933 to his friend A. Everett Austin about his invitation to Balanchine to come to America and found a school and a company, stated, "For the first he would take 4 white girls and 4 white boys, about sixteen yrs. old and 8 of the same, *negros* [sic]" (Lincoln Kirstein, Letter to A. Everett Austin, July 16, 1933, reprinted in Francis Mason, *I Remember Balanchine: Recollections of the Ballet Master by Those Who Knew Him* [New York: Doubleday, 1991], p. 116). Croce writes, "As Mitchell likes to point out, Balanchine enjoyed and exploited the contrast in skin color. Back in the forties, he had said to Ruthanna Boris, 'I wish I had a company half white and half black. Then I could play checkers'" (Croce, "Spelling," p. 90).

92 This is documented in Robert Craft, ed., *Stravinsky: Selected Correspondence* I (New York: Knopf, 1982), pp. 271–273, 276–277, 280–282, 284–290.

93 For an account of the ballet's creation, see Irene Alm, "Stravinsky, Balanchine, and *Agon*: An Analysis Based on the Collaborative Process," *Journal of Musicology*, Vol. 7, no. 2 (Spring 1989): 254–256; and Croce, "Spelling," p. 88–92.

94 Balanchine and Mason, *101 Stories*, p. 2.

95 Kirstein, *Four Centuries*, p. 242; Craft, *Correspondence*, p. 287.

96 Kirstein, *Four Centuries*, p. 242.

97 Kirstein, *Four Centuries*, p. 243.

98 In "Spelling," p. 92, Croce notes some of the similarities between *Apollo* and *Agon*.

99 I am basing my description of *Agon* on my live viewings of the New York City Ballet's performances and on several film or video recordings, especially: a film telecast, probably in 1960, on *L'Heure du concert*, Canadian Broadcasting Corporation, with Diana Adams and Arthur Mitchell dancing the Pas de Deux; "Balanchine Celebrates Stravinsky," prod. Judy Kinberg, dir. Emile Ardolino, *Dance in America*, Great Performances, PBS, WNET, New York, 14 February 1983, with Heather Watts and Mel Tomlinson dancing the Pas de Deux. My own viewings have also been aided immensely by Stilwell's meticulous musical and choreographic descriptions.

100 Stilwell mentions the likeness to Rockettes in a later section – the Galliard – but doesn't associate the opening grand battement in this section with the famous chorus-line kicks.

101 Denby, "Three Sides," p. 460.

102 Stilwell, "Stravinsky and Balanchine," p. 140.

103 See Stilwell, "Stravinsky and Balanchine," p. 140.

104 Denby, "Three Sides," p. 461.

105 Denby, "Three Sides," p. 461.

106 Arlene Croce, "Momentous," *The New Yorker* (8 December 1975), reprinted in Croce, *Afterimages*, p. 188.

107 Stilwell points out that originally the men left the stage, but in later versions they remained to clap the castanet rhythm ("Stravinsky and Balanchine," p. 177).

108 See Stilwell, "Stravinsky and Balanchine," pp. 178–179.

109 Croce, "Spelling," p. 90.

110 Croce, "Spelling," p. 89; Arlene Croce, "Love-Song Waltzes," *The New Yorker* (4 June 1984), reprinted in Arlene Croce, *Sight Lines* (New York: Knopf, 1987), p. 202; Croce, "Spelling," p. 88.

111 Deborah Jowitt, *Time and the Dancing Image* (New York: William Morrow, 1988), pp. 254–255.

112 Siegel, *Shapes*, pp. 232–233.

113 Quoted in Stilwell, "Stravinsky and Balanchine," p. 186.

114 Jordan, "*Agon*," p. 9. In fact, Mitchell was quoting Balanchine's instructions to him (quoted in Reynolds, *Repertory*, p. 183).

115 Denby, "Three Sides," p. 462.

116 Robert Garis, *Following Balanchine* (New Haven, CT: Yale University Press, 1995), p. 118.
117 Croce, "Balanchine's Girls," p. 419.
118 Denby, "Three Sides," p. 462.
119 Kirstein, *Four Centuries*, p. 242.
120 Stilwell, "Stravinsky and Balanchine," p. 188.
121 See Stilwell, "Stravinsky and Balanchine," pp. 194–205, for a detailed description of the entire Finale.
122 Denby, "Three Sides," pp. 459–460.
123 Stilwell, "Stravinsky and Balanchine," pp. 116–119.
124 Kirstein, *Four Centuries*, p. 242.
125 Stilwell, "Stravinsky and Balanchine," p. 125. Balanchine uses the term "symmetrical asymmetry" in regard to *Agon*'s musical score in "A Word from George Balanchine," *Dance Magazine*, Vol. 32, no. 1 (January 1958): 35.
126 Kirstein writes, "Bodies are digits; the atmosphere derives from the area where geometry governs anatomy, projecting a new measurement based on the twelve-tone system" (Lincoln Kirstein, Notes for *Agon*, Souvenir Program, Stravinsky Centennial Celebration, New York City Ballet, New York, 1982).
127 Denby, "Three Sides," p. 462; Siegel, *Shapes*, p. 228.
128 Stilwell, "Stravinsky and Balanchine," p. 40.
129 Ann Daly, "The Balanchine Woman: Of Hummingbirds and Channel Swimmers," *The Drama Review*, Vol. 31, no. 1 (Spring 1987; T113): 9–21.
130 Daly, "The Balanchine Woman," p. 9.
131 Daly, "The Balanchine Woman," p. 17.
132 Arlene Croce, "Free and More Than Equal," *The New Yorker* (24 February 1975), reprinted in Croce, *Afterimages*, p. 126; emphasis added.
133 Croce, "Free," p. 128.
134 Lincoln Kirstein, "*Apollo*: *Orpheus*: *Agon*," Souvenir Program, Stravinsky Centennial Celebration; Kirstein, *Four Centuries*, p. 242.
135 For an elegant interpretation of the Act II pas de deux from *A Midsummer Night's Dream*, see Joan Acocella, "Imagining Dance," *Dance Ink* (December 1990): 7–11.

ENVOI: RECENT DEVELOPMENTS

1 Alwin Nikolais, "No Man from Mars," in Selma Jeanne Cohen, ed., *The Modern Dance: Seven Statements of Belief* (Middletown, CT: Wesleyan University Press, 1966), pp. 64–65.
2 Ramsay Burt notes: "It could be said that [Cunningham], more or less, pioneered . . . unisex choreography – theatre dance in which, superficially at least, differences between male and female dancers are not especially important to the sorts of formal, aesthetic qualities presented in dance material." However, he contends that "a real blurring of masculinity and femininity rarely if ever occurs . . . in the work of Cunningham." Rather, even in what might be seen as ungendered movement, "masculinity is . . . taken as axiomatic, an unproblematic norm. Women thus get to be 'normal,'" by doing masculine movements, while men are seldom assigned movements associated with the feminine canon (*The Male Dancer: Bodies, Spectacle, Sexualities* [London: Routledge, 1995], pp. 137, 157–158). However, it seems to me an argument can be made that Cunningham does create androgynous movement, and that Burt is mistaken when he says that the women's "normality" consists in mimicking men. Nevertheless, I do agree that Cunningham preserves gender distinctions in his pas de deux.
3 Jill Johnston comments on this in her discussion of the lift in *Roaratorio*, in "Jigs, Japes, and Joyce," *Art in America*, Vol. 75, no. 1 (January 1987): 103–105.

4 In my interview with Lucinda Childs, 16 April 1980, she explained the character's psychological motivations for the final section.
5 Yvonne Rainer, *Work 1961–73* (Halifax, Nova Scotia: The Press of the Nova Scotia College of Art and Design; New York: New York University Press, 1974), p. 286.
6 Jill Johnston, "Rainer," program note, "Two Evenings of Dances by Yvonne Rainer," Avery Theater, Wadsworth Atheneum, Hartford, Connecticut, March 6 and 7, 1965, reprinted in Rainer, *Work*, p. 316.
7 *Judson Dance Theater 1962–1966*, exhibition catalog, Bennington, VT, 1981, p. 58.
8 This mixing of genres appeared in Rainer's work again, shortly thereafter, in "Duet" from *Terrain* (1963) – in which she and Trisha Brown wore push-up bras and tights; Rainer's ballet adagio contrasted with Brown's split body, performing a ballet port de bras with the upper half and burlesque bump-and-grind with the lower half.
9 Yvonne Rainer, *Work*, p. 317.
10 John Martin, *The Modern Dance* (New York: A.S. Barnes, 1933; reprint ed. New York: Dance Horizons, 1965), pp. 18, 14. In referring to Greek tragedy, Martin quotes Gilbert Murray.
11 Simone Forti, *Handbook in Motion* (Halifax, Nova Scotia: The Press of the Nova Scotia College of Art and Design; New York: New York University Press, 1974), p. 44.
12 Yvonne Rainer, "A Quasi Survey of Some 'Minimalist' Tendencies in the Quantitatively Minimal Dance Activity Midst the Plethora, or an Analysis of *Trio A*," in Gregory Battcock, ed., *Minimal Art* (New York: E.P. Dutton, 1968), reprinted in Rainer, *Work*, p. 65.
13 Rainer, "A Quasi Survey," p. 65.
14 Anne Livet, ed., *Contemporary Dance* (New York: Abbeville Press, 1978), p. 45.
15 Quoted in my *Terpsichore in Sneakers: Post-Modern Dance* (Boston: Houghton Mifflin, 1980; 2nd ed. Middletown, CT: Wesleyan University Press, 1987), pp. 79–80.
16 Yvonne Rainer, "Notes on Two Dances by Deborah Hay," unpublished manuscript, New York, 22 August 1966.
17 Yvonne Rainer, "Some retrospective notes on a dance for 10 people and 12 mattresses called *Parts of Some Sextets*, performed at the Wadsworth Atheneum, Hartford, Connecticut, and Judson Memorial Church, New York, in March, 1965," *Tulane Drama Review*, Vol. 10, no. 2 (Winter 1965), reprinted in Rainer, *Work*, p. 51; emphasis added.
18 In the soundtrack to "Beyond the Mainstream" (narr. Alan Titus, prod. Merrill Brockway and Carl Charlson, dir. Merrill Brockway, *Dance in America*, WNET-TV, New York, 21 May 1980), Rainer reads her manifesto to a silent interviewer and comments, "no to moving or being moved – whatever *that* means!"
19 Rainer, "Some retrospective notes," p. 51.
20 Frances Herridge, "The Avant-Garde Is at It Again," *New York Post*, 7 February 1969: 70; Margo Miller, Letter to the Editor, *New York Times*, 2 March 1969; Clive Barnes, "Critic's Concern – And Ford's," *New York Times*, 2 March 1969; all reprinted in Rainer, *Work*, pp. 155–157.
21 Noël Carroll, "Cracks in the Acoustic Mirror," in Noël Carroll, *Theorizing the Moving Image* (Cambridge: Cambridge University Press, 1996), p. 341. In the context of his article, Carroll makes this argument in order to criticize Kaja Silverman's psychoanalytic approach to film theory.
22 Yvonne Rainer, program notes, *The Mind is a Muscle*, March 1968, reprinted in *Work*, p. 71.
23 Rainer, "A Quasi Survey," p. 68.
24 Rainer, "A Quasi Survey," p. 68.
25 Rainer lists the elements she eliminated or minimized in a chart at the beginning of "A Quasi Survey," p. 63.
26 Rainer, "A Quasi Survey," p. 65.

27 Roger Copeland, "Dance, Feminism, and the Critique of the Visual," in Helen Thomas, ed., *Dance, Gender and Culture* (London: Macmillan, 1993), p. 147.
28 Copeland, "Dance, Feminism," p. 143.
29 The dance is recorded on "Beyond the Mainstream."
30 Copeland, "Dance, Feminism," p. 143.
31 Copeland interprets these dances differently – as "austere, cerebral, anti-voluptuous" products of "the new chastity" ("Dance, Feminism," pp. 142–143).
32 Yvonne Rainer, Letter to Nan Piene, 27 January, 1973, reprinted in *Work*, p. 238.
33 See *Bad Girls*, exhibition catalog, New Museum of Contemporary Art, New York (Cambridge, MA: MIT Press, 1994).

INDEX